THE MAYA TROPICAL FOREST

The Maya Tropical Forest

PEOPLE, PARKS, & ANCIENT CITIES

JAMES D. NATIONS

University of Texas Press · Austin

Material from *The Maya Textile Tradition*, edited by Margot Schevill (New York: Harry N. Abrams, Inc., 1997), reprinted by permission of the publisher.

Material from Chapter 1 of *Timber, Tourists, and Temples*, edited by Richard Primack, David Bray, Hugo Galletti, and Ismael Ponciano (Washington, D.C.: Island Press, 1998), reprinted by permission of the publisher.

Material from Jan de Vos, *Oro verde: la conquista de la Selva Lacandona por los madereros tabasqueños, 1822–1949* (Mexico City: Fondo de Cultura Económica, 1988) reprinted by permission of the author.

Material from Jan de Vos, *Viajes al desierto de la soledad: cuando la Selva Lacandona aún era selva* (Mexico City: Secretaría de Educación Pública, 1988) reprinted by permission of the author.

Requests for permission to reproduce material from this work should be sent to:

Permissions
University of Texas Press
P.O. Box 7819
Austin, TX 78713-7819
www.utexas.edu/utpress/about/bpermission.html

∞ The paper used in this book meets the minimum requirements of ANSI/NISO Z39.48-1992 (R1997) (Permanence of Paper).

Library of Congress Cataloging-in-Publication Data

Nations, James D.
   The Maya tropical forest : people, parks, and ancient cities / James D. Nations. — 1st ed.
       p.   cm.
   Includes bibliographical references and index.
   ISBN 0-292-71282-0 (hardcover : alk. paper) — ISBN 0-292-71318-5 (pbk. : alk. paper)
   1. Mayas—Ethnobotany.   2. Mayas—Ethnozoology.   3. Rain forest ecology—Yucatán Peninsula.   4. Human ecology—Yucatán Peninsula.
   5. Yucatán Peninsula—Environmental aspects.   I. Title.
   F1435.3.E74N38   2006
   304.2'09726—dc22
                                                2005023469

To my parents, Charlie and Em Nations, for such an excellent beginning.

To the memory of Carlos Soza Manzanero and Carlos Catalán, the finest community conservationists in the Guatemalan Petén.

To Mary E. Hartman, Chris Nations, Jamie Nations, and Nick Nations, for making it all worthwhile. Mary has been my kind and compassionate companion throughout the years covered by this book. I could not, and would not, have done this without her.

Contents

PREFACE *ix*

ACKNOWLEDGMENTS *xiii*

NOTES ON NAMES AND ORTHOGRAPHY *xvii*

ON DISTANCES AND MEASUREMENTS *xix*

EPOCHS OF CIVILIZATION IN THE MAYA TROPICAL FOREST *xx*

Part One: Time, Land, and Forest *1*

1. INTRODUCTION TO THE MAYA TROPICAL FOREST *3*

Sidebar: Biosphere Reserves *15*

2. HISTORY OF THE MAYA TROPICAL FOREST *18*

The New Land's Form *18*
The Rise of Maya Civilization *19*
The Classic Maya *22*
First Encounters *30*
A Mysterious Poison *31*
Conquest of the Lowland Maya *35*
The Rise of the Western World *44*

3. NATURAL HISTORY OF THE MAYA TROPICAL FOREST *46*

Introduction *46*
Weather *50*
Animals *51*
Sidebar: *U kunyah chäk k'ek'en* *59*
  (Lacandón Maya Chant to Cure the Coatimundi Growling Disease)
Wild Plants *93*

Part Two: Mexico, Guatemala, and Belize   111

4. MEXICO   113

The Selva Lacandona   113
Sidebar: The Best Pilot in Chiapas   128
People of the Selva Lacandona   129
Protected Areas   142
Archaeological Sites   149
Sidebar: Letter from Calakmul   170

5. GUATEMALA   172

Introduction   172
The Maya Tropical Forest in Guatemala   175
Modern Peoples in the Guatemalan Petén   177
Sidebar: The Lacandón Maya in Guatemala   180
Protected Areas   186
Major Archaeological Sites in the Guatemalan Petén   200

6. BELIZE   225

Introduction   225
Geography of Belize   228
Modern Peoples   233
Protected Areas   239
Archaeological Sites   248

Part Three: The Future of the Maya Tropical Forest   257

7. THE FUTURE OF THE SELVA MAYA   259

Protected Areas: Threats and Solutions   262
Archaeology: Threats and Solutions   268
Cultural Diversity: Threats and Solutions   270
The Challenge of Population Growth   276
The Promise of Ecological Tourism   280
Regional Incentives   282
Lessons from the Ancient Maya   283

GLOSSARY   287

REFERENCES CITED   289

INDEX   313

Photos following p. 110

Preface

Working in the Maya Tropical Forest for more than 25 years gave me the opportunity to examine scores of books on the region, but my research in libraries and bookstores never turned up the one book I was looking for. I was seeking a book that brought together the basic information on the region's people, archaeology, and natural resource conservation. Most of all, the book would tell interesting stories about the people, history, and wildlife of the Maya Tropical Forest. This volume represents my effort to create that book for future travelers and researchers.

The Maya Tropical Forest: People, Parks, and Ancient Cities tells a unified story of the lowland tropical forest of southern Mexico, Guatemala, and Belize. The Maya Tropical Forest is the closest rainforest to the United States and one of the most visited tourist sites in the Western Hemisphere. Journalists have called the Maya the most fascinating ancient culture since Egyptian pharaohs first inspired the public imagination, and few months go by without at least one major article on the ancient or modern Maya in *National Geographic, Natural History, Newsweek,* or *Time.* Descriptions of Maya archaeology appear regularly in the *New York Times, Washington Post,* and *Los Angeles Times.* Simultaneously, questions about the fate of the world's rainforests have seeped deep into public concern during the past 25 years, and generations of students are seeking to learn more about the fate of these forests.

The Maya Tropical Forest: People, Parks, and Ancient Cities guides the reader through the past and future of southern Mexico, Guatemala, and Belize, telling some of the stories I have heard and experienced in the region's archaeological sites, national parks, and communities. The book describes the region's plants and wildlife, explains how the ancient Maya used and guarded these resources, and shows how indigenous people utilize these same plants and animals today in village life and international trade.

Sections within the chapters on Mexico, Guatemala, and Belize take the reader on quick tours of the protected areas of the Maya Tropical Forest, from Mexico's Montes Azules Biosphere Reserve to the Cockscomb Basin Jaguar Reserve of southern Belize. On these pages, you will learn how the protection of these parks and reserves also protects the artifacts of ancient Maya civilization and the biological germplasm that will help define the future of humankind. You will also find an explanation of how the expanding industry of ecotourism helps protect both national parks and archaeological sites.

The book is intended for travelers to the Maya region and students of the region's environment and natural history. Tourism, especially nature-based tourism, is increasing every year in the Maya Tropical Forest. Among the most visited states in Mexico are Chiapas and Quintana Roo, homeland of the Maya Tropical Forest. The 1994 Zapatista rebellion in Chiapas, Mexico, focused world attention on the rainforest of the Selva Lacandona, the westernmost part of the Maya Tropical Forest, and tourism to the state is again on the rise, now that the rebellion has calmed.

Tourism in Guatemala is increasing by 9 percent per year, in the wake of the 1996 Peace Accords that ended civil strife between the Guatemalan government and leftist guerrilla forces. Since 1985 the number of visitors to Tikal National Park has increased 29 percent annually.

In Belize, the government has recognized tourism as the number one generator of foreign exchange, and new ecological tourism facilities, hotels, and archaeological excavations bring thousands more visitors each year. The number of annual visitors has increased by more than 80 percent since the early 1990s.

But *The Maya Tropical Forest: People, Parks, and Ancient Cities* is designed to be a reader's book, rather than a tourist guide. I have not attempted to write an on-site handbook to the area's attractions ("Turn left at Temple II and proceed north 150 meters (492 feet) . . ."). Instead, the book answers questions: Why did the Maya build the stone skyscraper city of Tikal in the middle of a tropical forest? How did Hernán Cortés's wounded horse change the history of the Maya people? Why do the descendants of the ancient Maya gather wild products from the forest, and which of their products will you find in your kitchen? How did Maya fish harvesting lead to the development of birth control pills? How does wildlife conservation assist efforts to protect Maya heritage and traditional cultures? What happened to the ancient Maya people, and what is the fate of their forest?

Structure of the Book

I have divided *The Maya Tropical Forest: People, Parks, and Ancient Cities* into three parts. Part One introduces the Maya Tropical Forest, describes the history of the Maya people, and surveys the most interesting aspects of the region's ecology, plants, and animals.

Part Two is divided into chapters on Mexico, Guatemala, and Belize. In turn, each country chapter presents sections on (a) modern peoples, (b) national parks and wildlife reserves, and (c) archaeological sites. Through this structure, a reader traveling to Guatemala can focus on the sites, people, and protected areas of that country, while a researcher interested in environmental conservation throughout the area can turn to the sections on protected areas for each of the three countries.

Part Three of the book is a concluding chapter, "The Future of the Maya Tropical Forest." Here, I have pulled together information from 25 years of research in the region to predict how current trends in the Maya Tropical Forest will likely impact its future: increasing ecotourism, expanding population growth, and—with luck and hard work—a renewed focus on the economic and intrinsic benefits of its natural areas.

If You Go . . . The Maya Tropical Forest

At the end of the description of each protected area and archaeological site, I have included a short section aimed at individuals who plan to travel to these areas. There, you will find an overview of the parks and sites and notes on their importance. But you should also carry a recent tourist guide to the region, so you can access information on restaurants, travel arrangements, and accommodations. Among the best of these guides are Lonely Planet's *The Maya Route*, Rough Guides' *The Maya World*, and *The Route of the Mayas*, each of which lists restaurant and hotel prices, along with brief descriptions of towns and attractions in the Maya region.

Keep in mind that accommodations in the Maya Tropical Forest range from the luxurious to the ludicrous. At the high end of the continuum, you can check into five-star hotels in Flores, Palenque, and Belize City and loll around the swimming pool after a sweaty morning of touring ruins. On the other end of the continuum, you can fall sleep in a hammock in a Maya village, sharing a mud-floored house with chickens and dogs, while wide-eyed children stare at you through gaps in the walls.

Traveling in the Maya Tropical Forest is an adventure. From a mule trip to Mirador in Guatemala, to a climb up Little Quartz Ridge in Belize, to a raft ride down the Río Usumacinta in Mexico, getting there is more than half the fun. The author's message here is simple: Let the mystery of the forest, its history, and its people set their own appropriate pace. Don't fixate on time schedules from the outside world. Recognize that in the Maya Tropical Forest, things move at their own natural tempo and everything is subject to change. Keep your wits about you and never stop going on adventures.

$\mathcal{A}$cknowledgments

Tall thanks to the Wilburys—Santiago Billy, Tom Sever, Dan Lee, Alfred Nakatsuma, and Frank "El Diablo" Miller—for hilarious adventures in the Maya Tropical Forest; to the leadership and staff of the National Parks Conservation Association and Conservation International for dedicating their careers and lives to protecting the earth's biological and cultural diversity; and to Ingrid Neubauer for a decade of assistance and steady good humor. Special thanks to friends and colleagues who read specific chapters with a critical eye: Norman Schwartz, Sharon Matola, David Freidel, Ronald B. Nigh, John Cloud, Peter Hubbell, Letitia Blalock, Ignacio March Mifsut, Joy Grant, and one anonymous reviewer. All remaining errors result from my failure to take their sage advice.

My sincere thanks for fine companionship on field expeditions to Mike Balick, Manuel "Chup" Baños, Steve Bartz, Karen "Kiki Chup" Buhler, Genoveva "Nuk" Buot, Juan José Castillo Mont, Fernando Castro, Reginaldo Chayax Huex, John Clarke, T. Pat Culbert, Juan Carlos Godoy, Ian Graham, Liza Grandia, Ramón Guerrero, Bob Heinzman, Ricardo Hernández Sánchez, Brian Houseal, Ruth Jiménez, Hank Kaestner, Jaime Kibben, Keith Kline, Chepe Krasborn, Andreas Lehnhoff, Greg Love, Ignacio March Mifsut, Simon Martin, Javier de la Maza, Martin Meadows, Luis Morales, Walter F. X. "Chip" Morris, José Hernández Nava, Brad Peirce, Victor Perera, Ismael Ponciano, Julián Tesucun Q'ixchan, Matt Quinlan, Conrad Reining, Alejandro Robles, Jon Schneeberger, Debra A. Schumann, Carlos Soza Manzanero, David Stuart, Chan K'in Pepe Valenzuela, Enrique Valenzuela, José Chan K'in Valenzuela, Koh Valenzuela, Michu Valenzuela, Jan de Vos, Ben J. Wallace, and John N. Williams.

For enabling me to carry out research in the Maya Tropical Forest, I thank Conservation International, Daniel I. Komer, Alyse Laemmle, Peter and Carlene Mennen, François Berger, Nini de Berger, Adam and Rachel Albright, Peter Morgridge, the Fulbright Scholars Program, the Tinker Foundation, the Inter-American Foundation, the National Science Foundation, the Summit Foundation, Aria Foundation, Prospect Hill Foundation, The Nature Conservancy, World Wildlife Fund–U.S., Compton Foundation, and the United States Agency for International Development, especially the missions in Guatemala and Mexico.

For friendship, encouragement, and assistance in the field, I thank Ira R. Abrams, Richard N. Adams, Scott Atran, Jim Barborak, Michel Batisse, John Beavers, Robin Bell, Donna Birdwell, Didier Boremanse, Jill Brody, Nick Brokaw, Doug Bryant, Jeanie and Harry Burn, John Burstein, Alfred Bush, Kraig Butrum, Jorge Cabrera Hidalgo, Judy and David Campbell, Haroldo Castro, Denis Caudill, Ray Cesca, Diane and Arlen Chase, John Cloud, Amy Coen, Carlos "Chup" Conde, John V. Cotter, Arthur Demarest, Barbara Dugelby, Glenn and Judy Elvington, Bob Engelman, Mercedes Estevez, Pliny Fisk, Gail Fisk-Vittori, Willy Folan, Anabel Ford, Adrian Forsyth, Dennis Fruitt, Ed I. Fry, Fumiko Fukuoka, Robert Goodland, Joy Grant, Kees Grootenbroer, Richard Hansen, Alex Harris, Catherine and Dick Hartman, Rick Hartman and Melissa Huffman, Susanna Hecht, Harold Hietala, Rick Holdridge, Stew Hudson, Dan Irwin, Kevin Johnston, Cristina Jorquera, Daniel Juhn, Carol Karasik, Sol Katz, Tom Lacher, Bob and Mimi Laughlin, Gary and Candace Love, Tom Lovejoy, Luisa Maffi, Mario Mancilla, Rod Mast, Caleb and Nan McCarry, Jane and Karl Miller, Cristina Mittermeier, Russ Mittermeier, Chan Mortimer, Doug Muchoney, John Musinsky, Ron and Kippy Nigh, Tom Outlaw, Mike and Trina Overlock, Ana Livingstone Paddock, Bill and Liz Paddock, Mariclaire Pais, Joe Palacio, James Parsons, Ambar Past, Tobey Pierce, Mark Plotkin, Anabela Pomes, Kathryn Cameron Porter, Darrel Posey, Milena Prem, Glenn Prickett, Bill Pulte, Chris Rader, Manuel Ramirez, Abbe Reis, Stacy Rhodes, Mike and Julia Richards, Hilda Rivera, Billy Roberts, Carlos Rodriguez Olivet, Bill Rogers, Carlos Saavedra, Carlos Salazar, Yvonne Sánchez, Sue and Peter Sawyer, Marianne Schminck, Susan Scott, Peter Seligmann, Nigel Smith, Pam Spruell, Laura and Bob Stevenson, Amanda Stronza, John and Kirsten Swift, Kirk Talbot, Jane Taylor, Adolfo Tovar, Edilberto Ukan Ek', Mark Walker, Rob Wasserstrom, Ron Weatherington, David Whitacre, Vicki Whitaker, Paul White, E. O. Wilson, Percy and Nancy Wood, Frank Zinn, John and Tracy Zykowski, the families of the Lacandón Maya communities of Mensäbäk, Naja, and Lacanjá Chan Sayab, and the members of the U.S. Man and the Biosphere Tropical Ecosystems Directorate: Twig Johnson, John Wilson, Roger Soles, David Bray, Francisco Dallmeier, Gary Hartshorn, Richard B. Primack, Anthony Stocks, Aaron Zazueta, Tom Ankersen, Laura Snook, Meg Symington, Kathy Moser, and Archie Carr III.

Notes on Names and Orthography

The Academia de Lenguas Mayas de Guatemala (ALMG), formed in Guatemala in 1986, is dedicated to the preservation and revitalization of Maya languages. Among the group's accomplishments is the publication of recommended spellings for Maya language names. Some of these spellings are logical and easily adopted: "Q'eqchi'" "Kaqchikel," "K'iche'" are good examples. Others go beyond long-accepted usage. I have respectfully chosen not to use their recommended term "Yukateko" for the people who live in Yucatán or "Lakantún" for the traditional Lacandón. "Yucateco" is a commonly used spelling in modern Spanish, including among the Yucatec Maya themselves. Modern Lacandones refer to themselves as "Lacandones" or "Caribes" when speaking Spanish. When speaking their native language, they call themselves "Hach Winik" and their language "Hach T'an."

I have used Spanish accents where appropriate, even in a few cases where the words are actually Maya that have been Hispanicized. The best example is Petén Itzá, the northern Guatemalan lake, which is written and pronounced in Spanish with the accent on the final syllables. But the words are Maya, properly pronounced with the accent on the first syllables; thus, *Peten Itza*.

The ALMG recommends Itzá for the Itza Maya people, but the Itza Maya themselves, most of whom are literate, have not adopted this spelling nor the indicated change in pronunciation. In these pages, I bow to the tradition of the Itza people.

Finally, some scholars use the term "Maya" for people and cultures, reserving the term "Mayan" for the written and spoken languages. I have utilized the more accepted "Maya" for all of these references.

Lacandón Maya vowels and consonants are pronounced as they would be in Spanish, although I have changed the Spanish *j* to *h* in Lacandón transcriptions that appear here. Lacandón also has two vowels that do not appear in Spanish: The vowel *ä*, as in the Lacandón Maya word for yellow, *kän*, is pronounced like the *u* in the English word "but." The Lacandón vowel *i*, as in the word for hill, *witz*, is pronounced as in the English word "wit."

Unless otherwise noted, all translations are mine.

On Distances
and Measurements

This book uses the metric system of distances and measurements: meters instead of feet, kilometers instead of miles, hectares instead of acres. The following list will aid readers not accustomed to these units.

Distance

- 1 meter = 1.1 yards or approximately 3.3 feet
  To convert meters to yards, divide the number of meters by 0.9144.
- 1 kilometer = 0.6 miles
  To convert kilometers to miles, multiply the number of kilometers by 0.6.
- 1 centimeter = 0.4 inch
  To convert centimeters to inches, divide the number of centimeters by 2.54.

Surface Area

- 1 hectare = 2.47 acres
  To convert hectares into acres, multiply the number of hectares by 2.471.
- 1 square kilometer = 0.4 square miles or 247 acres
  To convert square kilometers to square miles, multiply the number of square kilometers by 0.386.

Epochs of Civilization in the Maya Tropical Forest

Modern	1821–present
Colonial	1521–1821
Postclassic	(AD 900–1521)
Late Postclassic	AD 1200–1521
Early Postclassic	AD 900–1200
Classic	(AD 200–900)
Late Classic	AD 500–900
Early Classic	AD 200–500
Preclassic	(1800 BC–AD 200)
Late Preclassic	300 BC–AD 200
Middle Preclassic	1000–300 BC
Early Preclassic	1800–1000 BC

(After M. Coe 1993:9; Sharer 1994:46–47.)

PART ONE — Time, Land, and Forest

Introduction to the Maya Tropical Forest

February 16, 1990. Department of Petén, Guatemala.

We woke up to the raucous, barking growl of howler monkeys in the trees overhead—a sound much louder than animals their size should make and one that raises the hair on the back of your neck the first time you hear it in the rainforest. We had slept in the thousand-year-old ruins of the Maya city of Piedras Negras, on a sandy bank above the dark, rushing water of the Río Usumacinta, in northwestern Guatemala. Fifty meters (164 feet) across the water, on the other side of the river, was Mexico, where the same species of tropical trees dipped branches down to the sediment-laden water as it slid by underneath.

In a satellite view of where we were, we would have been microscopic specks in an ocean of trees, with the river running though it like a twisting, green ribbon. From our camp on the Guatemalan side of the Río Usumacinta, the forest stretched eastward for 50 uninterrupted kilometers (31 miles) before the first muddy logging road cut through the canopy of trees. This block of tropical forest hid the ruins of a dozen more ancient stone cities, a wealth of wildlife and plants, and 500 furtive Guatemalan revolutionaries who operated under the rubric of the Unión Revolucionaria Nacional Guatemalteca (URNG). Their stated goal was to overthrow the government of Guatemala and declare a Marxist state.

Shaking sand from our sleeping bags, we ignored the howlers 30 meters (98 feet) overhead, but we perked up when Santiago Billy yelled, "Avena y café para todos" (Oatmeal and coffee for everyone). We gathered around the smoking fire that Santiago had built in a fire pit on the beach and slurped oatmeal and sipped coffee and blinked the sleep from our eyes. Ten meters (33 feet) below us, fog began to rise from the fast-moving swirls

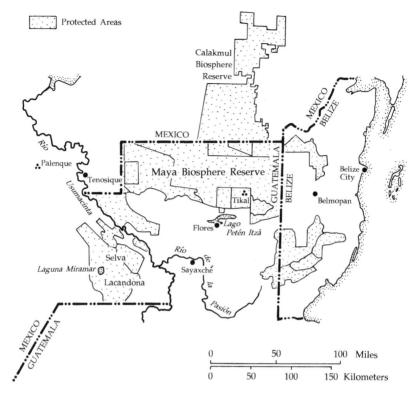

MAP 1. The Maya Tropical Forest

of the river. Slender, white royal herons picked their way along the shore downstream, and tiny blue kingfishers darted in and out of the foliage, watching the water for minnows.

Standing around the fire in the early morning chill, we were eight people in all: Tom Sever, Dan Lee, and Frank Miller, respectively an archaeologist, remote sensing specialist, and forester, working on a project with the National Aeronautics and Space Administration (NASA); Alfred Nakatsuma, the environmental officer with the Guatemala office of the United States Agency for International Development (USAID); two boat drivers, Israel Martínez Calderón and Rudy García, whom we had hired in the town of Sayaxché; Santiago Billy, a senior researcher with Guatemala's Comisión Nacional del Medio Ambiente (CONAMA); and me, a U.S. anthropologist turned conservationist. Together, we were the field team responsible for ground-truthing the first satellite image of the month-old 16,000 square kilometer

(6,178 sq. mi.; 3 million acre) Maya Biosphere Reserve, a newly created protected area in the lowland tropical forest of northern Guatemala. Informally, we called ourselves the Traveling Wilburys, after the singing group on the only cassette tape we had brought along on a previous expedition. Today—although we didn't know it yet—we were about to be captured by Guatemalan guerrilla fighters, who at that precise moment were locking and loading their weapons and settling into ambush positions 10 kilometers (6 miles) upriver.

After breakfast, we rinsed our dishes and gathered up our gear to pile it into the front of the two 4-meter (13-foot) aluminum boats we had hired in Sayaxché, Petén, a riverside town on the shore of the Río de la Pasión, one of a half-dozen tributaries of the Río Usumacinta. Our two boat drivers, Israel and Rudy, who lived in Sayaxché, were remarkably adept at maneuvering the small boats through the whirlpools and rapids of the river. Because we were headed upriver, against the current, they strained the 35-horsepower motors to push against the rushing flow of dark green water, and the boat yawed in the front, swishing from side to side as the drivers dodged boulders hidden beneath the water. Frank Miller—"El Diablo" because of his Lucifer-like goatee and diabolical laugh—grabbed the tie-down rope from the bow of the boat he was in and stood on the front aluminum bench, riding the bounce of the rapids like an urban cowboy on a mechanical bull. The rest of us took photos, half expecting him to pitch into the water at any minute.

As the boats curved around a slow bend in the river, we recognized the wide sandy beach on the Guatemalan shore as the site called El Desempeño. Half a century ago, the few remaining Lacandón Maya in Guatemala had lived in the forest above this beach. The last of the non-Christianized Maya, the Lacandones were the most traditional of the indigenous groups who lived in the Maya forest. Even into the twenty-first century, most Lacandón men wear their black hair long and flowing over white cotton tunics; married women tie toucan breast feathers in long, single hair braids. Together, they look like archetypes for the carved sculptures of Maya leaders on the limestone monuments that lie in the ruins of the surrounding Maya cities.

The last Lacandones in Guatemala had abandoned this site 50 years ago to join their relatives in the isolation of the Selva Lacandona, the Mexican tropical forest just across the river. But the Lacandones had left their mark on the region. Guatemalans use the name Laguna del Lacandón for the large lake that lies 5 kilometers (3 miles) inland from the beach at El

Desempeño, in recognition of the Lacandones' former settlement there. It was this lake that had drawn us to this place on the river on this particular morning.

We had seen the lake, isolated and incandescent blue, on the satellite images Tom and Dan had processed at NASA's Stennis Space Center. Our job here in Guatemala was to use handheld global positioning devices (GPSs) that looked like oversized calculators to "fix points" at recognizable sites in the Maya forest—determining exact longitude and latitude of physical features so that, once back in the NASA lab, Dan could electronically bend the satellite image to adjust for the curvature of the earth.

The result would be an accurate, photolike image of the entire Maya Biosphere Reserve, the first ever produced for this new conservation area. Santiago and I would use this image to help Guatemala's National Council of Protected Areas (CONAP) monitor the newly created reserve for illegal settlements and timber poachers. Tom and Dan would use the same image to correlate water sources and topography to predict the location of unknown Maya cities, hidden beneath the canopy of the forest. El Diablo would help us classify the various types of forest represented in the image. As an environmental officer with the U.S. Agency for International Development, Alfred would use the data to make the case for a US$12 million cooperative agreement with the government of Guatemala to finance the new biosphere reserve, preserving both forest and ancient cities in one fell swoop.

As we neared the beach at El Desempeño, Santiago pointed out wildlife—a crocodile slipping off the bank into the water, a tiger heron hidden in the foliage, two scarlet macaws flying overhead from Mexico into Guatemala.

Across the Usumacinta from the beach of El Desempeño, we first pulled to shore on the Mexican side of the river. We had stopped here yesterday on our way downriver to the ruins of Piedras Negras. We knew we would need a guide to take us into Laguna del Lacandón, and we thought the Mexican families who lived across the river might be willing to help us. A man had come down to the shore when we pulled in yesterday, making his way down from a thatched-roof house built in a cornfield on the steep bank five meters (16.5 feet) above us.

We asked the man if there were someone there who could guide us the next day to Laguna Lacandón. His first response was a question.

"¿Llevan armas?" (Are you carrying weapons?)

We assured him we had no weapons and turned the conversation to details: We could pay in Guatemalan quetzales or in food, but we had no

Mexican pesos. We agreed to return the next morning at seven thirty. Three times the man asked, "¿Seguro?" (For sure?)

"Yes, yes, for sure, we'll be here tomorrow morning."

And here we were pulling to shore beneath his house, only a half hour behind for our scheduled meeting.

But today, three athletic-looking men made their way down the steep embankment, eyeing us and our boats from end to end. One of the men wore an incongruous broad-brimmed straw hat, making him look like a caricature of a Mexican campesino. During 16 years of work in the region, I'd never seen a farmer wear a hat like that. As he neared the boats, the man in the hat began to pepper us with questions about what we were doing here, where we had slept last night, where we were headed.

"¿Llevan armas?" (Are you carrying weapons?) he asked us three times.

"No, no llevamos armas. Somos científicos." (No, no weapons, we're scientists.)

"¿Seguro?" (For sure?)

"Sí, seguro."

Once we had convinced the man we were harmless, he nodded to the younger of his two companions. The boy, probably 19 years old, climbed into the nearer of our two boats, moving Santiago's backpack over to make a space to sit down.

Israel and Rudy revved the outboards and cut sharply across the river to head directly to the Guatemalan shore, juicing the motors one final time to push the bows up onto the sand. We jumped out of the boats onto the beach and pulled out the gear we needed for the hike to Laguna del Lacandón—water, food, maps, the satellite image, compasses, our GPS units. Israel sat down in the shade of a tree to guard the boats while the rest of us hiked to the lake.

We climbed up the embankment on the Guatemalan side of the river and looked across the river into Mexico. Except for the small cornfield cut from the vegetation above the river where we had picked up our guide, the tropical forest extended into the distance as far as we could see. Behind us on the Guatemalan side of the river, an equally huge block of forest stretched toward the horizon. Divided only by the twisting ribbon of the Río Usumacinta, these blankets of lowland tropical forest join with equal expanses in Belize and southern Yucatán to create the largest tropical forest north of the Amazon basin. Increasingly, researchers and conservationists are coming to see this forest as a single, regional ecosystem called the Maya Tropical Forest.

Viewed from the vantage point of space, the Maya Tropical Forest is a single swath of green splashed across the midriff of Mesoamerica, where Mexico and Central America join together. On closer examination, it reveals itself as a mosaic of high and low tropical forest, grassland savannas, and oxbow lakes stretching from the eastern lowlands of the state of Chiapas across northern Guatemala, connecting to the Yucatán Peninsula, and spreading into the Central American republic of Belize.

On the ground, human history has divided the Maya Tropical Forest into three sovereign nations. As if in defiance of political borders, though, the flora and fauna of this region are remarkably similar. The vegetation includes montane tropical forest, lowland moist tropical forest, large, seasonally flooded scrub forests called *bajos,* pine savannas, and the largest freshwater wetland in Central America. Wildlife is abundant and varied, with jaguars, pumas, tapirs, monkeys, kinkajous, and peccaries among the larger mammals, and macaws, harpy eagles, and jabiru storks among the multiple hundreds of species of birds. Every year, the Maya Tropical Forest also becomes home to up to one billion migratory birds escaping winter in Canada and the United States (Nations, Primack, and Bray 1998:xiii).

The three nations that share the Maya Tropical Forest are also tied together by the rich cultural roots of the Maya peoples who have lived in this forest for millennia. The Maya Tropical Forest hides the decaying stone cities of the Classic Maya—a group that flourished here for a thousand years, between 100 BC and AD 900. The Maya turned the biological riches of this forest into the ecological foundation for one of the most developed civilizations of its time, with sophisticated mathematics, astronomy, water control, and art and a calendar that measured time more accurately than does our modern Gregorian version. They invented the only indigenous written language in the Western Hemisphere.

When Classic Maya civilization disintegrated around AD 900, the Maya left behind a forest filled with species useful to modern human communities—and one of the world's premier ecotourism attractions. The forest, in fact, is largely a human artifact, the result of centuries of selective clearing and manipulation by the Maya people who lived in this region for thousands of years, then watched it reclaim the land when their civilization collapsed. Archaeologist Anabel Ford makes the point succinctly: "The Maya Forest is a feral forest, gone wild after the collapse of Maya civilization" (Ford 2001).

At its peak of population around the year AD 700, the Maya Tropical Forest was probably home to as many as 4 to 5 million Maya people (Denevan 1992:370; Webster 2002:174). Today, there are fewer than 1 million people in the region—only a small percentage of them Maya—yet the area is rapidly being transformed from forest to pastures and wasteland. This transformation is bringing little benefit to the people who live in the Maya forest, many of whom continue to live lives of poverty and desperation. A host of solutions to this situation have been suggested, but too few politicians and citizens are focused on implementing them.

All of this information was unspoken background as we shrugged our day packs onto our shoulders and headed down the narrow forest trail toward Laguna del Lacandón in the Guatemalan tropical forest. Our hired guide urged us along, as if he were in a hurry to get to the lake and return. We walked through dense forest, admiring the height of the trees, and we held our hands out like tightrope walkers as we walked cautiously over thin logs thrown across streams that crossed the trail.

I stayed behind the rest of the team at one of the streams to take photos of a small waterfall. That's how I came to be the last man captured.

As I was putting away my camera, I suddenly heard yelling and what sounded like scuffling on the trail ahead of me. We had known the area was guerrilla territory when we started the hike, but I hadn't really expected this. The thought of running back to the boat flashed through my mind, but just as quickly I realized that I would be leaving behind the rest of the group. So, I gritted my teeth and walked slowly forward until I saw the team on the trail ahead. Santiago, Tom, Dan, El Diablo, Alfred, and Rudy were on their knees with their hands locked together behind their head, elbows in the air. Spread along the forest trail, they looked like beginners learning a duckwalk line dance. Then I focused on the yelling. On both sides of my teammates, on either side of the trail, uniformed men were jabbing automatic rifles at their heads and yelling, "¡Manos arriba!" (Put your hands up!) "Throw down your bags, get on your knees, hands over your head."

I saw our guide scramble away from the group on all fours, looking like a land crab scuttling into the forest. Obviously, he was getting out of the line of fire if someone started to shoot. The 14 guerrillas paid no attention to him, as if his escape had been prearranged.

I took my place at the end of the line as unobtrusively as I could, dropped to my knees, and threw my prized camera bag, filled with lenses and film, two meters to my left. One of the guerrilla leaders shouted, "Now, get on your feet, walk forward very slowly, line up right here."

We stood up and walked forward cautiously as the guerrillas encircled us. Two men held M-16 rifles on us while a third patted each of us down, looking for weapons.

All of the guerrillas were wearing new-looking, blue denim uniforms and black and tan Vietnam style, canvas-sided combat boots. Most of the men carried new M-16 A1 automatic rifles, which I recognized from my stint in the Army 15 years before. Two men carried AK-47s, Russian-style Kalashnikov rifles.

"No tienen nada" (They don't have anything), the searcher reported to his jefe, and the jefe said, "Put your hands down now, but don't move from where you are."

The guerrillas gathered up our bags, and one of the men pointed to the forest on the left side of the trail and said gruffly, "Walk."

Led off the trail into the forest, surrounded by men pointing automatic weapons at us, I realized that if the guerrillas were going to kill us, this was the moment of truth. I breathed a sigh of relief when, instead, they pointed to a clearing ahead in the forest and told us to sit down in a circle. Three men surrounded us, forming a triangle from 10 meters (33 feet) away and stood at the ready in case someone tried to make a break for it. One short and very muscular guerrilla with a broad, Maya face scowled as he looked us over, seemingly eager to kill us if given any possible justification.

Just into the forest toward the trail, we heard the jefe speaking into a walkie-talkie. A woman's voice responded, but we were too far away to make out the dialogue.

Militarily, the guerrillas made a mistake by putting all of us together in a circle, because we immediately began to talk to each other in English. I knew that in the boat we had duffle bags with documents, maps, satellite images, and electronic global positioning devices—all equipment that would make us suspicious characters inside guerrilla territory. So, we began to coordinate our stories.

"What are we doing here?" we asked each other.

"We're ecologists and archaeologists [true enough] examining Maya ruins."

"What are the GPS devices?"

"They measure the height of the pyramids in the Maya ruins."

And we agreed that we would all remind the guerrillas that we didn't represent a threat to them. We simply wanted to get back on the river and get back to work.

Santiago, though cool and collected, was still worried that the guerrillas would find his official credentials from the Guatemalan government, identifying him as a government employee and therefore as a valid target for guerrilla forces. Alfred was sweating the fact that his backpack contained his diplomatic passport, making him too a valuable target for kidnapping and negotiation. And Tom Sever was holding his head, lamenting the fact that his U.S. government official passport, identifying him as a NASA employee, was inside his duffle bag back at the boat. We also remembered that our prized 1:50,000 topographic maps were hidden under the bow of the boat back on the river. Because their detail makes them valuable for military action, their distribution was carefully restricted from civilian hands. But by carefully cultivating contacts in the Military Geographic Institute, Santiago had been able to secure a full set of topo sheets of the Petén. We figured that if the guerrillas found these, we were toast. At the least, we'd lose our hard-won maps.

About the time we had agreed on a common story about who we were and what we were doing in guerrilla territory, the jefe of the group ended a walkie-talkie conversation and walked over to the men guarding us. "Separate them," he commanded, and our three guards dispersed us in a large circle around the clearing, out of range of conversation with one another.

After a few minutes, one of the guerrillas walked out of the forest and approached Tom Sever. "Come with me," he said in Spanish. Tom responded in English: "I don't speak Spanish." Having always served as the team's unofficial translator, I automatically blurted out what Tom had said in English, and the guerrilla looked at me with a frown and said, "You come instead."

Again, I had a momentary flash that if they were going to shoot us, they would do it by taking us off individually into the forest. Goaded by the guerrilla's AK-47, I followed the trail through the forest to a large tree, where I saw all of our gear piled up in a mound. A young guerrilla stood guard off to the side of a small clearing while the jefe spoke into a walkie-talkie. He had a wire antenna strung between two trees about head high. Again, a woman's voice answered as the man talked into the radio.

Ending his conversation, the jefe pulled out a journalist's steno pad and began to ask questions.

"What's your name?"

"James, but Jaime in Spanish. Jaime is better. The *apellido* is Nations, like Naciones, but with a *t*."

"Where are you from?"

"The United States."

"What are you doing here?"

"Archaeology—looking at the ruins. Yaxchilán. Last night we slept at Piedras Negras."

"What work do you do?"

"I'm an ecologist—plants and animals. The others are archaeologists; one is a forester."

"Where are you going?"

"To Laguna del Lacandón to see the wildlife and take pictures."

"How do you know about the lake?"

"We saw it on a tourist map and it looked close to the river, so we asked someone to guide us to see it."

"How many of you are there?"

"Just the ones you see. Seven of us. There was a guide, but I don't know where he is now. He's not with us now. I guess he got lost."

"Do you know his name?"

"No, we just asked along the river for someone to guide us."

"Did you pay him?"

"Not yet, but we were going to."

"Where else have you been? What other countries?"

I respond with a shortened list: "Belize and Mexico, to Ecuador, Brazil, Peru, but not on this trip."

"Who are your boat pilots?"

"Men we hired in Sayaxché."

"Who owns the boats?"

"I don't know. I don't know if they belong to the pilots or if they rented them from someone."

"Do you know who we are?"

I figured this was my chance to soften the fellow up, so I responded, "I have an idea. I suspect you are the armed resistance to the government of Guatemala. You work for honesty and integrity. You're working to help the people. You work against those who work just for the rich. We've read about the Guatemalan Army, how they kill people and cause refugees to flee into Mexico. We're not against you. We know you are working for the people."

The jefe seemed to like the speech. He told me to identify my bag from the pile at the base of the tree. I did so, and he said, "Revísalo" (Make sure everything is there).

I was relieved to see that all my cameras and lenses were intact.

I said, "Gracias, muy amable," and he sent me back to the group.

As quickly as I sat down, the guerrillas guarding us took Rudy, the captured boat pilot, then Santiago Billy into the forest to be interviewed. They all returned safely, smiling, and we realized that we were all responding to the jefe's questions with the same, harmless story.

Then, they pulled Tom out of the group and told me to come with him to translate. Back in front of the jefe, Tom and I were surprised when he began to show us gear that we knew we had left back in the boat. We would later find out that three of the original 14 guerrillas had hiked to the river, captured Israel, the other boat driver, gone through our gear, and held Israel face down on the bank of the river all day at gunpoint.

The jefe thrust out the GPS device and asked, "What is this?"

I translated as Tom explained that the apparatus measures the height of archaeological sites. The jefe seemed satisfied with the answer. He showed us a battery-powered Snake Doctor, a small electric stun gun I was carrying as immediate treatment for snakebite and which they had found in my duffle bag back at the boat. (Field-tested over several years in the Ecuadorian Amazon, the devices have saved many lives, according to missionary doctors there; other physicians discount them, saying they are worthless.)

"It treats snakebites," I said.

"There are no snakes here," the second guerrilla said, and he laughed.

Half trying to convince them not to confiscate the Snake Doctor, I said, "We don't know if it works; we haven't had to use it yet. It's best that we never have to."

Both of the guerrillas laughed.

They told Tom to pick up his bag, and we returned to the group.

After interviewing Alfred and Dan and hearing the same responses again about who we were and what we were doing in their territory, the guerrillas seemed satisfied that we were indeed harmless and represented no threat.

We spent the rest of the day in anticipation of what would happen next. Would they march us to Laguna del Lacandón as hostages? Would we become pawns in a political negotiation? Unable to talk with each other, we exchanged glances across the expanse of the circle we were still being held in, guarded by the scowl-faced Maya guerrillas with the automatic weapons.

I was convinced we would be okay, so I took advantage of the downtime and cleaned my prized 35-millimeter camera and lenses. Furtively, I tried to snap a photo of my companions on the other side of the clearing, but I couldn't lift the camera to my face to get a light meter reading and had to guess the proper exposure. I misjudged, and the only photo I was able to snap off while innocently looking in the other direction captured nothing but a splash of blue from Tom Sever's field shirt, surrounded by the dark green of the forest.

At four in the afternoon—some six hours after we had been captured—one of the guards brought us cans of food from our stash in the boat. We ate, sitting on the ground in the forest, with the guards keeping a wary eye on us.

Finally, at six fifteen, as the sun was setting over the forest canopy and the forest was taking on a golden glow, the event defused. The jefe came into our clearing and told us to gather round him. We sat on the ground in a group as he stood before us. He asked me to translate as he began.

"First," he said, "we want to ask your forgiveness for any inconvenience we've caused you. We want you to understand that we captured you because of where you are.

"This is our territory. We control it. The army comes here searching for us. It is a zone of conflict. We were afraid that by coming here, you might accidentally get caught in the middle of a fight.

"When we captured you, we didn't know who you were. We thought you might have been sent by the army.

"We are the regular forces of the URNG—la Unión Revolucionario Nacional Guatemalteco. We are fighting against the oppression of the army of Guatemala. Their oppression is directed against *el pueblo campesino del país.* Now, we know that you are tourists. Because this is a dangerous area, it is better that you not come here. We have taken two compasses and some maps from your packs. These serve us to orient ourselves in the *monte* and are very useful to us. We want to thank you for letting us have them.

"You are free to go now. But we want to ask you to tell people in your country or in any other country about our struggle again repression. Again, we ask your forgiveness and wish you a safe trip."

With that, the guards indicated that we should pick up our bags and file out of the clearing. Santiago gave the jefe our remaining cans of food left over from our makeshift lunch. The jefe stood at the front of the column of guerrillas, as if in a reception line, and shook hands with us as we filed past.

One of the young guerrillas ran us back to the boats, his rifle slung over his shoulder, at a pace that none of us could keep up with. I had spent three years hiking with Lacandón Maya in Chiapas, following men who had grown up in the tropical forest, but I had never seen anyone move that fast down a forest trail. This fellow moved like a deer, his feet barely touching the fallen logs and mud holes as he zipped down the narrow path.

"Keep up, keep up," he snarled. "You move like children."

We finally arrived at the bank of the river, exhausted but happy to be reunited with our missing boatman. Still, we wasted no time. We quickly loaded our gear into the boats and cranked up the outboards. We were taking no chances that the guerrillas would change their minds and decide to keep us.

Loaded into the two aluminum boats, we had just enough time to head directly across the river to the Mexican side before dark. The boatmen reminded us that we couldn't navigate the rapids in the dark, so we dashed for the other side of the river and piled out of the boat onto the beach to set up camp for the night. Tom looked through the boat, then walked up to our campsite and told us that our topographic maps were still hidden beneath the bow of the boat. The guerrillas hadn't found them. The maps they had taken were copies of *National Geographic*'s Ruta Maya map.

Around a campfire on the riverbank in Mexico, we celebrated our survival and talked about the experience late into the night, then collapsed into our hammocks and tents.

Early the following morning, we were happy to climb back into the boats and head up the Río Usumacinta toward the riverside town of Sayaxché. As we pulled away from the shore, Santiago told us in a low voice to casually look at the tree line on the Guatemalan side of the river—"Not all at once," he said.

Half hidden behind a large tree across the river, one of the guerrillas was carefully watching us disappear upriver.

Biosphere Reserves

Biosphere reserves are natural protected areas included in a global network organized by the United Nations Educational, Scientific and Cultural Organization (UNESCO). Participating countries propose land and water sites within their boundaries as potential biosphere reserves, and accepted sites are designated at the international level by UNESCO's Man and the Biosphere (MAB) Program. To qualify for acceptance as a biosphere reserve, a protected area must have global or regional significance for biological conservation, one or more inviolate core zones, and one or more surrounding buffer zones where human communities utilize natural resources in ecologically sustainable ways.

The central tenet of biosphere reserves is the conservation of natural resources alongside their utilization for human benefit. The overall goal of biosphere reserves is the protection of biological diversity, but they differ from strictly protected areas such as national parks and wilderness areas by accepting human settlement as a feature of the landscape. Biosphere reserves represent an attempt, not to wall out the external world, but to incorporate human populations into sustainable land-use systems. In most biosphere reserves, landownership remains unchanged upon acceptance of the reserve into the global network: private landowners retain their holdings but agree to manage them in ways compatible with the reserve's maintenance. In other biosphere reserves, all land areas are owned and controlled by the nation's government.

Approval of a biosphere reserve site by the MAB Program morally commits the host country to manage the protected area according to designated standards and to participate in MAB's international biosphere reserve network. On-the-ground management of biosphere reserves continues to be the obligation of the individual countries, following their national legislation. Participation in the MAB biosphere reserve system is voluntary; countries are not required to designate biosphere reserves. UNESCO's role in the biosphere reserve network focuses on facilitating information exchange, providing guidance and technical assistance, encouraging international cooperation, and promoting financial and technical support from governments and international organizations. A small secretariat staffed by professional conservationists coordinates the biosphere reserve program from UNESCO's headquarters in Paris. As of early 2005, 459 biosphere reserves had been established in 97 countries (UNESCOPRESS 2004).

Like biosphere reserves throughout the world, those of the Maya Tropical Forest combine the goals of conservation, scientific investigation, and sustainable economic development. The purpose of a biosphere reserve is not to exclude people from the protected area, but to identify ways in which people and nature can coexist to the benefit of both. All biosphere reserves have core areas that are designed to remain inviolate except for visiting scientists and, sometimes, ecotourists. Many reserves have multiple-use areas inhabited by indigenous peoples and other communities that, ideally, practice sustainable harvesting of natural resources. And all biosphere reserves have buffer zones aimed at providing a transition zone between the protected reserve and activities of the outside world.

Both Mexico and Guatemala have enacted specific legislation declaring new protected areas as national biosphere reserves, which are later submitted to UNESCO for inclusion in the global network. However, most biosphere reserves encompass areas previously protected under other categories, such as national parks or wildlife reserves. Biosphere reserves may also be recognized through other international designations, such as World Heritage Sites and Ramsar Wetland Sites. In Guatemala, Tikal National Park, one of the core areas of the Maya Biosphere Reserve, is also a World Heritage Site. Laguna del Tigre National Park, also a core area of the Maya Biosphere Reserve, was Guatemala's first Ramsar Wetland Site. Belize has not yet secured designation of any of its many protected areas as a biosphere reserve, but an application has been submitted for UNESCO recognition of the Río Bravo lands of the Programme for Belize (Nations 2001).

2 $\mathcal{H}$istory of the $\mathcal{M}$aya Tropical Forest

The New Land's Form

Legend has it that when the Spanish conquistador Hernán Cortés first returned to Spain from the New World in the early sixteenth century, the king asked him what this new land looked like. Cortés reached for a sheet of parchment, crumpled it into a ball, and partially smoothed it out on the table before him. Pointing to the convoluted ridges and folds of the paper, he said, "This is the new land's form."

But Cortés already knew that there was more to this region of the world than crumpled mountains and steep river valleys. He had also encountered wild expanses of tropical rainforest, wetland savannas, and short, dry scrub forest growing on the flat limestone shelf of the Yucatán Peninsula. In 1525 Cortés had set out from the Valley of Mexico toward the Caribbean coastal settlement of Nito, near the mouth of the Río Dulce in modern-day Guatemala. The captain Cortés had sent to conquer that region had rebelled with all his ships and soldiers, and Cortés was determined to punish the man in person.

Cortés left Mexico City for the coast with 230 Spanish infantry and cavalry and 3,500 Indian warriors from the Valley of Mexico. Traveling southeast by ship, he disembarked in Maya territory in present-day Tabasco. Pushing toward Nito, his army spent week after week cutting their way through immense, flat stretches of tropical forest, suffering "hunger, bruises, illnesses, hard roads, worse lodgings, and other insupportable trials," according to the Spanish chronicler Juan de Villagutiérrez (Means 1917:17).

As Cortés struggled along this route through the land of the Maya, he encountered small family settlements dispersed in the forest and the island

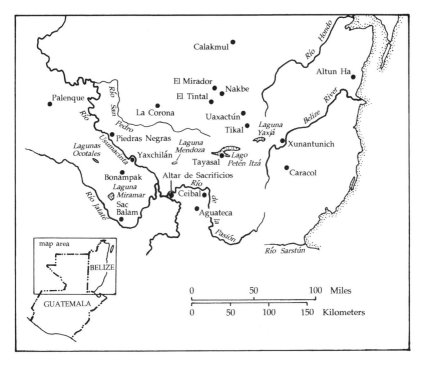

MAP 2. Major archaeological sites of the Maya Tropical Forest

city of Nohpeten, where thousands of Itza Maya still worshipped a pantheon of ancient gods in giant stone temples. Hacking a pathway through the forest, Cortés also stumbled over the ruins of ancient Maya cities, most of which by the time of his adventure had already been abandoned for more than six centuries. These ruins were the stone remnants of the Classic Maya civilization, which flourished in southeastern Mexico and northern Central America for almost a thousand years.

When their civilization disintegrated around AD 900, the Classic Maya left behind a legacy of mythology, technology, and ecology that was still very much alive in the time of Cortés's travels and that today continues to echo down the canyons of a dozen centuries of New World history.

The Rise of Maya Civilization

While the land itself divides the Maya region into highlands and lowlands, it was left to the archaeologists and historians to divide human time into five periods of Maya history: the Preclassic (1500 BC–AD 200), Classic (AD 200–900), Postclassic (AD 900–1521), Colonial (1521–1821), and Modern (1821–present).

Sometime after 5000 BC, groups in the Maya region began to turn from hunting and gathering to a more settled life in village communities, supported by agriculture that included maize (corn), squash, avocados, chili peppers, and beans. The earliest of these sites appeared along the Pacific coast of Mexico and Guatemala, in the region known today as the Soconusco. By the period between 2500 and 2000 BC, the villagers began to produce well-made clay pottery, and by 1000 BC almost all of the Maya region was inhabited by villagers living in family compounds similar to those that can still be found in the Maya region today.

Houses were built around a framework of wood poles with walls of poles or stones slathered with mud—a technique called wattle and daub. Roofs of palm or thatched grass were lashed together with vines, leaving wings that extended out over the walls to keep out the torrential tropical rains (Gallenkamp 1987:60–61).

This earliest era of Maya history, called the Preclassic or Formative period (1500 BC–AD 200), also saw the development of the first Maya pyramids—low, flat-topped earthen platforms with a simple Maya house perched on top and used for religious ceremonies. Mayanist Charles Gallenkamp notes that gradually, through the centuries, "this religious architecture became more elaborate, incorporating masonry, sculptural embellishments, and stairways; and important temples were arranged around open courtyards to form ceremonial precincts within the core of each settlement" (Gallenkamp 1987:61–62). Recent excavations at the site of Nakbe, in what is now the Guatemalan Petén, reveal a settlement that by 750 BC could properly be classified as an early city.

Through the centuries, these villages and incipient cities evolved into vibrant centers of economic and ceremonial activities, and the temples and courtyards grew larger and more complex. Structures at some of the sites reached 20 to 30 meters (66–99 feet) in height. The southern Maya lowland site of El Mirador, in the Guatemalan Petén, is the largest known site for this period. Flourishing between 150 BC and AD 150, it grew to cover 16 square kilometers (6 sq. mi.) of tropical forest land and was one of the first large cities on the North American continent. One of its pyramids, Tigre, may be the largest structure ever built by the Maya. It looms upward to 55 meters (180 feet) through a sequence of earth and stone platforms.

Standing inside the tropical forest that today covers the Preclassic city of El Mirador, you find it difficult to form a picture of what the city must have looked like in its glory. The forest hides enormous mounds of earth that the site map indicates are the eroded temples of El Mirador—once the largest city in the Maya world. Only when you climb the tallest of the mounds—Danta (the tapir), Tigre (the jaguar), or Monos (the spider monkeys)—and look out over the ocean of tropical forest to see other temples poking their heads through the dense canopy do you get a sense of the absolute size of this abandoned city.

From the high perch of Danta, you can watch the sun set on tropical forest that radiates out from the pyramid in all directions as far as you can see. Yet beneath the green waves of this living ocean lie the bones and stones and distant dreams of a city that flourished here for more than three centuries: traders hawking cotton cloth and fine-slipped pottery from the open-walled stalls of the marketplace, priests garbed in wooden masks and macaw feathers chanting whispered prayers to a pantheon of gods, hunters straggling in from the edge of the forest with red brocket deer thrown over their shoulders.

Today, El Mirador is mute. Only the distant roar of a howler monkey and the gliding circles of an orange-breasted falcon overhead remind you that it is still a place of life.

On the horizon, a full day's walk away—if you have water and know the way—lies the slightly earlier Preclassic Maya site of Nakbe. The forbidden city, it lies shrouded in jungle like a child's toy shoved under a carpet of green.

Located at the base of the Yucatán Peninsula, Nakbe lay at the conjunction of the canoe portages for the primary Maya trade routes. Through this early city flowed the lifeblood of early Maya commerce: jade, obsidian, feathers, skins, cacao, and salt.

Through time, El Mirador wrenched control of the trade routes from Nakbe and went on to become the major power in the Maya lowlands prior to the Classic period. Similar patterns emerged in the Maya highlands; Preclassic cities such as Kaminaljuyú and Chalchuapa grew up along major trade routes and vied with one another for control.

Strangely, most of the Preclassic cities of the southern Maya lowlands were abandoned between AD 150 and 250. Some archaeologists point to drought or shifts in trade patterns as the cause of this hiatus. More recently, hypotheses have focused on the fiery eruptions of Ilopango Volcano around AD 200–250 in what is now west-central El Salvador. Today,

Ilopango is a giant caldera filled with water—the modern Lake Ilopango. But when it exploded 1,800 years ago, the volcano destroyed 3,000 square kilometers (1,160 sq. mi.) of Maya homeland, expelling the population for hundreds of years (D. Wallace 1997a:31).

Archaeologists Robert Sharer and Payson Sheets excavated the Maya city Joya del Cerén, a New World Pompeii, a Preclassic Maya city that lies buried in hardened volcanic ash from one of Ilopango's explosions. The ashfall wrought a devastating blow to agricultural production in the southeastern Maya region. Population decline followed drops in food production, cities were abandoned, and trade routes were disrupted, "affecting even those southern Maya populations not directly impacted by the volcanic eruption" (Sharer 1994:133).

This natural disaster, it is believed, joined with still unknown economic and political changes during the Preclassic period to replace the influence of some cities with that of others. Before Ilopango exploded, major Maya trade routes followed along the Pacific coast of what are now Mexico, Guatemala, and El Salvador. Subsequent to the explosion, trade routes wound through the lowland rainforest of the Maya Tropical Forest.

The Classic Maya

There was no transition between the Preclassic and Classic periods that the Maya themselves would have recognized. Archaeologists point to the Classic as the period when traits of civilization that had begun in the Preclassic period blossomed into the full glory we think of when we say "ancient Maya." The city most closely associated with this rise to glory is Tikal, in today's Guatemalan Petén. As Tikal rose to power in the Maya Tropical Forest, it began to overshadow cities of previous prosperity, some of which, like El Mirador, were completely abandoned to the forest.

From a stone platform on the top of Temple IV in the ancient Maya city of Tikal, travelers look out on an expanse of green that stretches to the horizon in all directions. The forests hides the traces of all human activity save four other limestone pyramids that pop their roof combs through the blanket of vegetation. During the rainy season, the forest turns a hundred shades of green, and bursts of yellow, white, and purple flowers splotch the canopy. In the dry season, the forest fades to a paler green than its wet season's glory. Some of the trees turn chartreuse; others—especially the cedars and ceibas—lose their leaves completely. And some trees shed their leaves only to immediately break out in brilliant red-orange flowers.

At 70 meters (231 feet), Temple IV is the tallest Maya structure ever built. It also symbolizes the heights to which Maya civilization ascended, to become, as Gallenkamp describes it, "the most brilliant civilization ever known in pre-Columbian America" (Gallenkamp 1987:2).

Look out in any direction from the highest platform of Temple IV and you will see ridge after ridge of forested landscape fading across the slope of the Guatemalan Petén. On some of these ridges, jungle-covered mounds form silhouettes against the sunset. Other ridges look unperturbed. That all these ridges—and the valleys in between—were deforested for Maya agriculture, as some archaeologists believe, seems illogical. As archaeologist Tom Sever of NASA's Marshall Space Flight Center notes, "The bajos and valleys were deforested for certain. But many of the hilltops were almost certainly still in forest during the days of the Classic Maya." One team of geographers, specialists in Latin America, estimated that the Maya had modified 75 percent of the environment by AD 800 (Whitmore et al. 1990:35).

The dozens of Maya cities that spread over the landscape of the Maya Tropical Forest demonstrate the importance of the region during the Classic period. Of these cities, the largest are Tikal, in Guatemala, and Calakmul, in what is now southern Campeche, Mexico. Tikal had more than 3,000 structures—from skyscraper temples to simple palm-thatched huts—at its peak around AD 800. A system of defensive earthworks on the north and south enclose an area of 123 square kilometers (48 sq. mi.). As many as 90,000 people may have called the city home, making it as large as many post-Roman cities of the Old World (M. Coe 1993:91).

During this peak period of Maya civilization, the lowlands hosted an interconnected web of cities and ceremonial centers interspersed with food-producing settlements that lay in the forest between. Surrounding the region's major cities, hundreds of smaller towns dotted the forests. In Belize, the sites of Altun Ha and Xunantunich joined in trade networks that may have stretched to Copán, Honduras, across Guatemala, and to cities such as Bonampak, Toniná, and Palenque in Chiapas, Mexico.

Along the Río Usumacinta, which today separates Mexico from Guatemala, the Classic Maya cities of Yaxchilán and Piedras Negras controlled river traffic of trade canoes loaded with animal skins, macaw and quetzal feathers, polychrome pottery, incense, medicinal plants, and tobacco.

It was during the Classic period that Maya civilization expounded on the characteristics first developed during the Preclassic, among them writing, astronomy, water control, sophisticated architecture, and a precise annual calendar. These years were the golden age of the Maya, during which as many as 4 to 5 million people lived in 60 regional capitals (Webster 2002:174).

In the highlands of Guatemala, Maya characteristics flourished until around AD 400, when warriors from the city of Teotihuacán, near today's Mexico City, seized such sites as Kaminaljuyú and began to rule over the Maya population. The Mexican invaders added Maya ways to their own, but the vanquished Maya of the highlands began to depend culturally, if not politically, on the Mexican altiplano (de Vos 1993:22).

Teotihuacán imposes it influence in the cities of the Maya Tropical Forest in AD 378, with the arrival of a Teotihuacano warrior called Siyah K'ak'. Arriving via the site of El Perú/Waka', Siyah K'ak' takes possession of Tikal and defeats the rival city of Uaxactún in battle, killing its royal family and imposing military and political dominance over much of what is today the Guatemalan Petén (Stuart 1998; Martin and Grube 2000:29).

This Teotihuacán-influenced dominance dissipates in the second half of the sixth century after a period in which no stelae are erected and many stone monuments are defaced and mutilated. But the cities of the tropical lowlands are not abandoned, and by AD 620 Classic Maya characteristics take off again without Teotihuacán influences. Not unpredictably, this blip in history coincides with the sacking of Teotihuacán around AD 600. After Teotihuacán falls into ruins, the lowland Maya go on to unparalleled heights of glory, producing the pottery, ornate sculptures, and sprawling cities that we associate with the Classic Maya civilization.

THE DISINTEGRATION

But several centuries later, between AD 700 and 900, lowland Maya civilization also begins to disintegrate. One by one, the star cities of the Maya constellation blink and go dark. In some places, religious and political monuments are broken and vandalized. As much as 90 percent of the population either dies or abandons the area.

Archaeologists have debated the cause of this disintegration for decades, and they have found plenty of fuel for hypotheses. Some authors cite evidence for soil exhaustion, overpopulation, mysterious diseases, military invasions. The late J. Eric S. Thompson proposed that Maya civilization collapsed in the area from the "overthrow of the small ruling group" by the peasant underclass. Invited once to a seminar on the mystery of the Maya collapse, Thompson telegraphed back: "No need for seminar—peasant uprising."

Robert Sharer writes that the dramatic decline in population and civilization that shook the southern Maya lowlands between AD 800 and 900 resulted from many causes, "but in the end it was because people lost faith in their kings. The people no longer supported a political system that had failed—the deified rulers and the elite class could not solve their problems" (1996:75).

Over a period of 100 years, the working families of Maya civilization "drifted away from the declining cities," Sharer notes. "Some went to the coasts; others went south into the highlands, or north into Yucatán. The influx created a renewal of Maya civilization and a new era of prosperity in these regions, especially the northern lowlands" (1996:76).

More recently, archaeologists have begun to consider the Maya collapse not in terms of a single cause, but in terms of "the stresses that were inherent in the very fabric of Late Classic Maya society," as T. Patrick Culbert puts it (Culbert 1974:113). These internal stresses included population increase, growing demands for food production, malnutrition and disease, warfare between political units, and increased appropriation of wealth by the society's ruling elite.

Archaeologist Richardson B. Gill caused a stir in Maya studies with a well-documented book in which he argues that severe and sustained drought prompted both the Hiatus of AD 535–593 and the Collapse of AD 790–910 (Gill 2000). Gill points out that most Classic-era Maya relied on surface water reservoirs to sustain their communities, and depended on rainwater to replenish these reservoirs (Gill 2000:247). Pointing to historical parallels, Gill concludes that "the Collapse and disappearance of Classic Maya civilization was the result of a series of brutal droughts which ravaged the Maya Lowlands between A.D. 800 and 1000" (Gill 2000:363).

Gill proposes that "the flow of food and water was shut off, the people died from hunger and thirst, and the social system collapsed from the bottom up." By his argument, "Those cities that had water survived and those that did not died" (Gill 2000:104, 371). Gill presents strong evidence, endorsed by other disciplines, that severe drought devastated much of Central America, including the Maya area, during the Late Classic period. Lasting at least two centuries, this dry period combined with, and may have hastened, a process of decline already initiated by population growth, environmental degradation, and war.

Other researchers, while acknowledging the logic of Gill's argument, hold that drought was "just one more factor in what happened" (Webster 2002:247). Pennsylvania State University archaeologist David Webster holds that the Maya Collapse was triggered by three interrelated factors, in this order of importance: "One, a worsening relationship of Maya popula- tion to their agricultural and other resources; two, the destabilizing effects of warfare and competition, and three, the rejection of the ideology and institution of kingship" (Webster 2002:328).

In a wide-ranging study of the collapse of civilizations around the world, Jared Diamond proposes that a major factor in the Maya collapse "was environmental degradation by people: deforestation, soil erosion and water management problems, all of which resulted in less food." Diamond notes that these problems were exacerbated by droughts. "Chronic warfare made matters worse," Diamond goes on, "as more and more people fought over less and less land and resources" (Diamond 2005a:A21).

Summing it up, Diamond notes that "when it comes to historical col- lapses, five groups of interacting factors have been especially important: the damage that people have inflicted on their environment; climate change; enemies; changes in friendly trading partners; and the society's political, economic and social responses to these shifts" (Diamond 2005a:A21).

The middle ground scenario is that all of these stresses tore at the fabric of Classic Maya society, bringing about a gradual but final disintegration of Classic-era civilization, an event that archaeologist Michael Coe called "surely one of the most profound social and demographic catastrophes of all human history" (M. Coe 1993:127).

As the cities of the Maya Tropical Forest declined, cities in the north- ern lowlands of the Yucatán Peninsula—places such as Uxmal, Chichén Itzá, Kabah, and Sayil—began to reach their greatest levels of prosper- ity and power. In the depleted cities of the Maya Tropical Forest, foreign groups moved in to take advantage of the disintegration and simultane- ously helped bring about the rise of the northern Postclassic cities around AD 900.

These changes are associated with the geographic expansion of groups of warrior-merchants from the coastal lowlands of the Gulf of Mexico in what is now Tabasco, Mexico. Collectively called the Putun Maya, they were a Chontal Maya-speaking association of communities living as geo- graphical intermediaries between the Maya and the Toltecs of the Valley of Mexico. Allied with the Toltecs, the Putun brought many Mexican traits into the Maya regions they began to occupy.

Using large seaworthy canoes, the Putun began to dominate trade in both the Usumacinta watershed and around the Yucatán Peninsula. Thompson called them "the Phoenicians of the New World." They expanded up the Usumacinta to exert control at such sites as Altar de Sacrificios and Ceibal; they appear, as well, to have extended into the Maya highlands. Some sites in the highlands were abruptly abandoned around AD 800 and replaced by fortified strongholds on hills or mountains bordered by steep ravines. In the Maya highlands, Mexicanized groups seem to have conquered the K'iche', Kaqchikel, and other Maya groups, though they adopted these highland languages as their own. The new foreign rulers may well have maintained cultural—and physical—ties to the new Putun rulers of the rising cities of Yucatán (de Vos 1993:24).

The Putun also established new coastal trading centers, including ports on islands along the coast of Yucatán, and went on to establish their capital city at Chichén Itzá, a city that would reign over the northern Maya lowlands for the next two hundred years. Thus, in archaeology, the Putun came to be known in some regions as the Putun Itza and finally as simply the Itza.

Still, neither the Maya highlands nor the Maya Tropical Forest were depopulated after the collapse of the Classic Maya. Although the majority of Maya people disappeared from the Maya Tropical Forest when Classic civilization disintegrated, thousands of people continued to live there, just as they did in the highlands and in the flourishing Yucatán Peninsula. Archaeologist Jeremy Sabloff notes that while "most large centers in the southern lowlands" ceased to function by the end of the ninth century, "centers in other parts of the lowlands were still alive and thriving. There was no massive, overall collapse," he writes, "but a partial one, leading to large-scale demographic, political, and economic rearrangements." Sabloff notes that the Classic tradition did not die out entirely, "but its focus shifted from the southern to the northern lowlands" (Sabloff 1994:145).

Archaeological data even indicate that small groups of Maya continued to occupy a few decaying cities in the Maya forest, including Tikal. They set broken stelae back on their bases, and attempted to re-create some measure of the civilization's former glory. As well, some southern lowland cities with favorable locations and plentiful water—in northern Belize, the Lake Petén Itzá region, and along the western and southern borders of the southern lowlands—continued to flourish (Sabloff 1994:122).

As in the highlands, some of the Postclassic Maya of the Maya Tropical Forest established fortified villages, but they did so on islands in large lakes and rivers. These villages were built mostly of perishable materials that disappeared over time, but the inhabitants constructed some stone buildings that survive today as ruins. Among the known sites are Lacantún (Lake Miramar, Chiapas), Topiltepec (in the Río Jataté, Chiapas), Pochutla (Lake Ocotal Grande, Chiapas), Nohpeten (now the island city of Flores, Petén), Topoxté (on Lake Yaxjá, Guatemala), and still unexplored and unnamed ruins on islands in Laguna Puerto Arturo and Laguna Mendoza in the Guatemalan Petén.

These ruins have been largely neglected by archaeologists. Some sites—Laguna Mendoza and Laguna Puerto Arturo, for example—are known only from tales of local farmers, who find stone walls and broken pottery on the surface of the islands. Frans Blom's 1953 archaeological map of the Selva Lacandona, Chiapas, indicates that he explored and mapped the ruins of Lacantún, the island in Lake Miramar, Chiapas, but the notes from this exploration lie unpublished in the library of Na Balom Museum, in San Cristóbal de las Casas. More recently, Mexican archaeologist Sonia E. Rivero published a detailed description of the island (1992).

Finally, one of these fortified Postclassic sites, that of Nohpeten, known now as the island city of Flores, Petén, has been continuously occupied at least since Classic Maya times. As the capital of Guatemala's Department of Petén, Flores is today home to 2,500 people and the focus of a thriving tourist industry.

But it was on the flat, dry plains of the Yucatán Peninsula where the Postclassic Maya continued to develop and expand after the Classic Maya collapse. The first 300 years of the Postclassic period were dominated by the city of Chichén Itzá, located in the center of the modern Mexican state of Yucatán. These first three centuries are viewed as a period of Mexicanization of the Maya of Yucatán, meaning that the Putun Itza, heavily influenced by populations from the Valley of Mexico, came to dominate developments in the Yucatán. Sharer points out that the expansion of Putun Itza influence throughout the Yucatán and into the highlands "brought the heartland Maya into contact with new political ideas, military tactics, and religious practices" (Sharer 1994:385).

Around AD 1221, Chichén Itzá was attacked and sacked, apparently by warriors from a rival city, Mayapán, located 100 kilometers (60 miles) to the west. Although it thrived for more than 200 years after the fall of Chichén Itzá, Mayapán too was sacked and abandoned, around 1441. This warfare was part of a process of internal Maya struggles, during which all the larger cities of Yucatán began a period of decline. Maya leadership broke into separate states headed by rival noble lineages at small cities such as Tecoh, Tibolón, Maní, and Santa Rita Corozal.

Just as the Putun Maya of the Tabasco lowlands spread their dominance over the northern lowlands of Yucatán during the Postclassic period, so also did Mexicanized groups come to dominate the highlands to the south. The Putun appear to have extended their influence into the southern highlands by following the Río Usumacinta southward along its tributaries, which flow out of the highlands, and by extending their coastal trading routes around Yucatán, up the Río Motagua, and into the heart of today's Guatemala. As Mexicanized groups came to dominate the Maya highlands, Postclassic settlement patterns changed in reaction. The open-valley sites of the highlands were abandoned and replaced by fortified communities constructed on hilltops bordered by ravines. The conquering warriors who wrought these changes adopted local Maya languages and married into local Maya lineages, but they established political dominance over these populations.

According to historian Jan de Vos, the Popol Vuh, a highland Maya book, records the route taken by Toltec warriors, who appear as the founders of the dynasty of the Utatlán K'iche'. De Vos notes that the legend probably deals with the route taken two centuries earlier by the Putunes when they wiped out the Maya cities of the Usumacinta and Chixoy river valleys. A similar tale, he says, appears in the *Annals of the Cakchiquels,* who trace their elite ancestry to a conquering group that penetrated the Cuchumatanes Mountains of Guatemala from the valley of the upper Grijalva (de Vos 1993:26).

Groups such as the K'iche' and Kaqchikel Maya competed for control of Maya communities that lay between their fortified highland cities. Some of these cities can be identified with Maya linguistic groups that survive in the highlands today—among them Utatlán (K'iche' Maya), Mixco Viejo (Poqomam Maya), Atitlán (Tz'utujil Maya), Zaculeu (Mam Maya), and Iximché (Kaqchikel Maya).

The basin of Lake Atitlán, in highland Guatemala, was occupied by at least two Maya groups in addition to the Tz'utujil of the city of Atitlán. The Kaqchikel controlled the north and east sides of the basin, and the K'iche' the northwest side. The groups created a mosaic of agricultural landscapes—including irrigated fields, sophisticated terracing systems, and drained cultivation fields—on the deltas of the rivers leading into the lake (Whitmore and Turner 1992:416).

Such was the scene among the Maya when the first Spaniards arrived in the New World, bringing upheaval and an entirely new future to the land of the Maya.

First Encounters

The first known encounter between Maya and Europeans came in 1502, on Christopher Columbus's fourth and final voyage to the Western hemisphere. As his ships lay off Guanaja, one of the Bay Islands near the north coast of today's Honduras, Columbus sighted and pursued an eight-foot-wide dugout canoe filled with Maya traders. In the canoe were two dozen men, plus a captain and an unnamed number of women and children, who rode in a palm-covered structure mid-ship. The bewildered Maya told the Spaniards that they came from a province called Maia, the word from which the modern spelling of Maya eventually developed.

According to Christopher's son Ferdinand, who accompanied his father and later wrote about the encounter, Christopher Columbus ordered that "there should be taken from the canoe whatever appeared to be most attractive and valuable, such as cloths and sleeveless shirts of cotton that had been worked and dyed in different colors and designs, also pantaloons of the same workmanship with which they cover their private parts, also cloth in which the Indian women of the canoe were dressed" (Sauer 1967:128).

Columbus also seized what he wanted of the Maya's cargo of pottery, cacao, wooden swords set with obsidian blades, and copper bells and axes. He ordered the Maya captain to henceforth serve as his guide, renaming him Juan Pérez. While the traders continued on their way to an unknown port, Columbus and Juan Pérez sailed on into history.

Fifteen years later, three Spanish ships commanded by Francisco Hernández de Córdova were blown off course to founder at the northeastern tip of the peninsula of Yucatán. Most of those who survived this shipwreck made it back to Cuba, where they told stories of fierce battles with Maya warriors. Córdova himself died of wounds from one of these battles. But some of the Spaniards managed to loot some Maya temples before their escape, and the small gold trinkets they brought back to Cuba fueled a Spanish rush to find more gold.

The governor of Cuba organized an expedition under Juan de Grijalva, who sailed off in April 1518 to travel around the northern coast of Yucatán, reaching the Laguna de Términos, the area from which the Putun Itza had earlier launched their dominance of the Maya region. Enticed by gold that he found near the mouth of the river which would later bear his name, Grijalva headed in the direction the Maya pointed—toward the Aztec empire in today's Mexico. Near the present-day city of Veracruz, Grijalva met Aztec emissaries sent by Montezuma and received their gifts of large quantities of gold.

Those initial gifts would prompt Hernán Cortés to march into the heart of the Aztec empire in 1519, setting off a series of historic events that would forever alter the history of the New World's indigenous peoples. Four years later, the Aztec world conquered and its leaders deposed or killed, Cortés sent Pedro de Alvarado to conquer the territories that would become Guatemala and El Salvador, an assignment that Alvarado "carried out with relentless brutality," as Gallenkamp noted (Gallenkamp 1987:6). Alvarado marched along the Pacific coast of Mexico to today's Guatemalan coast, then turned northward toward the fortified cities of the Maya high-lands. Following Cortés's example in the conquest of Mexico, Alvarado marched at the head of a column of thousands of indigenous warriors—in this case, the previously conquered Aztecs and Tlaxcalans—who fought the highland Maya in a series of heinous battles.

In 1524 Cortés sent Cristóbal de Olid to conquer and colonize the region known today as Honduras. This event led to Spanish dominance of that region of the Maya world as well, although Olid himself was killed in a re-bellion against Cortés—the same rebellion that prompted Cortés to tramp across the Maya world. Two years later, in 1526, Francisco de Montego was authorized by the king of Spain to conquer and subdue Yucatán, a process that would take a series of Spanish leaders two decades to accomplish.

A Mysterious Poison

Within 50 years of Columbus's sighting of the hapless Maya trade canoe, Spanish hegemony over the Maya world—and over the areas known today as Mexico and the Caribbean—was complete. But it was not Spanish fire-power alone that wrought this victory.

Despite the advantage the Spaniards carried over the Maya in the form of horses, metal weapons, firearms, and dogs trained to attack and kill, it was something the Spaniards carried unwittingly in their bodies that allowed them to vanquish the indigenous populations of the Americas. The native populations of the New World had lived for millennia without contact with Old World diseases such as measles, smallpox, influenza, and pulmonary plague. Pulmonary plague is a form of bubonic plague, caused by a bacterium, *Yersinia pestis,* which spreads by hitching a ride on fleas. In humans, the bacteria infect the lymph nodes, causing bubonic plague. When the bacteria spread to the lungs, the disease is known as pneumonic or pulmonary plague. When Spanish soldiers unknowingly brought pulmonary plague and other diseases into Mexico and Central America, they ran rampant among the indigenous people. Even relatively benign diseases of Europe turned killer.

Before the conquering Spaniards themselves entered the Maya area, their diseases spread over trade routes and down rainforest trails to decimate Maya families. As a result, by the time Spanish friars and scribes produced their initial descriptions of the region, a significant percentage of the aboriginal Maya inhabitants already lay buried beneath the tropical soil.

The first and best documented of the epidemics to ravage the Maya region was a complex of diseases, of which the most destructive was small-pox. Beginning in the Greater Antilles in 1519, this pandemic spread over Mexico and Central America, killing "a third or a half of the Indian population," according to historian Murdo MacLeod (1973:19). Historian Henry Dobyns called it "in all likelihood the most severe single loss of aboriginal population that ever occurred" (Dobyns 1963:514). This epidemic entered Guatemala four or five years before Pedro de Alvarado set out to conquer the highlands, prompting MacLeod to call disease "the shock troops of the conquest" (MacLeod 1973:40–41). The best estimates indicate that "depopulation probably approached 90 percent by 1600" (Whitmore and Turner 1992:421).

The historical records report plagues that swept off large numbers of indigenous people throughout the sixteenth century. Half the Indians of Honduras succumbed to measles in the 1530s. Ninety percent of the Indians of Tabasco died between first contact and 1579 of "measles, small-pox, catarrhs, coughs, nasal catarrhs, hemorrhages, bloody stools and high fevers," according to one of the early chroniclers.

A few years later, during the seventeenth century, a new scourge—yellow fever—took a heavy toll among those women and men who had survived the earlier plagues. Beginning in 1638 in the Leeward Islands, the disease spread to Campeche and Mérida, then south through the Maya area. (The Leeward Islands are one of two island groups in the Lesser Antilles. The Leeward Islands—those less exposed to the trade winds—are

Anguilla, St. Martin/St. Maarten, Saba, Statia, St. Barts, St. Kitts, Nevis, Antigua, Barbuda, Montserrat, and Guadeloupe.) The fierceness of the disease prompted a Yucatec Maya commentator to note stoically in the Chilam Balam of Chumayel: "1648. Yellow fever occurred and the sickness began" (Roys 1968:120). Historians Frances Scholes and Ralph Roys wrote that in some towns, probably half the population died in seventeenth-century yellow fever epidemics (Scholes and Roys 1968:304).

Epidemic diseases were not the only killers. While smallpox, measles, influenza, typhus, and plague swept through populations like tidal waves, they were followed by endemic disorders such as tuberculosis, malaria, pneumonia, and the Old World varieties of hookworm and amebic dysentery. Overall, the tropical lowlands lost 95 percent of their population, and the highlands lost 85 percent, according to geographer Karl Butzer (1992:352). Butzer goes on to state that without the population loss wrought by European diseases, the Spaniards never would have been able to subdue and control the peoples of Middle America.

So great was the devastation of consecutive rounds of disease that even decades later, some Europeans could not believe that the depopulation of the New World was caused by foreign pathogens. Thus, Sir Basil Thompson could declare in 1894 that "apart from bacilli of foreign diseases, there is now no doubt that the different races of man are themselves uncongenial, and that their first meeting generates a mysterious poison fatal to the weaker race" (MacLeod 1973:15).

If the historical demographers are correct that approximately 5 million people lived in the Maya region at the time of Spanish contact, more than 4 million persons died of disease in the first hundred years after the Spaniards arrived (Butzer 1992:347; Denevan 1992:370). Even then, disease and war were not the only factors that decimated the Maya. Traveling behind them came other predators to feed upon the native population: the Spanish colonists themselves. In the face of this information, the surprising fact is that any Maya traditions survived at all to reverberate in the modern world.

The conquest affected every facet of the Maya world, not the least of which were alterations on the face of the land itself. Through the expansion of population and agriculture, the Maya had transformed the vegetation of Mexico and Central America long before the Spaniards knew the New World existed. They cleared large areas of forest for crop production and periodically burned some areas to maintain grassland savannas.

The Spanish conquest altered this landscape in two profound ways. First, the intensive agricultural systems of the Maya—terraces, irrigation, and raised fields—could not be sustained after such phenomenal losses in human numbers. Lack of upkeep eventually led to abandonment, which weakened Indian claims on the land and allowed Spaniards to occupy the territory for themselves. Second, the introduction of Old World species—especially cattle and sheep—led to dramatic changes in land use, as formerly cultivated fields, tropical forests, and savannas were burned and turned into pastures. Wheat for Spaniards' bread was planted throughout the highlands, and sugarcane sprouted on Spanish estates in the lowlands (Whitmore and Turner 1992:416).

The Spaniards also brought crops that indigenous people came to adopt as their own, among them rice, sugarcane, watermelons, sour oranges, lemons, limes, bananas, plantains, mangos, and coconut palms. The Spaniards had learned of these crops from the Muslim Moors of southern Spain, who in turn had received them from Baghdad by way of Egypt, Tunisia, and Morocco. The Muslims of Baghdad had received these crops and their cultivation techniques from Asia, mostly from India (F. Gies and J. Gies 1994:102–103).

Disappointed not to find the wealth of gold and silver they had hoped for, the Spaniards set about to exploit the land and labor of the region's indigenous people. By 1550 Spanish colonists in the Maya region had turned to cattle ranching, sugarcane, and the production of cotton and woven cotton cloth to produce the riches they desired. Both cotton cloth and cochineal—a scarlet dye produced by cactus-eating insects—"were simply demanded of Indian tributaries, who subsequently bore the risks and difficulties of cultivation," according to anthropologist Robert Wasserstrom (1983:13).

The conquering Spaniards soon found that their most lucrative enterprise was the exploitation of native labor. In this endeavor, religious and economic interests worked hand in hand. In return for title to territory in the New World, Spanish authorities were required by the papal donation of 1493 to Christianize the inhabitants of these domains. To fulfill this requirement, and more importantly, to incorporate the Maya into the Spanish economic system, the Spaniards brought dispersed Indian communities together in programs of resettlement called *reducciones*. Once under firm Spanish control and nominally Christianized, the Maya were divided among Spanish landowners under the systems of *encomienda* and *repartimiento*. Through these systems, Indians labored for their Spanish patrons; in exchange, the Spaniards provided for the religious well-being of their Indian wards.

Other groups of Maya became debt peons on Spanish haciendas. Under the hacienda system, the Spanish landowner paid the Indians' tribute requirements and protected them from further harassment in exchange for their labor. Still other groups provided a stable labor pool for the Spaniards as sharecroppers—often on lands they had formerly owned. And other Indians, seeking respite from exorbitant Spanish demands for tribute, "simply became attached to a hacienda or plantation by a multitude of interlocking arrangements" (MacLeod 1973:225–226).

Conquest of the Lowland Maya

Not all the Maya were forced into such direct and relentless contact with the colonial Spaniards. The Spanish colonists were drawn more to the highlands than to the lowlands of the Maya region, which seemed disease-ridden, inhospitable to people and domestic animals, dark, and filled with death.

This Spanish vision of the tropical forest provided the lowland Maya some measure of protection from invading Spanish overlords. But as the highland Maya fell victim to the effects of relocation and work demands, Spanish officials were forced to search for additional laborers and slaves. In answer, throughout the sixteenth and seventeenth centuries, they sought to subdue the inhabitants of the Maya Tropical Forest and incorporate them into the colonial economy.

Between 1559 and 1697, the Maya of the lowland tropical forest were either killed, enslaved, or relocated by Spanish authorities and soldiers in a series of military and religious *entradas* (incursions). In Chiapas, Spanish soldiers attacked an island fortress in Lake Miramar. From the name of the island fortress, Lacantún or Lacam Tun (Fallen Stones), the Spaniards fashioned the name of the people they sought to subdue—the Lacandón. Spanish authorities eventually would go on to apply this term to all apostate and non-Christian Maya in the region.

Pedro Ramírez de Quiñones, Oidor (Judge) of the Audiencia (High Court) of Guatemala, led the expedition against the Choltí-speaking Lacandón Maya of Lake Miramar in 1559. Ramírez marched east from Comitán, Chiapas, with 100 Spanish soldiers, 3 priests, 200 Zinacanteco Maya cargo bearers, 600 Chiapaneco Indian warriors, and 100 Guatemalan (probably Chortí Maya) warriors. The group carried the parts and fittings for two 100-man sailing ships to use in the attack on the Choltí island village (Remesal 1966, vol. 4, bk. 10, chap. 12:1524–1526; Trens 1957, vol. 1:203).

Arriving at the lake, the Spaniards built and launched the two ships against the waiting Maya. In the ensuing battle, "many" Choltís were killed and 150 were captured, according to the Spanish chronicler Fray Antonio de Remesal. After plundering the island, the Spaniards burned the houses and destroyed the fortifications. Then they pushed on in search of more lowland Maya settlements. With them were 150 Choltí Maya prisoners, to be sold in Guatemala. (By royal fiat, Spaniards were allowed to enslave indigenous families who resisted obeisance to the Spanish crown.)

The Spaniards marched to a second fortified village, called Topiltepec, probably on an island in the Río Jataté in southern Chiapas, which they also attacked and destroyed. Then they pushed on to the Chol Maya fortress of Pochutla, situated on an island in the lake known today as Lake Ocotal Grande, near today's Tzeltal Maya town of Palestina.

Neither of the two brigantines the Spaniards had constructed at Lake Miramar survived the trip to Pochutla. One lay at the bottom of Lake Miramar; the second was abandoned during the march. To attack the island stronghold, the Spaniards constructed balsa rafts. Their Chiapaneco Indian allies pushed cane floats into the water and unleashed showers of arrows as the Spaniards fired harquebuses point-blank into the Chol Maya defense. Although the Choles counterattacked by canoe, Spanish firearms forced them to abandon the lake completely. With their Indian allies, the Spaniards occupied Pochutla without further resistance. They found no one alive on the island: the women and children had hidden in the forest prior to the battle.

Returning to Comitán with a train of Chol and Choltí captives, the Spanish soldiers were rewarded by colonial officials. Their Chiapaneco allies received a reduction in the amount of tribute they were required to pay and were given the swords and halberds (pikes) used in the campaign. The Zinacanteco allies were given nothing. Their complaints were soon joined by those of the Chiapanecos, whose halberds were confiscated. Halberds, a Spanish judge informed them, were not fit weapons for Indians (Remesal 1966, vol. 4, bk. 10, chap. 12:1531).

Over the course of the following century, Spanish military and missionary expeditions sought out the lowland Maya to kill, capture, or relocate and Christianize them. As a result, the populations of Spanish-controlled towns on the fringes of the forest swelled with former pagans and provided new tributaries for Spanish authorities.

During the 1690s, Spanish authorities began an accelerated program of pacification and *reducción* that eliminated the last lowland Maya holdouts once and for all. Economics provided the impetus. During the seventeenth century, raids on Spanish shipping by French and English pirates threatened trade between Spain and colonial towns in Guatemala and Yucatán. English pirates sailing out of Belize attacked as far inland as the town of Palenque. The raids increased so drastically in the 1690s that Spanish authorities planned an overland trade road between Guatemala City and Mérida. They called it the Camino Real, the Royal Road.

But along the trajectory of the Royal Road lay the provinces of the still-pagan Choltí Lacandones of the southern Chiapas jungle and the Itza Maya of the northern Guatemalan Petén. Until the two groups were subdued, no overland route was viable.

In 1695 military *entradas* accompanied by Spanish missionaries were launched against the Choltí Lacandones and Itza Maya to defeat the unconquered groups "once and for all and briefly and completely," as Spanish officials determined (Ximénez 1973, vol. 5, bk. 5, chap. 57:307). On February 28, 1695, a group of soldiers under the command of Melchor Rodríguez Mazariegos marched north from Huehuetenango, while other forces marched east from Ocosingo and northwest from Alta Verapaz. Mazariegos arrived first at a Choltí Lacandón settlement called Sac Balam (White Jaguar). Through the adroit work of an accompanying Spanish friar, Spanish troops were able to occupy the Choltí town peacefully. They renamed the settlement Nuestra Señora de los Dolores, erected a palisade, and constructed a wood fort, from which they undertook several futile attempts to reach Itza territory. Exploring the surrounding forest of the Selva Lacandona, the Spaniards brought in an additional 700 lowland Maya from dispersed settlements they encountered (Tozzer 1968:499; Ximénez 1973, vol. 5, bk. 7, chap. 63:349; Nolasco Pérez 1966:78).

Interest in the conquered Choltí Maya town of Los Dolores eventually waned, and the Spaniards abandoned it. What happened to its Maya inhabitants is a mystery left unrecorded in Spanish chronicles. Some reports indicate that the town remained a Spanish settlement until at least 1712, when the Choltí were resettled near Huehuetenango or Comitán. There, they either died off or were absorbed by highland Maya groups. Other reports say that half the people of Los Dolores died of disease, and the rest slipped back into the jungle to take up Maya ways again. Only one thing is clear: by 1712 the Spanish-dominated village of Sac Balam–Los Dolores was abandoned to the tropical forest from which it had emerged, and its fate and even its precise location were buried beneath the jungle vegetation for almost 300 years.

Today, the fading traces of Sac Balam lie within the Montes Azules Biosphere Reserve, the 3,312 square kilometer (1,279 sq. mi.) rainforest area established by the Mexican government in 1978. Designed to protect the wildlife and tropical forest of the Selva Lacandona, Montes Azules also protects a range of Postclassic Maya ruins: Lacantún at Lake Miramar, Pochutla on Lake Ocotal Grande, and the lost city of Sac Balam, found again only in 1997. One of the enticing clues that led to its rediscovery came in the 1980s, when Guatemalan Maya families fled into the rainforest of southern Chiapas to escape the violence of Guatemala's civil war.

Weeks later, as they filtered back out of the jungle into Mexican communities along the Mexico-Guatemala border, they spoke of finding a cave deep within the forest where swords and metal armor were stored against the walls. (The rediscovery of Sac Balam is detailed in Chapter 4.)

In pacifying the Choltí Maya of the southern Chiapas jungle, the Spaniards had finally wrenched control of the Selva Lacandona from its aboriginal inhabitants. But their occupation of lowland Chiapas, though prolonged and costly, proved in the end to be a Pyrrhic victory. Aside from a thousand or so new vassals, the conquest of the Chiapas jungle yielded little of immediate value to the Spaniards. The lowland Maya possessed no great wealth in precious metals, and few Spaniards were willing to establish haciendas in the rainforest.

Although they managed almost to depopulate the Selva Lacandona, the Spaniards soon learned that the Maya they had missed in their jungle round-ups were mixing with refugees from occupied territories in Yucatán and Guatemala to reoccupy the population vacuum they had left behind. As these refugees moved across the Río Usumacinta into the Selva Lacandona, they too became known as Lacandones. Escaping disease and disruption in other regions of the tropical lowlands, these new Lacandones managed to remain aloof from Spanish—and later, Mexican—dominance until the 1960s, when logging companies and immigrating colonists found Yucatec Maya-speaking Lacandones living in quiet settlements hidden in the forest.

Known today simply as the Lacandón Maya, these families have managed to hold on to a surprising array of traditions—mythology, agriculture, and ecology among them. Their lives provide researchers with tantalizing clues to some of the secrets of the tropical forest Maya who have lived so long within the biological riches of lowland Mexico, Guatemala, and Belize.

NOHPETEN AND THE ITZA MAYA

The story of the Choltí Maya is not unlike that of the Itza. The Putun or Itza Maya had come to dominate much of the Maya world during the Postclassic period. Although of Maya stock, they bore Mexicanized cultural traits because their original location in the coastal lowlands of Tabasco lay between the Toltec region of the Valley of Mexico and the Maya region itself.

As seafaring traders between the two groups, the Putun Itza introduced Mexican traits into Yucatán, later into the Maya highlands, and eventually came to dominate Yucatán through such cities as Chichén Itzá. Driven from Chichén Itzá by the rise to power of the city of Mayapán, at least some of the Itza escaped southward into the forest of the Guatemalan Petén, where they established themselves on an island fortress in the middle of Lake Petén Itzá, the island known today as Flores. The Itza settlement lay precisely on the route the Spaniards chose for their Royal Road between Guatemala City and Mérida. This economic impetus prompted the Spaniards to try to establish control over the resisting Itza.

In 1696 a Spanish friar, Alonso Cano, would describe the Itza as "well featured and of perfect stature" but frightening in appearance: "They have their faces cut and rubbed in with black. . . . painting themselves or cutting on their faces the form of the animal which they have as a charm."

Friar Cano noted that the men tied up their hair with bands of woven cotton, "with many curious colors, with cords and tassels at the ends, made very beautifully. They clothe themselves with something like jackets with half sleeves, and all from top to bottom woven at intervals with stripes of various designs and incorporated in the same woof—very lovely to look at" (Means 1917:22–23).

"And with all these elegantly ornamented clothes," he wrote, "they always paint themselves red and black." The women, Cano stated, "wear only some skirts of cotton from their waist down, but from the waist up they go bare and uncovered, with their hair rolled up without as much care as the men." At night, Friar Cano went on, the women "muffle themselves up with sheets woven of various stripes and designs of different colors, like cloaks" (Means 1917:22–23).

The Itza were no strangers to Spanish conquistadores. Hernán Cortés himself had passed through Nohpeten on his route from Mexico to the Caribbean, to put down the rebellion of Captain Olid in 1524–1525 (G. Jones 1998:29 ff.). Traveling months through tropical forest, Cortés arrived at Lake Petén Itzá on March 13, 1525. The Itza ruler Ajaw Kan Ek' met the Spaniard and his 600 Chontal Maya bearers on the northern shore of the lake. Ajaw Kan Ek' was the leader then and one in a long history of leaders who bore the same name; this line sequentially reigned over the 22 districts of Itza-controlled territory, including the island city of Nohpeten and a total of 25,000 people.

By all accounts, Cortés was kindly received by the Itza on his arrival in 1525. The Itza, though, were amazed by the Spaniards' clothes, firearms, horses, and beards. As Cortés camped on the northern shore of Lake Petén Itzá, the Itza ruler, Ajaw Kan Ek', and 32 of his chiefs arrived in canoes to visit him. The Spaniards sang a Mass with all available Spanish instruments and decorations. The music especially delighted Ajaw Kan Ek', who said that "such a thing had never been heard before" (Means 1917:33).

Cortés gave the Itza leader a shirt, a black velvet cap, and metal scissors and knives and urged him to give up his traditional gods to become a Christian vassal of Emperor Charles V of Spain. Ajaw Kan Ek' declined, and Cortés was forced to content himself with a tour of the Itza island city of Nohpeten. He traveled by boat, accompanied by 30 crossbowmen, while the rest of the Spanish expedition traveled on land around the long length of the lake to the southern shore.

On the island of Nohpeten, Ajaw Kan Ek' gave Cortés a few gold trinkets (which the Spaniards described as of poor quality and little value) and some woven cotton cloth. The Itza told Cortés how to proceed toward his destination of Nito, bringing "great joy to Cortés and his men on account of the great desire they all had to find the Spaniards in search of whom they had undertaken this perilous journey" (Means 1917:35).

As Cortés and his troops prepared to leave the Itza to continue toward Nito, Cortés asked one last favor. His horse, Morzillo, had injured a hoof and had become a burden to the expedition. Cortés asked Ajaw Kan Ek' to take care of Morzillo until he could send for the animal after the expedition arrived in Nito. Leaving Morzillo behind, Cortés rode a canoe across Lake Petén Itzá to join his army and continue his journey.

Perplexed by the wounded horse, the first such animal they had seen, the Itza of Nohpeten fed it flowers, fowl, and meat. Morzillo promptly died.

Either out of respect for this mysterious animal or fear of Cortés's reaction, the Itza carved a stone statue of the horse and erected it in one of their island temples. They preserved one of its thigh bones in a second temple. The Itza named the horse-god Tzimin Chac, "Tapir Lightning." Tzimin is the Itza word for tapir, the rainforest animal that most closely resembles the horse.

Cortés never returned to retrieve Morzillo, and 95 years passed before the Itza saw another horse or another Spaniard in Nohpeten. In 1616 or 1617, a Franciscan friar, Juan de Orbita, and a fellow priest traveled from Yucatán to Nohpeten in another attempt to convince the Itza to submit to the Spanish crown (Jones 1998:43). The friars met with some success, for they returned to Yucatán accompanied by 150 Itza from the island city. After paying homage to Governor Antonio de Figueroa of Mérida, the Itza returned to Nohpeten, and Juan de Orbita and another friar, Bartolomé de Fuensalida, both of whom spoke Yucatec, initiated plans to join them there. The two friars reached Nohpeten in 1618 with an entourage of singers and sacristans. Their songs and ceremonies pleased the Itza, but Ajaw Kan Ek' diplomatically declared that the time had not yet arrived for the Itza to renounce their traditional religion.

Things might have been left there, but events soured when the missionaries happened upon the stone horse in the temple, with flowers and incense arrayed around it. Infuriated at finding a domestic animal transformed into a heathen god, Father Orbita attacked and smashed the idol. The Itza immediately overpowered Orbita, but Fuensalida, talking quickly, convinced them not to kill his brother friar. The two missionaries rather contritely headed back to Yucatán, and the Itza built a replacement statue to the horse-god, Tzimin Chac. (Local lore in the modern Petén holds that this second horse was carved from stone on the northern shore of the lake and was being transported by canoe to the island when a strong wind rose up and dumped the statue into the water. Some boatmen in modern Flores claim that when the lake's water level is low, you can see the horse's outline beneath the waves.)

Frustrated by the unsuccessful attempt to pacify the Itza Maya of Nohpeten, the governor of Yucatán authorized Captain Francisco de Mirones to mount a military expedition against the island. A Franciscan missionary, Father Diego Delgado, joined the forces but, slipping ahead of them, continued on alone with 80 converted Yucatec Indians and 13 soldiers. Delgado, the soldiers, and the Christian Indians arrived on the island of Nohpeten in 1622 to an initially peaceful reception, but the Itza suddenly ambushed them, killed the entire group, cut off the soldiers' heads, and set them on stakes around the island. Then they cut Father Diego Delgado into pieces and sacrificed the 80 Yucatec Indians to the gods.

Determined to prevent another *entrada,* the Itza then traveled north until they found the rest of the military expedition of Captain Mirones, who was camped on his way to subdue Nohpeten. The Itza killed that group as well. Thus ended Spanish attempts to conquer the Itza, either militarily or peacefully, for another 55 years.

The final chapter came in 1697, when the planned Mérida-Guatemala road was halted only 20 kilometers (12 miles) north of the lake and the Itza were still resisting all attempts at pacification. A military expedition of 235 Spanish soldiers, cavalry, and more than 100 Indian mule drivers and carriers pushed to the edge of Lake Petén Itzá and built two boats, "una galeota y una piragua menor," (a 14-meter (46-foot) rowing galley and a longboat with three oars on each side), which they fitted with artillery they had brought from Yucatán (G. Jones 1998:268).

On March 13, 1697, the force celebrated Mass, ate breakfast, and waited for instructions. As the sun rose, the Spanish vice-general granted the men a general Catholic absolution of their previous sins. Then, the men boarded the *galeota* to row across the lake to attack the Itza stronghold of Nohpeten. The Itza launched canoes from the island and paddled toward the Spaniards.

As the floating battle lines converged, the Itza tried to flank the Spaniards with two waves of canoes, while the Itza on shore loosed a hail of arrows. According to an official Spanish report, as the *galeota* neared the island an interpreter called out that the Spaniards had come in peace and friendship. The Itza answered with another shower of arrows, wounding two Spaniards. Angered, one of the wounded men fired his harquebus into the Itza stronghold. At this, the Spanish soldiers began firing at will and began leaping into the water to attack the Itza island. Using firearms and swords, the Spaniards overran the shore defenses and put the Itza to flight. As the *galeota* rowed back and forth before the island with men firing from its deck, Captain Martín de Ursua and his troops pushed up the hill to the top of Nohpeten.

The surviving Itza leaped into the lake and swam for the mainland, while Ursua struggled to plant the Spanish flag. The battle was over by eight that morning. Not a single Spaniard had been killed.

After a ceremony of thanks and prayer, Ursua ceremoniously renamed the Itza island Nuestra Señora de los Remedios y San Pablo de los Itzaes. The Spaniards scourged the island's temples and smashed the Itza idols, presumably including the stone horse. One chronicler wrote that "so vast was the number of idols that their destruction took the entire Spanish force from nine in the morning to half past five in the afternoon" (Morley and Brainerd 1956:127). Ursua selected the site of the principal Itza temple for the construction of a Christian church. The Catholic Church of Flores still stands on this site today.

"Thus," wrote Morley and Brainerd, "in the morning of a single day the power of the Itza was crushed, and the last independent Maya political entity was brought under the domination of the Spanish Crown" (Morley and Brainerd 1956:127). Michael Coe notes the irony of the fact that in the year Nohpeten fell to the conquering Spaniards, students at Harvard College were already scratching their heads over Cotton Mather's theology, "while Itza priests 2,000 miles away were still chanting ritual from hieroglyphic books" (M. Coe 1993:158).

J. Eric S. Thompson lamented the fact that despite the solid descriptions the Spaniards left of the battle of Nohpeten, no one had the foresight to produce a detailed account of life in the "Maya fossil" of Nohpeten. Strangely, records indicate that at the time of the final Itza battle, a red-headed man was living with the Itza of Nohpeten, married to an Itza woman. Before the battle, Itza visitors had told the Spaniards that the man was a Castilian, with two sons and a book like that carried by the Spanish friars (G. Jones 1998:235).

Under the impression that the man was an Englishman, Thompson wrote, "When one recalls that the writing of books on native life was for long a leading British occupation, one regrets that this sojourner among the Itza never returned to civilization to indulge in the national pastime; his observations would have been of inestimable importance" (M. Coe 1993:158).

But history pushed on in different directions. The glory of the Maya—even the fading ripples of the Itza holdouts—was gone, destined to become the stuff that archaeologists' careers are made of.

Still, the Itza Maya hardly disappeared. Numbering 150,000 at the time of their conquest in 1697, the Itza have seriously diminished in number, but several hundred Itza Maya still live today in the town of San José on the northern shore of Lake Petén Itzá (Atran 1993b:633–700). Aware that their cultural traditions, agricultural systems, and language were disappearing, however, in 1991 the Itza Maya established the Bio-Itza, a 36 square kilometer (14 sq. mi.) tropical forest reserve dedicated to Itza survival. The Bio-Itza has become the focal point of a movement to revitalize the Itza language and an impressive agroforestry system based on traditional forest management and Itza oral history.

The Bio-Itza forms part of the southern buffer zone of the 16,000 square kilometer (6,178 sq. mi.) Maya Biosphere Reserve, created in 1990 to protect the tropical forest, wetlands, and Maya archaeological ruins of Guatemala's Department of Petén. The largest tropical forest protected area north of the Amazon basin, the Maya Biosphere Reserve simultaneously protects the largest collection of Preclassic, Classic, and Postclassic Maya ruins anywhere in the Maya world. As the only aboriginal inhabitants of the Maya Biosphere Reserve or its buffer zone, the Itza Maya are the appropriate standard-bearers for the region; they carry on traditions that originated in the preconquest history of the Maya world.

The Rise of the Western World

After the Spaniards had finally come to dominate—at least politically—the entire Maya world, history took a decidedly Western tack. Forces both regional and international gradually led the Maya and non-Maya inhabitants to join with the rest of Mexico and Central America in declaring independence from Spain in 1821. The Maya of Chiapas learned in 1824 that they were no longer part of Guatemala, but were now Mexican. Maya from Yucatán were even pressed into military service to defend Mexican territory, and some marched northward into Texas with General Santa Ana in 1836 to storm the Alamo in San Antonio (Howren 1913).

Guatemala's Maya became part of the Mexican empire for a few years, then were told that Guatemala had reasserted its independence to join the United Provinces of Central America. Later, Guatemala became a separate republic, which it remains today. The Yucatec, Q'eqchi, and Mopán Maya residents of Belize became part of the British empire and eventually became citizens of an independent Belize in 1981.

Despite these political maneuverings through the decades, Maya village life changed slowly. Viewed as second-class citizens during the colonial period and well into the modern period, the Maya held tight to tradition where they could and adapted to change when survival required it. As centuries of oppression began to slowly lift, Maya traits began to reassert themselves. In several places, this reemergence boiled into outright revolt—as in the Yucatec Maya Caste War of 1847 (G. Jones 2001). Inspired by a talking cross, the Yucatec Maya rose up against their Spanish overlords and pushed them to seek refuge in the capital city of Mérida in 1848. When the Maya retired to plant their fields at the start of the rainy season, the Spaniards brought in reinforcements and began the slow march toward reclaiming the Yucatán Peninsula as their own, a process that some Yucatec Maya declare still has not been accomplished.

Guerrilla warfare between the two sides flared for another 50 years, until the Spaniards unilaterally declared in 1901 that peace had come. During the decades in between, however, the Maya had briefly created a Yucatán ruled by Maya warriors and religious leaders.

Other rebellions punctuated the late nineteenth and early twentieth centuries in Chiapas, Guatemala, and the Yucatán Peninsula. Guatemala's civil strife took on a Maya face during the 1970s through 1990s, as highland Maya farmers were transformed into warriors fighting against the Guatemalan Army. In an ironic twist of history, Maya guerrilla fighters frequently found themselves shooting at Maya cousins forcibly drafted into the army by the Guatemalan government.

As recently as 1994, Tzeltal, Tzotzil, and Tojolobal Maya—united as the Zapatista National Liberation Army—rose in armed rebellion against Spanish-speaking landowners and soldiers in Chiapas, demanding justice, democracy, and land. Modern politics have so far prevented a full military assault on these historical and linguistic cousins of the Choltí, Itza, and Yucatec warriors of previous centuries, but at this writing several hundred of them continue to hide in the hills above the island fortress of Lacantún.

These continuing struggles remind the non-Maya citizens of Mexico and Central America that the Maya are far more than an archaeological memory. Today, 7 million Maya live in Mexico, Guatemala, Belize, and Honduras. Another 1 million live in the United States. At least 4 million people continue to speak one of 30 living Maya languages as their primary tongue. Almost half of modern Guatemala's 13 million people are of Maya descent. The Maya are the second-largest group of indigenous people in the Western Hemisphere, after the Quechua speakers of the Andean republics of Ecuador, Peru, and Bolivia.

Far from being an echo of a jungle-covered past, modern Maya communities display a blend of survival skills learned during centuries of conflict and traditions that reach back to the Preclassic past. Adaptability, ethnic cohesion, and deep cultural roots have allowed the Maya to weave ancient views and technological advances into the fabric of the future.

The story of the people and traditions of the Maya Tropical Forest is one of change, resilience, and determination. That the Maya and their traditions have been so adaptable is nothing short of miraculous. That so much has survived is a joyous relief.

3 Natural History of the Maya Tropical Forest

Introduction

Long before humans came to occupy the Maya region, geology had divided it into highlands and lowlands. Photographs taken from NASA's space shuttles as they pass over Guatemala show a long chain of volcanic mountains streaming westward along the Pacific Ocean into Chiapas and eastward into El Salvador and Honduras. Here and there, a few volcanoes belch smoke and ash and spew red, iridescent lava down slopes blanketed with pine and oak trees.

In the scores of river valleys that lie north of this long chain of volcanoes, today's highland Maya families live in dispersed villages surrounded by forests of pine, oak, laurel, and madrone trees. Wheat and cabbages—crops introduced by Spaniards in the sixteenth century—grow on hillsides with the native corn, squashes, and beans that the Maya have depended on for millennia. Sheep and cows, also brought to the New World by Spaniards, graze in small clearings, while young women dressed in colorful *huipiles* (blouses) weave on backstrap looms in the shelter of nearby trees.

In the volcanic highlands, much of Maya history seems to be still alive. The Sunday markets of Chichicastenango, Antigua, and San Cristóbal de las Casas are kaleidoscope theaters of colored textiles, exotic vegetables, and burning incense. Weekend excursions will take you to centuries-old highland Maya cities—Iximché and Mixco Viejo—where French and Italian tourists sort through Maya weavings at handicraft stalls and black-haired boys with Maya features chase soccer balls between the ancient mounds.

Immediately south of the volcanic chain lies a thin edge of coastal lowlands that slope into the Pacific Ocean. During the time of the ancient

Maya, and later during the centuries of Spanish occupation, this fertile Pacific coast was the source of great agricultural wealth. Some of the earliest Maya villages appeared along this thin edge of prime land between the mountains and the sea, and its easy riches of cacao—later sugarcane and coffee—have made it prized territory for millennia.

Looking north toward the Gulf of Mexico and the Caribbean, photographs taken from the space shuttle show the Maya highlands of Mexico and Central America fading gradually into a lower lying area we call the Maya lowlands. This region too can be divided into two regions—northern and southern. In the north lies the flat Yucatán Peninsula, which juts like a swollen thumb into the Caribbean Sea. Yucatán is an ancient limestone shelf left suspended between gulf and sea by geological upheaval and aeons of lowered ocean levels. The northern Maya lowlands of the Yucatán Peninsula encompass the dry, flat Mexican states of Campeche, Yucatán, and Quintana Roo. Moving northward across the landscape of the Yucatán Peninsula, the land becomes flatter and the forest progressively drier, until the peninsula, covered with thorny scrub brush and dotted with sinkholes called *cenotes*, disappears into the sea.

The southern lowlands include the low-lying wetlands and savannas of the Mexican state of Tabasco, the Selva Lacandona of eastern Chiapas, the Guatemalan Petén and nearby Lake Izabal, and the nation of Belize—the latter despite the sudden appearance of a small repeat of the highland ranges in southern Belize called, appropriately, the Maya Mountains. The ancient Maya cities of the southern Maya lowlands range from Copán, Honduras, in the east to the sites of Yaxchilán, Palenque, and Toniná, Chiapas, in the west.

Within the southern Maya lowlands is the forested area we call the Maya Tropical Forest—eastern Chiapas, the Guatemalan Petén, the forests of southern Yucatán, and all of Belize. Here, the traveler must search for history in the dense vegetation. The tropical forest has long since reclaimed the Maya cities of Bonampak, Caracol, Yaxchilán, and Mirador, which flourished in this region more than 1,000 years ago.

Given its impact on New World history and on the careers of hundreds of explorers, archaeologists, and photographers, the Maya Tropical Forest is surprisingly small. The entire Maya region, including the Maya Tropical Forest and the adjoining Maya highlands, covers an area about half the size of Texas, or two and one-half times the size of England.

For almost 10,000 years, the vegetation of the Maya Tropical Forest has been a mixture of moist tropical forest, tropical savanna, and wetlands

called *bajos*, the latter dominated by vines, lianas, bromeliads, and logwood (Méndez 1999:33). During the past 30 years, though, much of this
vegetation has fallen victim to loggers, settlers' axes, and the giant fires of
cattle ranchers.

The first writer to recognize the Maya Tropical Forest as a single ecosystem was the lawyer Rodulfo Brito Foucher, who traveled through the region in 1924, visiting the early logging camps where mahogany and Spanish
cedar trees were being cut and rolled into the rivers to float downstream
for capture and export to Europe and the United States. In a long article
published in a university journal, Brito Foucher began his account of the
logging camps with a description of the forest itself (Brito Foucher 1931).
Almost 80 years later, what Brito Foucher saw in 1924 still holds true.

> In the southeast of Mexico, in Belize, and in the north of the Republic
> of Guatemala exists a grand territorial extension that geographically
> can be considered one unit, although politically it is divided between
> the three mentioned countries. It is an immense region of virgin
> forests that, in part, remain unexplored by man until today. (Brito
> Foucher 1931, cited in de Vos 1988b:201)

The Maya Tropical Forest is the second-largest block of continuous tropical forest in the Western Hemisphere, bested only by the Amazon forest
of South America. The Maya forest also is one of the most biologically
diverse regions on the planet, surpassed in its number of plant and animal
species only by lowland Amazonia and the lowland forests of the tropical Andean region—the tropical forests of Colombia, Ecuador, Peru, and
Bolivia. All told, the Maya Tropical Forest is home to more than 3,400
species of vascular plants, 60 species of freshwater fish, 42 of amphibians,
121 of reptiles, at least 571 of birds, and 163 of mammals (Conservation
International 2003).

This impressive biological diversity has its roots in the geological past.
During most of the last 65 million years—the era that paleontologists call
the Age of Mammals—the North American and South American continents remained separate from one another, and their very different life-
forms evolved in isolation from one another. On the northern continent,
rabbits, gophers, squirrels, cats, raccoons, bears, tapirs, primitive horses,
deer, and peccaries roamed the forests and savannas. In the south, the land
teemed with opossums, armadillos, porcupines, sloths, anteaters, monkeys, agoutis, and capybaras.

It was only 3 million years ago—very recently, in geological time—that crucial sections of Central America were lifted out of the sea, creating a land bridge between the North and South American continents. Gradually, species began to flow in both directions across the Central American land bridge, in what paleontologists call the Great American Biotic Interchange (Webb 1997; D. Wallace 1997a). In the tropical rainforest of the newest major piece of real estate on earth, South American monkeys and opossums met North American squirrels and deer for the first time.

Over millions of years, the broken topography and microclimates of the Central American land bridge also produced its own wealth of biodiversity, resulting in high rates of endemism—species that appear nowhere else on earth—in plants, birds, mammals, reptiles, and amphibians. This rare combination of regional endemism and the mixing of species from two continents crowds Central America with so much life that the region supports 7 percent of our planet's species diversity on less than 0.5 percent of its land (D. Wallace 1997a:xiii). Nature writer David Rains Wallace calls the region "a miniature continent in the number and distinctiveness of its regions" (D. Wallace 1997b:72).

In the twenty-first century, the single largest expanse of this original wealth of Mesoamerican biological diversity is the Maya Tropical Forest of southern Mexico, northern Guatemala, and Belize. Here, North and South American species mix with native plants and animals in forests and grasslands that grow on thin topsoil covering a limestone shelf 3,000 meters (9,840 feet) thick (Coates 1997:32). Geological forces lifted this great limestone shelf from the sea at the end of the Cretaceous period. Drenched with tropical rains, the land weathered into distinctive convolutions of limestone towers, subterranean caverns, and karst basins marked by a paucity of surface drainage, giving the region "a unique regional character" within Mexico and Central America (Coates 1997:33).

One of the elemental features of the Maya Tropical Forest is its plant diversity, both in types of forest and in the variety of plant species within those forest types. The region known today as the Maya Tropical Forest (la Selva Maya, in Spanish) includes forests that range from the true rainforest of extreme southeastern Chiapas and southwestern Petén to the semi-deciduous tropical forest of the northern Petén and southern Yucatán Peninsula. In Chiapas, the Selva Lacandona is mostly a lower montane tropical rainforest that lies between the pine and oak forest of the Chiapas highlands and the lowland swamp forests of the state of Tabasco. The Selva Lacandona itself is marked by various ecological zones, including moist tropical forest and even pine forest on mountains of 1,000 meters (3,300 feet) (Breedlove 1973:149; 1981).

The key point here is that what appears at first to be a homogenous splatter of green vegetation reveals itself as a highly diverse collection of vegetation types. But diversity is also the hallmark within these vegetation types. While forests in temperate zones of the globe are generally dominated by only a few tree species, a tropical forest like the Maya forest supports up to 200 different species of trees—as well as hundreds of species of vines, fungi, shrubs, and ferns—on a single hectare (2.47 acres) of forest.

Weather

Biologist Marston Bates published an early book about the tropics, entitled *Where Winter Never Comes* (1963). Bates was alluding to the fact that tropical forests do not experience four seasons, as in the world's temperate zones, but only two—wet and dry. This holds true in the Maya Tropical Forest as well. But to confuse issues, Spanish speakers call the rainy season *invierno* (winter) and the dry season *verano* (summer).

Rainy season in the Maya Tropical Forest occurs between late May and late November, a six-month period when up to 3 meters (118 inches) of rain fall in some parts of the forest. In the early part of the rainy season—from late May to early June—the days are almost predictable. The season brings foggy dawns, followed by bright, sunny mornings with scattered white, puffy cumulus clouds. Yet the mornings sag with elevated humidity from yesterday's rains, and cloudy afternoons guarantee more rain to come. I have seen Maya Indians look up at the morning sky and predict, accurately, within 15 minutes of when the rain would begin to fall in the afternoon.

The rain may begin gently enough, but as it builds in intensity it gives true meaning to the term "tropical downpour." The rain pounds the thatched palm roofs of forest communities, bringing conversation to a halt. Rivulets of runoff appear everywhere, joining together in their search for the nearest stream. The streams overflow their narrow banks, flooding the neighboring forest as they merge into the rushing rivers.

The rivers run the color of café au lait from sediment released from the exposed soil by the heavy deluges. The rain washes dust from the vegetation, and the forest glistens green from new growth brought on by the moisture. Animals disperse away from the rivers to eat and drink in what is now a well-watered forest.

As if following an unseen calendar, most rainy seasons in the Maya Tropical Forest are punctuated by a two-week period during July or August when the rains suddenly cease for a mini-dry season. The forest shakes off the clouds for a brief period of rapid growth, spurred by the intensely hot sun. Spanish speakers in Mexico and Guatemala call this two-week dry period *la canícula* (the dog days). Belizeans refer to it as "the mauger season," from the Creole word for "meager" (but pronounced "maga").

Then the rains return with a vengeance, bringing periods of three to four days when nothing happens but cold rain. Maya families huddle beneath the dripping eaves of their thatch-roof houses, watching for a break in the clouds, or work inside around the fire in quality family time. The Lacandón Maya call these long downpours *shaman*, which means "north," referring to the direction from which the storms emerge. Spanish speakers call them *nortes* for the same reason.

When the rain finally ceases in late November or early December, the days remain humid. During the short days of December and January, nights are chilly and families sit around the fire to warm themselves. As the months progress, the weather begins to warm, and the lack of rain turns the forest dry and brittle. Animals dash furtively to drink at the edge of the river, keeping a wary eye alert for predators. Farmers clear undergrowth and fell trees to make new agricultural plots, leaving the vegetation to dry in the increasingly hot sun. In March, at the peak of the dry season, they set fire to the dried mounds of branches, leaves, and tree trunks, sending furious plumes of white smoke into the atmosphere and sometimes inadvertently setting fire to the adjoining forest, creating forest fires that devour the dried out tropical forest.

The land smolders from the fires and the sun's heat until the sky begins to turn purple-gray with clouds and the rains begin another green year of tropical growth.

Animals

No matter what the time of year, one of the delights of visiting the Maya Tropical Forest is experiencing its animal life: glimpsing a jaguarundi crossing the trail, watching a crocodile slip into the river at the approach of your boat, waking up to the sounds of a dozen bird species celebrating the coming of dawn—the protesting shriek of brown jays, the owl-like "hoo hoo" of the motmots, the catlike mewing of the clay-colored robins, and the peculiar church-organ roll of the oropendulas.

Here are descriptions of some of the most interesting of these creatures. Before you begin, recognize that my introduction to many of these animals began with a peculiar bias. I worked with the Lacandón Maya in the lowland forest of eastern Chiapas for more than three years, and—as lifelong residents of the Maya Tropical Forest—the Lacandones and other Maya families view many of these animals as food resources. I have reported here on indigenous use of these creatures as bushmeat for its ethnographic value, but my interest is in conserving these increasingly rare animals, not in eating them. I urge you to consider them in the same light.

MAMMALS

The Maya Tropical Forest hosts a wealth of wild mammals, some of them easier to spot than others, ranging from retiring nocturnal opossums to cats of various sizes and ecological niches. You would be very lucky if you caught a glimpse of the rare but present puma (*Puma concolor*), the margay cat (*Leopardus wiedii*), or the ground-dwelling ocelot (*Leopardus pardalis*). You are likely to see the rare silky anteater (*Cyclopes didactylus*) only in the zoo. But you may be lucky enough to see a kinkajou (*Potos flavus*), a large-eyed nocturnal tree-dweller that the Lacandón Maya call *ak'maash*, "night monkey," and you are very likely to see the gray fox (*Urocyon cinereoargenteus*) bounding up the stone stairs in the ruins of Tikal, or one of the smaller carnivores such as the grison (*Galictis vittata*) or tayra (*Eira barbara*) in one of the more remote Maya ruins.

Also, keep your eyes out for the mammals described in the next few pages.

PACAS AND AGOUTIS   Two large rodents, the paca (*Agouti paca*) and the agouti (*Dasyprocta punctata*) live throughout the Maya Tropical Forest and are favored foods among families in the region. The larger of these rodents—reaching up to 10 kilograms (22 pounds)—is the paca (Spanish = *tepesquintle* or *tuza*; Belizean English = gibnut; Lacandón Maya = *ha'ale*). They are reddish-brown, pig-shaped animals with heads like a fat-cheeked squirrel. Lines of white stippling trace across their sides, aiding no doubt in camouflaging them as they walk the forest floor at night, searching for tree fruits and seeds.

As you would expect, pacas (and agoutis) have the four large incisor teeth that are characteristic of rodents, helping them gnaw on fruits, nuts, and seeds. During the dry season, the nocturnal paca eats leaves and lives off its accumulated fat. Agoutis bury seeds in the forest floor during the rainy season and seek them out during the dryer months. Because they fail to find some of the tree seeds they have buried, the agoutis serve as effective seed dispersers, planting new trees throughout the forest.

Pacas are nocturnal animals, so the preferred method of hunting them is to seek out their hiding places in hollow logs or in burrows in hillsides or at the base of trees. Today, hunters walk through the forest with their hunting dogs, waiting for the dogs to pick up the scent of the paca (or another edible mammal). If a dog can trace the scent to a paca's hiding place, the hunter will dig the animal out, or sometimes attempt to smoke it out with burning brush pushed down into the hole. When the animal emerges, either fleeing the fire or pulled out by the hunter, the man kills it with a machete.

The agouti (Spanish = *guaqueque*; Belizean English = Indian rabbit or bush rabbit; Lacandón Maya = *tzup*) is similar to the paca in shape but is completely orange-brown, with taller, thinner legs. Again, its head looks like that of a large squirrel. Agoutis are related to pacas, as well as to guinea pigs. You may see them in well-protected forests, such as that of Tikal National Park, searching the forest floor for seeds and nuts. They eat by sitting on their back haunches and holding their food in their front paws, working it over much the way a mouse or squirrel eats. The agouti is a diurnal animal. The Maya hunt them during the day with dogs and machete.

DEER Three species of deer live in the Maya Tropical Forest: the familiar Virginia white-tailed (*Odocoileus virginianus*; Spanish = *venado cola blanca*; Belizean English = savanna deer; Lacandón Maya = *keh*) and two species of the more exotic brocket deer (*Mazama americana* and *Mazama pandora*; Spanish = *temezate*; Belizean English = antelope; Lacandón Maya and Itza Maya = *yuk*). The white-tailed deer of the Maya forest is smaller than its North American counterpart and favors mixed forest-grasslands areas. By contrast, the smaller brocket deer is a forest dweller that is difficult to spot in the dense undergrowth. When frightened, the white-tail deer escapes with great speed, flashing its characteristic white tail. Brocket deer are more likely to slip away into the forest, although they will jump into water to escape.

Taxonomists now recognize that both the red brocket deer (*Mazama americana*) and the brown brocket deer (*Mazama pandora*) live in the

Maya Tropical Forest (Medellín, Gardner, and Aranda 1998). Traditional Maya in the region point out that during the dry season, the brown brocket deer move into the open swampy areas (*bajos*), while the red brocket deer remain in the forest and gravitate toward streams and other permanent water sources (Peter Hubbell, personal communication, January 2005). Unlike the red brocket, the brown brocket deer occupy the drier deciduous forest habitats of the Yucatán Peninsula, but Guatemalan conservationist Santiago Billy found skulls of the brown brocket in the tropical forest of the Guatemalan Petén as well (Medellín, Gardner, and Aranda 1998; Santiago Billy, personal communication, 1987).

All three species of deer are hunted for their meat and skins. Among the Lacandón Maya of Chiapas, many houses still have hides of the tiny brocket deer hanging from the rafters to dry or in use on the dirt floor as small rugs. Throughout the Maya forest today, the brocket deer is more commonly seen; the white-tailed deer has been largely hunted out.

JAGUARS   The most regal and most feared mammal in the Maya Tropical Forest is the jaguar (*Panthera onca;* Spanish = *tigre* or *jaguar;* Belizean English = tiger; Yucatec Maya and Itza Maya = *hach balum*). A large, powerful cat, the jaguar was a symbol of royalty among the ancient Maya, and their skins were a status symbol among Maya rulers, judging by the frequency with which these people appear dressed in them on carved stelae and painted ceramics. As the top predator in the forest, jaguars feed on a variety of other animals, including deer, pacas, peccaries, and armadillos. They also eat turtles, iguanas, and some birds and fish (Reid 1997:274). They can grow to a supersized 136 kilograms (300 pounds) and stretch to 2 meters (6.5 feet) from head to toe.

Despite their fearsome reputation, jaguars are not known to attack human beings with any frequency. Naturalist Victoria Schlesinger writes that "jaguars very rarely attack people; it is most common when their cubs are threatened" (Schlesinger 2001:165). Belize Zoo director Sharon Matola points out that she has never heard of any confirmed report in Central America of a jaguar attack on a human (S. Matola, e-mail to author, December 20, 2004). At the same time, Lacandón Maya have a traditional prayer, chanted to the gods while holding palm leaves over the smoke of burning copal incense, that includes the lines "Do not permit the snake to bite me; do not permit the jaguar to bite me. For this I am well; cease all evil" (Tozzer 1907:175), an indication that whether or not jaguars have attacked humans in the Maya forest, the Lacandones, the most traditional of the Maya forest's people, still give them a healthy dose of respect and distance.

The Maya Tropical Forest has the largest population of jaguars north of the equator (Swank and Teer 1989). Calakmul Biosphere Reserve has an estimated 400 individuals, but Belize probably has more jaguars than any other Central American country (Barry and Vernon 1995:129). They are also the best researched (Rabinowitz 2000).

Despite scores of trips through the Maya forest and despite seeing fresh jaguar prints on a dozen occasions in all three countries, I have yet to see a jaguar in the wild. They very likely saw me, however.

"Jaguars are so hard to find," Dr. Eduardo Carrillo, a Costa Rican biologist, reported in *The New York Times*. "I can be standing right next to one, and I know it because I have picked up the signal from its radio collar, and still I may never see it" (Angier 2003:D1).

To my knowledge, the closest I came to a jaguar was in the northern Guatemala archaeological site of Mirador. Tom Sever, Santiago Billy, Dan Lee, Frank Miller, Will Garrett, and I had spent the late afternoon on top of the tallest of the temples, Danta, and climbed down at sunset with two guards from Guatemala's Instituto de Antropología e Historia (IDAEH). We returned to the IDAEH camp a mile away in two groups, some of us walking ahead, Tom Sever and the two guards walking about 10 minutes behind. We were already puttering around the camp when Tom and the guards came in and excitedly told us that two jaguars had stalked them all the way back to camp. When Tom and the guards had stopped walking, the jaguars had stopped walking. When the three moved forward again, the jaguars followed. As Tom and the two frightened guards reached the camp and the fire we were lighting, the pair of jaguars peeled away and sauntered into the forest. Jaguars are notoriously curious, and it is very likely that the pair were simply trying to figure out what was going on in their territory.

In past decades, hunters killed jaguars for their pelts. Until Mexico signed the Convention on International Trade in Endangered Species (CITES) in 1991, Guatemalan jaguar hunters killed hundreds of the animals in the northern Petén and sold them across the northern border of the country to Mexican dealers who then exported them to Europe, the United States, and Asia. Mexico's entry into the CITES treaty helped calm this illegal trade.

According to former jaguar hunters I interviewed in the Guatemalan Petén, they lured jaguars into a trap through two methods. Some hunters began by killing a monkey with a rifle shot, then dragging the dead monkey through the forest to lay a scent trail. The hunter would then hang the monkey from a vine or tree in an open spot and hide in ambush until a jaguar showed up to investigate. If an unsuspecting jaguar appeared, the hunter bagged it.

Other hunters told me they used a jaguar call known in Spanish as a *tecomate*. To make a *tecomate*, the hunter buys or grows a bottom-heavy, hour-glass shaped gourd about 30 centimeters (1 foot) tall. He slices off both ends of the gourd and stretches the skin of a horse, deer, or cow over the larger end, sewing it in place. He punches a small hole in the middle of the skin and feeds a 45-centimeter-long (18-inch) length of horse tail hair through it, securing it with a knot above the skin. The rest of the horsehair hangs down inside the gourd. The hunter reaches into the gourd, grasps the horsehair between his thumb and bent index finger, and pulls on the hair slowly to create a moaning, jaguar-like call. Successful hunters say the *tecomate*, in the hands of a skillful user, will call forth curious jaguars that can then be shot for their pelts.

MONKEYS The Maya Tropical Forest has two types of monkeys, spiders and howlers. The Central American spider monkey (*Ateles geoffroyi*; Spanish = *mono araña, chango*; Lacandón Maya = *ma'ash*) is characterized by long, thin arms and legs—hence the name, spider monkey—and feeds on fruit and leaves high in the trees during the day in groups of two to five, although several dozen may gather at night to sleep on tree branches. In the Maya forest, spider monkeys have almost black fur on their backs and lighter fur, brown to tan, on their undersides and rump. Spider monkeys are curious and will sometimes stop to watch humans walking along the forest floor. If they feel you are intruding in their territory, they may bark and growl and break dry branches from the trees and drop them on your head. More obnoxiously, they will sometimes urinate or defecate on unwanted intruders. Nonetheless, they are fun to watch from a distance. You may see small baby monkeys slung under the mother's chest, holding on tightly to her fur as she leaps from one tree branch to another.

The second monkey in the Maya forest is the endangered Yucatán black howler (*Alouatta pigra*; Spanish = *saraguato, mono aullador*; Belizean English = baboon; Yucatec Maya and Lacandón Maya = *batz'*), best known for its loud call, which carries for several miles through forest vegetation in the evening and early morning. Howlers are larger and more robust than the spider monkey, and their heads are larger. Their long fur is entirely black. While spider monkeys tend to like undisturbed forest and travel in large groups, howler monkeys will live in less than pristine areas and travel in families of two to six. They are frequently seen near water sources, sometimes feeding or lounging on tree branches along rivers. Howlers eat leaves, fruit, and flowers; they are especially fond of the chicozapote (*Manilkara zapota*) and ramon (*Brosimum alicastrum*).

The Lacandón Maya report that a second type of howler, likely the mantled howler monkey, *Alouatta palliata,* lived in the Selva Lacandona of Chiapas as recently as 40 years ago. The mantled howler is black, like the Yucatán black howler, but has long, yellowish fur on the sides of its body. This report certainly seems plausible; the mantled howler's natural range includes southern Tabasco and northern Chiapas, Mexico. The mantled howler has not been reported in the Selva Lacandona for decades. It does appear, however, in the Punta Manabique Wildlife Refuge in Izabal, Guatemala (Steury 2003).

Monkeys are important animals in tropical forest ecology, because they are major seed dispersers. Highly mobile, and with a diet high in fruit, monkeys drop partially eaten fruit to the forest floor, or eat the fruit from a seed, which they then drop to the forest floor, thus casting seeds in a wider pattern than the seeds would otherwise reach. Notwithstanding their importance to forest ecology, monkeys have ended up in the cooking pots of many Maya families. The Lacandón Maya claim that their gods' favorite food is tamales made from monkey meat, and Lacandones formerly hunted both spider and howler monkeys to treat the gods (Lacandones themselves are also inordinately fond of monkey tamales.) The traditional Lacandón bow and arrow set includes an arrow with a specially carved, wooden foreshaft (*k'ek' che'*), which has carved barbs (*k'ek'*) along its length. The barbs prevent a pierced monkey from pulling out the arrow and disappearing into the forest canopy. Instead, with the arrow firmly seated in his body, the monkey bleeds out and falls to the forest floor, where the hunter, who has been following beneath the monkey, has only to pick it up and take it home to cook and eat.

During the mid-1970s, I lived for a month with the family of Pancho Na Bor of Lacanjá Chan Sayab, a Lacandón Maya community in the southern Selva Lacandona, Chiapas. I ate meals with the family and became totally and secretly enamored with one of Pancho Na Bor's younger wives (he had three at the time). While we ate meals, I would watch her from the end of the table, as she pushed her long, black hair back from her delicately beautiful Maya face. But I lost my crush on her one morning when I came to the breakfast table and saw her munching on the cooked head of a howler monkey, as if she were eating an apple: crunch, crunch, slurp, peel, chomp.

TAPIRS   The Central American tapir (*Tapirus bairdii*; Spanish = *danta* or *tapir*; Belizean English = mountain cows; Lacandón Maya = *k'ash tzimin*) is not common in the Maya Tropical Forest, but you can find them in the more remote regions of the protected areas: Montes Azules Biosphere Reserve in Chiapas, Laguna del Tigre National Park in Guatemala, and in the Cockscomb Basin Wildlife Preserve of Belize. Tapirs are the largest land animals in Central America—150 to 300 kilograms (330–660 pounds). They have a long proboscis that they use to browse for leaves, fruits, flowers, and grasses. Tapirs spend most of their time foraging, but rest during both night and day in mud wallows or shallow water. They tend to freeze in place when disturbed, trying to blend into the shadows of the forest undergrowth, but they may crash through the vegetation or jump into a stream or river to escape if they feel threatened. Tapirs communicate with one another through a system of grunts and whispers and whistle to one another over long distances (Reid 1997:279).

Many rural Belizeans incorrectly believe that tapirs will attack and kill human beings, peeling their victim's skin directly off the muscle.

COATIMUNDIS   Coatimundis (*Nasua narica*; Spanish = *pisote* or *tejón*; Belizean English = quash; Lacandón Maya = *chäk k'eken* or *susu*) look like red-brown, elongated raccoons, with especially pointed snouts. Hikers in the forest frequently see them in groups of 2 to 12, moving through the forest undergrowth with their long, ringed tails upright. They are especially common in Tikal National Park and walk among hikers and tourists with no fear. Coatis forage for invertebrates under logs and in leaf litter, but they will also climb trees to eat fruits such as wild figs or wild hog plums (*Spondias mombin*).

Families near Calakmul Biosphere Reserve, Mexico, prize coatimundi meat for roasting. They dig a hole in the ground, build a fire in it, then place stones on top of the hot coals. They place the skinned coatimundi on top of the stones, then cover it with leaves and let it bake for an hour. The resulting meat is delicious, I have been told.

The Lacandón Maya blame some infant disorders on the coatimundi. Tradition holds that a father who walks along a trail that coatimundis have followed will sometimes pick up the animals' secretions on his feet. When he returns home, the father spreads this contamination to his newborn infant, who develops an illness characterized, according to Lacandón informants, by "sticky skin, sleeplessness, and failure to suckle" (possibly infant colic). The only cure for the illness is a chant that a male relative must perform, and he must perform it flawlessly. The man holds the baby in his lap and leans over it to whisper the rhythmic healing chant (called a *kunyah* in Lacandón). The coatimundi chant entices the animals with their favorite forest foods, "paying" the coatis to leave the child in peace. (This system of magical healing mimics the Lacandones' own payments to the gods of copal incense and rubber figures to heal human diseases.) The coatimundi chant's list of preferred foods illustrates the depth of knowledge that Lacandones have about animal ecology.

Modern research on infant colic reveals that the Lacandón Maya may be on to something. Although colic is a normal and inevitable phase of early infant development, getting a colicky baby to stop crying tries the patience of parents from any cultural group. According to a 2005 article in the *New York Times*, California physician Harvey Karp discovered that re-creating an infant's sensation in the womb can help calm it down. The method is to hold the baby tightly, jiggle it gently, and make a whooshing sound (which simulates the sound of blood rushing through the placenta). According to Dr. Karp, the practice puts the baby back into the trancelike state it experienced inside the womb. Testimony that the system works comes in the fact that Dr. Karp's book describing the technique has sold 350,000 copies and been translated into 12 languages (Blakeslee 2005:D6). The Lacandones independently discovered the same technique. Their tradition of holding a colicky baby tightly and bouncing it lightly while whispering the coatimundi healing chant in its ear produces exactly the same successful effect that Dr. Karp describes.

U kunyah chäk k'ek'en
Lacandón Maya Chant to Cure the Coatimundi Growling Disease

Hash poiteh	Truly wash it
ti tam beh	on the deep road
ti tu sum beh	there all bunched together
ne tam beh	very deep road
hach koton beh	very male road
ti ton beh	there on the road

ti ku man on beh	where they move on the road
wawa näk u neh u man on beh	with tails raised in the air they move
tan u yawät ton beh	they are growling on the road
ti ton beh	there on the road
hash palil on beh	true child
u kat ulen	must come home
u kat u che'eneh	must be cured
u kat u che'eneh tech on beh	must cure you
u kat ki hach b'oteh	must be truly paid
ne ton beh	very male road
u kat ki hash bo'ot on beh	must be truly paid
u kat u che'enech on beh	must cure you
yawät on beh	growling on the road
hash palil on beh	true child
ti ton beh	there on the road
tan yawät ton beh	they are growling
ne nah beh	very big road
chuikak u man on beh	moving through the trees
u kat u kichil on beh	they must arrive
ti ton beh	there on the road
kat kulen	it wants me to come home
lahi yawät ton beh	all growling on the road
ti ton beh	there on the road
lah u yoch on beh	that is their food
säkatz on beh	sonzapote
lahi u yoch on beh	that is their food
ti ton beh	there on the road
ha'as on beh	mamey
lahi yoch on beh	that is their food
ne ton beh	very male road
ti sinah witz on beh	from the tops of hills
ti yamyam man hebon beh	through the valleys
ti ku tal on beh	they come on the road
tan tu näk tantik y yahi on beh	brushing their disease on the road
ti ton beh	there on the road
suwik u tan	squeeze its calcium
u kat u ki hash bo'oteh	it must be truly paid
u kat u ki tak chaeh ton beh	it must be rubbed (on the infant)
u sayab na witz on beh	with virgin spring water

u kat ki in hash bo'otah on beh	it must be truly well paid
ti ton beh	there on the road
yetel k'uhtan	with holy words
u kat u ki hash bo'toteh	it must be truly well paid
u kabi u ni on beh	excretions of their noses
ti ton beh	there on the road
u kabi u tan u käp	excretions of the soles of their feet
u kabi u neh on beh	excretions of their tails
ti ton beh	there on the road
u kat u che'enih u yawät ton beh	it must be cured, the growling
hash palil on beh	true child
u kat u ki hash bo'oteh ton beh	it must be truly paid
lahi u yoch ton beh	that is their food
kopoh beh	wild figs
ti ton beh	there on the road
op che ton beh	wild anona
lahi u yoch on beh	that is their food
ti ton beh	there on the road
u kat ulen	it must come home
uch on beh	wild black persimmon
lahi u yoch on beh	that is their food
ek' bache on beh	black balche
ah kopoh beh	wild figs
ti ku man on beh	where they move on the road
chiukak u man on beh	through the trees they move
ti ton beh	there on the road
u kat u ulen on beh	it must come home
u kat ulen ti hash palil on beh	it must come home to the true child
u kat ulen ti u hash bo'otik on beh	it must come home to be truly paid
suwik ton beh	to squeeze it in the water
u kat u ki hash bo'otech	it must be truly well paid
u kat u tupi ton beh	it must be finished
u kabi u ni on beh	the excretions of their noses
u kabi u yok on beh	the excretions of their feet
ti ton beh	there on the road
u kat ch'eneh ton beh	it must be cured
ti ku man on beh	where they move on the road
säkätz on beh	sonzapote
lahi u yoch on beh	that is their food

ti ton beh	there on the road
ha'as on beh	mamey
lahi u yoch on beh	that is their food
ti ton beh	there on the road
ti ton beh	there on the road
u kat ulen ton beh	it must come home
ah koyok on beh	wild avocado fruit
lahi u yoch on beh	that is their food
on ton beh	avocado
lahi u yoch on beh	that is their food
le ten ton beh	there on the road
u oni wïtz on beh	wild mountain avocado
koyok on beh	wild avocado fruit
lahi u yoch on beh	that is their food
hach bämäsh on beh	ramon fruit
lahi u yoch on beh	that is their food
ti ton beh	there on the road
ti ku man ti u käp on beh	where they move with their legs (through the branches)
tan u yawät u man on beh	they are growling
koton beh	male road
u kat u ki hash bo'oteh	they must be truly well paid
u kat u che'eneh u yawät on beh	their growling must be cured
ti ton beh	there on the road
ha'as che on beh	mamey
lahi u yoch on beh	that is their food
ti ton beh	there on the road
u kat ulen on beh	it must come home
sismuk on beh	thorned berry vine
lahi u yoch on beh	that is their food
ti ton beh	there on the road
u kat u ki lukseh on beh	it must be well erased
u yawät on beh	their growling
hash palil on beh	true child
u kat ch'eneh on beh	it must be cured
u yawät ton beh	its disease
u kat ki hash bo'otech	it must be truly well paid
u hash palil on beh	its true child
u kat u che'eneh yawät on beh	the growling disease must be cured

ti ton beh	there on the road
ti ku man on beh	where they move on the road
lahi u yoch on beh	that is their food
sotz bämäsh on beh	"covered ramon" fruit
lahi u yoch on beh	that is their food
mehen kopoh on beh	little fig
u kat che'eneh on beh	it must be cured
u kat u ulen on beh	it must come home
ten ton beh	me on the road
ha'as on beh	mamey
ti ton beh	there on the road
on te' on beh	avocado tree
mehen on te'	little avocado tree
lahi u yoch on beh	that is their food
säk on te	white avocado tree
lahi u yoch on beh	that is their food
ne ton beh	very male road
u kat ulen on beh	it needs to come home
ek' on te	black avocado tree
lahi u yoch on beh	that is their food
säk on te	white avocado tree
lahi u yoch on beh	that is their food
hoch on beh	Nectandra fruit
lahi u yoch on beh	that is their food
u kat u ki luksah on beh	it must be well erased
mehen on te	small avocado tree
lahi u yoch on beh	that is their food
ti ton beh	there on the road
uch on beh	wild black persimmon
ti ton beh	there on the road
shoyok on beh	red dye plant
lahi u yoch on beh	that is their food
chimon beh	chimon fruit
lahi u yoch on beh	that is their food
u kat u ki lukah on beh	it must be well erased
u kat u ki tak chaeh suwik u tan	the calcium must be squeezed
u kat u ki hash bo'oteh	it must be truly well paid
u kat u che'eneh u yahi on beh	the disease must be cured
u sayab wɨtz on beh	virgin water

lahi u ya'alil on beh — that is its liquid
u sayab u wɨtz on beh — virgin water
u kat u kunik on beh — it must be chanted
u kat u ki hash bo'otech — they must be truly well paid
u kat u che'eneh yawät on beh — the disease must be cured
hash palil on beh. — true child on the road.

As chanted by Chan K'in José Valenzuela, February 1976, Mensabak, Selva Lacandona, Chiapas.

According to Lacandón Maya informants in Mensabak, Chiapas, "They are growling" can also mean "They are spreading disease."

The calcium referred to is made from the shells of the *jute* snail, *Pachichilus indiorum*.

Virgin water comes from a spring or cave where few or no people have touched it.

Säk'ätz = sansapote (*cabeza mico, sonza; Licania platypus*).

Ha'as = mamey (*Pouteria sapota*).

Kopoh = wild fig (*Ficus cookii* and *Ficus involuta*).

Op che = unidentified wild anona.

Uch' = wild black persimmon (*zapote negro; Diospyros ebenaster*).

Ek' bache = zopo (*Guatteria anomala*).

Koyok = unidentified wild avocado-like fruit.

On = avocado (*Persea americanus*).

Oni wɨtz = wild mountain avocado.

Hach bämäsh = unidentified ramon species (*Brosimum* sp.).

Ha'as che = mamey-like fruit inedible by humans.

Sismuk = unidentified thorned vine with edible berries.

Sotz bämäsh = "covered bamash," unidentified, inedible by humans.

Mehen kopoh = small type of *Ficus*.

On te = *Nectandra* sp.

Mehen on te = *Nectandra raticulata*.

Säk on te = white avocado, probably *Nectandra* sp.

Ek' on te = black avocado, probably *Nectandra* sp.

Hoch = unidentified avocado-type fruit, perhaps *Nectandra* sp., but inedible by humans.

Shoyok = red dye plant (*Morinda yucatanensis*).

Chimon = unidentified.

OTTER   Neotropical river otters (*Lutra longicaudis;* Spanish = *perro de agua;* Belizean English = water dog; Lacandón Maya = *u peki ha'* "water dog") live in the rivers, streams, and river-connected lakes of the Maya Tropical Forest. They dig burrows along the shore and feed on fish, crustaceans, and mollusks (Reid 1997:269). Despite their status as an endangered species, hunters sometimes kill them for their fur. I have seen them along the shores of Lake Dzibatnah, near Mensabak, in the Selva Lacandona; Rivero reports them archaeologically at Lacam Tún, the Postclassic Choltí Maya island in Lake Miramar (Rivero 1992).

PECCARIES   Two types of wild, piglike mammals called peccaries live in the Maya Tropical Forest. The collared peccary (*Tayassu tajacu;* Spanish = *puerco de monte;* Lacandón Maya = *kitam*) is the smaller of the two and has a cream-colored collar on its coarse, grizzled, gray-brown fur. In wilderness areas, you may see collared peccaries in herds of 15 or so, but they usually forage on the forest floor in groups of 2 to 5 animals. They also frequent agricultural areas, where they sometimes eat families' crops. Collared peccaries create mud wallows in the forest, and the areas take on the odor of the animals' scent glands—a ripe, cheesy smell that travelers find obnoxious but which the peccaries obviously enjoy. It is not unusual to smell the path that collared peccaries have marched along, for their peculiar odor seems to cling to the ground and vegetation. They root along the forest floor, gobbling up underground stems, bulbs, roots, fruits, and seeds, especially ficus figs, palm nuts, zapotes, and acorns (Reid 1997:281).

The white-lipped peccary (*Dicotyles pecari;* Spanish = *jabalí* or *senso;* Lacandón Maya = *hach k'ek'en*) is larger and darker colored than the collared peccary, and it has a white patch of hair on its lower jaw, cheek, and throat. The white-lipped peccary may live in herds of 40 to 200 individuals, and they travel long distances through the forest in search of fruits, roots, seeds, and nuts. They also eat insects and worms and have attacked human beings who were in their path. A large herd moves through the forest like a vacuum cleaner, rooting up the topsoil and snapping up food items.

Jungle lore in the Maya Tropical Forest holds that white-lipped peccaries chomp their powerful jaws together as they march through the forest. If you hear this sound, experienced forest workers will tell you, immediately climb a tree so that the herd can pass beneath you (the animals do not climb). Santiago Billy, a Guatemalan conservationist, told me of the time he was forced to climb a tree to avoid an approaching herd of white-lipped peccaries, but found that the only tree within reach was a thin sapling. He climbed the tree, and just as the herd of chomping peccaries approached him, the sapling began to bend over toward the ground. Luckily, even after the tree bent he was still a meter above the ground, though upside down, and the peccaries passed, unaware, under him.

BIRDS

More than 570 species of birds live in the Maya Tropical Forest—some of them as permanent residents and some as migrants who spend the months of the North American winter there. Of the estimated 2 to 5 billion birds that migrate between North America and Central and South America each year, somewhere between 1 and 2 billion of them stop over or pass the winter in the Maya Tropical Forest, making the area a vitally important wintering home for North American birds (Greenberg 1990:5). Some of these birds fly along the coast of Mexico, staying over land as they move southward. Others—including at least one species of hummingbird—take the leap of faith and cross from the United States into Mexico and Central America by flying over the Gulf of Mexico.

HARPY EAGLE   Of the hundreds of bird species that live full-time in the Maya forest, the most majestic is the rare harpy eagle (*Harpia harpyja*). Before the twentieth century, harpies ranged throughout the dense tropical forests of Veracruz and Oaxaca, Mexico, through Central America, and south to Argentina and Bolivia (Davis 1972:23). A meter (3.3 feet) tall and weighing more than 4.5 kilograms (10 pounds), the harpy, according to wildlife biologist Les Beletsky, "is perhaps the world's most powerful eagle" (Beletsky 1999a:146). The bird's wingspan can reach 2 meters (6.5 feet). Their prey includes opossums, iguanas, coatimundis, kinkajous, porcupines, and monkeys.

The name "harpy," taken from Greek and Roman mythology, refers to a flying monster that is half-woman and half-bird. The word itself comes from the Greek term that means "to snatch," a fitting description for an animal known for grabbing unsuspecting animals from the branches of tropical trees. The Lacandón Maya call harpies "*kot ma'ash*," which literally means "tears apart monkeys." In at least one Lacandón ceremony, men stick feathers into the back of their hair in imitation of harpy eagles.

Sightings of live harpy eagles are exceptionally rare today in the Maya Tropical Forest. David Whitacre of the Peregrine Fund researched evidence for the bird from Honduras to Mexico during 2000. He reported a number of recent records from the southern half of Belize, primarily in the Maya Mountains, with several repeated sightings at the archaeological site of Caracol. As well, he heard of harpy sightings in Chiapas' Montes Azules Biosphere Reserve, saw a recent photograph from Yaxchilán, and learned of sightings at Chajul and Bonampak. Harpies have also been seen in Guatemala's Sierra del Lacandón National Park, and at least one was sighted in the Sierra de las Minas of southern Guatemala during 2000. Ornithologist Robin Bjork reported sighting a harpy in the Chiquibul Biosphere Reserve of southeastern Petén, also during 2000 (R. Bjork, personal communication, March 2001, La Milpa, Belize).

"Existing records are virtually all from areas with at least 2,000 mm of rainfall," Whitacre writes. He notes that, "the eastern two-thirds of [Guatemala's] Maya Biosphere Reserve may be too dry for them," although in the eastern one-third of the reserve, near the Sierra del Lacandón, two harpy skeletons turned up during the 1980s." Whitacre proposes that the primary habitat of the harpy in Guatemala may have been the tropical forest of the southern Petén, where deforestation eradicated most of the habitat between 1960 and 1990 (Whitacre 2000).

Guatemala's best-known photographer, Ricardo Mata, told me during the late 1980s that the first time he traveled to Tikal National Park, around 1970, he stepped down from his jeep just at the moment that a harpy eagle flew out of the forest canopy with a monkey in its talons. Moving rapidly overhead, the bird was gone before Mata could grab his camera.

SCARLET MACAWS Another magnificent bird of the Maya Tropical Forest is the scarlet macaw (*Ara macao cyanoptera;* Spanish = *guacamaya;* Lacandón Maya and Itza Maya = *mo'*). The birds' red, yellow, blue, and purple feathers were highly prized by the ancient Maya, and are frequently depicted on headdresses in sculptures.

Although the scarlet macaw ranges from southern Mexico to Brazil, the subspecies that inhabits the Maya Tropical Forest is restricted to northern Central America and southern Mexico, where fewer than 1,000 individuals were estimated to live as of 2001 (Paiz 2001). The birds have been seriously depleted by habitat destruction and by the illegal practice of stealing young birds from their nest to sell as pets. Because scarlet macaws are highly dependent on riparian habitat and specific tree species for nesting and feeding, they are highly vulnerable to perturbations of habitat. Scarlet macaws are also threatened by the spread of Africanized honeybees into the Maya Tropical Forest. The bees take over the birds' nesting sites and sometimes sting the baby chicks to death (Paiz 2001).

Scarlet macaws mate for life, and you will usually see them flying overhead in pairs. They are long lived, surviving for 50 to 70 years. Breeding pairs nest in preexisting cavities in specific trees. The female lays one or two eggs in early spring, and the hatchlings fledge and fly away in late spring.

In the Petén, scarlet macaws nest almost exclusively in the leguminous *cantemó* tree (*Acacia angustissima;* Guatemalan Spanish = *cantemó;* Lacandón Maya = *kän te' mo,* "yellow tree of the macaw"). Nesting sites have been identified in Belize in the Upper Macal and Raspaculo river valleys, where the birds nest in the quamwood tree (*Schizolobium parahybum*). They also nest along the Río San Pedro, Río Chajul, and Río Usumacinta in the Guatemalan Petén, and at Yaxchilán and along the Río Lacantún in the Selva Lacandona (Matola 2001; Billy 1999; Iñigo-Elías 1996; Eduardo Iñigo-Elías, personal communication, 1992).

In Belize, scarlet macaws are restricted to the river valleys on the flanks of the Maya Mountains. Research shows that the birds cross from Belize into Guatemala and from Guatemala into Chiapas and back again. A scarlet macaw radio-collared in late 2000 in the Guatemalan Petén was tracked 120 kilometers (72 miles) to the south in the Selva Lacandona of Chiapas. Others have been observed by field biologists crossing from Belize into the Petén (Matola 2001). One promising development in macaw conservation is the formation in 2001 of Guacamayas sin Fronteras (Macaws without Borders), an international network of conservation biologists from Mexico, Guatemala, and Belize, focused on the fact that the birds inhabit the region rather than individual countries and that their protection should likewise be regionally focused (for information, contact Eduardo E. Iñigo-Elías, http://birds.cornell.edu/).

PARROTS The Maya Tropical Forest is home to many species of parrots, from the small, white-fronted parrot (*Amazona albifrons;* Lacandón Maya = *t'uut'* or *kurish*) to the large blue-crowned parrot (*Amazona farinosa;* Lacandón Maya = *kacho*). The former fly in large flocks, devouring tree fruit in a noisy, messy fashion, with half-eaten fruit and husks falling to the forest floor. They sometimes attack Maya cornfields, in which case they are considered serious pests. Maya families sometimes take young birds as household pets.

The larger blue-crowned, or mealy, parrot travels over the Maya forest from one end to the other. Working in western Guatemala, ornithologist

Robin Bjork radio-tagged 19 mealy parrots in 1999 and traced them into Quintana Roo, Mexico, and southwest to the Sayaxché-Petexbatún region of the Petén. In 2000 the birds moved north to near the community of Uaxactún in the Maya Biosphere Reserve, then across the Lacantún Biosphere Reserve and northeastern Montes Azules Biosphere Reserve, and into the Chan K'in Reserve and Bonampak protected areas, in a pattern that Bjork called "the parrot polygon" (Bjork 2001).

TOUCANS   Keel-billed toucans (*Ramphastos sulfuratus;* Spanish = *tucán;* Lacandón Maya = *pan*) are one of the more delightful-looking birds of the Maya Tropical Forest. The bird is unmistakable, with its bright yellow breast feathers and red rump feathers offsetting a black body and giant, multicolored beak, which the bird uses to grasp palm and fig fruits to toss down the beak into its throat. The toucan's measured "creek, creek, creek" call sounds at first like a frog. Pairs of toucans frequently sit on the same tree branch, with the male rocking back and forth as the two birds chant together.

Northern Lacandón Maya men give their wives the yellow breast feathers of toucans, and the women tie them to their long hair braids in a symbol of marriage. Toucan breast feathers are also visible as decorations on the costumes of warriors in the mural at the archaeological site of Bonampak, Chiapas.

REPTILES

SNAKES   Of the 2,500 species of snakes known in the world, most live in the tropics, and the Maya Tropical Forest has a generous share. More than 60 kinds of snakes from six families slither through the Maya Tropical Forest (Campbell 1998; Garel and Matola 1996). Most are harmless to humans, specializing in smaller prey such as rodents, frogs, lizards, birds, and other snakes. In turn, some birds of prey eat the snakes.

The Maya Tropical Forest is home to four species of snail-eating snakes that feed on snails and slugs, including *Dipsas brevifacies,* which has specialized teeth for extracting snails from their shells (Garel and Matola 1996:59). Another species, Freminville's scorpion-hunter (*Stenorrhina freminvillei,* Spanish = *alacranera de Freminville* or *sabanera;* Belizean English = spider-eating snake), eats spiders, scorpions, and other invertebrates. It is rumored to be immune to scorpion stings.

At the same time, there are nine venomous snakes in the Maya Tropical Forest. (Beletsky points out that Mexico has more species of venomous snakes—about 60—than any other country in the Western Hemisphere, but many of these are found in the drier region of northern Mexico [Beletsky 1999a:105].) In the Maya forest, venomous snakes fall into two general categories, based on the type of venom they produce. Snake venom, a modified saliva, is classified as hemotoxic or neurotoxic. Hemotoxic venom is produced by snakes that feed on warm-blooded animals, such as birds and rodents. The hemotoxins introduced through the bite impair blood function by breaking down the victim's capillary walls, which causes blood and lymph to leak into surrounding tissues and produce swelling. The venom also destroys the integrity of the prey's blood cells (Garel and Matola 1996:36).

By contrast, neurotoxic venom impairs the central nervous system of the prey, leading to death by respiratory failure. Snakes with neurotoxic venom prey on cold-blooded animals, such as lizards, frogs, and other snakes. To confuse the issue, however, the neotropical rattlesnake (*Crotalus durissus*) carries both hemotoxic and neurotoxic venoms, making them doubly lethal to prey.

The most feared of the venomous snakes in the Maya Tropical Forest are the hemotoxic vipers, of the Family Viperidae. The vipers that live in the region have long, hollow fangs that inject venom into the prey (or victim, as it were). Jonathan A. Campbell, one of the foremost herpetologists on the Maya region, points out that most vipers are not aggressive unless provoked and that most viper bites do not result in death; nonetheless, he states, "the serious nature of envenomation from a viper should never be underestimated."

In other words, watch your step out there—also your hands. Campbell notes that most people hiking through the forest probably pass within a few meters of venomous snakes on a regular basis without ever seeing them. "Viper bites most frequently occur," he warns, "when people are careless about where they place their hands and feet" (Campbell 1998:269). (An interesting sidelight here: 50,000 people die annually from snakebite, but 30,000 of these deaths occur in India, the remaining 20,000 divided among all other countries of the world.)

All New World vipers, those of the Maya Tropical Forest included, are pit vipers, a term that comes from the heat-sensitive pit on the side of their head that allows them to detect very small changes in temperature. This ability allows the snake to sense heat emanating from warm-blooded prey.

The most deadly of these pit vipers is the fer-de-lance (*Bothrops asper*), known in Guatemala as the *barba amarilla* (for its pale, yellow throat), the yellow-jaw tommygoff in Belize, and the *equis* or *nauyaca* in Chiapas and Calakmul. The Lacandón Maya call the fer-de-lance *hach kan*, "the true snake."

The fer-de-lance has large fangs and strong, fast-acting hemotoxic venom. Growing up to 2.3 meters (almost 8 feet) long, the snake normally feeds on rodents, birds, small mammals, and frogs. A nocturnal predator, it is the most common venomous snake in the Maya Tropical Forest and the rest of Central America. Small individuals are equally at home in trees or on the ground, but large adults are usually seen in shallow depressions or under low vegetation (Garel and Matola 1996:133; Campbell 1998:274).

I encountered the fer-de-lance under several challenging circumstances in the Maya Tropical Forest. Beginning a four-hour hike from the Lacandón settlement of Mensabak to Naja, I came upon a medium-sized fer-de-lance coiled exactly in the middle of the forest trail, staring up at me. I took the encounter as an omen and returned to my thatched roof hut in Mensabak.

Two years later, I was hiking a trail toward the compound of a Lacandón family who still lived isolated in the forest, away from the larger settlement of Mensabak, when the forest trail halted at the edge of a harvested milpa and disappeared. I knew that the trail began again somewhere on the opposite side of the milpa, 100 meters (330 feet) away, but where, beyond this expanse of doubled corn stalks and ripening squashes, did it emerge? I jumped up on a huge, felled log, half-burned from the spring milpa fire, to try to spot the trail. The vibration of my feet landing on the tree trunk flushed an enormous fer-de-lance from underneath. Fortunately, the snake slithered deeper into the milpa. I immediately turned around and went back to my hut in the settlement of Mensabak.

There are five other pit vipers to watch out for in the Maya Tropical Forest. One is the aggressive cantil (*Agkistrodon bilineatus russeolus*; Spanish = *cantil* or *wolpoch*; Belizean English = moccasin), which uses its tail to mimic a worm to lure frogs, lizards, rodents, and birds (Garel and Matola 1996:127). Another is the jumping tommygoff (*Atropoides nummifer*; Spanish = *víbora saltadora* or *chalpate*; Belizean English = jumping pit viper), which eats rodents and holds its mouth open in a wide gape when threatened. The snake's common name in English derives from the misguided belief that it can jump at its prey. The jumping tommygoff actually throws itself backward about one-third of its body length when threatened (Campbell 1998:272; Garel and Matola 1996:129).

The eyelash viper (*Bothriechis schlegelii*; Spanish = *víbora de pestaña* or *nauyaca cornuda*; Belizean English = green tommygoff, eyelash palm-pitviper) is camouflaged green, brown, yellow, and white to blend into the vegetation of the humid forest. Usually arboreal, rarely seen on the ground, the snake eats birds, rodents, and bats, but has strong hemotoxic venom. Campbell found them at night, coiled on palm trees near streams and in deep, shaded ravines (Campbell 1998:273). The snake earns its name from the spinelike scales that grow above its eyes, giving the appearance of eyelashes.

Another unusual poisonous snake, the hognose viper (*Porthidium nasutum*; Spanish = *víbora chatilla de la selva*; Belizean English = tommygoff), usually less than two feet long, is characterized by a pointed, up-turned snout. The snake is normally found in open forests around fallen logs and especially around Maya ruins. Adults eat small rodents, lizards, and frogs but have strong hemotoxic venom.

Finally, the tropical rattlesnake (*Crotalus durissus*; Spanish = *cascabel, víbora real*) is one of 30 species of rattlesnakes, all of them from the New World, and the only one to appear south of Mexico's Isthmus of Tehuantepec. Adults grow to 1.7 meters (5 feet). Rattlesnakes are known for the tail rattles they use to warn away potential threats. The snake seems to prefer open, drier areas, but they have been found in Tikal National Park (Campbell 1998:280). Tropical rattlesnakes feed on rodents, ground-nesting birds, lizards, mice, and black iguanas. They have a strong hemotoxic poison as well as neurotoxic venom, a rarity among snakes of the Maya forest.

Coral snakes are the only New World representatives of the Family Elapidae, which includes cobras, sea snakes, and black mambas. Three species appear in the Maya Tropical Forest: the variable coral snake (*Micrurus diastema*), which is the only coral snake in the Guatemalan Petén, the Mayan coral snake (*Micrurus hippocrepis*), which appears in central and southern Belize, and the Central American coral snake (*Micrurus nigrocinctus*), also from Belize (Campbell 1998:262–268; Garel and Matola 1996:120–123). All three of them are known in Spanish as *coralillo* (little coral) or *gargantilla* (little throat).

The Mayan coral snake is mostly brilliant red, with small yellow and black bands around it. The other two species look more like the classic coral snake, with wider, alternating bands of red, yellow, and black. To confuse the issue, the Maya Tropical Forest also hosts two false corals, the white-bellied false coral (*Oxyrhopus petola*) and long-tailed false coral (*Pliocercus elapoides* or *Urotheca elapoides*), both known in Spanish as *falso coral.* Just in case you have forgotten your Scout lore, the red bands of true coral snakes always touch the yellow bands; in false corals, the red bands normally touch the black bands. ("Red and yellow, kill a fellow; red and black, venom lack.") But to further confuse the issue, the long-tailed false coral *Urotheca elapoides* bears red and yellow bands that do touch one another. Still, it is possible to tell it from a true coral. "The head and large eye of the *Urotheca* are the giveaway," says Belize Zoo director Sharon Matola, "but who wants to get that close to be certain?"

Many people believe that because coral snakes do not have long front fangs, they represent little threat to human beings. Herpetologist Jonathan Campbell points out, however, that the short, relatively immobile fangs of the coral snakes make them "dangerously venomous to humans." As he writes, "The common belief that because of their relatively small size, coral snakes are unable to bite unless they happen to grab a small part of the body, such as the web between fingers, is pure hokum" (Campbell 1998:184).

Instead, he points out, coral snakes have a wide mouth gape. Anywhere you have skin loose enough to be even slightly pinched is a danger point for a coral snake bite. Because coral snake venom acts on the nervous system, they do not usually produce swelling, leading people who have been bitten to dismiss the bite. But the neurotoxic venom impairs the central nervous system, causing respiratory and cardiac failure. Victims should be transported to the hospital immediately. "Unfortunately," as Campbell warns, "antivenin for coral snake venom is rarely available in Central American hospitals" (1998:263).

If no hospital is available, you can turn to traditional remedies. In 1996, two experienced *chicleros* (chicle extractors) in the Guatemalan Petén, Carlos Catalán and Luis Morales, told me of a snakebite cure that they swore by. On a Friday, they said, cut a piece of the *contrayerba* herb (*Dorstenia contrajerva,* Fam. Moraceae), mash it up, and place it in a bottle filled with water and a little alcohol (preferably *aguardiente,* a distilled sugarcane liquor popular throughout the Maya forest). Always carry the concoction with you while in the forest. If someone gets bitten by a poisonous snake, they must immediately drink the contents of the bottle. Doing so will make the victim very thirsty, the *chicleros* told me, but the herb will produce a cure. However, they also pointed out that the potion will not cure the victim if they are bitten by a snake on a Tuesday or Friday.

Another misunderstood and mostly harmless snake of the Maya Tropical Forest is the boa constrictor (*Boa constrictor*; Spanish = *boa* or *mazacuata*; Lacandón Maya = *ach kan*; Belizean English = wowla). Although they are not poisonous, boas are feared for their size and for the belief that they can wrap around victims and squeeze them to death.

The boa is, in fact, the largest snake in the Maya Tropical Forest, growing to a length of 2.5 meters (8 feet). They feed mainly on birds, rodents, and other small mammals, such as coatimundis and opossums, though they will capture an occasional lizard or iguana. They hiss and strike at anything that threatens them, and large boas may bite, although the bite is not poisonous. Boas are found on the forest floor, in trees, in mammal burrows, and hidden on rock shelves, not infrequently in unexcavated Maya ruins.

While I was living with a Lacandón Maya family in Chiapas during the late 1970s, I sat in the half-light of a palm-thatched hut talking with a visiting French bush doctor, Geneviève Buot. After half an hour or so, Geneviève stood up to walk toward the door, and we both heard something hit the bark platform exactly where she had been sitting. We looked down to see a meter-long boa recovering from its fall from the roof thatching. Once we determined that the snake was indeed a boa, we shooed it outside with the long blade of a machete. I slept that night in the same hut, hanging in my cocoon of a hammock, but I kept a wary eye on the roof all night, waiting for the snake's return visit.

Naturalist Peter Hubbell heard claims from numerous rural families in Chiapas and Guatemala that boa constrictors "were poisonous," but he was able to identify only one case where a boa constrictor bite led to human death. According to the rural families he talked with, "The 'poison' only showed up on the third day after the bite," reported Hubbell. "From the description of the patient's condition, it appears he died of blood poisoning from a bacterial infection caused by the bite" (Peter Hubbell, personal communication, 2005).

CROCODILES Of the world's 23 living species of crocodilians (members of the family Crocodylidae), two occur in the Maya Tropical Forest—the American crocodile and Morelet's crocodile (Beletsky 1999a:95; Campbell 1998:283–292). The American crocodile (*Crocodylus acutus*; Spanish = *cocodrilo del río*; Lacandón and Itza Maya = *ayim*) appears in southern Florida, coastal Mexico, and Central America, and in northern

South America, mainly in river mouths and mangrove swamps. In the Maya forest, it is restricted to the Río Usumacinta and the coastal mangrove forests of Belize. By contrast, Morelet's crocodile (Spanish = *cocodrilo morelete, cocodrilo de pantano;* Lacandón and Itza Maya = *ayim*) is an endemic species for the Maya Tropical Forest; the animal appears in nature nowhere else in the world. Morelet's crocodile appears in Tabasco, Mexico, the southern Yucatán Peninsula, the Selva Lacandona of Chiapas, the Guatemalan Petén, and throughout Belize, primarily in inland freshwater sites such as lagoons, marshy edges of lakes, and sluggish rivers (Beletsky 1999b:95; Kamstra 1987, cited in Rath 1990:19; Lee 2000:134). Morelet's crocodile is named for the French explorer Pierre Marie Arthur Morelet (1809–1892), who took specimens back to France from his explorations of the Petén during the 1840s (Morelet 1990).

Morelet's crocodile, 2.5 meters (7–8 feet) long, is smaller than the American crocodile, which can reach 4 to 7 meters (13–23 feet). They spend much of their time in the water, with only their eyes, snout, and sometimes part of their back above the surface, but you can also spot them basking in the sun on the riverbank or find them at night by the reflection of their eyes in the beam of a flashlight.

Morelet's crocodiles mainly eat small mammals, fish, aquatic birds, frogs, and mud turtles. They can be distinguished from the American crocodile primarily by habitat, but where the species overlap, the Morelet's is generally of a smaller size and has a wider snout. Both species of crocodile can be distinguished from alligators and caimans by the snout (alligators and caimans do not appear in the Maya Tropical Forest). Alligators tend to have broader, rounded snouts; those of crocodiles are longer and more pointed.

Guides at Tikal National Park and other parks and archaeological sites tell hair-raising stories of crocodiles attacking humans, and at least some of the stories are true. A Morelet's crocodile in the main *aguada,* a Classic Maya water reservoir, at Tikal killed at least two men and wounded two children before being shot by a park ranger (Campbell 1998:291). Guides at the site like to taunt tourists with tales of finding the remains of hapless visitors on the edge of the *aguada,* with nothing but their camera and tattered t-shirt left behind. The owners at the Tikal Inn recount that they found a crocodile in the hotel's swimming pool one morning, to the surprise of tourists who had looked forward to a dip after visiting the ruins.

At nearby Lake Yaxja, a 2.2-meter (7-foot) crocodile attacked a Dutch tourist in full daylight in November 1994. The man was saved by Gabriella Moretti, owner of El Sombrero Lodge, who rowed out in an aluminum boat to aid him. Gabriella smashed the crocodile repeatedly with the boat's oars and managed to pull the struggling man from the animal's jaws. The tourist was flown to Guatemala City for treatment and survived the ordeal (G. Moretti, personal communication, 1995; cf. Campbell 1998:291–292). The co-owner of El Sombrero Lodge, Juan José de la Hoz, later dispatched the offending crocodile. Its skull is on display at the lodge, with a bullet hole neatly piercing the top.

Belize Zoo director Sharon Matola stunned her fellow participants at a conservation workshop at the Hotel Villa Maya in the Guatemala Petén in 1998 when she announced that on her morning swim in the lake in front of the hotel, she had lifted her head from the water to find that she was staring directly into the eyes of a crocodile only two meters away. "I knew it was large," she said, "because its eyes were very far apart." Well aware of crocodile behavior from observing those at the Belize Zoo, Matola lifted herself out of the water and slammed down as hard as she could as close as she could to the crocodile, knowing, she said, "that these animals are easily intimidated by sudden, strong movement and noise. This behavior is very far from what prey behavior would be," she continued. "My objective was to not appear in any way like a prey item to this fellow" (S. Matola, e-mail to author, November 2004).

As herpetologist Jonathan Campbell warns, "Although I hardly consider crocodile attacks to be of major concern in Petén, I would think twice before swimming in some of the more remote and isolated lagunas, and swimming after dark anywhere that crocodiles are known to exist is probably not a good idea" (1998:292).

IGUANAS   In the Maya forest, green iguanas (*Iguana iguana rhinolopha*; Spanish = *iguana de ribera*; Lacandón Maya = *huh*; Yucatec Maya = *itzam*) spend most of their time in the canopy of trees that overhang rivers or streams. The adults are herbivores, eating tree leaves and fruit, but young iguanas will also eat insects. People traveling by boat along the region's rivers frequently see iguanas draped over branches of trees that stretch over the water, and the iguanas will drop into the water and swim away if they feel threatened. Some rural families in Chiapas, the Petén, and southern Belize eat the eggs and meat of green iguanas. Schlesinger reports that the Q'eqchi' and Mopan of southern Belize value iguana fat as a remedy for various illnesses (Schlesinger 2001:227).

Campbell reports a singularly gruesome practice of commercial iguana hunters in Guatemala:

> The unlaid, yellow eggs of iguanas were considered a special treat and females were sometimes doomed to a particularly horrible death. An incision was made on the bellies of females that were obviously gravid and the eggs were removed; the abdominal cavity of the female was then filled with leaves and she was released under the mistaken assumption that she would recover and go on to produce more eggs that could be harvested at a later date. (Campbell 1998:147)

While we have to admire the attempt at sustainable harvest, it is clear that none of the iguanas survive after being treated in this fashion.

TURTLES　The Maya Tropical Forest is home to a variety of turtles, and turtles have been important to Maya peoples at least since the Preclassic era. Turtle shells and bones turn up in archaeological excavations in sites from the Preclassic through the Classic periods, and they are "the most abundant reptile bone discovered" in excavations in the center of Tikal (Schlesinger 2001:223). Images of turtles appear in Maya codices, and turtle shells mounted on a stick as a rattle were a traditional lowland Maya musical instrument. The Lacandón Maya refer to this type of musician as *"u hätzik u bosh ak,"* "He hits the turtle shell."

Lacandones capture turtles by hand when possible; otherwise, they attempt to spear them through the head or neck. If they boil the meat, they remove the shell and intestines; if they roast the meat, they leave the animal in its shell and its intestines intact, removing them as they eat. Lacandones gather turtle eggs at the edge of rivers, when the guanacaste tree (*Enterolobium cyclocarpum*) blooms, usually during the month of April (Baer and Merrifield 1971:240).

One of the turtles most frequently mentioned in conversations with modern families in the Maya forest is the Central American snapping turtle (*Chelydra serpentina;* Spanish = *zambundango, tortuga lagarto,* or *tortuga cocodrilo*). The animal is easily recognized by its hooked upper jaw and pointed snout extending over powerful jaws (Campbell 1998:102). Snapping turtles grow as large as 15 kilograms (33 pounds) and are remarkably fast strikers when angered. They can inflict serious bites. They tend to live in quiet backwaters and oxbow lakes, but also show up in larger rivers. They do not appear in the northern Petén, but are well known in the tributaries of the Río de la Pasión, near Sayaxché, Petén, as well as in the Selva Lacandona of Chiapas. The Central American snapping turtle eats smaller animals, including birds and mammals, but also feeds on aquatic vegetation (Beletsky 1999a:98).

The Central American river turtle (*Dermatemys mawii*; Spanish = *tortuga del río* or *tortuga blanca*; Lacandón Maya = *hach ak*) is a large, aquatic, herbivorous turtle that rarely leaves the water. They are hunted throughout the Maya forest for their meat and are sometimes seen for sale in urban markets. Nonetheless, the species is listed as endangered in Appendix II of the Convention on International Trade in Endangered Species of Wild Flora and Fauna, CITES (Polisar and Horwich 1994:338). They are known locally as hicatees in Belize, and as *jicoteas* in Guatemala and Chiapas, a name that is also applied to the Meso-American slider (*Trachemys scripta*), which is also hunted for food. In northern Belize, families have a strong tradition of eating hicatees for Easter dinner (Polisar and Horwich 1994:339). The turtles are harpooned, captured in nets, and gathered by hand. Their natural predators include river otters (*Lutra longicaudis*). That the species was eaten by the ancient Maya seems evident from remains found in human burials, including at Uaxactún, Petén (Campbell 1998:113).

The Meso-American slider (*Trachemys scripta*; Spanish = *jicotea*) has distinctive yellow and dark brown lines familiar to anyone who has frequented pet stores. In the United States, this same animal is known as the red-eared slider and is sold in huge quantities as pet turtles (Campbell 1998:115). They are frequently seen on logs sticking out the water, basking in the sun. They are omnivorous, feeding on aquatic vegetation, tree fruits, fish, and aquatic invertebrates, as well as carrion (Campbell 1998:115). Sliders sometimes become the prey of Morelet's crocodiles.

Finally, the northern giant musk turtle (*Staurotypus triporcatus*; Spanish = *guao* or *tres lomos*; Lacandón Maya = *let*), has three distinctive keels that run the length of its carapace. They have large heads and powerful jaws, matched by an aggressive temper. They live in large lakes and large, slow-moving rivers but also show up in flooded grasslands and marshy areas. The turtles eat smaller turtle species, mollusks, and crustaceans, as well as fish, tree seeds, and fruits that fall into the water (Campbell 1998:107). The giant musk turtle is also highly prized for its meat, but hunters capture them cautiously; they are aggressive biters and inflict painful wounds (Lee

2000:151). Herpetologist Jonathan Campbell warns that "this turtle is capable of delivering a severe bite and readily defends itself. It should never be handled just for the hell of it" (Campbell 1998:107).

Another well-known herpetologist in the Maya forest, Julian Lee, notes this myth about the musk turtle: "Many rural inhabitants of southern Mexico [and] northern Central America believe that these turtles are swallowed alive by crocodiles, which are then killed when the turtle chews its way out" (Lee 2000:151).

FISH

The Maya Tropical Forest is dotted with lakes, and streams and rivers crisscross much of it, providing habitat for a high diversity of freshwater fish. For the Río Usumacinta watershed, Miller (1988) reports 112 species of fish, including 18 of marine origin and 10 endemic to the Usumacinta region.

A 1999 Rapid Assessment Program expedition to Laguna del Tigre National Park, in the northwestern corner of the Guatemalan Petén, identified 55 species of freshwater fish in the lakes, lagoons, and rivers of the park and surrounding area (Bestelmeyer and Alonso 2000:199–203). The Selva Lacandona of Chiapas has 67 known species, representing 45 percent of the fresh water fish in the state (SEMARNAP 2000:29; Lazcano-Barrero and Vogt 1992:135). Lake Petén Itzá, in the Guatemalan Petén, has at least 20 fish species, including catfish, tetras, mollies, mosquito fish, and 8 known cichlids (Castro 1988).

Several introduced species also show up in aquatic surveys of the Maya forest. A Chinese government project introduced Nile tilapia (*Oreochromys niloticus*) to Lake Petén Itzá in the late 1980s; others were brought into the Lacanjá Chan Sayab region of the Selva Lacandona by a misguided Mexican government project. Prolific breeders, tilapia showed up in marine Rapid Assessment Program surveys in Laguna del Tigre National Park, Guatemala, in 1999 (Bestelmeyer and Alonso 2000). The grass carp (*Ctenopharyngodon idella*) has also been introduced, and occasionally shows up in illegal nets set along the banks of the Río San Pedro.

Families in the region still catch fish in traditional ways. During several decades of research in the Maya Tropical Forest, I found that the most common fishing gear is a hand line—very simply, a 3- to 7-meter (10- to 23-foot length of monofilament fishing line with a lead weight and hook on the end. The scarcity of store-bought lead weights leads some men and boys (who do most of the fishing in the Maya Tropical Forest) to hammer a .22 caliber rifle bullet—or any other small lead object they can find—around the fishing line. The line is usually stored on a small piece of wood carved into a Y at each end. That and a half-dozen worms or grubs dug from the soil are all they need to catch fish in the Maya forest (although a little knowledge of fish ecology and some skill go a long way).

The Lacandón Maya—and probably other indigenous groups in the past—make long fishing spears (*semet*) using a climbing bamboo (*Merostrachys* sp.) or thin reeds of carrizo cane (*Phragmites comunis;* Spanish = *caña brava;* Lacandón Maya = *oh*). Lacandón friends told me that before contact with the outside world became frequent, they tipped the spear with a foot-long barbed foreshaft of Guatapil palm (*Chamaedorea* sp.; Lacandón Maya = *paho*). Today, they are more likely to use the straightened wire bail of an old bucket, with a barb shaped at the piercing end.

In the past, indigenous groups in the Maya forest also captured fish using forest plants that stun fish for easy capture. The most commonly used was the barbasco vine (*Dioscorea* spp.), a forest floor tuber that produces a climbing vine. Casting the broken part of a barbasco tuber in a slowly moving stream stuns fish, which float to the surface for easy harvest. (Barbasco is discussed in this chapter's Plants section.) The southern Lacandón Maya formerly used a dozen strips of bark from either the mahogany tree (*Swietenia macrophylla*) or black poisonwood tree (*Metopium brownei*) for the same purpose (Baer and Merrifield 1971:247).

Yet another traditional fishing method is the fish trap. Women and men weave one-meter-tall pear-shaped fish traps from the climbing vine of the Swiss cheese plant (*Monstera* spp.), with a trapdoor that can be slapped closed by pulling on an attached vine. They place ground cornmeal in the bottom of the fish trap and lower it into shallow water, then wait for a swarm of minnows to swim into the trap. When that happens, the fisherman pulls on the vine to close the door or quickly lifts the fish trap from the water, capturing the fish. Smaller minnows are used as bait on hand lines to catch larger fish. Larger minnows are fried and eaten, with heads and tails intact.

In recent decades, more acculturated fishermen have purchased gillnets, which they stretch across narrow rivers to capture every fish that swims by. Understandably, this is a less conservation-minded form of fishing, and some traditional inhabitants of the Maya forest point to its wasteful nature. The practice is also illegal, although the scarcity of park guards or police makes enforcement difficult.

Subsistence and, more recently, commercial fishing in the region tend to focus on six types of edible fish: *blanco, mojarras, machabil,* snook, alligator gar, and catfish.

The *blanco* (white) fish, known in Belize as the bay snook, is endemic to the Maya Tropical Forest. Scientifically *Petenia splendida,* the *blanco* is a member of the Cichlidae family, which includes various smaller cousins called *mojarras.* Similar in appearance to a large-mouth bass, the *blanco* grows up to 38 centimeters (15 inches) long and has a large, tubelike mouth that opens surprisingly wide to take in the smaller fish the *blanco* preys on. Spanish speakers in the Selva Lacandona call the fish *tenguayaca;* Lacandones call it *sohom.* By any name, it makes a tasty meal and is highly prized by fishermen throughout the region. Restaurants around Lake Petén Itzá sometimes offer *blanco* on their menus, but local residents point to the decreasing size of individual fish as a sign that the species is being overexploited.

The related *mojarras* are smaller than the *blanco* but equally prized as food. The most abundant species are *Cichlasoma octofasciatum* (*negrita*), *Cichlasoma urophtalmus* (*bule*), and *Eugerres mexicanus* (*mojarra*). Taken on hand lines, these fish are either fried in oil or boiled and drizzled with lemon as a fish stew eaten with tortillas.

The numerous bones of the *macabil* (*Brycon guatemalensis*), known in the Petén as the *machaca* (Lacandón Maya = *ch'ikar*), require that this fish be cooked by boiling in fish stews. It is still not uncommon for Guatemalan commercial fishermen to harvest *machacas* by the thousands before Easter. Using illegal gillnets, they vacuum the fish from rivers such as the Río de la Pasión, in southwestern Petén, and the Río San Pedro Mártir, in the northwest. They construct large latticeworks of poles and dry the captured fish in the sun on the banks of the river before transporting them to major cities in Guatemala for sale to unsuspecting Easter celebrants.

Surprisingly, one of the most prized fish for eating in the Maya Tropical Forest is the anadromous snook (meaning that it is a saltwater fish that migrates up rivers to breed in freshwater). Snook (*Centropomus undecimalis;* Spanish = *robalo blanco;* Lacandón Maya = *shokla*) grow to almost 1.5 meters (5 feet) in the ocean, but those seen in the Maya Tropical Forest tend to be less than 1 meter (3.3 feet) long. They feed in tributaries of the Río Usumacinta when the water is clear during April and May, and return to the Gulf of Mexico during the rest of the year. (There are, however, landlocked snook that live year-round in lakes left by ancient meanders of the Usumacinta near the towns of Tenosique and Balacán de

Domínguez in Tabasco, Mexico.) The northern families of the Lacandón Maya call the Río Usumacinta the *Shokla,* because of the annual appearance of the migrating snook. Proposals by the federal government of Mexico to construct hydroelectric dams on the Río Usumacinta threaten the timeless migration of snook and of tarpon (*Megalops atlanticus*), which also show up occasionally in the river's many tributaries.

Alligator gar (*Atractosteus tropicus;* Spanish = *peje lagarto;* Lacandón Maya = *ayim kai,* "crocodile fish") are plentiful in lakes and rivers of the Maya forest. They are frightening-looking fish, with mouths filled with needle-sharp teeth in a jaw one-quarter the length of the fish itself. As their morphology would indicate, gar are predatory, feeding on unsuspecting fish that lurk in the same lakes and rivers. On hot days, alligator gar sometimes float motionless near the surface of the water, looking like so many silver logs just under the water. Despite their appearance, alligator gar are prized as food. Fishermen capture them on hand lines or in nets, cut off the stiff armor-like skin, and either fry or boil them. The roe, however, are regarded as poisonous.

Various kinds of catfish also are prey for fishermen of the Maya Tropical Forest. Among the most sought after in the Selva Lacandona are the *bobo liso* (*Ictalurus meridionalis*) and two species called *bagre* (*Ariopsis felis* and *Cathorops melanolopus*). In neighboring Petén, the most common catfish are *curruco, cabeza de fierro, jolote,* and *filin* (respectively, *Potamarius nelsoni, Cathorops aguadulce, Ictalurus furcatus,* and *Rhamdia guatemalensis*) (Lazcano-Barrero and Vogt 1992, Bestelmeyer and Alonso 2000). Many fishermen seek catfish with hooks and hand lines under trees and other vegetation along the shores of the larger rivers.

SNAILS

Some families of the Maya Tropical Forest eat two types of freshwater snails, although many families eat only the smaller of these. Almost every indigenous group in the lowland forest eats *Pachychilus indiorum* from time to time. *Pachychilus* is a 7-centimeter-long (3-inch) snail that forms a progressively widening cone that ends in an opening, through which the animal pokes his head and "foot" to attach to the streambed and take in food. The snails are abundant in streams of the lowland forest. They are known in Spanish as *jutes* (pronounced "hooties" in Belize) and *t'unu'* in Lacandón Maya.

Families intent on a meal of *jute* snails collect them in streams and leave them for 24 hours in a bucket of clear water to purge them of grit and digesting food. Then, they boil the snails and cut off the end tip of the small end of the shell in order to suck the snails out of their shells through the larger, open end. The Lacandón Maya sometimes serve snails on a large, toasted tortilla smeared with sweet potatoes (*Ipomoea batatas*) or taro (*Colocasia esculenta*), an Old World cultigen (Nations 1979b:569). In Belize, the snails are said to have medicinal properties for treating eye irritations and cataracts.

The ancient Maya (and modern Lacandón Maya) use *Pachychilus* shells to make lime for cooking corn (Nations 1979b). Burned in open fires, then slaked with water, the snail shells become powdered lime, which is added to water for boiling corn for tortillas and corn gruels. Lacandones say that lime loosens the outer shell, or pericarp, of corn kernels, but combining lime with corn also has important nutritional values. As anthropologist Sol Katz and colleagues point out, "Maize [corn] is deficient in the essential amino acids lysine and tryptophan, and in niacin, a member of the vitamin B complex" (Katz, Hediger, and Valleroy 1974:766). Cooking corn with lime minimizes the effects of niacin deficiency and increases the availability of lysine. It enhances the grain's nutritional value and helps prevent pellagra. Adding lime to boiling corn also loosens the pericarp for easy removal, as the Lacandones correctly point out. Katz et al. demonstrated that societies that depend on corn as a major dietary staple of necessity prepare it with lime or another prime source of alkali. Without such treatment malnutrition would be rampant, especially among children.

Although the Maya Tropical Forest grows on top of an ancient karst seabed that is essentially a giant limestone formation, the Lacandones declare the rock unsuitable for edible lime production. Instead, they gather *Pachychilus* shells and transform them into lime. It is also clear that the ancient Maya used *Pachychilus* shells for the same purpose, as well as eating the animals inside (Moholy-Nagy 1978).

Some Guatemalan families also eat the *Pomacea flagellata* snail (Belizean English = apple snail; Lacandón Maya = *t'at'*). These are large, rounded snails that grow up to 9 centimeters (3.5 inches) in diameter and are similar in shape to *escargot de Bourgogne* (*Helix pomatia*), the western European restaurant snail. Families of the island town of Flores, Petén, eat *Pomacea* snails as ceviche—removed from their shells and "cooked" in lime juice. The Lacandón Maya of neighboring Chiapas, however, refuse to eat *Pomacea*, saying that eating them will make you sick. *Pomacea* snails are abundant in lakes of the Maya Tropical Forest, and their shells are often seen washed up on the shore, bleaching in the sun. Both the snail kite (*Rostrhamus sociabilis;* Spanish = *gavilán caracolero*), a raptor, and the limpkin (*Aramus guarauna;* Spanish = *totolaca correa*), a large, brown, cranelike shore bird with a long, thin bill, eat *Pomacea* snails. The snail kite uses its hooked bill to force open the snail's operculum and dig out the snail's body. The limpkin uses its long bill to drill a hole in the shell and savor the insides (S. Matola, e-mail to author, December 2004).

INSECTS

Tropical forests are supposedly renowned for the number and ferocity of their insects, and you will find thousands of insect species in the Maya Tropical Forest. Beetles and ants are especially numerous. The insects' ferocity is mostly overrated, although some of the ants do bite or sting, and the mosquitoes can be especially troublesome during certain times of the year. Long pants, a long-sleeved shirt, a hat, and a dab of insect repellent will keep you happy and hiking.

As the most numerous inhabitants of the Maya forest, insects also serve up some interesting encounters. I once watched a Lacandón Maya family use feather fans made from the black tail feathers of the great curassow (*Crax rubra;* Spanish = *hocofaisán, pajuil;* Lacandón Maya = *kosh*) to redirect an enormous column of army ants that were headed directly toward the family's house. (Lacandones normally use the fans to breathe life into the kitchen fire.) By brushing the lead ants in the long column in a new direction, the family prompted the entire battalion of ants to march off into the forest, away from their thatched-roof house.

On one of several trips to explore the Maya site of La Corona, inside Guatemala's Maya Biosphere Reserve, one of our guides, Carlos Catalán, came into camp with a large, live katydid poised on a dry stick. The insect had very long, thin legs and a body that looked exactly like a green tree leaf, complete with pseudo caterpillar bites taken out of one side of it and speckles of faux fungus all over. Impressed with the success of its camouflage, I took a photograph of the insect and weeks later sent it to Sacha Spector, an entomologist then at the Smithsonian's American Museum of Natural History. Spector wrote back in an e-mail message that there are only four scientifically known katydids in the region, and this was not one of them. "If you had brought it back as a specimen," he wrote, "I would have named it for you."

Most of the insects you will encounter in the Maya Tropical Forest are harmless, as well as interesting. But here are a few to watch out for.

AHORCADORA WASP   The *ahorcadora* wasp is an insect 5 to 7.5 centimeters (2–3 inches) in length that delivers a sting as painful as a snakebite. The wasps have metallic blue-black bodies and orange-brown wings, displaying what entomologists call aposematic coloring—coloring so conspicuous that it warns away potential predators, which have come to associate the coloring with the insects' powerful sting. Known in English as the tarantula hawk wasp (*Pepsis* spp.), the *ahorcadora* (in Spanish) is one of almost 300 species of spider wasps that occur between Argentina and Utah. A subset of spider wasps, the tarantula hawk wasps occur wherever tarantulas live, for a simple reason: female wasps require a tarantula in order to reproduce.

Female tarantula hawk wasps move over the ground, using their sense of smell to locate a female tarantula within its burrow or a male tarantula in the open. If the wasp finds a female tarantula, she expels it from the burrow, then attacks it, stinging it with her powerful venom. The venom paralyzes but does not kill the tarantula, which the wasp then drags back into its own burrow. If the wasp finds a male tarantula, she attacks and stings it, then digs a new burrow and drags the paralyzed male tarantula inside it. The tarantula wasp then lays a single egg on the tarantula's abdomen and seals off the burrow, which has now become a burial chamber and nursery. When the wasp egg hatches, the grub begins to suck the body fluids from the comatose tarantula. Once the grub has gone through its final molt, the newly emerged tarantula wasp tears open the tarantula's body abdomen and eats the remaining goods before emerging from the burrow.

Powerful enough to paralyze a tarantula, the sting of a tarantula hawk wasp is one of the most painful of all insect bites. Carlos Catalán of Carmelita, Petén, told me in 1997 that during his many years in the Maya forest he had been bitten by a poisonous snake, the fer de lance (*Bothrops asper*), and by a tarantula wasp, and that the tarantula wasp experience was worse. "With a snake bite, you feel like you may die," he said. "With the wasp, you're certain you will."

While tarantula hawk wasp bites are not, in fact, lethal, a bite from the wasp does put a human victim into anaphylactic shock. The victim's head and neck begin to swell, constricting their trachea and making it difficult to breathe (hence the name *ahorcadora*, "strangler"). Near the archaeological site of La Corona, Petén, Santiago Billy and I were fishing for dinner in an *aguada* (water hole) when he caught his fishing line in a branch overhead. Pulling on the line to release it, he somehow disturbed a tarantula wasp, which promptly bit him on the arm. Santiago fell to the ground, disoriented, and began asking for water. As I gave him sips from a canteen, he described his symptoms: he said his face felt like it had swollen to twice its size and he felt like his eyes were popping out of his head. His heart was palpitating, and his throat was constricted. Tom Sever and I walked him back to our nearby camp, gave him Tylenol to ease the pain, and helped him lie down in his tent. He woke up two or three hours later much relieved and almost back to normal. Had we known better, we would have been carrying antihistamines, which are the indicated treatment for anaphylactic shock, and therefore for a tarantula hawk wasp bite.

BEES   What we normally think of as the honeybee, *Apis mellifera*, was brought to the Americas by European colonists in the early seventeenth century. Before this introduction, the Maya harvested honey from stingless Maya bees, *Melipona beecheii* and *Trigona* spp., which are native to the New World. Only about half the size of the stinging, European honeybee, the Maya stingless bee lives in hollows in trees and rocks in the lowland forest. Maya hunters who come upon a cache of stingless bee honey will sometimes climb the tree to harvest the honey. The honey itself is dark and thin and as strongly flavored as whiskey, almost taking your breath away if you drink a tablespoon or more of it.

The Yucatec and Lacandón Maya, and probably other Maya as well, have long maintained bees in sections of hollow logs or pear-shaped gourds, treating the insects with religious respect (Baer and Merrifield 1971:252; Weaver and Weaver 1981; Schlesinger 2001:247). The Lacandón have traditionally kept stingless bee hives in the family godhouse, where the only other residents are clay representations of the multiple gods of the Lacandón pantheon. Prior to the introduction of sugarcane into the Americas, the lowland Maya made *balche,* their sacred fermented drink, from fermented honey, water, and the bark of the *hach balche* tree (*Lonchocarpus longistylus*).

Africanized European honeybees, also known as "killer bees," migrated northward into the Maya Tropical Forest during the late 1980s. In 1956 a Brazilian geneticist brought a race of European honeybees (*Apis mellifera adansonii*) from Africa to Brazil with the goal of breeding a more productive honeybee. Only a few months after they were imported, however, 26 swarms of the new bees escaped. Mixing with other hives, they have been aggressively spreading northward ever since, at rates of 320 to 480 kilometers (200–300 miles) per year, outcompeting, outbreeding, and displacing other European honeybees and possibly the Maya stingless bee as well (*Science* 1978; Winston 1979:642; Wilson, Nunamaker, and Maki 1984:448–449).

Africanized honeybees are more aggressive and more easily provoked than normal honeybees, and some people have died after being stung up to 1,000 times, but their reputation as "killer" bees is exaggerated nonetheless. Still, being attacked by these bees is no walk in the park. On the trail to Lake Miramar, Chiapas, in September 1997, two fellow conservationists and I were attacked by Africanized bees that swarmed out of a forest tree when a companion in front of us shook a liana growing on the tree that held their hive. As the bees swarmed out of the cavity in the tree, they stung me six times, José Hernández Nava eight times, and Hank Kaesner five times. It was every man for himself when the bees hit us. José and Hank ran like crazed men. I dashed for the first stream that crossed the trail and dived into it face first—glasses, cap, backpack and all. Our stings swelled into red welts, and the sting on my left ear hurt for a week. Days later, returning from the lake, José pointed to a narrow log laid over a deep gully along the trail.

"Normally, I would have walked very carefully over that log," he said. "But when those bees hit us, I ran over it so fast, my feet barely touched the surface."

THE BOTFLY (*COLMOYOTE*) Most everyone who spends enough time in deep forest ends up with a "mosquito bite" that doesn't seem to heal but instead swells into a hard lump. They have become a host for one of the least appealing insects of the Maya Tropical Forest, the botfly or beef worm (*Dermatobia hominis*). Part of the Oestridae family of insects, botfly adults are large bumblebee-like insects that feed on flower nectars. But the immature botfly larvae are carnivorous. They eat muscle, and they are indiscriminate about their hosts. Tapirs, deer, peccaries, monkeys, and humans are all fair game.

Because they have no way to insert their eggs beneath an animal's skin, bot flies depend on mosquitoes to do their drilling for them. Bot flies capture a mosquito and lay a single egg on the mosquito's hypodermic proboscis. Released, the mosquito goes back to normal life and eventually drills its nose into an animal to suck its blood. When it does so, the botfly egg slides beneath the skin, where it eventually hatches. The young maggot then begins to feed on the mammal's flesh (Berenbaum 1993:238–239; c.f. Kricher 1989:57).

Ensconced in its habitat of choice, the botfly maggot eats muscle for sustenance. The created wound begins to hurt, because the larva's body is covered with sharp spines, and the larva turns in its hole as it grows. Left alone, the maggot will emerge to pupate in 40 to 50 days. Tropical ecologist Daniel Janzen is famous for once having left a Costa Rican botfly in his arm to pupate and emerge to fly away.

The botfly skin lesion, referred to medically as "specific myiasis," can be remedied in a variety of ways: with tape, petroleum jelly, bacon, or tobacco. All of these treatments function because the botfly larva breathes through a tiny abdominal tube that must remain in contact with the air. Even though the larva lives beneath your skin, his breathing hole links him to the outside world, like a skin diver's snorkel. Cut the maggot's supply of oxygen and you suffocate him.

To do this, modern travelers sometimes stretch a piece of adhesive tape across the wound, leave it for several days, then pull the tape off. Sometimes removing the tape pulls the now-dead maggot out of his hole. Otherwise, you can squeeze it out like solidified toothpaste. Petroleum jelly works much the same way to suffocate the maggot, but you have to keep the wound and jelly covered to ensure that it remains in place until the worm is dead. A more interesting trick is to tape a small piece of raw bacon over the wound. The botfly moves upward to maintain his breathing hole, but nonetheless suffocates and dies. But when you pull the bacon off your skin, the maggot is exposed, and you can grab him with tweezers and extract him from your skin.

The Lacandón Maya use a time-honored technique of applying a poultice of masticated cigar tobacco to the wound. The nicotine in the tobacco serves as an insecticide to kill the maggot, and the animal can be squeezed out of the muscle.

Sharon Matola, director of the Belize Zoo and an intrepid forest explorer, states that the worst place to get bot flies is in your head. (She has had as many as 16 in her scalp at one time—"the reason I wear a hat when I am outside," she says. "Always.") Having bot flies in your scalp, she reports, is like having "someone inside your head jamming it with an ice pick to get out." As well, she says, "they keep you awake at night with all their gnawing and chewing."

LEAF-CUTTER ANTS   Most any hiker on a trail through the Maya Tropical Forest will come across a narrow, denuded path that passes through the leaf litter like an insect's highway. In fact, that's exactly what it is. Worker leaf-cutter ants (*Atta* spp.; Spanish = *zompopes;* Belizean English = *wi wi;* Lacandón Maya = *sai*) climb trees and use their mandibles to clip rounded bits of leaf, which they hoist above their heads and carry along their trails to the large mounds that are their nests. So numerous are they that their movement creates trails through the vegetation. Victoria Schlesinger (2001:241) describes the leaf-cutter ants as looking "like a parade of sailboats, their green sails teetering and flapping in the wind."

Once inside their large nest, the worker leaf-cutter ants turn their leaf clippings over to specialized ant castes, which grind the cuttings into a soft pulp. They add tufts of fungi that feed on the pulp, creating the ant colony's food source. Unable to survive in the wild, these particular species of fungi are the ants' domesticated plants, dependent on the leaf-cutter ants for their survival. The fungi, in turn, are the ants' only food source, making the species codependent. While all of this is going on, the hive's queen ant—which is the size of a small mouse—spends her entire life laying eggs and being tended to by female worker ants.

Lacandón Maya traditionally began their garden plots on a clearing created by leaf-cutter ants (*u mul äh sai*). Even today, traditional Lacandones will say a prayer to the ants before clearing a new agricultural site. No doubt, this practice stems from days before metal tools were available. When clearing a hectare or half-hectare plot of tropical forest with stone tools, having the help of leaf-cutter ants in defoliating and killing the vegetation would have been grounds for gratitude. It is also likely that the large mass of organic material accumulated by the ants increased crop fertility.

BITING BLACK FLY   One animal you will want to avoid if you visit the Maya Tropical Forest is the biting black fly, sometimes known as the sandfly (*Phlebotomus* spp.), which occasionally transmits one or more species of protozoa that cause the infection called leishmaniasis. Leishmaniasis is variously known as *chiclero*'s ulcer, cutaneous leishmaniasis, tropical sore, or forest yaws. In the Maya forest region, biting black flies can spread at least two species of protozoa: *Leishmania mexicana mexicana* and *Leishmania braziliensis braziliensis.*

The skin sores that result from infection with these protozoa are open, ulcerating, granulose lesions that may heal spontaneously in 2 to 18 months but leave a deep scar on the skin. On the other hand, secondary infection of the sore is common, so—beyond being unsightly—the infection is nothing to trifle with. Treatment includes injections of antimony, a heavy metal that some patients describe as only slightly less obnoxious than the infection itself. The most frightening cases of leishmaniasis involve infection of the nose, mouth, and throat, which if left untreated can lead to serious disfigurement and death from secondary infection.

The saving grace of leishmaniasis is that it is not common. One researcher from the U.S. Department of Health and Human Services who studied the disease for more than three years in Guatemala noted that the annual incidence of cutaneous leishmaniasis in the Petén is estimated to be only 1 percent of the population (Navin 1989). In today's Petén population of 700,000 people, that would indicate 7,000 cases of leishmaniasis at any given time.

MYTHOLOGICAL ANIMALS

A forest as large as the Maya Tropical Forest still has many animal species not yet reported by science. It also has room for creatures that are reported but which may or may not actually exist. Among the possibilities are the *sisimite, sikismiki, pupo,* and *duende,* four creatures that are periodically sighted by forest residents and visitors but which remain unrecorded by scientific researchers.

The *sisimite* is a large, primate-like creature reported throughout the Maya forest. It occurs in the oral tradition of the Itza Maya and the Ladino *chicleros* (chicle collectors) of the Petén, the Yucatec Maya of the Calakmul region, the Maya of southern Belize, and the Lacandón Maya (who call them *lok'in,* "the wooden people"). In the Selva Lacandona of Chiapas, the creature is known as *el sinsimite* or *el salvaje.* Only a few people will actually admit that they have seen the creature, but many relate that a relative—their father, their grandfather, a person they have known all their life—has seen it in the forest. Those who have encountered a *sisimite* describe it as an abnormally tall, human-like creature, 3 meters (10 feet) tall, and totally covered with hair, much like the yeti or sasquatch reported in other regions of the world.

The *sisimite* walks through the forest, they say, making loud noises. In Calakmul, Mexico, where the creature is also known as Juan T'otalin, people told me that he carries a small, ukelele-sized guitar. He travels the trails playing his guitar and singing a song in Maya:

I walk these roads. If I find you, I'll break your back, put you in my net bag, and continue on my way.

In southern Belize, where the creature is called Big Foot Hairy Man, he lives in caves on mountainsides and screams like a human being (TMCC and TAA 1997:23). He tears men into pieces and carries women off for unknown purposes.

If the *sisimite* encounters you in the forest, the reports go, he will devour you. But according to the Yucatec Maya, you have one chance to escape. The *sisimite* has the peculiar characteristic of having no knees. (In the Itza Maya version, the *sisimite* has its feet on backwards but has knees.) As a result, he walks in a stiff-gaited, jack-boot marching fashion. On the off chance that you run across a *sisimite* in the forest, you should always have a red bandanna in your pocket. If you see the creature, you quickly pull the bandanna from your pocket, take off all your clothes, twirl the bandanna above your head, and begin to sing. When the *sisimite* sees this, he starts to laugh so hard that he falls down and rolls on the forest floor. While he is down and laughing riotously, you grab your clothes and run the other direction as fast as you can. Because the *sisimite* doesn't have knees, it takes him so long to stand up to chase after you that you have the chance to escape. Many a man reports that he knows someone who escaped being eaten because of the *sisimite*'s lack of knees.

During the 1990s, French-trained Guatemalan conservationist Santiago Billy operated the Las Guacamayas Biological Station on the Río San Pedro in the Maya Biosphere Reserve. He hired Miguel (Tío Mio) Manzanero, one of the most experienced *chicleros* of the region, a man who had lived in and worked in the Maya forest for 50 years, to conduct monthly surveys of wildlife in the forest around the station. Each month, Tío Mio dutifully produced a report on the animals he had seen on his rounds in the forest—for example, 15 toucans, two tapirs, 12 howler monkeys, one jaguar. But when Santiago read one of his regular, monthly reports, in 1992, he came across a reported encounter with a *sisimite*. Santiago laughed and handed the report back to the fellow, saying, "What's this?"

Tío Mio was visibly offended.

"What do you mean?" he asked indignantly. "I've lived in this forest for 50 years, and I know what I saw with these eyes. I saw a *sisimite*."

Realizing how serious Tío Mio was, Santiago turned back to the report, "Fine," he said. "Fifteen toucans, two tapirs, 12 howler monkeys, one jaguar, and one *sisimite*."

The *sisimite* is joined in the forest by another creature, the *sikismiki*, which is short in stature, has reversed feet, and tricks travelers in the forest by taking on the voice of someone the traveler knows in order to lure him deep into the forest, where he gets lost. According to experienced forest workers in Chiapas and the Guatemalan Petén, the only way to avoid the *sikismiki's* tricks is to wear your shirt inside out. Before I heard the story of the *sikismiki*, I had seen seriously experienced guides and *chicleros* do exactly this. When I asked them why they were wearing their shirts inside out, they replied, "To avoid getting lost." Several years passed before I finally learned why these men—who had spent their entire lives hiking in the Maya forest—feared they would get lost.

Another reported creature in the Maya forest is called *doohende* or *duende* in the Petén, Belize, and Mexico, *arux* (or *alux*) among the Itza Maya, and *kisin* among the Lacandón Maya. These are small, wood fairy–type creatures who protect the ramon trees and heal the chicozapote trees after chicle tappers cut hatchmarks in them to extract latex (Atran and Ukan Ek' 1999:55). The Itza hold that the *arux* recently have been scared away from frequently visited sites such as Tikal by the noise of tourists, radios, and television (Atran and Ukan Ek' 1999:55). Some Peteneros say that *duendes* wear a sombrero, like to play the guitar, and spend lots of time preening in front of the mirror.

In Belize, anyone walking in the forest who comes upon a *duende* hides his thumbs, because *duendes* have no thumbs and are so jealous of those who do have them that they will cut them off out of spite. (You will know you are suspect if travelers you encounter on the trail seem to have only four digits on each hand.)

Lacandones believe that short, black-colored *kisin* live in caves in the Maya Tropical Forest, smell terrible, and cause earthquakes by grabbing the earth and shaking it. To the Lacandones, this is serious business. I was sleeping in the house of José Chan K'in Valenzuela, in the Lacandón Maya settlement of Mensabak, Chiapas, during the February, 1976, late night earthquake that devastated Guatemala. The tremors were strong even kilometers away in Chiapas. After the first strong tremor, José Venezuela's next door neighbor, a Lacandón man of 40-plus years, came running to the door of the house yelling, "Tan u peksik luum kisin!" (The *kisin* are shaking the earth!). The men spent the rest of the night awake, terrified that the *kisin* would produce more tremors.

The *ixtabai*, who appears among the Itza Maya and Belizean forest farmers, is a shapely, horse-faced female with long hair, who lures unsuspecting men into the forest. In Spanish, she is called La Llorona, "the crier," for the crying sound she makes to attract the attention of her hapless victims. Of course, men who follow what appears to be a beautiful woman into the forest are surprised—and killed—when the *ixtabai* turns around to reveal her horse face and evil demeanor. One wonders if the *ixtabai* is a myth perpetuated by wives to keep potentially wayward men in check.

Guatemalan refugees who fled into Mexico's Montes Azules Biosphere Reserve in the Selva Lacandona, Chiapas, during the 1980s reported sightings in the region between Arroyo Azul and Arroyo Miranda, just north of the Río Lacantún, of a large mammal "like a tapir, but spotted and with horns and a short tail." According to the refugees, the same creature exists in the Guatemalan Petén, where it is called *el pupo*. Ramón Guerrero, then Conservation International–Mexico's Director for the Ixcán Ecolodge project, searched the area of the reported sightings in 1994, but never found the *pupo*, he said.

Local Maya farmers who live around Lake Miramar, in the Montes Azules Biosphere Reserve of eastern Chiapas (most of them are 1970–1980 colonists from the Chiapas highlands) report sightings in Lake Miramar of a large, unidentified animal "like a fish" that jumps above the surface and back into the water. Mexican archaeologist Sonia Rivero proposes that the animal might be a manatee (*Trichechus manatus*), an aquatic mammal, "which has caused fear among the indigenous people who navigate the lake" (Rivero 1992:20).

Wild Plants

ASPIDOSPERMA   The Lacandón Maya utilize beams, powdered bark, and sap from the tree they call *tzayok* (*Aspidosperma megalocarpon*, or *A. megalocarpum;* Belizean English = "my lady") as a natural insecticide against cockroaches. They cut beams from the tree to use as roof supports, because the wood releases chemicals that are unnoticed by humans but toxic to cockroaches. Lacandones also sprinkle powered bark near doorways and daub the tree sap on ropes and twine that suspend food-filled baskets from the ceiling. Cockroaches will climb down the ropes from the ceiling, attempting to get to the food, but die when they encounter the sap of the *tzayok* tree. In Belize, *Aspidosperma* is prized for rafters and house framing because it can be cut into long, straight, flexible lengths, depending on the age of the tree, but there is no indication that the Belizean builders also recognize the wood's pest-repellent qualities (Heinzman and Reining 1989:19).

ALLSPICE Allspice is the berry of a tree (*Pimenta dioica*) that grows wild and is plentiful in the Maya Tropical Forest. It is most abundant in the north-central and northeastern Petén. In Spanish-speaking Mexico and Guatemala, the plant and fruit are called *pimienta gorda* (fat pepper); in Belize, it is the clove tree, and to the Itza Maya it is *naba kuk* (in England, it is known as the pimento berry).

Allspice berries smell like a mixture of cloves, cinnamon, nutmeg, and ginger—hence, the name allspice. The allspice tree grows to a height of 20–25 meters (66–83 feet), though some older individuals in natural forest may reach 30 meters (100 feet). It is easy to spot in the forest because of its smooth yellow and light gray bark, which peels off in thin sheets like birch. Allspice trees are nominally male or female, though some male trees bear small numbers of berries (Rosengarten 1973:103). Female trees produce an average of about 2 kilograms (4.4 pounds) of berries per year, although Don Zacarias Q'ishchan, of the Guatemalan Petén, notes that he has harvested up to 136 kilograms (300 pounds) of green berries from a single wild tree.

During June, July, and August, *pimenteros* climb into fruit-bearing (female) allspice trees using *espalones,* spikes strapped onto their shoes, like telephone linemen. In a process technically known as pollarding, they cut off the branches that bear fruit, then climb down to strip the berries from their stems. Although the process sounds destructive, the trees do not die. Instead, they soon sprout new branches to replace those removed. The same trees can be harvested again after six years of regrowth. Properly done, allspice harvesting is a renewable industry.

Pimenteros dry the mature but still slightly green allspice berries in the sun—the preferred method—for four or five days, or dry them over a wood fire, which is faster but diminishes the quality and economic value of the product. As they dry, the berries turn red-brown. Drying accomplishes two goals simultaneously: it reduces the weight of the berries, which have to be packed out of the forest on mules or—if near a road—in the back of a pickup truck. Drying the berries also prevents mold from growing on them, given that harvesting takes place during the rainy season. The resulting berries are sold nationally and exported to the United States.

The primary competition for wild-gathered allspice from the Maya Tropical Forest comes from industrial plantations in Jamaica. Allspice is the only major spice produced on a commercial basis exclusively in the Western Hemisphere (Rosengarten 1973:100). Enough trees grow wild in the Guatemalan Petén to support the export of up to 400,000 kilograms

(880,000 pounds) of allspice berries each year, although some years result in almost no harvest at all, due to insufficient rainfall. Guatemala currently supplies about 30 percent of the international allspice market, trailing Jamaica, which benefits from plantation production (Heinzman and Reining 1989).

Today, allspice is used primarily in food products—in ketchup, sausages, meat broths, jams, fruitcakes, and fruit pies. It is also used in spice teas, in potpourris, and as a pickling agent, especially for pickling fish (pickled herring is pickled in salt and allspice). You will also find it amid other spices in the bottom of jars of dill pickles. Allspice is a key ingredient in Benedictine and chartreuse liqueurs. Steeped or boiled in water, the leaves make an excellent tea, which is used to settle the stomach. Allspice oil is used in men's aftershave and cologne fragrances, but must be distinguished from a related member of the myrtle family, *Pimenta acris,* which is the key ingredient in bay rum, a traditional men's aftershave lotion (Rosengarten 1973:100).

Allspice was harvested and used by the ancient Maya as well, and allspice trees are abundant in the ruins of many Classic Maya sites today, the forest around Tikal especially abounding in them. Spice researcher Frederic Rosengarten Jr. states that the Maya "used allspice berries to embalm and help preserve the bodies of important leaders" (Rosengarten 1973:101). They may also have used it to preserve meat, as did ship crews during long voyages of the seventeenth to nineteenth centuries.

Friar Diego de Landa, in his 1566 manuscript *Relación de las cosas de Yucatán,* noted that the Maya of sixteenth-century Yucatán used allspice as an additive to toasted corn gruel: "They also toast the maize and then grind and mix it with water into a very refreshing drink, putting into it a little Indian pepper [allspice] or cacao" (Landa 1978:34).

AMATE   The ancient Maya made paper (*hu'un*) from the inner bark of the amate tree (*Ficus* spp.; Itza and Lacandón Maya = *kopo'*). Maya codices were made from amate paper cut into strips up to a meter long. Maya scribes folded the paper screens into accordion-like books and coated the pages with white calcium. They painted hieroglyphs on the prepared surface with dyes made from plants, clay, snails, and minerals, to record information about astronomy, agricultural cycles, and prophecies.

Both the ancient Maya and modern Lacandón Maya made long strips of amate paper for ritual bleeding ceremonies. The ancient Maya pierced their tongues and genitals with obsidian blades and dripped the blood onto the paper. Most modern Lacandones color the paper with red dye from the annatto plant (*Bixa orellana;* Spanish = *achiote;* Lacandón Maya = *k'ushu*), rather than blood, although obsidian blades and amate strips occasionally show up in sacred caves in Lacandón territory, indicating that a few Lacandones may still be following the ancient ways. Either way, Lacandones burn the resulting paper in ceremonies or leave it in sacred caves in bundles of long strips.

BALSAM Powdered bark from the balsam tree (*Myroxylon balsamum*) has an ethereal, incense-like smell. The Lacandón Maya sometimes sprinkle this powder onto tobacco leaves as they roll homemade cigars from tobacco grown in their milpa plots, especially when the tobacco has too much bite. The *naba,* as the Lacandones call balsam, smoothes the taste of the cigar and gives it a pleasant aroma.

The Maya of southern Belize also use the word *naba* to refer to balsam, but they burn the powdered bark with copal as incense in clay incense burners during ceremonies to their traditional gods.

BARBASCO VINE The barbasco vine (*Dioscorea* spp.), common throughout the Maya Tropical Forest, has had a marked impact on modern civilization. The barbasco vine grows out of the ground as a large tuberous bulb with heart-shaped leaves on a green climbing vine. Maya families in the region have long used barbasco as a fish poison. They cut up the bulbous root and disperse it into slowly moving water in a stream or river. The root releases chemical substances that stun but do not kill fish that move through the affected water. As the fish float to the surface, the Maya fishermen have only to wade through the water, grabbing the fish and dropping them into a basket.

Laboratory analysis of the 25 species of barbasco vine have revealed several with large quantities of the alkaloid diosgenin (*D. spiculiflora, D. escuintlensis;* and *D. floribunda*). During the mid-twentieth century, chemists worked with diosgenin to produce oral contraceptives and cortisone for skin ailments and deep joint problems. The Selva Lacandona of Chiapas became the initial, primary source of barbasco for the production of these products, but attempts to manipulate the supply and price backfired and edged the Mexican industry out of the market. Similar East Indian plants took over the market, especially for the production of birth control pills.

BAYAL   If you travel down a lowland forest trail by mule, you can be suddenly ripped out of your wooden saddle by the unfriendly *bayal* vine (*Desmoncus orthocanthos;* formerly *D. schippii* and *D. martius;* Lacandón Maya = *jenen;* Belizean English = basket ti tai; tie tie), a tall, slender climbing palm that sends out a long shoot covered with sharp spines and tipped by an arrowhead-shaped hook on its end. This hook will catch on clothing or straps and is strong enough to pull a traveler off his mule. *Xateros* (*xate* harvesters; see *Xate,* below) and *chicleros* traveling narrow roads through thick forest have also been pulled out the back of pickup trucks by the *bayal* vine.

Lacandones use *bayal* to make baskets (*shak*) for washing corn. Carefully avoiding the many inch-long spines that cover the vine, they pull the inner core of the plant away from its outer spiny covering to reveal a long, strong cord that is flexible and durable, much like rattan. Woven into round baskets 36 centimeters (14 inches) across, the core makes an excellent, long-lasting implement for washing corn or holding harvested crops such as *chayotes.* Belizeans weave *bayal* into baskets, hats, and handicrafts for tourists.

RAMON   Ramon (*Brosimum alicastrum;* Yucatec Maya = *osh;* Lacandón Maya = *ya'ash osh* and *hach osh*) is the most frequently occurring tree in the northern Petén (8–9 percent of all trees). It appears throughout the Maya Tropical Forest (Atran and Ukan Ek' 1999:53). It is especially common in and around archaeological sites, a fact that has prompted several interesting hypotheses. The most frequently cited is the possibility that the ancient Maya cultivated the species for its food value in garden plots near their stone cities. Several studies point to the use of cooked and ground ramon nuts to make tortillas, especially during times of corn scarcity (Puleston 1968). Following this idea, the abundant ramon trees in and around today's ruins are the descendants of trees cultivated by the Maya 1,000 years ago. A second hypothesis holds that because the ramon is adapted to well-drained, stony soils in the Maya forest, the trees are naturally abundant on stone ruins, which are covered with well-drained, stony soils (Schulze and Whitacre 1999:217).

It is definitely the case that, because the ramon provides foliage and nuts for such a wide variety of wildlife—deer, peccary, pacas, squirrels, monkeys, bats, tinamous, parrots, and toucans, among others—the animals disperse ramon seeds over wide areas of the lowland forest. The resourceful muleteers (*arrieros*) who haul food and forest products in and out of *chiclero* and *xatero* camps in the Maya forest feed their mules and horses ramon. Before sunset, the *arrieros* climb up ramon trees by strapping on the same *espalones* they use to climb chicle or allspice trees for harvesting. They pollard the branches from the trees, dropping them to the ground. Back on the ground, they pile the branches—replete with leaves and sometimes ramon nuts—in a long row, much like a stacked cord of wood. Then they tie the mules and horses within reach of the pile, and the animals eat ramon during much of the night. In the morning, all the *arriero* finds is a pile of peeled ramon poles; the mules and horses have eaten every leaf and even gnawed the bark off the branches. One *arriero* from Carmelita, Petén, told me that mules and horses eat better in the forest, because of ramon trees, than they do in their communities at home. "They come back from their weeks in the forest fat, fat, fat," he said. The process does not kill the ramon trees, which begin to sprout new branches.

Various groups of Maya formerly toasted ramon nuts—they have a branlike flavor—or boiled and ground them for use in tortillas. Ramon is high in protein and similar to corn in providing critical protein groups, but contains twice as much tryptophane, an amino acid commonly lacking in diets made up chiefly of corn (Pardo-Tejeda and Sánchez Muñoz 1981:20). Still, eating ramon nuts carries some social stigma. Some Maya families will only reluctantly admit that they eat ramon during periods of food scarcity, as if consuming the nuts were a marker of a family's poverty. On the other hand, the Itza Maya mark some special occasions by cooking half-meter (19 inch) wide tortillas made of ground ramon and corn.

According to the early Mayanist Teobert Maler, the Maya placed ramon seeds inside a gourd to create a diviner's rattle. The dissolved sap of ramon, consumed with warm water, has also been used in ethnomedicine as a remedy for asthma, coughs, phlegm, hoarseness, and fever (Roys 1931:4, 272).

Ramon trees can grow as tall as 40 meters (130 feet). The female trees drop their round fruit, still encased in a thin covering that looks like the peel of an orange, during April and May. A single tree can produce as many as 1,000 kilograms (2,200 pounds) of ramon nuts. Many ground-feeding animals, such as pacas and peccaries, feast on the nuts and peels at this time. As the peel is eaten or rots away, a golden brown nut appears, covered at first with a papery membrane. This is the form of ramon utilized by the Maya as a food source.

CACAO   The cacao tree (*Theobroma cacao*), the source of cocoa powder and chocolate, has been utilized in the Mexican and Central American tropics for thousands of years, first by the Olmec, who lived in the region of the modern Mexican states of Veracruz and Tabasco, and later by the Maya. The Classic Maya consumed cacao (later to be called chocolate) in what Sophie and Michael Coe call "a vast and complex array of drink, gruels, porridges, powders, and probably solid substances, to all of which could be added a wide variety of flavorings," including chilies, vanilla, allspice, honey, annatto, and dried and powdered flowers (S. Coe and M. Coe 1996:51, 89).

The ancient Maya drank ground, toasted cacao bean powder mixed with water—cold and usually unsweetened unless there was honey on hand (cane sugar came to the New World with Europeans), frequently pouring the liquid from one vessel to another to build up a frothy foam. They also put thickened chocolate froth on corn gruel drinks, much like you and I might pour frothy milk foam on coffee. Cacao was so prized by the Classic Maya that they used the unground beans as money, even to the point that some unscrupulous souls hollowed out the insides to make counterfeit money of the emptied beans.

Columbus found cacao beans among the many trade items stuffed into the Maya trading canoe he encountered off the coast of Honduras during his fourth voyage to the Americas in 1502. But it apparently fell to a group of highland Maya, the Q'eqchi', to introduce cacao to Europe. In 1544 Dominican missionaries returning to Spain from Alta Verapaz, Guatemala, brought with them a group of Q'eqchi' Maya nobles. Among the gifts these Q'eqchi' presented to Prince Philip (later King Philip II) were quetzal feathers, chilies, corn, beans, copal incense, and chocolate. Within a few decades, cacao was added to the stock of trade items that made their way from the New World to Europe. The Spaniards, who drank their chocolate hot, went on to develop solid chocolate sweets and to introduce the substance to other nations. Eventually, the Englishman Nicholas Sanders, in 1727, combined chocolate with milk to make the first milk chocolate, and two Swiss men, Henri Nestlé and Daniel Peter, in the 1860s and 1870s, produced the first milk chocolate bars (S. Coe and M. Coe 1996:249–250).

All this is a far cry from the lowland tropical forest of the Maya world, where the chocolate tree still grows in the courtyard gardens of some Maya families. Lacandones plant the tree in their garden plots but use the toasted, ground seeds today mainly as a topping for corn gruel drinks. Just as likely, they will be found today eating a commercial Carlos Quinto milk chocolate bar, purchased in a nearby town.

Hikers in the Maya forest occasionally come across a feral cacao tree, which the Lacandones call *barum te,* "jaguar tree," indicating its respected status. The plants are likely survivors from previous generations of Indian plantings.

CECROPIA/GUARUMO Shield leaf pumpwood (*Cecropia peltata;* Spanish = *guarumo;* Lacandón Maya = *k'och*) is a fast-growing tree in disturbed forest areas. The tree is common in old milpa plots and along roads and other cleared areas in the early stages of regrowth, reaching a height of 20 meters (66 feet). Because the *Cecropia* quickly colonizes disturbed areas, it is useful in holding the thin tropical soil in place as shade-demanding, slower-growing tree species gradually take over. Like the acacia tree, *Cecropia* is colonized and protected by ants. The ants live on and inside the hollow trunk of the *Cecropia* tree and, in turn, keep the tree cleaned of vines and predators. In Belize, the *Cecropia* is called the trumpet tree and the top shoot of the tree when boiled is used to treat arthritis. Maya families throughout the region use split *Cecropia* trunks as house walls. Toucans, monkeys, and bats eat the plentiful seeds of the *Cecropia* tree, dispersing the species throughout the forest.

CHECHEM NEGRO In addition to the many useful plants in the Maya Tropical Forest, the natural vegetation also includes plants that locals try to avoid. One of these is the black poisonwood tree. Commonly known throughout the Maya Tropical Forest as *chechem negro,* the black poisonwood tree (*Metopium brownei*) produces a sap that burns human skin like a third-degree burn if a person comes into contact with it. Touching the tree, climbing it, or chopping it, for example, will produce an itching, then sharply burning sensation. People unfortunate enough to unknowingly climb a *chechem* tree can end up with serious burns over much of their body. The caustic effects of the tree are carried even by its smoke. Chechem limbs used as firewood give off smoke that will itself burn those closely downwind. Stories exist as well of individuals who sought refuge under a chechem tree during a rainstorm and quickly found themselves with burns covering their body. Among the Lacandón Maya of Chiapas, Mexico, oral history holds that at least one man eliminated a rival by lacing his corn gruel with the sap of the chechem tree.

In a situation that seems to prove the adage that nature always seeks a balance, wherever the noxious chechem tree grows in the forest you will almost always find its antidote, red gumbo limbo, growing nearby (*Bursera simaruba; Indio desnudo* in Chiapas and gumbo limbo or "tourist tree" in Belize, because its skin turns red and peels off). Ecologically, this is the result of both species preferring similar microclimatic conditions. Forest dwellers in the Maya Tropical Forest treat burns caused by the chechem tree with ground bark of the gumbo limbo tree. Studies by ethnobotanists Mike Balick and Rosita Arvigo demonstrated that the tree's bark does in fact heal skin wounds. Today, in Belize, you can even buy a commercially produced skin salve made from *Bursera*.

CHICLE The extracted latex of the *chicozapote* tree (*Manilkara zapota*), called *chicle* in Spanish and *ya* in Lacandón Maya and Itza Maya, was once the primary ingredient in chewing gum. Tough forest workers known as *chicleros* harvest chicle from February to June each year by cutting hatch marks in the outer bark of the chicle tree in a herringbone design. They work only during the early rainy season because the trees do not produce a steady flow of latex during the dry season. *Chicleros* almost always work in groups, basing themselves in a deep forest camp where they hang their hammocks and mosquito nets and eat beans, rice, tortillas, and chilies prepared by a cook—frequently a woman with children—who prepares the meals while the men work the chicle trees in the surrounding forest (Dugelby 1998).

The density of chicle trees in the Maya forest varies from region to region but ranges from 58 per hectare (23 trees per acre) in northern Belize to 27 trees per hectare (11 trees per acre) in Quintana Roo, Mexico. Anthropologist Norman Schwartz reports densities in the western Petén that range from as few as 15 per hectare (6 trees per acre) up to 50 per hectare (20 trees per acre) (Heinzman and Reining 1989:17).

When the *chicleros* cut hatch marks in the trees, the latex bleeds from the inner bark and runs down the crisscrossing pattern to drip into a paraffin-coated cotton bag hung on a peg tapped into the base of the tree. Some *chicleros* use burlap bags coated with natural rubber (*castillo* or *hule*). A good tree will produce five pounds of raw chicle latex during every tapping season, but the same trees are not tapped every year. Instead, the *chiclero* rests the harvested trees for several years to allow them to rebuild their strength and productivity.

If the *chiclero* cuts the trees properly—if he cuts only the outer bark of the trees, without damaging the heart—the chicle trees heal their wounds and can be harvested again in four or five years. Cutting too deeply into a tree creates wounds that are exploited by insects or plant pathogens, leading to the death of the tree. Studies indicate that mortality reaches about 5 percent of all chicle trees tapped.

After gathering the latex from his tapped trees in the forest, the *chiclero* returns to his forest camp and boils the liquid in a large, open-mouthed pot that looks like a meter-wide Chinese restaurant wok. Boiling evaporates water from the gum, and when it reaches the proper percentage of moisture content—about 25–30 percent—the *chiclero* pulls the gum from the fire and begins to dry and cool it by stirring it with a small pole, much like taffy makers pull taffy. (The chicle has the consistency of taffy candy at this point in preparation.)

While the gum cools, the *chiclero* flattens out rough henequen gunnysacks on the ground and places rectangular wooden molds on them. After protecting his hands and upper arms with a thick soap paste made from commercial detergent or bar soap, he dips his hands into the wok and grabs a large blob of the hot gum. He quickly drops it into the wooden mold and spreads it evenly like cake batter in a cake pan. When the gum is almost cool in the mold, the *chiclero* carves his initials into the top of the chicle loaf, which is turning a golden brown on the outside, like a baked loaf of bread. He then allows the block to dry. The resulting hardened block of chicle weighs 9 kilograms (20 pounds). Marking the blocks with his initials allows the *chiclero* to distinguish his product from that of the *chicleros* with whom he shares the camp, especially if the blocks produced by several *chicleros* are packed onto the same mule train to be transported out of the forest.

During the late 1980s, *chicleros* received about US$2 per pound for their work. During a good week, a top notch *chiclero* can produce 100 pounds per week, although most harvest only 50 to 70 pounds per week (Heinzman and Reining 1989:15). Official Guatemalan statistics indicate that the value of exploiting chicle has reached as high as US$1.4 million per year in Guatemala alone, but official statistics on forest products are notoriously underreported to avoid taxes on the extracted products.

In the United States, cheaper substitutes have pulled the bottom out of the market for natural chicle. Today, chicle is exported mostly to Japan and Europe, where it is still used in chewing gum production. Italy especially is undergoing a surge in the use of natural chewing gum. The chicle industry in Guatemala has suffered from industry substitutes of sorva, a gum base from Brazil. During 1985, Brazil exported almost US$29 million of sorva from Manaus alone (Ghillean Prance, personal communication, 1988). Chewing gum produced in the United States today is largely plastic mixed with sugar and flavorings. Instead of using natural chicle, producers make chewing gum from polyvinyl acetate, a synthetic resin. In creating this synthetic gum, manufacturers add plasticizers to a synthetic gum base to imitate the flexibility of real chicle gum.

A secondary grade of gum latex called *chiquibul* in Spanish and "crown gum" in Belizean English, is tapped in southern Belize and some regions of the Petén. It comes from the closely related tree *Manilkara chicle*. Unscrupulous *chicleros* sometimes adulterate the higher quality chicle, or white gum, by adding *chiquibul* to it to increase the volume of gum they have to sell. (They have also been known to place a large rock in the middle of the wooden mold as they drop in the chicle, leading to the purchasers' common practice of breaking apart each block of chicle gum as they examine it.)

The wood of the chicle tree is dense, splits well, and is decay resistant, so it is prized for use in construction. The ancient Maya used chicle for roof beams in their corbeled arches, and some beams are still supporting weight a thousand years after being laid in place. The Classic Maya also carved lintels (overhead doorway supports) from chicle and carved them with intricate scenes, some of which are preserved today in museums. The best known and best preserved are from the major temples of Tikal, although others have been found in the sites of Chichén Itzá and Uxmal, in northern Yucatán (Sharer 1994:657).

CHOK BERRIES The plant that Lacandón Maya call *chok* is known in Spanish as *chilillo, chilil, xilil, morrito,* or *zapote faisán* (curassow's mamey). Known scientifically as *Ardisia paschalis* (Myrsinaceae), the plant produces yellow round fruit favored by birds in the Maya forest. As one of the plant's Spanish names implies, *chok* berries are a favored food of the Central American curassow, *Crax rubra*. At the same time, the curassow is one of the favored foods of Maya peoples, because these large, plump birds are not difficult to hunt. They tend to be somewhat slow in the forest canopy, and their large wings make noticeable noise when they fly from branch to branch.

Lacandón and Itza Maya hunters told me that if they bag a curassow that has dined on chok berries, they have to be exceptionally careful that their dogs don't eat any part of the bird, most especially the intestines. Although people can eat such a curassow without problems, dogs that do so go into violent, yowling pain in reaction to some toxic substance in the berries.

COHUNE   Cohune palms (*Attalea cohune,* formerly *Orbignya cohune;* Spanish = *corrozo*) are tall trees with draping leaves that may reach a surprising 18 meters (59 feet) in length. The trees are common throughout the Petén and southern Belize, where they have multiple uses among local people. Maya families split the long fronds lengthwise to create thatch for a roof that will last 7 to 10 years. The cohune's oil-rich seeds, when cracked and boiled, produce a slick, edible oil used in cooking. Workers boil the cohune nuts to soften them, then crack them using a wood mortar and pestle. They then boil the nuts again to extract the oil. One worker can make up to 10 quarts of oil per day, which sells for a few dollars per quart (*Belize Times* 1991).

Chicleros sometimes burn the dense, hard nuts of the cohune in a slow, smoldering fire to produce an incense to ward off mosquitoes. During World War II, part of the filtering effect of gas masks came from charcoal made from cohune nuts, as well as pits from peaches and apricots. Because cohune trees are resistant to fire, they are frequently the only trees standing—and the only shade provided—in pastures cleared from tropical forest.

COPAL   The resin of the copal tree (*Protium copal;* Maya = *pom*) is one of the most sacred substances among the traditional people of the Maya Tropical Forest. Trees are bled up to twice a year by cutting small patches of bark from the trunk and scraping the resin that bleeds from the resulting wound with a wooden paddle over a period of several weeks. The result is a sticky, fragrant gray-white gel with the consistency of butter. In southern Belize, the Maya gather about 20 grams (two-thirds of an ounce) of resin from each tree during each collection (Wilk 1997: 149–150).

The ancient Maya burned copal (as well as rubber and chicle and probably balsam) in elaborate, cylindrical ceramic incense burners. The Lacandón Maya still burn copal as payment to their traditional gods. While chanting traditional prayers, they line up dozens of small mounds of copal on flat mahogany prayer boards with handles. They then place these mounds, one by one, into their godpots—or on stones if they are praying in sacred caves or ancient ruins. Smoke from the highly combustible copal helps carry the Lacandones' prayers to the gods.

Bishop Landa, in his 1566 book on the Maya of Yucatán, made this reference to copal: "They cut the incense tree a great deal, for the demons; this they extract cutting the bark with a stone for the sap to run out. This tree is fresh, tall, and with fine leafage and shade, but its flower turns the wax black when it is present" (Landa 1978:103).

EPIPHYTES   Epiphytes grow on so many lowland tropical forest trees that they constitute up to one-quarter of the total plant species in the forest. Often called air plants, epiphytes are not parasites but simply live on other plants; hence their name: *epi* "upon," *phytes* "plants." More than 15,500 species of epiphytes grow in Central and South America. Of these, 2,000 are members of the pineapple family, Bromeliaceae. Most orchids are epiphytes.

All epiphytes attach themselves to a tree branch and live from soil nutrients blown into the canopy. They develop root systems that gradually accumulate organic matter and build an organic litter base called an epiphyte mat and trap falling leaves, fruits, and insects, which provide additional nutrients (Kricher 1989:43). A few large bromeliad species grow leaves that create small cisterns, which collect water and debris high in the canopy and provide homes and sustenance for frogs, salamanders, and insects, including mosquitoes.

GUANO   The guano palm (*Sabal mauritiiformis, Sabal morrisiana;* Spanish = *guano;* Belizean English = bay leaf; Lacandón Maya = *sha'an*) has large, water-resistant fronds that make it the most highly prized roofing palm in the Maya forest. A roof made of guano palm fronds will last up to 15 years, although Maya harvesters point out that the leaves must be cut when the moon is full; otherwise, the stems become susceptible to insect damage. The roof for a 46 square meter (500 sq. ft.) house requires around 1,500 guano leaves. As guano palms mature, they develop a dense and very hard trunk, difficult to chop with an axe. At this point, the tree earns a new name: *botán,* to distinguish it from the shorter, more easily harvested guano palms (O'Hara 1998:198).

Maya families eat the heart of the guano palm either by boiling it or roasting it in hot coals. Before commercial salt became readily available through trade, the Lacandón Maya of Chiapas used the stems of young guano palms to make salt. They placed small pieces of the palm's trunk on top of a cooking fire to sweat out the palm's sap, so that it dripped onto the fire's ashes. Later, they gathered the black, hardened sap from the cooled ashes and stored it in a leaf for subsequent use. To utilize the hardened palm sap as salt, the Maya placed it in a pot of water to dissolve. They used the salty water for cooking foods such as meat, squash, or beans (Baer and Merrifield 1971:220–221).

LOGWOOD   Logwood (*Haematoxylon campechianum;* Spanish = *tinte* or *palo de Campeche;* Itza and Lacandón Maya = *ek'*) is a swamp forest legume tree that grows in dense stands in seasonally inundated areas of the Selva Lacandona, Guatemalan Petén, and lowland Belize. Guatemalans calls these stands *tintales* or *bajos;* Belizeans call them logwood thickets. Growing to only 8 meters (26 feet), logwood is not a tall tree, but it grows in almost impenetrable stands along the edges of lakes and in low-lying wet areas. Mexican novelist Pablo Montañez describes logwood thickets and the plants associated with them in the hot, humid bajos as "the only vegetation that can live with its feet in water and its head in hell" (Montañez 1971, cited in de Vos 1988b:213).

Logwood trees played a major role in the history of Belize, for it was the abundance of logwood that prompted British loggers to colonize the Belizean coast, leading to a British challenge to Spanish rule of the area that eventually would become British Honduras and later Belize. (The Belizean flag preserves an image of two logwood cutters, one black, one white.) Logwood was prized during the eighteenth and nineteenth centuries by the British wool industry, whose entrepreneurs imported the logs to dye woolen thread. The discovery of chemical dyes during the 1850s decreased the export of logwood and other plant dyes, such as indigo, from Mexico and Guatemala, but exports from Belize continued into the twentieth century, peaking in 1928 with more than 1,000 metric tons sold. Logwood exports then lay dormant for five decades, until Japanese companies began importing the product as a natural dye during the late 1980s (Heinzman and Reining 1989:47).

The dye produced from logwood, sometimes called fustic, is extracted by cutting off complete branches or trunks of trees, then mashing the dense heartwood into bits and boiling it in water. The heartwood contains approximately 10 percent of a colorless compound called haematoxylin, which oxidizes to a violet blue substance, haematein. The color that results depends on the additives, called fixatives or mordants, that are boiled with the logwood chips. Possible colors include red-orange and yellow, but black is the most common (Heinzman and Reining 1989:21).

Logwood is still used as a dye in the production of biological stains. Most exports today—primarily to Western Europe, the United States, and

Japan—originate in the Caribbean island nations of Jamaica, Haiti, and the Dominican Republic.

In Chiapas, I learned that the Lacandón Maya still seek out logwood trunks for use as house corner-posts because they are impervious to moisture rot and last for years. They also value fallen trunks and limbs as firewood. A fire made from three logwood limbs in a star-shaped pattern will produce embers that glow all night, making it easy to revive the fire the next morning.

PALO SANTO *Palo santo* is a flowering liana (*Clematis* spp.?) that drapes down from the forest canopy. Lacandón Maya, Tzeltal Maya, Itza Maya, and Guatemalan *chicleros* cut down sections of the liana and chop it into 15-centimeter (6-inch) pieces, which they use to make a refreshing drink that tastes like sassafras tea. A cross-section of the liana reveals the design of a cross, hence one of the plant's names in Spanish: *palo santo*, "holy stick." The Maya and *chicleros* boil the short sections in a pot of water until the pieces give a deep red color to the water, which can be drunk either hot or cold. Most modern Maya families add white sugar to the drink, which is absolutely refreshing on a hot day or very warming when served hot on a chilly morning. Lacandones call the plant—and the drink— *nɨkte' ak*, "nectar flower vine." Tzeltales call it *t'utum*, and in Spanish it is variously called *bejuco de pimienta* or *palo santo*. Different groups assign various medicinal properties to the vine, including cures for kidney problems and blood disorders. The Lacandón Maya drink it to cure bone and muscle aches (Kashanipour and McGee 2004:63).

PIPER Several species of the genus *Piper* (Lacandón Maya = *mäk u lin*; Spanish = *ubil*; Belizean English = cow foot leaf) grow abundantly in the Maya Tropical Forest. The plants have large, heart-shaped leaves with the peculiar characteristic of a densely packed stalk of flowers that stands up from the base of the leaf like an obelisk. Lacandones showed me how to take advantage of the leaves' clovelike aroma by placing them in the bottom of the cooking pot when steaming tamales. *Piper* leaves are also used to wrap fish for cooking.

Medicinally, several indigenous groups of the Maya forest boil the root of *Piper* for half an hour and drip the juice on an aching tooth to relieve pain. Tea from the leaves helps babies purge intestinal worms. Adults use it to treat indigestion and stomach gas. Women tie the leaves around their waist in pairs, under a tight wrap, to ease menstrual cramps.

RUBBER Inhabitants of the Maya Tropical Forest have found several uses for native rubber (*Castilla elastica;* Spanish = *hule;* Lacandón Maya = *k'ik'*). *Chicleros* create waterproof bags by coating gunnysacks or cotton bags with latex bled from the rubber tree. The ancient Maya made rubber balls for the Maya ballgame from *Castilla elastica.* Spaniards described the manufacture of these balls in the sixteenth century and commented on the bounce the balls produced. They also noted that the Maya mixed rubber latex with juice squeezed from the morning glory vine, creating a white blob that could be shaped into a ball.

More recently, researchers from the Massachusetts Institute of Technology analyzed rubber artifacts from archaeological sites in Veracruz, Mexico, and verified this process. Morning glory juice contains sulfur compounds that cause polymer molecules in rubber to cross-link, giving rubber its bounciness. Vulcanization, invented during the 1800s, produces the same effect (*Science News* 1999:31).

Small amounts of native rubber have been exported from the Maya region, but both there and throughout the world the industry is dominated by the *Hevea brasiliensis* rubber tree, a native of the Amazon basin, which produces superior latex.

SOAPBERRY Landa noted the harvest of soapberry by the sixteenth-century Yucatec Maya: "There is another kind [of tree] that bears a fruit like filberts, of whose kernels they make fine beads, and whose bark is used for washing clothes the same as soap, making a fine lather" (Landa 1978:103).

The modern Lacandón Maya refer to soapberry trees with the same term, *bahbah*, that they use for commercial bars of soap. The tree's scientific name is *Sapindus saponaria;* in Spanish it is *amole, palo blanco,* or *tabancillo.*

STRANGLER FIG (*FICUS CRASSIUSCULA;* SPANISH = *MATAPALO*) Like something from a science fiction movie, the strangler fig begins its life cycle innocently enough, but gradually transforms into a killer. Birds and monkeys eat the tasty figs that the strangler fig produces and later expel the seeds onto the branch of a forest tree. When one of the seeds germinates, it sends thin tendrils downward to wrap around the trunk of the tree, anastomosing, or fusing together, dozens of tendrils in an organic web that envelops the tree trunk. Eventually, the strangler's tendrils reach the ground, and it develops its own root system. As the strangler fig grows, its expanding tendrils constrict the bole of the original tree and begin to shade out its crown. One or the other of these processes gradually kills the original tree, leaving the strangler fig standing in its place to produce its own crop of figs and perpetuate its species.

XATE   *Xate* (pronounced *sha*-te, from the Itza and Lacandón term *ish yat*) is the Spanish-language term for several species of *Chamaedorea* palms that grow in the understory of the Maya Tropical Forest. Millions of stems of these palms are exported every year, mainly from Chiapas and the Guatemalan Petén, destined for use in the floral industry in the United States, Switzerland, Germany, and the Netherlands. Florists use the fronds as the green backdrop for cut flowers, especially for large arrangements used in weddings and funerals.

Although 60–65 species of *Chamaedorea* palms grow in Mexico and Central America, the *xate* industry concentrates on two, known in Spanish as *hembra* and *jade* (or *macho*). *Hembra* palm (*Chamaedorea elegans*) is the smaller and more delicate looking of the two plants, usually growing from 45 centimeters (18 inches) to 1 meter (37 inches) in height. By contrast, *jade* (*Chamaedorea oblongata*), with larger, leathery leaves, grows to triple this height, sometimes reaching 3 meters (10 feet) (Dugelby 1991:27).

Both species of *xate* palm are prized in the floral industry, because the fronds remain green and fresh looking for up to 60 days after they are harvested in the forest. Forest workers known in Spanish as *xateros* harvest *xate* fronds by searching for the palms in the forest understory and cutting only two or three leaves from each plant. Using a pocket knife, they take only mature green leaves, being careful not to kill the plant so they can harvest it again in two to three months. The fact that the plants are not killed means that *xate* is a renewable resource that can be maintained as long as the forest remains uncleared.

In Guatemala, *xateros* (almost always men) are organized into harvesting teams by contractors (mostly men, some women), who are based in small urban areas such as Flores or San Benito, Petén. The contractors provide the *xateros* with food and transportation, delivering them to a forested region where they set up camp and begin to work the forest. Every other day, the contractor returns to the camp to bring in more food and rush the *xate* fronds to processing warehouses in urban areas. In the warehouses, workers (usually women) sort and grade the fronds, discarding leaves that are discolored or missing leaves. The fronds selected for sale are bundled and shipped by refrigerated truck either to the airport for export to Europe, New York, and Florida, or all the way to San Antonio, Texas, the distribution center for *xate* that enters the United States by refrigerated truck from Mexico.

Xate harvesters are paid by the number of leaves they cut, so the *xateros'* goal is to move through the forest as quickly as possible, cutting as many palm fronds as possible but leaving the palms alive for future work in the area. On an excellent day, a *xatero* may make as much as US$32, but half of this is not uncommon. Over the year, the average take is about US$8 per day, an amount that surpasses that earned by laborers on cattle ranches (Carlos Soza, personal communication, Flores, Petén, 2000). At least 6,000 people work as *xateros* in the Guatemalan Petén, probably half that many in neighboring Chiapas. In addition, another 1,000 farmers gather *xate* during a few months of the year to earn additional income. University of Delaware anthropologist Norman Schwartz found that at least half of the farmers in communities of the central Petén earned additional income harvesting *xate*. He reported that more than a quarter of household heads in some communities were supporting themselves exclusively as *xate* gatherers (Schwartz 1990).

The *xate* industry is threatened by deforestation of the natural forest and by inexperienced harvesters—many of them immigrants into the lowland forest—who sometimes cut down the entire palm to secure the maximum number of leaves.

Stela glyphs, Tikal

Tourists exploring Palenque, Chiapas

Photos are by James D. Nations unless otherwise indicated.

Central Plaza, Tikal

Island city of Flores, Petén, Guatemala

Temple of the Inscriptions, Palenque

Stucco frieze at Xunantunich

El Mirador pyramids covered with forest, Maya Biosphere Reserve, Guatemala

Kinkajou, *Potos flavus,* in Montes Azules Biosphere Reserve, Chiapas, Mexico

Río San Pedro, Laguna del Tigre National Park, inside the Maya Biosphere Reserve, Guatemala

Guatemalan botanist Juan José Castillo Mont examines a palm inside Sierra del Lacandón National Park, Maya Biosphere Reserve, Guatemala.

Buttresses of a ficus tree, El Perú/ Waka' archaeological site, Laguna del Tigre National Park, Maya Biosphere Reserve, Guatemala

Lacandón Maya family, Chiapas, Mexico

Q'eqchi' Maya families, Belize

Young Mopan Maya girls, southern
Belize

Koh, Lacandón Maya, settlement of
Mensabak, Chiapas, Mexico

Belizean men and boys, Temash River, Belize

Chiclero tapping *chicozapote* tree (*Manilkara zapota*)

Chan K'in Valenzuela, Lacandón boy, settlement of Mensabak, Chiapas, Mexico

LANDSAT satellite image of northwestern Guatemala, 1988, contrasting forested area of the Department of Petén with deforested areas of Tabasco and Chiapas states, Mexico (photo courtesy of Tom Sever, NASA Marshall Space Flight Center)

Colonist's house, Laguna Ixcoch, Río Usumacinta, Guatemala

Colonist's house and deforestation inside Laguna del Tigre National Park, Maya
Biosphere Reserve, Guatemala

Colonists' settlement, road to El Naranjo, Department of Petén, Guatemala

Guatemalan *chiclero* with 10-kilogram (22-pound) block of hardened chicle from the *chicozapote* tree (*Manilkara zapota*)

Xatero with collected *xate* palms (*Chamaedorea oblongata*) near the archaeological site of Bonampak, Chiapas, Mexico

Luis Morales, muleteer and forest guide, at Nakbe archaeological site, Maya Biosphere Reserve, Guatemala

Xateros sorting *xate* palms (*Chamaedorea oblongata*), multiple-use zone of the Maya Biosphere Reserve, Guatemala

Loggers loading boles of mahogany trees (*Swietenia macrophylla*) for transport to sawmills, Department of Petén, Guatemala

Workmen grading and sorting planks of sawed mahogany (*Swietenia macrophylla*) and tropical cedar (*Cedrela odorata*) for export, Department of Petén, Guatemala

Brenda and Jorge Zapata, Carmelita, Petén, Guatemala

Q'eqchi' Maya hunters, southern Belize

Ramon nuts (*Brosimum alicastrum*)

Rafters running the Río Usumacinta stop for the night at Piedras Negras, Petén, Guatemala.

Mexico, Guatemala, and Belize

4   *Mexico*

The Selva Lacandona

The Río Usumacinta slides enormous quantities of thick, brown water past overhanging forest and jagged rock formations in the heartland of Classic Maya territory, draining a major portion of the Maya Tropical Forest. Twelve centuries ago, the river was the principal route for a trade network that exchanged jade, feathers, ceramic pots, salt, obsidian, and copal incense between major cities of the Maya world. Traders, warriors, and ceremonial retinues paddled dugout canoes up and down the river and its numerous tributaries, in territory that now forms part of Mexico and Guatemala.

Today on the Río Usumacinta, long wooden boats propelled by outboard motors move live cattle from Guatemala into Mexico and *xate* palm harvesters from one site to another all along its shores. Excited tourists in inflatable rafts glide over the river's rapids to visit the ancient Maya cities of Yaxchilán and Piedras Negras. The river's banks are dotted intermittently with small settlements of farm families, who live in mud-floored huts with roofs made of guano palm thatch.

The Río Usumacinta also marks the international boundary between Mexico and northern Guatemala. On the eastern, Guatemalan, side of the river lies the forest of the Petén. On the western, Mexican side of this watershed, the region and the forest are known as the Selva Lacandona.

Part of Mexico's southeastern state of Chiapas, the Selva Lacandona hides its history in a dense forest traversed by a dozen tributaries of the Usumacinta, all of them stained a tea-colored brown by natural tannins in the tropical vegetation. The Selva Lacandona is home to one of Mexico's

MAP 3. La Selva Lacandona, Chiapas, Mexico

last large remnants of lowland tropical forest, a forest that takes its name from the Lacandón Maya, the traditional Maya people who have lived here for centuries.

Until the twentieth century, the Selva Lacandona covered 13,000 square kilometers (5,000 sq. mi.) of eastern Chiapas, stretching eastward from the towns of Ocosingo and Las Margaritas to the Río Usumacinta. Today, two-thirds of this forest has been cleared and burned for farmland and pasture-land, leaving less than 4,000 square kilometers (1,500 sq. mi.) in its original vegetation. Most of this remaining forest is protected today as the Montes Azules Biosphere Reserve and the six other protected areas that adjoin it.

Political ecologist Karen O'Brien aptly describes the Selva Lacandona today as "a frontier agricultural region with forests increasingly restricted to the crests and slopes of mountains, along with a core of the forest within the protected confines of the Montes Azules Biosphere Reserve" (O'Brien 1998:35–36).

A mountain chain that runs northwest to southeast through the Selva Lacandona turns the hydrology of this eastern part of Chiapas on its head. The rivers Santo Domingo, Perlas, Negro, and Tzendales, along with their many tributaries, flow from the northwest to the southeast to join with the Río Jataté as it evolves into the Río Lacantún. The Lacantún then flows northeast to meet the Río Salinas, emerging out of Guatemala, to create the Río Usumacinta. The Usumacinta then carries all these waters directly northwest—back in the direction they came from—to mix them at the last minute with the Río Grijalva and spill into the Gulf of Mexico. This complex of intermingling rivers creates the largest watershed in Mexico and the seventh-largest watershed in the world (SEMARNAP 2000:13).

Over several decades of research in the Selva Lacandona, I traveled on almost all of these rivers, but the best trip took place in September 1999, when I traveled on the Río Lacantún and Río Tzendales with a team of five Mexican biologists and another U.S.-based researcher. (The other members of the expedition were Ignacio [Nacho] March Mifsut, Ricardo Hernández, Patricia [Paty] González Domínguez, Ramón Guerrero, Manuel de Jesús Gómez, and John N. Williams.)

Our goals were to evaluate biodiversity protection efforts in the southern region of the Montes Azules Biosphere Reserve and to look for the ruins of an infamous nineteenth-century logging camp that three of the expedition's members had come upon several months earlier.

We found that this region of the reserve was in good condition—plenty of wildlife and no illegal settlements. We found one abandoned hunting camp, but it appeared not to have been used for more than a year. As we glided up the rivers, listening to howler monkeys in the distance, we talked about what we knew of the ruined logging camp we were searching for, a camp called La Constancia.

La Constancia gained a nefarious reputation through the works of journalist Berick Traven Torsvan, who wrote in the early twentieth century under the name B. Traven. Traven is best known for the Mexico-based novel *Treasure of the Sierra Madre* (published in the United States in 1935), which was made into a movie with Humphrey Bogart. In 1925, 1929, and 1930, Traven traveled in the Selva Lacandona and interviewed workers who had labored in the logging camps of La Casa Romano, a profitable enterprise owned by two brothers from Spain. The novel that resulted from this investigation, *Rebellion of the Hanged,* established La Constancia as the scene of cruel, forced labor under terrifying conditions (Zogbaum 1992:97; Tello Díaz 2004:34).

Between 1880 and 1933, using the toil of indentured Maya Indians from the highlands of Chiapas, the Romano brothers built an economic empire focused on wrenching giant mahogany and tropical cedar trees from the forest and dragging them to the rivers, using teams of oxen. Rolled into the water, the felled tree trunks floated six weeks down the turbid, twisting rivers that roil through the Selva Lacandona. Downriver, in the town of Tenosique, Tabasco, waiting boatmen captured the logs and roped them into rafts of 200–300 trunks, which they floated out the mouth of the river into the nearby Gulf of Mexico. There, giant cranes lifted the logs, one by one, into the holds of oceangoing ships for transport to England and the United States. Transported to the industrialized world, the hardwood trees of the Selva Lacandona were carved into elegant dining room tables, office paneling, and the famous Chippendale furniture.

The highland Maya men and women who were tricked into working in the logging camps of the Romano brothers entered the forest to pay off debts of 50 to 100 pesos, debts which were frequently incurred because of family illnesses or during drinking bouts at fiestas. Special recruiters called *enganchadores* supplied money or alcohol to indigenous men during fiestas, obligating them to work in the *monterías* (logging camps) to pay off the debt. Alternatively, the *enganchadores* paid the fines of Maya serving time in jail, gaining their release in return for a signed work contract (O'Brien 1998:73).

Six months into their labor, the hapless workers would find that their food and equipment accounts at the company store had risen to 300 or 400 pesos, locking them into a downward spiral of debt from which they could never escape. Maya who tried to flee this forced servitude were chased through the forest by pairs of snarling mastiffs led by ruthless overseers, in a scene reminiscent of a Hollywood prison movie. Once captured, the laborers were whipped with cat-o'-nine-tails and forced once again to chop giant trees in the forest. The few who eluded capture found themselves faced with a two-week walk through uninhabited tropical forest toward the first town. No one is known to have ever escaped alive.

For the Romano brothers and dozens like them, extracting timber from the Selva Lacandona in the late nineteenth century required financial capital, political connections, and a large pool of laborers. The capital and connections were functions of financing and friendships, the laborers a legacy of centuries of exploitation of the indigenous poor of Chiapas. Political ecologist Karen O'Brien points out that "these workers were essential to the selective logging of millions of cubic meters of tropical hardwoods" (O'Brien 1998:21). The highland Maya were especially vulnerable.

To reach La Constancia in 1999, our group drove southwest from Tuxtla Gutiérrez, the capital city of Chiapas, past cornfields and weedy cattle pastures, to arrive late the same day in the Ejido Ixcán, a community on the southern edge of the Montes Azules Biosphere Reserve. Ejido Ixcán lies on the western bank of the Río Ixcán, which flows into Chiapas from nearby Guatemala. The *ejido*, a cooperative farming community, is one of a dozen legal settlements whose territory overlies the boundaries of the Montes Azules Biosphere Reserve, due to the creation decades ago of separate decrees by competing elements of the Mexican federal government. One ministry created a protected area; another created *ejidos* on the same land. One of the challenges of conservation in the region is working with these communities to maintain forest cover in the overlapping sections; the competing decrees sometimes pit conservation against agriculture. To meet this challenge, the nonprofit organization Conservation International works with the *ejidos* to develop income-producing alternatives to forest destruction.

In the Ejido Ixcán, this economic alternative comes in the form of an ecotourism lodge and biological station built on land that legally belongs to the Ejido Ixcán but which is located within the boundaries of the reserve. The national decree that created Montes Azules Biosphere Reserve in 1979 restricts the ways the community can use this portion of the land, so the ecotourism lodge is a positive compromise that produces income for the community but simultaneously preserves the region's biological diversity. In other regions of the Montes Azules reserve, conservation efforts are sometimes complicated by illegal squatters who have moved into the forest from other regions of Chiapas or other states of Mexico. Although they have no legal claim to the land, they clear and burn the forest to plant corn and coffee, and to create pastureland to graze cattle. Government efforts to relocate these illegal squatters have been stymied since 1994 by the Zapatista movement, an armed rebellion of indigenous farmers who seek more land for families from the Chiapas highlands. The Mexican government has hesitated to relocate the invading families for fear of setting off another armed rebellion.

As we approach Ejido Ixcán, Ricardo Hernández, then ecotourism coordinator—and now director—of Conservation International–Chiapas, notes that "if it weren't for the Zapatista movement, the government of

Mexico would be carrying out strong relocations of invaders in the Montes Azules Biosphere Reserve."

"Even with this problem," he says, "some advances are being made in preventing illegal invasions."

"The Procuraduría de Protección al Ambiente [PROFEPA], the director of Montes Azules Biosphere Reserve, and 20 soldiers from the Mexican Army recently removed a group of invaders from an illegal settlement called Playa de Corozal," Ricardo tells us." The authorities had made several attempts to negotiate with the families, but the leaders refused to talk, saying they wouldn't leave.

"As a result," says Ricardo, "they were removed by force, and the two leaders were temporarily jailed. The families went back to their original community outside the Selva Lacandona."

When we arrive at the *ejido,* we unload our gear at the edge of the Río Ixcán and make arrangements to leave our two vehicles with one of the community leaders. Then we climb into a 7-meter (23-foot) fiberglass boat with a 50-horsepower outboard motor and head downstream toward Ixcán Lodge. As the sun slides behind the 500-meter (1,650-foot) hills along the north side of the river, we watch large white egrets (*Ardea alba*) fly gracefully over sandbanks along the edge of the forest. The boat motor is loud enough to preempt meaningful conversation, so everyone sinks into their own thoughts about the day.

Shortly after we leave the *ejido,* I look over my left shoulder to see the Y formed by the confluence of the Río Ixcán and Río Jataté. The juncture of the two rivers mixes the clear waters of the Jataté with the café au lait water of the Ixcán, forming a wide, bicolored seam you can see clearly for a hundred meters. I have seen this admixture of different colored rivers in only one other place, near Manaus, in the Brazilian Amazon. Here in Chiapas, the two rivers swirl clear water together with the sediment-loaded waters running off cattle pastures and farm fields in neighboring Guatemala to create a new color and a new river—the Río Lacantún.

Our boatman, Manuel de Jesús Gómez, slows the motor and guides the boat to the northern bank of the Lacantún. Looking up the steep bank above our boat, we see that we have arrived at the Ixcán Ecotourism Lodge and Biological Station. Because we have arrived late after dark, we haul our gear up to the lodge and settle in. After a few minutes of moving our gear around in the dark, we climb into sleeping bags and eventually fall asleep inside the sound chamber of frog calls and insect whines that passes, for quiet in the tropical forest.

The following day, we wake up early in our small rooms in the Ixcán Station, blinking our way into the day to the roars of howler monkeys in the distance and the shrieks of worried brown jays along the edge of the forest that surrounds the lodge. Daylight reveals that we have slept in a two-story octagonal structure, with a roof that pitches off, star-shaped, in eight directions. Inside, each of our small guest rooms has a rough wooden floor and a bed with a foam mattress, a table, and an open closet to store gear. The outside wall of each room is a screen that keeps out mosquitoes. Visitors step through a screen door onto an open balcony that overlooks the surrounding forest.

In the bright morning light, we wash up, one by one, in the two showers that are heated by wood fires at the base of meter-tall water tanks attached to the bathroom wall. Then we sit down to a full Mexican breakfast in the *comedor* on a cement terrace above the river—fried eggs, black beans, coffee, chilies, and tortillas. Women and men from Ejido Ixcán work in the lodge as cooks—also as builders and guides—earning far more money than they would clearing forest to plant corn and jalapeño chilies. It is this income, and the income paid to the Ixcán community fund from visitors' lodging fees, that CI hopes will convince the families of Ejido Ixcán that the forest of the Montes Azules Biosphere Reserve is worth more to them alive than cleared and burned and planted in crops.

After breakfast, our team loads into the fiberglass *lancha* and heads up the Río Jataté to see the Cañón del Colorado. There, the normally wide Río Jataté squeezes itself into a narrow ribbon to flow between giant red rocks that border both sides of the river. Above the rocks, forest cascades down steep hills to create a dramatic tropical setting where visitors can bathe in jacuzzi-sized basins created by the river's centuries of eating away at red sandstone.

Logically, many visitors assume that the Cañón del Colorado got its name from the red-colored (*colorado*) rocks that created it. But the name came, in fact, from a Mexican engineer, Cornelio Colorado, who drowned here in 1878. Colorado and five other men were hired by a logging company, the Casa Bulnes Hermanos, to determine the feasibility of floating felled mahogany trees down the Río Jataté to the Gulf of Mexico, hundreds of kilometers to the northeast. The logging enterprise proposed to fell trees in the forest drained by the Jataté and its tributaries, drag the logs to the river with oxen, and roll them into the water to float them downstream. During a six-week trip, the logs would float down the Río Lacantún, then down the Río Usumacinta, and on hundreds of kilometers toward the town of

Tenosique, Tabasco, where men working from canoes would tie the logs together in rafts and float them the last few kilometers to ships waiting in the Gulf of Mexico.

Colorado proved that all this was, in fact, possible, but he and three other members of the expedition lost their lives in doing so. After days of paddling down the unexplored Jataté in their dugout mahogany canoes, one named La Malinche, the men suddenly found themselves rushed into the narrow, rock-lined canyon that would later bear the engineer's name. In a violent explosion of churning water and splintered wood, the canoes smashed against the rocks, and the men were catapulted from the canoes into the river and whisked downstream by the rush of water. Two of the men thrashed their way to overhanging branches and hung on for dear life; the other four, including Cornelio Colorado, drowned in the raging river.

Ironically, six weeks later their battered dugout canoe La Malinche, with its name still clearly lettered on its side, was pulled from the Río Usumacinta in Tenosique, proving that it was in fact possible to float mahogany logs from the Selva Lacandona down the network of rivers to the Gulf of Mexico. The costly experiment set off a race between competing logging companies to harvest timber from the Selva Lacandona for export to England and the United States (de Vos 1988a:69).

Leaving behind the Cañón del Colorado and its history, we travel downriver several kilometers and pull over to the northern bank to hike Las Guacamayas trail into the Montes Azules Biosphere Reserve. Walking only 15 minutes down a trace of trail through the forest, we arrive at a 30-foot waterfall that throws itself over a cliff of limestone and travertine. We climb around to the top of the waterfall on a trail that winds to the top of the hill and find a nice pool for swimming.

After enjoying the water, we walk back along the trail through the forest, watching spider monkeys eating ramon leaves (*Brosimum alicastrum*) in the canopy overhead. We also come upon the tracks of tiny brocket deer. Ramón Guerrero, CI's director of the Ixcán Station project and consummate forest guide, points out a patch of a half-dozen pita plants (*Bromelia penguin;* Lacandón Maya = *ch'am*), a ground-growing bromeliad with round, astringent fruit that grow from its center like a hundred tiny pineapples. He tells us, "The fruits are not red and ripe yet, so they're not edible," and we miss the dubious treat of eating the sweet fruit until the skin peels off our tongues.

We sleep again at the Ixcán Lodge and the following day are up at sunrise for breakfast and final packing for the trip to La Constancia. Overhead, the day is overcast with gray skies. We climb into the boat and head down the Río Lacantún toward the mouth of the Río Tzendales. An hour and a half later, we turn northward into the Río Tzendales, then stop to change propellers on our 50-horsepower outboard motor. The dark waters of the Tzendales hide dozens of submerged tree branches and hidden rocks, and we don't want to risk damaging the new propeller we have been using on the larger Río Lacantún.

While we wait for our boatman, Manuel, to make the change, we watch two pairs of *guacamayas* (scarlet macaws) fly overhead and another pair in a *palo de gusano* (a legume tree) on the western bank. The river is high here, says Ramón, a meter and a half above what it was during the last trip, when his team first came upon the ruins of the logging camp, La Constancia. Pure stands of forest grow on both banks of the river, but the water is so high this week that many of the trees are growing directly out of the river.

With the propeller successfully exchanged, we continue upriver on the Tzendales and the wildlife show continues. This area of Montes Azules Biosphere Reserve is still largely undisturbed. As we travel under gray skies and intermittent rain showers, we see a crocodile crash through the vegetation on the riverbank and slide into the water as we approach. Overhead, six howler monkeys sit in a 30-meter (100-foot) tree hanging over the river, each of them hunkered down from the moist, chilly air. As we slip by underneath, the monkeys look like six fur balls attached to the high tree branches. Heading upriver, we lift our binoculars to watch a group of five toucans resting in a tall, leafless tree.

The rain for the past weeks has raised the river level so much that the anticipated portage points identified by the previous expedition are now passable with the outboard. Rather than having to jump out of the boat to manually lift the boat into the next pool of the river, we skim over the rock barriers that divide one pool from the next.

Around noon, though, we finally meet our match. Ahead in the river, we see the largest of the cascades, its large rocks exposed in the water, with the water rushing forcefully around them. We pull over to the bank of the river and off-load all our gear to lighten the boat. Ramón and Manuel slowly prod the unloaded boat up the cascade while the rest of us form a human chain to pass the equipment, food, and 10-gallon gasoline containers over a ridge, through the forest, and down to the river on the far side of the waterfall. There, we hook up again with Ramón and Manuel, safely up the cascade, reload the boat, and head upriver again. The rain has stopped completely and the day is bright, but the sky remains gray overhead.

Ramón and Ricardo were on the previous expedition here in April, and they are surprised at how soon we reach the arroyo that marks the entrance to the nineteenth-century logging camp La Constancia. Because we have had to portage only once, we have arrived here much faster than anyone expected. We pull our boat to the bank of the river under overhanging trees. The area is dense with tropical vegetation—large trees stretching overhead, a half-dozen kinds of waist-high palms on the forest floor, and gnarled vines twisting down from the canopy. We reconnoiter the area quickly and pick a campsite that is close to the river, but on more or less high ground. Preparing the site amounts to little more than using a machete to chop back just enough ground vegetation to pitch four tents and clear a safe place for a campfire.

Once we are installed, Ramón and Ricardo lead us to the area where they found ruins on their last trip here. Only 100 meters (330 feet) into the forest, we begin to encounter stacks of red clay bricks and curved, Spanish-style roofing tiles (*tejas*) lying on the forest floor—the remnants of the turn-of-the-century *montería* La Constancia. The ruins are mostly jagged, chest-high brick walls covered with vines and strangler figs. Some of the walls are taller than we are—3 meters (10 feet) or so—and in one or two places they reveal openings where large windows would have had wooden shutters. Twelve-meter-tall (40-foot) strangler figs grow over several of the taller red brick faces, their tentacles flowing in and out of gaps, testifying to the 70 years that have passed since the site was abandoned to the tropical forest.

The logging camp La Constancia came into being in early 1894, when two engineers and 11 workmen established the first palm thatch huts on this site on the arroyo El Colorado, one hour north from its conjunction with the Río Tzendales. The operation was owned by La Casa Romano, one of the oldest and most prosperous logging operations in the state of Tabasco, Mexico. The enterprise's owners were two brothers, Román and Manuel Romano, Spaniards born in La Villa de Llanos, Province of Oviedo, Spain. The brothers were heavily involved in marine and river transport—they were the first to operate steamships in the Gulf of Mexico—and they had been engaged for many years in the exploitation of mahogany and logwood (dyewood) in Tabasco. Knowing that Tabasco timber resources were almost exhausted, the Romano brothers began to search for new timber sources in the state of Chiapas.

At the time, the Selva Lacandona was part of a disputed zone between Mexico and Guatemala known as el Desierto de Tzendales. Groups from both countries carried out periodic expeditions in the region, carrying guns and hand-drawn maps with competing versions of national ownership. For the most part, the territorial dispute revolved around competing logging companies, some based in Guatemala and others in Mexico, but all of them with designs on the rich timber resources of the Desierto de Tzendales. Beyond the owners of these hungry timber companies, few people cared about this tropical wilderness at the turn of the twentieth century (de Vos 1988a:114–121).

Timber operations in the Selva Lacandona during the 1800s were modest affairs at first. Using hand axes, loggers cut 100–200 trees per year along the margins of the region's major rivers. To find these trees, the operator would conduct a *monteo*, an exploration of the territory to determine the quantity of commercial timber available. If he encountered a promising stand of mahogany or tropical cedar, the operator would construct a main house and workers' quarters on the banks of the river closest to the stand of trees. The names of the emerging camps expressed faith in the potential bonanza to be generated by these *monterías:* Hope, Destiny, Forthcoming, Desire, Paradise, Progress, and Constancy—"La Constancia" (de Vos 1988a:55–56).

Historian Jan de Vos points out that La Constancia had an infamous reputation even in its day. "The administrator, Fernando Mijares Escandón, was known and feared throughout the forest for the cruelty with which he punished his workmen" (de Vos 1988b:202).

In evidence of this statement, we have the report of a European lawyer named Rodulfo Brito Foucher, who visited La Constancia in the 1920s and wrote a scathing exposé of living conditions there.

> The life of the workmen, from the day they arrive until they die, is one of monotony and indescribable difficulty. At three or four in the morning, the foreman sounds his horn, and the workmen wake up and breakfast on black coffee and black beans. When the sun rises, they must be at the foot of the tree they will cut or beside the felled tree trunk they are to debark. There they work until noon, when they pause for a meager lunch. In the afternoon, they return to camp, ingest more

black coffee and beans, and fall asleep, only to rise again the following day and continue this eternal drill. They dress in twill pants, cotton shirts, sombreros, and straw sandals. (Brito Foucher 1931)

Walking over the site of La Constancia, we find remnant pieces of the old steam-powered sawmill scattered over the forest floor, overgrown with *Chamaedorea* palms and covered with leaf litter. Decades ago, this equipment cut mahogany boards for the construction of the logging camp itself. Most of the mahoganies and tropical cedars the workmen felled were dragged as whole tree trunks to the edge of the river and rolled into the water, using teams of oxen. The 10-meter-long (33-foot) logs floated down the Río Tzendales, tumbling over the rock cascades in the river, working their way to the faster Río Lacantún and on to the giant Usumacinta, traveling toward the town of Tenosique. Waiting in Tenosique were the teams of logrollers in canoes, assigned the dangerous task of wrestling the logs to the riverbank, where they could be tied into giant rafts of logs.

Historian de Vos describes the scene in Tenosique: "The trunks of mahogany that floated down the rivers were captured by logrollers who fished the trees from the Usumacinta where it flattens out onto the plains of Tabasco. The men gathered the individual trees and tied them together in enormous rafts to float them down the river to the Gulf of Mexico. As the river approaches the Gulf, it divides into three principal branches. At the mouth of each branch lay a port, where the rafts of logs were broken up and the trees lifted individually into the hulls of ships destined for New York, London, and Liverpool" (de Vos 1988a:27). In Europe and the United States, the trunks were sold on the docks at fantastic prices under the name *madera de Tabasco* (Tabasco wood).

Aware that some of the valuable logs were slipping past the Tabasco logrollers and being lost in the Gulf of Mexico, the Romano brothers hired a Belgian engineer to deal with the problem. The engineer constructed a web of giant metal anchor chains across the river to capture and contain the multi-ton tree trunks.

*U*nfortunately, the trees came floating downriver faster than the capture teams could deal with them. The web of chains quickly filled with tangled logs. They strained at the contraption's restraints on shore and burst in a nightmare of screaming metal and splitting wood. The hapless men caught downriver in their fragile canoes were swept away like drowned rats. Confronted with their death and the failure of his design, the Belgian engineer committed suicide. The logging company went back to wrestling logs out the river one by one and resigned itself to losing a few from time to time.

In the evening, a light drizzle begins to splatter our campsite, and we help Ramón stretch a hemp rope head-high between two trees and spread a large piece of clear plastic over it, using twine to tie the four corners to other trees and create a dry shelter. We stoke up the fire, begin cooking instant rice and refried beans, and heat up the last of the beefsteak and tortillas we brought with us in an iceless plastic cooler. Then we open the bar. I make *misteriosas,* using a recipe a retired psychiatrist friend, Percy Wood, revealed to me in San Cristóbal de las Casas 10 years ago: a shot of tequila, the juice of a whole lime, then fill the glass—or plastic cup, in this case—with orange juice. We have brought two bottles of tequila and two half-gallon cartons of Mexican orange juice with us; we gather freshly fallen feral limes beneath a tree growing near the shore of the Río Tzendales where we tied up the boat. Planted by the men who felled the trees, worked the oxen, and rolled the green gold of the forest into the river, the lime tree—or its descendant—still dutifully produces plump, juicy limes a century later.

Lifting our cups, we toast the memory of the workers who lived on this spot a hundred years ago and left their lives and walls in the forest to be covered once again by the wilderness of the Selva Lacandona.

*F*ollowing a plan hatched at night during dinner, we arise early the following morning for a quick cup of coffee, then load into the boat to search upriver for wildlife. Our early morning zeal is rewarded only 30 minutes into the trip, when a full-grown tapir splashes off the shore and swims directly toward our boat as we round a curve. Nacho flashes a quick photo of the animal, its eyes reflecting the sudden light, and the tapir submerges and appears on the other side of the boat behind us. It scrambles up the muddy bank and disappears into the forest undergrowth.

Back at camp, after a breakfast of smoked pork chops and more refried beans, we walk to the ruins to map them. During a two-hour period, using a 25-meter measuring tape Nacho has brought along, we map out the brick structures of La Constancia, discovering one long brick building, now completely in ruins, with a series of brick columns in front of it, and what must have been a *teja*-roofed shed behind it.

FIGURE 1. La Constancia timber camp, Selva Lacandona, Chiapas, Mexico, as it was circa 1920. Drawing by Peter Sawyer, 2005, from a field sketch by Ignacio March, 1999.

The structure looked something like Figure 1.

As we examine the emerging diagram, Ricardo is reminded of a passage from Brito Foucher's 1931 work, in which he describes the living arrangements at La Constancia.

> In the main house, there were 10 or 15 people; they told me that the workmen of the enterprise, who added up to several hundred, were distributed in groups within the forest. A few indiscreet servants told me of a famous administrator who was there, that every morning he formed up the workers and passed by them in military-style review. The unhappy men trembled beneath the view of the fierce administrator, as soldiers surely have never trembled in front of the most cruel instructor of the army. (Brito Foucher 1931)

Today, only a few brick columns remain standing at La Constancia; most have fallen onto the forest floor, leaving a trail of bricks 3 meters (10 feet) long through the undergrowth, looking like a child's precarious stack of dominoes tumbled onto a carpet. Enough walls of the brick building are still standing to give us a sense of the huge size of the building, but everywhere palms and ficus grow over bricks and tiles and foundations. Strangler figs have draped themselves over the standing walls, weaving roots in and out of crevices and holes to create an effect reminiscent of the ancient city of Angkor Wat in Cambodia.

After mapping the site, we head back to the campsite. We take quick baths in the river by jumping out of the boat to get wet, climbing back in to lather up with soap and shampoo, then jumping back in to rinse off. We have to do all of this quickly to avoid the clouds of mosquitoes and *chaquistes* (tiny, black biting flies) that follow us like a movable haze wherever we go.

The day has been remarkably dry, so it is little surprise when at midnight, tucked into our tents, we hear the initial drops of rain, followed by a torrential downpour that lasts through the night.

On Saturday, we awake in a camp of mud and puddles and begin the soggy process of packing wet clothes, wet tents, and wet tarps into wet plastic bags. Everything is covered in mud, including us. Where we brush away mud, we find tiny seed ticks enjoying a breakfast of blood. They find paths between the raised mosquito bites and crawl up and down our arms and legs. Yet the camaraderie and sheer adventure of it all keep us in high spirits, with lots of verbal banter and laughter.

Once loaded into the white fiberglass boat, we head downstream, gliding over the cascades like kids on a Disney World ride. Only once—again for the largest of the rapids—do we have to put to shore to off-load and carry our gear downstream through the forest. Manuel, Ramón, and Ricardo (who sits in the front of the boat to photograph the adventure) take the boat over the rapids, and we join them on the other side of the hill.

Edging into the Río Lacantún, we proceed upriver toward Ixcán, stopping once to change to the newer propeller and again at Ejido Chajul to buy cold beers for the evening. Along the way, we see a fishing eagle, a great blue heron, several hawks and toucans, parrots, and a king vulture, the famous *zopilote rey* (*Sarcoramphus papa*). We arrive at the Ixcán Lodge and off-load the boat, then spread our wet gear over the balconies and grassy areas to dry. And we take showers. The two women cooks from Ejido Ixcán serve us a nice *comida* of pot roast, carrots, and potatoes, accompanied by rice, guacamole, and soup. Excellent fare.

By late afternoon, we are relaxing in hammocks, waiting for our final things to dry, and reading and writing. I begin to thumb through Jan de Vos's book *Oro Verde* (1988a), on the history of the logging camps of the Selva Lacandona, and seize upon two passages:

> In 1913, as part of the Mexican Revolution, a small brigade of revolutionaries marched south from Tenosique to liberate the workers captured in the *monterías* of the Selva Lacandona. Although the group destroyed a half-dozen *monterías,* they did not find them all, and the Casa Romano continued operating in the southern Selva until 1933, when it closed, largely due to a presidential decree in 1925 that declared that foreigners such as the Spanish Romano brothers could not own large expanses of territory along Mexico's international borders. Although the Romano brothers challenged the edict and continued exploiting timber for another eleven years, they eventually went bankrupt and abandoned La Constancia and their other holdings in the Selva. (de Vos 1988a:228 ff.)

And this one:

> . . . in 1949 the Mexican government decided to prohibit the export of unprocessed timber, closing in this measure a lucrative business of more than seventy years. (de Vos 1988a:11)

The Best Pilot in Chiapas

September 5, 1996, 1:45 p.m.

After waiting several hours at the small asphalt airstrip on the outskirts of Comitán, Chiapas, our turn comes to fly in the small Cessna that has been traveling to and from settlements in the Selva Lacandona all morning. José Hernández Nava, Ricardo Hernández, Victor Hugo Hernández (none of whom are related), and I are headed toward the settlement of Zapata to meet with community leaders and examine the potential for ecotourism projects at Lake Miramar. When I appear skeptical of the worn-looking, four-seater airplane we're scheduled to fly in, Victor Hugo reassures me: "We'll have the best pilot in Chiapas."

Almost at that moment, a man Victor Hugo calls Capitán Tovar emerges from the corrugated tin-roof shack that serves as the airport headquarters. He is 45 years old with short gray hair, no more than 5 feet 6 inches tall, and sports a healthy beer belly that Mexicans laughingly call a *panza* ("Panza

llena, corazón felíz"/"Full belly, happy heart"). Capitán Tovar seems compe-
tent enough, so he and the three Hernándezes and I load our gear aboard
the plane and climb in. I sit up front as copilot to take photos while the *tres
Hernández* squeeze into the cramped back seat. As I am settling in, I look
around to figure out where the alcohol smell is coming from. Just when I realize it must be coming from the pilot, he lifts a beer from between his legs and
takes a big swig as he revs the engine to taxi down the runway.

I'm about to ask him where my seat belt is when, anticipating my question,
he says, "The only belt in here is the one holding up your pants. *Ni modo* [Any-
way], you know what seat belts are good for in an airplane?" he asks. "They
keep the *mierda* from getting all over the plane when it crashes."

Then, with a big belly laugh, he revs the engine, pulls back on the wheel,
and we skate half-sideways down the airstrip, roaring toward what looks
like sudden death in an attempt at a takeoff. But at the last minute, with the
cars on the nearby highway looming just 30 meters (100 feet) in front of us,
Capitán Tovar pulls on some magic lever and the tiny Cessna leaps over the
telephone wires of Comitán.

As I loosen my white-knuckle grip on the plane's door handle,
Victor Hugo's promise echoes in my ears: "We'll have the best pilot in
Chiapas." Turns out, this fellow—Capitán Tovar—is the man he was
talking about.

People of the Selva Lacandona

The many stories of Mexico's Selva Lacandona proceed both backward and
forward in time from the era of the logging camp of La Constancia. In the
past lies the history of the ancient Maya cities that today bring so many international travelers to the state of Chiapas. But travelers to southeastern
Mexico come to see not just its past but also its present in the form of the
region's indigenous people.

In the early sixteenth century, when Hernán Cortés touched shore
on the territory that would later become modern Mexico, more than 17
million indigenous people called the region home (Denevan 1992:370).
They hunted, fished, and farmed in scores of ecosystems, ranging from
the mountains of the Sierra Tarahumara of northwestern Mexico to the
lowland rainforest of the Selva Lacandona in the extreme southeast of the
country. The region was also the homeland of two of the New World's most
developed civilizations, one—the Aztecs—still in its heyday when Cortés
arrived, and a second—the Maya—that already lay in ruins.

Today, during the initial years of the twenty-first century, Mexico is still home to a diverse family of indigenous communities. Of the 120 languages spoken at the time of the conquest, 54 are still alive among Mexican Indian families today (Martínez Ruíz 1986, cited in Bye 1993). Ten percent of the nation's 95 million people are considered descendants of indigenous tribes with little or no European blood.

In fact, the total number of indigenous speakers in Mexico has been increasing since 1950, although with some internal disparities. The 13 Mexico states that have been classified by the Mexican census as "eminently indigenous" include the states that make up the Mexican portion of the Maya Tropical Forest: Chiapas, Quintana Roo, Campeche, and Yucatán (Barry and Vernon 1995:223). In this lowland forest region, speakers of Chol Maya, Tzeltal Maya, Tzotzil Maya, and Lacandón Maya are growing in number, while the number of people who speak Chontal Maya and Yucatec Maya is declining (Bye 1993:709). Throughout Mexico, indigenous groups have legal control of reserves measuring 160,000 square kilometers (61,800 sq. mi.)—8 percent of the national territory (Durning 1993:88). The largest of these indigenous reserves lies within the Mexican portion of the Maya Tropical Forest—the Comunidad Lacandona of eastern Chiapas.

Created in 1971, the Comunidad Lacandona declared 641,000 hectares (6,410 sq. km.; 2,475 sq. mi.) of lowland forest as the homeland of the 500 Lacandón Maya, 5,000 Tzeltal Maya, and 3,000 Chol Maya who lived inside the reserve at that time. Their numbers have since grown considerably. Simultaneously, this indigenous reserve overlaps 85 percent with the Montes Azules Biosphere Reserve, which was both established by Mexico and recognized by UNESCO in 1978. But the story of the indigenous reserve and the biosphere reserve begins in an earlier time.

When Spaniards invaded Chiapas in the early sixteenth century, as part of the conquest of Mexico, they found that the Chiapas highlands were occupied by Tzotzil Maya, the Chiapas foothills by Tzeltal and Tojolabal Maya, and the lowland forest of the Selva Lacandona by Chol and Choltí Maya. At that time, the people who we today call the Lacandón Maya occupied the tropical forest area of what is now southern Campeche and the Guatemalan Petén.

None of these groups fared well under Spanish colonial rule, but the lowland Chol and Choltí Maya fared even worse than the highland Tzotzil and Tzeltal. All of these groups were racked by Old World diseases, but in addition the tropical forest Chol and Choltí were attacked during a series of military and missionary expeditions in the sixteenth and seventeenth centuries, during which many of them were killed. Survivors were relocated into the northern Chiapas foothills (near today's towns of Bachajón and Yajalón) to work on Spanish haciendas. Their forced removal from the Selva Lacandona created a population vacuum that was gradually filled during the eighteenth and nineteenth centuries by Yucatec-speaking families fleeing disease and disruption in southern Campeche and the Guatemalan Petén. The Spaniards called these immigrants "Lacandones," a name they had previously applied to the Choltí in the same region.

The transformation of Chiapas from Spanish colony to Mexican republic during the nineteenth century had minimal impact on the Maya. Later, the Mexican Revolution of the early twentieth century did little to affect the area's dramatically skewed land ownership, in which Spanish-speaking landlords controlled both the land and the labor of the Maya families who lived on it. During the 1950s and 1960s, however, the agrarian reform laws of the Mexican Constitution gradually came to be applied in Chiapas, and thousands of Maya families were released from debt peonage on haciendas in the Chiapas foothills. Urged on by state and federal officials, these families migrated eastward into the valleys of the Selva Lacandona to create new communities on what were considered to be vacant forest lands. In some sense, the Chol were returning to the land of their ancestors. They were joined, however, by Tzeltal from the Ocosingo Valley, and later by Tojolabal and Tzotzil Maya from other regions of Chiapas.

This influx of indigenous immigrants turned into a steady flow during the mid-1960s after two U.S.-based timber enterprises sold their unworked timber concessions in the Selva Lacandona to a group of Mexican businessmen. The businessmen began to bulldoze roads through the Lacandón forest to take out mahogany and tropical cedar trees that the earlier, river-based logging enterprises, such as that of the Romano brothers, had failed to reach.

As trucks carried mahogany and cedar out of the forest on these new roads, landless Chol, Tzeltal, Tojolobal, and Tzotzil Maya families flowed into the forest seeking new land and new lives. Within a decade, these colonists were followed by a second wave of settlers—this time cattle ranchers from the Mexican states of Tabasco and Veracruz. These ranchers began to buy up the pioneer settlers' cleared plots and turn them into large cattle ranches. The farmers pushed farther into the forest to clear more land.

As immigrant Maya farmers and Ladino cattlemen set about clearing the Selva Lacandona, they unwittingly fulfilled a national strategy created by politicians in Mexico City, a policy that divided the republic into two regions of economic production. The northern states of Mexico were—and continue to be—used to produce beef cattle for export to the United States. The tropical lowlands of Veracruz, Tabasco, and Chiapas became the source of beef and corn for consumption in Mexican cities (González Pacheco 1983).

Profits from timber operations in the Selva Lacandona also fit into this plan, producing flushes of capital for state-owned as well as privately owned companies. By 1971, however, the individuals who controlled these companies realized that the farm families they had pushed into the Selva Lacandona were clearing and burning the forest before the loggers could extract the commercial hardwoods. In reaction, in 1971, the Mexican government decreed an indigenous reserve of 641,000 hectares (2,475 sq. mi.)—the Comunidad Lacandona—and declared 66 Yucatec-speaking Lacandón Maya men the sole owners of the area. Simultaneously, they flew into the isolated Lacandón communities and, in exchange for gifts of bolts of cotton cloth, secured the thumbprints of the available Lacandón men on Spanish-language documents that none of them could read. The Tzeltal and Chol families were at first denied any of the spoils of the hastily constructed timber operations.

Twelve months later, with legal contracts filed, the government-owned logging company that the businessmen represented bulldozed roads toward the Lacandón communities and began to rattle the hills with chain saws and falling trees. During the months that followed, they extracted thousands of mahogany and tropical cedar trees from Lacandón lands. According to the foreman of one logging team, in a single period of 20 days his team wrenched US$2 million worth of logs from the forest. The Lacandones grasped the full meaning of the contracts they had signed when workmen began to log the hillsides at the edge of their settlements.

Not all the Lacandones had been so quickly duped into selling their tropical forest heritage. Asked by government officials to sign the logging contracts, Chan K'in Viejo, the 80-year-old patriarch of the settlement of Naja, advised them that the mahogany trees weren't his to sell. "I didn't plant the trees," he told them. "They're God's," meaning Hachäkyum, the major Lacandón deity. "Go ask him."

As payment for Hachäkyum's trees, the Lacandones received periodic cash settlements and assurances of unseen deposits to a community fund in the state capital. They used the cash to buy medicines, kerosene, .22 caliber rifles, radios, battery-powered record players, and wristwatches. The community funds went to government-designed development projects, the most visible of which was the installation of a CONASUPO supermarket in each of the three major Lacandón settlements. In the stores, families could purchase such incongruous items as cookies, refined sugar, white flour, chewing gum, canned fruit juices, honey, and packaged ground corn. An engineer charged with easing the Lacandones' introduction into the commercial world told me, "We must teach these people how to live."

Within a year the stores' periodic resupply network had faltered, then ceased altogether. The three stores stood empty—fitting monuments to the frustrations of tropical development projects. When I inquired about the program in Tuxtla Gutiérrez, the Chiapas state capital, a government official insisted that the 7 million peso community fund had been totally exhausted; privately, other officials whispered that the fund had never existed.

Nonetheless, the Lacandón Maya's windfall of land and timber payments was met with protests from the Tzeltal and Chol Maya families who had colonized the new Comunidad Lacandona lands between the 1960s and 1971. Because they had already occupied forestlands within the reserve when the decree was issued, they had been transformed overnight into illegal settlers on Lacandón land. In reaction, Mexican officials recognized the land rights of 5,000 Tzeltal Maya and 3,000 Chol Maya who lived inside the boundaries of the Comunidad Lacandona. But in a move reminiscent of the sixteenth century Spanish *reducciones,* which concentrated scattered indigenous populations into colonial towns, the Mexican government required the Tzeltales to relocate into the community of Palestina, renamed Nuevo Centro de Población Velasco Suárez, after the Chiapas state governor at the time. They relocated the Chol Maya into the settlement of Frontera Corozal, renamed Nuevo Centro de Población Echeverría, after Mexico's president that year (Arizpe, Paz, y Velázquez 1996:24–25; Simon 1997:96–99). Within months, the centers became the largest settlements in the Selva Lacandona.

In such a fashion, the Comunidad Lacandona came to include three indigenous groups: the Tzeltal Maya of Palestina/Velasco Suárez, the Chol Maya of Frontera Corozal/Echeverría, and the Lacandón Maya of the communities of Lacanjá Chan Sayab, Mensabak, and Naja. This confusion of names continues to perplex the press and Mexican citizens, who are hard-pressed to distinguish between today's 700 members of the Lacandón Maya and the 19,000 Tzeltales and Choles who now live within the boundaries of the Comunidad Lacandona (SEMARNAP 2000:49).

The overlap between the Comunidad Lacandona lands and those of the Montes Azules Biosphere Reserve leads to constant conflict over land use.

Immigrant indigenous families seek to push into the reserve to utilize its forested soils for food crops and cattle pastures. Other indigenous groups, chiefly the Lacandón Maya and Chol Maya, seek to protect the forest for its many other uses, including watershed protection, wildlife, and building materials. This tension is exacerbated by the continuing uncertainty generated by the Zapatista rebellion of 1994. At the time of the January 1994 uprising, 10,000 people lived inside the Montes Azules Biosphere Reserve and another 17,000 lived along its borders (March 1994).

Perfunctory claims of ecological conscientiousness notwithstanding, the Zapatistas and their supporters have promoted colonization of the reserve by landless farm families, declaring the Lacandón Maya's attempt to protect the forest the result of manipulation by corporate interests (Stevenson 2001).

THE LACANDÓN MAYA

Of the three ethnic groups that make up the legal population of the Comunidad Lacandona, the most traditional are the Lacandón Maya. Until the mid-1960s, the immensity of the lowland tropical forest protected the Lacandones from many of the changes that rolled over other indigenous groups in Mexico. This isolation allowed the group to preserve environmental adaptations that are intimately tied to the forest ecosystem. From the biological diversity of eastern Chiapas, Lacandón families still gather fruit, wild animals, natural insecticides, fish poisons, fiber for rope, incense for religious ceremonies, wood for houses, furniture and canoes, and medicinal plants that may cure a toothache or snakebite.

The Lacandón Maya are divided into two distinct groups—northerners and southerners—by linguistic and historical differences, as well as by their location within the Selva Lacandona. Most southerners live today at Lacanjá Chan Sayab. Northerners live on the shores of Lake Naja and near Lake Mensabak, in the northern Selva Lacandona. During the late 1980s, however, a dozen northern Lacandón families moved into a new settlement, Betel, near the southern community of Lacanjá Chan Sayab, but the northern-southern differences in language persist.

Both northern and southern Lacandones speak dialects of the same language, appropriately called "Lacandón," though it is in fact a historical dialect of Yucatec Maya, with which it is mutually intelligible. Itza Maya of the Guatemalan Petén is likewise very similar to southern Lacandón and about 90 percent mutually intelligible with northern Lacandón.

Word and accent variation between the northern and southern dialects lead the Lacandones to state that they understand most, but not all, of the other group's speech. Despite their differences, both groups recognize one another, as well as the Yucatec and Itza Maya, as *winik* (people), though they retain for themselves the term "Hach Winik" (the true people).

Lacandón men let their long black hair fall over the shoulders of their white tunics. Northerners distinguish themselves from southern men by cutting bangs across their foreheads. Southern women leave their hair long and flowing, while northern women pull their hair back in a single braid, which they decorate with the yellow breast feathers of the toucan when they marry. Southern Lacandón women wear colorful, full-length tunics, while northern women wear a short version of the men's white tunic over a colorful skirt decorated with ribbons. For both men and women, the longer sleeves and hem of the southerners' tunics give outsiders a clue to their origin and provide the source of one of the northern Lacandones' names for their southern relatives—*chukuch nok,* "long clothes."

Traditionally, northerners have also had another name for their southern cousins: "those who kill their brothers," a reference to the feuds and wife-stealing raids that southern Lacandones conducted as recently as the 1950s. Among the southern Lacandones of Lacanjá Chan Sayab and the region around Lake Miramar, homicide was the single most frequent cause of death until 1940. Three-quarters of these deaths were the result of intragroup feuding over women, the consequence of seeking marriage-age females in a small population where most men aspired to have at least two wives. Until the years of World War II, it was not uncommon for southern Lacandón men to raid other southern Lacandón settlements to abduct the wives and daughters of other families. Oral history indicates that almost all of the 58 known Lacandón homicides were cases of southerners killing southerners.

The northern Lacandones of Naja, Mensabak, and the former settlement at El Censo/Monte Líbano heard rumors of these raids, although there are no indications they were directly attacked by southern Lacandones. Nonetheless, well into the 1970s some northern women would hide if a southern Lacandón man entered their settlement. Then, as today, northern Lacandones were more passive than their sometimes aggressive southern cousins, and they have always been more likely to die of respiratory infections or malaria than homicide.

Just as the forest itself has helped define Lacandón character, so also has the constant threat of death defined the way they have lived. Prominent in the multideity pantheon of Lacandón gods is Äkyantho, god of foreigners and traders. In modern Lacandón settlements, he is sometimes envisioned as a white man, a *tz'ul*, who wears a hat and carries a pistol. His current home is reportedly near the town of Tenosique, in a cave on a high cliff on the Río Usumacinta. His previous home and status are unknown, for both he and his creations came into being with the sixteenth-century Spanish invasion of the Maya world.

In Lacandón cosmology, the god Äkyantho created westerners and the objects they brought with them to the Americas: horses, gunpowder, cattle, metal, money. Even if responsible for nothing more, Äkyantho would have been a deity to deal with, to supplicate, and to appease. But his distinction results from less benevolent gifts. Äkyantho was also the creator of the foreigners' diseases—smallpox, influenza, measles, and yellow fever.

Fear of introduced diseases may have been the factor that prompted many Lacandones to cross the river from the Guatemalan Petén into the rainforest territory of southeastern Mexico in the late eighteenth, nineteenth, and early twentieth centuries. Inside the forest now known as the Selva Lacandona, they hid their houses in isolated compounds throughout the forest, so that each extended family was located several hours distant from the nearest neighbor. This dispersed settlement pattern guaranteed each family an abundant tract of primary forest for hunting and agriculture and, more important, a buffer zone against the transfer of epidemic disease.

By isolating their houses in the forest, Lacandones decreased their contact with outsiders and potential infection. When early Lacandones chose to interact with the outside world, it was usually to acquire trade goods— cloth, axes, salt, and machetes were highly prized items—and they were still exceedingly cautious. In 1902, when anthropologist Alfred Tozzer began fieldwork among the northern Lacandones of Lake Itzanok'uh, he found that he could enter their settlements only "after overcoming their fear that I would bring sickness of various kinds" (Tozzer 1903:46). Seventy-five years later, a Lacandón family of Granizo treated me in a similar fashion. I was allowed to sleep in the family compound only after I had repeatedly assured them that I had no respiratory disorders.

In the past, Lacandones sometimes abandoned their house if a visiting outsider coughed or sneezed inside. Families closed off the trails to their compound when one of their children fell ill, and they sometimes dismantled and moved the house if a family member died there. Even today, some Lacandones flee to small houses in their agricultural plots when respiratory infections make them noticeably ill.

Until the late twentieth century, the scene most characteristic of Lacandón life was one of isolated families secreted in the forest, quietly raising their families on the bounty of their rainforest garden plots and from hunting forest animals. More recently, Lacandones have witnessed a great decline in mortality rates due to access to Western medicine, and they have concentrated their families into three major settlements: Naja and Mensabak in the north, and Lacanjá Chan Sayab in the south. Constant communication with the outside world still brings disease into these larger communities, but this contact also brings in cures. Antibiotics administered by community health workers, missionaries, biologists, and anthropologists, as well as by the Lacandones themselves, have drastically cut death tolls from infection. Itinerant Mexican doctors regularly immunize children in Lacandón communities, and deaths from measles and diphtheria now are almost unknown. Modern Lacandones are not uncommon visitors to hospitals in Palenque, Tenosique, and San Cristóbal. Several individuals have undergone surgery in the state capital, and many young women give birth in San Cristóbal hospitals instead of in their mother's dirt-floored houses. More Lacandones are alive today—approximately 700—than at any other time in the past two centuries.

The past 30 years have brought rapid change in Lacandón life. All three major settlements are now connected to Mexico's growing system of rural roads. A few Lacandones own trucks, and several families have televisions on which they watch soccer games and soap operas broadcast from Mexico City. But step outside the settlement with a hunter or a small boy and you can travel a hundred years into the past. The hunter uses the same stealth and knowledge of rainforest ecology that Lacandones have used for centuries, and any nine-year-old boy can walk down a forest trail and name dozens of plants, telling you when they flower and which jungle animals eat them.

If you listen carefully in a Lacandón settlement, before the blare of the radio's mariachi music has begun, you may hear a grandmother singing within a cane-walled house, her voice wavering and catching on songs as old as the Maya themselves.

The sun comes up to see me grind my corn.
I am rolling it into a ball on this table.

The sun sees my table.
I am washing it with water.
I am grinding on it. I am grinding.
I make a ball of dough,
and I grind.
The sun is coming up.
Hot sun, the hot sun.
I am washing husks from the corn.
The sun clears the sky.
I see it rise up on the horizon.
It is picking up its corn husks.
It doesn't move fast.
It watches me grind.
It goes slow, slow.
It doesn't go down fast.
It takes its time.
Slow, slow sun,
It doesn't go fast,
and I grind.

(AS SUNG BY MARÍA KOH, MENSABAK;
RECORDED AND TRANSCRIBED BY THE AUTHOR, 1976)

Lacandones still visit the ruins of the Classic Maya city Yaxchilán, on the Río Usumacinta, where they offer the gods a traditional prayer board mounded with copal incense in a ceremony that is older than the ancient stone ruins around them. The headless, carved-stone statue in Structure 33 is a fear-inspiring Lacandón deity named Hach Bilam. (Archaeologists call it the statue of Bird Jaguar IV, a former ruler of Yaxchilán.) The Lacandones know that if Hach Bilam's stone head, which lies in a niche nearby, is ever replaced upon his body, the world will cease to exist.

Some Lacandón Maya still practice their traditional system of agroforestry, which produces food crops, trees, and animals on the same plot of land simultaneously. The Lacandón orchard-garden (Spanish = *milpa;* Lacandón Maya = *kol*), combines up to 79 varieties of food and fiber crops on single hectare (2.47-acre) plots cleared from the tropical forest. After burning the forest to clean the plot of insects and weeds, the farmer plants fast-growing tree crops and root crops in the nutrient-rich ash—papayas, bananas, chayote, manioc, sweet potatoes, and plantains. Then, during the course of the year, the farmer and his family add corn, chilies, limes, watermelons, squash, tomatoes, cotton, tobacco, rice, beans, sugarcane, cacao, and onions. Planting times for some of these crops are keyed to seasonal signals, like the flowering of specific forest tree species. When the flowers of the mahogany tree fall, for example, the Lacandón farmer knows that it is time to plant the spring corn crop. The falling of wild tamarind flowers indicates the days to plant tobacco.

The biological diversity of the Lacandón milpa has a corollary benefit: pacas, peccaries, brocket deer, and other edible mammals are drawn to the young shoots of the agricultural plot, and Lacandón hunters lie in wait for them to add vital protein to their families' diet. Studies by forest ecologists indicate that the presence of milpa plots in the tropical forest can actually increase the population of some wildlife (Linares 1976; Denevan 1992:375).

Over the past dozen years, most Lacandones have become fully incorporated into the economy of modern Mexico, and many practice milpa agriculture that has only traces of its former complexity. Paved roads now pass near all three of the major Lacandón communities—Naja, Mensabak, and Lacanjá Chan Sayab—and most children attend bilingual schools. Increasingly, only the older adults keep alive traditional knowledge about the ecological intricacies of the tropical forest that surrounds them.

The best ethnographies of the Lacandón Maya are the classic 1907 study by Alfred Tozzer, *A Comparative Study of the Mayas and the Lacandones,* and the more recent study by Belgian anthropologist Didier Boremanse, *Hach Winik: The Lacandón Maya of Chiapas, Southern Mexico* (1998). Other informative books on the Lacandones are Marie-Odile Marion's 1991 *Los hombres de la selva,* a Spanish-language study of material culture, and R. Jon McGee's 1990 detailed study, *Life, Ritual, and Religion among the Lacandón Maya.*

CHOL MAYA

The archaeological record indicates that ancestors of today's Chol Maya constructed the ancient Maya cities that now lie in ruins within the Selva Lacandona. After the sixteenth-century Spanish conquest of Chiapas, the surviving Chol were relocated into the Chiapas foothills, near the towns of Tila, Tumbalá, Sabanillas, Salto de Agua, and Palenque, where many of them remained until recolonization of the Selva Lacandona began in the 1960s. Among the leaders of that colonization process were Chol Maya families from the towns of Palenque, Chancalá, and the valley of the Río Tulijá (Marion 1997:82).

Most Chol Maya of the Selva Lacandona have given up their traditional clothing, although some women still wear colorful *huipil* blouses in towns such as Frontera Corozal (Echeverría). At the same time, the families have retained in-depth knowledge of folk medicine and traditional healing. The group is also known for their principles of organization, "based predominantly on respect for rules of procedure and institutional participation and regulated by an ancient system of responsibilities," according to the late Mexican anthropologist Marie-Odile Marion (1997:83).

The Choles are also respected as agriculturalists, less interested in coffee and cattle than their Tzeltal Maya cousins, and focused on conservation of the forest that surrounds their communities. The largest of the modern Chol Maya settlements is Frontera Corozal, on the shore of the Río Usumacinta. Many Chol Maya work today in the tourism industry, serving as guides and boatmen for visitors to Yaxchilán.

TZELTAL MAYA

With a population of 310,000 individuals (1990 census), the Tzeltal Maya are the largest ethnic group in the Selva Lacandona, as well as the largest in Chiapas. They represent 45 percent of the state's indigenous population. The Tzeltal are divided into highland and lowland groups. The highland Tzeltal live in towns such as Tenejapa and Bachajón in northern Chiapas. The lowland Tzeltal originated in the Ocosingo Valley, where the modern town called Ocosingo has existed for several centuries. Gradually, the lowland Tzeltal have moved eastward and southward into the Selva Lacandona, filling in the river valleys that lie between the region's tall mountains.

Beginning around 1980, lowland and highland Tzeltal Maya began to mix in the southern reaches of the Selva Lacandona, as highlanders moved into national forests southwest of Lake Miramar to colonize land and apply for *ejido* status. In towns such as Zapata and San Quintín, highland Tzeltal mix with their lowland cousins and with Tzotzil and Tojolabal Maya from farther west in the state.

RECENT MIGRANTS TO THE SELVA LACANDONA

The Mexican national oil company, Petróleos Mexicanos (PEMEX), constructed a vast network of new roads through the Selva Lacandona during the 1980s and early 1990s. Although very little forest was cleared for actual well construction, the road network and corresponding bridges prompted a new wave of colonization.

To avoid redistributing the large holding of Mexico's political/economic elite, the government gave away national lands to new colonists. By 1990, 568 *ejidos* were established in the Selva Lacandona and another 2,500 settlements had sprung up, made up of colonists from other regions of Chiapas—Tzeltal, Tzotzil, Tojolabal, and Chol Maya—and from the states of Oaxaca, Guerrero, Veracruz, and Puebla (O'Brien 1998:18, 28). Through a combination of rapid natural increase and continuing in-migration, the population of the region continues to grow. The 1960 population of 60,000 people had grown to 350,000 by 1995, to 603,000 by 2000, and is expected to reach 787,000 by the year 2010 (O'Brien 1998:18; Sánchez 2001).

Population growth rates in the Maya tropical forest—especially among indigenous families—are among the highest in the world (CARE/CI 1995). In the Selva Lacandona of eastern Chiapas, the current population of 603,000 people (including such towns as Ocosingo and Palenque) is growing at the rate of 7 percent per year, due mostly to in-migration from the highland Maya region, a rate of growth that would double the population within 10 years. Fifty-two percent of the population of the Selva Lacandona is under the age of 15 years (World Bank 1994).

WHY DO RURAL FAMILIES DO WHAT THEY DO?

Research by biologist Eduardo E. Iñigo-Elías demonstrated the economic logic that drives the principal activities of families in the Selva Lacandona (Iñigo-Elías 1996). Comparing the monetary return on the number of days worked, Iñigo-Elías showed that the most productive activity among *ejido* community farmers in the Selva Lacandona and neighboring Marqués de Comillas region is poaching baby macaws from their nests. A single young macaw was worth US$145 in 1993. In terms of the most successful economic return for days of labor, poaching macaws was followed by growing marijuana, then by raising cattle and pigs. The least productive activities

Table 1. Income from Various Production Activities, Selva Lacandona and Marqués de Comillas Regions, Chiapas, Mexico (Iñigo-Elías 1996)

Product	Amount	Income (US$)	Labor Required	Ratio of Income per Days Worked
Maize (corn)	100 kg	6.50	56 days over 3 months	0.11
Chili peppers	100 kg	38.70	140 days over 5 months	0.27
Cacao	100 kg	9.70	120 days over 10 months	0.08
Calf	500 kg	162	144 days over 12 months	1.12
Pig	25 kg	19.30	20 days over 5 months	0.96
Mahogany	1 cu. ft.	8.30	20 days over 1 month	0.41
Marijuana	100 kg	161	15 days over 4 months	9.66
Scarlet macaw	1 chick	145	1 day during 1 month	145

Source: Eduardo E. Iñigo-Elías, Landscape Ecology and Conservation Biology of the Scarlet Macaw (*Ara macao*) in the Gran Petén Region of Mexico and Guatemala. Ph.D. dissertation, University of Florida. Reproduced by permission.

for return on labor invested were raising chili peppers, maize (corn), and cacao, in that order (see Table 1).

Suffice it to say that illegal activities are the most productive of those listed, and the destructive activity of cattle ranching in the lowland tropical forest is lucrative enough to prompt many rural families to be, or dream of being, cattle ranchers.

Protected Areas

When they first entered the *selva* of eastern Chiapas two centuries ago, the Lacandones encountered an endless expanse of rainforest. Any direction they turned offered them a week's isolation from the closest non-Maya neighbor. When I began to visit the Lacandones in 1974, it still took two or three days of travel from San Cristóbal las Casas to reach the edge of Lake Tz'ibatnah and the northern settlement of Mensabak. The community of Naja lay farther south—down four hard hours of forest trail.

By contrast, during the mid-1990s I drove with my son Chris from San Cristóbal to Mensabak in a rented Volkswagen van down a network of Mexican oil company roads and parked in front of the house of Chan K'in José Valenzuela, overlooking the lake I once rowed across in search of Lacandón families. Twenty years ago, the trip to Mensabak or Naja took you through a wonderland of lowland forest with jungle rivers and soft-edged mounds that are the thousand-year-old ruins of Classic Maya civilization. Today, you will drive endless hours past eroding pastureland and smoldering agricultural fields. The original 13,000 square kilometers (5,000 sq. mi.) of the Selva Lacandona have been reduced by loggers, cattle raisers, oil roads, and colonizing farmers to fewer than 4,000 (1,500 sq. mi.), and it will be nip and tuck from now on to maintain what little forest remains.

The world is lucky that the Lacandones' dispersed settlements and isolation led the government of Mexico, in 1971, to deed 6,410 square kilometers (2,475 sq. mi.) of the Selva Lacandona to the Lacandón population as a communal reserve. Although the likely impetus for this land grant was a timber scam, not indigenous land rights, the action nonetheless gave legal title of this huge block of forest to the families who had lived within it for 200 years.

Six years after the Lacandón land grant, in 1978, the government of Mexico responded to international clamor for rainforest protection by establishing the 3,312 square kilometer (1,280 sq. mi.) Montes Azules Biosphere Reserve, 85 percent of which overlaps the 1971 Lacandón land grant. None of the forest's residents were queried about their desire for a protected area, but today most of them are pleased that the biosphere reserve gives them a buffer against the onslaught of forest destruction outside the reserve's boundaries. In 1992 President Carlos Salinas de Gortari—regardless of his later problems—did the world a favor when he declared four new protected areas adjoining Montes Azules Biosphere Reserve, effectively adding 810 square kilometers (313 sq. mi.) to the protected area network of the Selva Lacandona.

Still, neither the biosphere reserve nor Comunidad Lacandona designations have halted forest clearing. The Tzeltal Maya, originally from the Ocosingo Valley to the west, are ambitious forest farmers who dedicate exhausted cornfield land to pasture for beef cattle. They then clear more tropical forest for corn farming, and the process of converting forest to pasture continues. As a result, the Tzeltal are quickly exhausting the tropical forest of the northern half of the 6,143 square kilometer (2,475 sq. mi.) Comunidad Lacandona lands, causing their Chol and Lacandón Maya cousins in the southern portion of the territory to wonder how many years will pass before they find themselves defending their own forest lands from the land grant's co-owners.

Outside the land grant and its adjoining protected areas, the tropical forest is already a memory made hazy by the smoke of burning tree trunks. Most of it has fallen prey to Latin America's classic three-stage process of deforestation: logging roads are followed by landless families who clear the forest and move inexorably farther into the shrinking forest, as cattle ranchers follow in their wake, turning the exposed, thin soils into medio-cre pasturelands.

Inside the Montes Azules Biosphere Reserve, considerable hope comes from the fact that during the 1990s the more enlightened leaders of the Choles and Tzeltales awakened to realize that conservation of the remaining forest is their best ticket to a sustainable future. Increasingly, the Chol Maya of the Comunidad Lacandona are joining forces with the Lacandones to protect Montes Azules and to search for economic alternatives—ecotourism, handicrafts, new agricultural crops—to avoid having to clear and burn the forest for a few more years of corn and beans and squash.

The forest the group seeks to keep alive is, in fact, a biological marvel. It is the most species-rich ecosystem in Mexico—itself a mega-diverse country. A third of Mexico's bird species, almost half of its butterflies, and a fifth of the country's plants exist within Montes Azules—this in a country that stretches from the dry Texas border to the tropical Caribbean shores of Yucatán. No surprise, then, that the Lacandón forest is Mexico's number one conservation priority and the focus of millions of dollars of conservation investment from both national and international organizations and from forward-thinking Mexicans.

Mexican ecologist Rodrigo Medellín points out why the Selva Lacandona is probably the most diverse ecosystem in Mexico. "It is," he writes, "the largest remnant of tropical rainforest in Mexico and part of the largest expanse of that vegetation type in Central America" (1994:780). The Selva Lacandona has long been noted for its diversity of arthropods and plants; more recently, Medellín has noted that the Selva Lacandona's mammal fauna represents 25 percent of Mexico's total (1994:786). Bats, with 64 species, account for many of these mammal species, but combined with high numbers of marsupials, rodents, and carnivores, they make the Selva Lacandona second only to Cuzco Amazónico, Peru, in terms of number of mammal species in the entire Neotropics (1994:789).

MONTES AZULES BIOSPHERE RESERVE AND ADJOINING RESERVES

Most of these species are protected today in the 3,312 square kilometer (1,280 sq. mi.) Montes Azules Biosphere Reserve, established by the gov-

Table 2. Protected Areas in the Selva Lacandona, Chiapas

Name of Area	Established	Square Km.	(Square Mi.)
Reserva de la Biósfera Montes Azules	January 12, 1978	3,312	(1,279)
Refugio de Flora y Fauna Silvestre Chan K'in	August 24, 1992	121.84	(47)
Monumento Natural Bonampak	August 24, 1992	43.57	(16.8)
Reserva de la Biósfera Lacantún	August 24, 1992	618.73	(239)
Monumento Natural Yaxchilán	August 24, 1992	26.21	(10)
Reserva Comunal Sierra la Cojolita de la Comunidad Lacandona	1993	354.10	(136.7)
Area de Protección de Flora y Fauna Najá	1998	38.47	(15)
Area de Protección de Flora y Fauna Metzabok	1998	33.68	(13)

Source: *Diario oficial de la Federación, 23 de septiembre de 1998,* courtesy of Ignacio March, Tuxtla Gutiérrez, Chiapas, 2001.

ernment of Mexico in 1978. In 1992 a presidential decree added an additional 810 square kilometers (313 sq. mi.) to the reserve, and the Lacandón, Tzeltal, and Chol Maya inhabitants of the Comunidad Lacandona recently created a community conservation area, La Cojolita, that geographically connects the Montes Azules Biosphere Reserve to a similar reserve, the Maya Biosphere Reserve, in neighboring Guatemala. These adjoining reserves are listed in Table 2.

Montes Azules Biosphere Reserve is also rich in water sources. In the reserve's northern panhandle lie the Lagunas Ocotales, a series of a half-dozen finger lakes ringed by tropical forest and white limestone cliffs. (An island on one of these lakes, Laguna Ocotal, was the site for the Postclassic Choltí Maya town Pochutla). In the southwest of Montes Azules, the huge tropical Lake Miramar covers 79 square kilometers (30.5 sq. mi.). Modern Lacandón Maya call it Chan Kagnah, "Little Ocean." One of the lake's islands became the Postclassic town of Lacam Tun. In the northeast of Montes Azules is the 10-square-kilometer (4 sq. mi.) Laguna Lacanjá, long associated with the southern Lacandón Maya.

The reserve is also drained by a series of large rivers. The Ríos Santo

Domingo, Jataté, Perlas, Tzendales, and Lacanjá flow southeastward through forest and past farm settlements to join with the Río Ixcan as it flows in from the highlands of Guatemala. Together, these waters create the Río Lacantún, a wide, sediment-filled river that links with the Río Salinas to create the mighty Usumacinta.

It is important to note that both the Montes Azules Biosphere Reserve and Lacantún Biosphere Reserve were created by the Mexican federal government as biosphere reserves, rather than having that designation tacked on top of another category, much the way many national parks become biosphere reserves as well when recognized by UNESCO's Man and the Biosphere Program. Mexico was the first nation to create a national category of "biosphere reserve" (several others have since followed suit, Guatemala among them), and Montes Azules was the first such national biosphere reserve created. However, Montes Azules, and later Calakmul Biosphere Reserve, were submitted to UNESCO for international biosphere reserve designation, which both easily received. By contrast, the Lacantún Biosphere Reserve has not been submitted to nor recognized by UNESCO and remains a nationally declared biosphere reserve.

Fewer than 5 kilometers (3 miles) northeast of the Lacantún Biosphere Reserve lies the Refugio de Vida Silvestre Chan-K'in, also created on August 21, 1992, by President Carlos Salinas. At 121 square kilometers (47 sq. mi.), Chan-K'in is not a large protected area, but it conserves an important block of lowland forest between the Southern Frontier Highway and the Río Usumacinta. The reserve is surrounded on all sides by farming communities, making its future a bit uncertain. Today, however, this low-lying region (less than 200 meters [656 feet] above sea level) protects high and medium evergreen tropical forest and its wildlife community in one of the last redoubts of tropical forest in southeastern Mexico. The Refugio Chan-K'in is named for Chan K'in Viejo, the Lacandón Maya patriarch and religious leader, who died in 1996, well into his nineties.

Twenty-five kilometers (15 miles) northwest of the Refugio Chan-K'in, and also attached to the Montes Azules Biosphere Reserve, are two archaeological parks and a community reserve that connects them. The Monumento Natural Bonampak was created in August 1992 not so much for its wildlife as for the important Classic Maya ruins, site of the most famous painted mural in the Maya world (see Bonampak, under archaeological sites, below). Nonetheless, the site also protects 43 square kilometers (17 sq. mi.) of tropical forest, home to toucans, macaws, hummingbirds, and plant species such as orchids, palms and endemic ferns.

LA COJOLITA, CHIAPAS

Bonampak tucks into the southern end of a forest and wildlife conservation area called La Cojolita, created in 1993 by the Comunidad Lacandona. La Cojolita is not a federally sanctioned protected area under the control of the national government, but an area of *certificación,* a designation under Mexican law that allows the area's indigenous owners to protect the land as a community reserve but maintain it under their own control (Carlos Manterola, Conservation International–Mexico, e-mail to author, December 28, 2004).

La Cojolita is an indigenous community reserve created in 1995 by the three ethnic Maya groups of the Comunidad Lacandona: Tzeltal Maya, Chol Maya, and Lacandón Maya. The original goal of the reserve was local: to preserve a forest connection between the Classic Maya archaeological sites of Bonampak and Yaxchilán to promote income generation through ecotourism.

In creating this reserve, however, the community has promoted international conservation by establishing a legal mechanism to maintain a biological corridor between Montes Azules Biosphere Reserve and the Sierra del Lacandón National Park of the Maya Biosphere Reserve. Nonetheless, continuing protection of this community-established corridor is not assured. Threats to the area include a proposed new highway to the archaeological site of Yaxchilán, agricultural expansion from the communities of Frontera Corozal and El Desempeño, uncontrolled forest fires during agricultural burning, and illegal colonization by families not affiliated with the legally recognized Comunidad Lacandona.

On its northern extreme, La Cojolita attaches to the Monumento Natural Yaxchilán. Yaxchilán is one of the most magnificent and mysterious Maya ruins in the Selva Maya, a large Classic-era city built on an omega-shaped loop in the Río Usumacinta. The ruined city, as well as the tropical forest that covers it, are protected as the Monumento Natural Yaxchilán, covering 26 square kilometers (10 sq. mi.).

NAHA AND METZABOK FLORA AND FAUNA PROTECTION AREAS

The Lacandón Maya lived for centuries in a tropical forest inhabited by few other human beings. Population expansion, road construction, logging, and beef cattle production changed this situation drastically during the twentieth century. As farm families and cattle ranchers moved into the Selva Lacandona and cleared and burned its forest, the Lacandones found themselves increasingly surrounded by settlements and deforestation rather than tropical forest. Pressure on Lacandón land, especially in the northern communities of Naha and Mensabak, increased steadily between 1970 and 1994, when the Zapatista rebellion created an environment of lawlessness in the Selva Lacandona that prompted several neighboring Tzeltal communities to invade the forested land of the Lacandones.

In reaction to these pressures, the Lacandones sought federal protection by seeking to declare their lands as protected area. The result was the 1998 federal decree establishing Naja and Mensabak as Flora and Fauna Protected Areas in the *Diario oficial de la Federación, 23 de septiembre de 1998.* The decree declared 3,368 hectares (13 sq. mi.) surrounding Naja and 3,847 hectares (15 sq. mi.) surrounding Mensabak, both including their sizable lakes, to be federally protected areas (SEMARNAT 2000).

The regulations of the decree allow the Lacandón Maya to continue their traditional agricultural practices, but dedicate these sections of humid tropical forest to conservation rather than colonization and deforestation. Lacandón families, numbering 180 individuals in Naha and 69 in Mensabak, as of the year 2000, continue to live within the reserves. Both areas also have sizable and impressively beautiful lakes. Lake Naha covers 52 hectares (129 acres). The community of Mensabak includes 21 lakes of varying sizes. There are two large lakes: Dz'ibatnah (closest to the community) covers 179 hectares (442 acres); neighboring Lake Mensabak is 86 hectares (213 acres). Although much of the wildlife of the Naha and Mensabak reserves has been depleted by hunting, they remain one of the few places in the northern Selva Lacandona where you can find blocks of tropical forest in its original state.

IF YOU GO . . . NAHA AND MENSABAK

You can travel to Mensabak by traveling south from Palenque to the old sawmill town of Chancalá and taking the spur road to El Diamante. The turnoff to Mensabak is between El Diamante and the Tzeltal *ejido* of El Tumbo. The trip from Palenque takes about three hours. Naha is an hour farther south on the road. Both communities are also accessible from Ocosingo by passing through Monte Líbano, then northward to Naha and an hour farther north to Mensabak. You can make arrangements to camp in either of the communities or stay in rustic tourist lodging by asking for

Mexico 149

the community president. Most of the men and a few women speak at least
rudimentary Spanish.

Archaeological Sites

Like most of the Selva Maya, Mexico's Selva Lacandona is filled with Maya
ruins, large and small. Visitors find it difficult to walk more than a kilometer anywhere in the Selva Lacandona without stumbling over the stone
foundation of at least a Maya house mound. Many of these house mounds
surround the ruins of stone cities of the Classic era. Among the most important of these cities are the following.

BONAMPAK

In 1946 two Lacandón Maya men from the settlement of Lacanjá Chan
Sayab guided Karl Hermann Frey, a U.S. draft dodger, to ruins that the
Lacandones call Dz'ibatnah, "Painted House." Frey and a subsequent
visitor, Giles Healey (who was the first outsider to see the site's famous
murals), both reported the site to Mexican authorities. Renamed Bonampak, the site became world famous for the colorful, intricate paintings that
decorate three rooms of one of its buildings. Frey later drowned, under
suspicious circumstances, in the nearby Río Lacanjá.

Bonampak is dominated by a large acropolis composed of stairways, terraces, and buildings constructed on a hill. The acropolis overlooks a wide
plaza that is dotted with several stelae, one of them an enormous depiction of the ruler Chan Muan, who commissioned the famous Bonampak
murals.

Archaeological and hieroglyphic research indicates that Bonampak
was associated with Yaxchilán, which lies 30 kilometers (18 miles) northeast. A *sacbe* (Yucatec Maya, plural = *sacbeob*; English = white road)
that leads northeast from Bonampak may lead to Yaxchilán, though no
one has yet followed the road all the way. While there are hints of activity during the Early Classic period, Bonampak's glory years appear to
have come during the eighth century AD, under the ruler Knot-eye Jaguar, his son, Chan Muan, and Chan Muan's son, the baby who makes an
appearance in the murals. Bonampak was contemporary with Palenque
and appears to have subdued it once, around AD 600 (Schele and Mathews
1998:95). Nonetheless, the earliest recorded date at Bonampak is AD

740 and the final date only 50 years later, about when the murals' events took place.

The Bonampak murals were formerly believed to record the designation of an heir to the Bonampak kingship—the son of ruler Chan Muan, the ruler who plays the central role in the murals' historical events. More recent work indicates that the topic may actually be the payment of tribute by vassal lords incorporated into Bonampak's power structure after the great battle the mural depicts (A. Coe 2001:298).

Painted around AD 790, the scenes include a court celebration with elaborately dressed participants and orchestra members playing large trumpets, gourd rattles, drums, and beating turtle shells. Another scene depicts a raid on another Maya city, with gory battle details, including a spear piercing the forehead of an enemy warrior. A subsequent scene indicates that fighters captured in the raid were taken back to Bonampak to have their fingernails pulled out and their heads cut off. The story ends in a mural that illustrates a ritual dance and a royal bloodletting ceremony.

Maya artists painted the Bonampak murals with colors made from minerals and natural vegetation. Hematite provided red, and clays and soils produced yellow and blue. Carbon provided black (Sharer 1994:665). Tree latexes, including that of *Trichospermum mexicanum* (Spanish = *corcho rojo;* Lacandón Maya = *tz'itz'*) added other colors. Today, the paintings are faded and difficult to decipher, the result of exposure to the air and the 1960s practice of daubing them with kerosene to intensify the colors. Fortunately, excellent color drawings and life-sized reproductions were made by Guatemalan, Mexican, and Dutch archaeologists and artists, among them Antonio Tejeda, Rina Lazo, Agustín Villagra, and Kees Grootenbroer. You can see these at the anthropology museum in Villahermosa or the one in Mexico City or at the Florida State Museum in Gainesville.

IF YOU GO . . . BONAMPAK   Infrastructure completed by Mexico's Instituto Nacional de Antropología e Historia in 2000 allows travelers to drive directly to a visitor's center at the site of Bonampak and buy soft drinks and souvenirs from Lacandones from the nearby communities of Lacanjá Chan Sayab and San Javier. The more interesting way to visit the site is to hire a Lacandón Maya guide in Lacanjá Chan Sayab or San Javier and hike an hour down a forest trail to encounter the site much the way Frey and Healey first found it in the mid-twentieth century. Along the way, the Lacandones will point out interesting plants and wildlife and tell you the Maya perspective on the discovery of the monuments and murals.

You can camp in one of several Lacandón-owned campsites in Lacanjá Chan Sayab or continue on to hotels or campsites in Frontera Corozal or Palenque. Bonampak receives about 16,000 visitors per year.

LACANJÁ

The Classic-era site of Lacanjá is just over an hour's walk from the modern Lacandón Maya settlement of Lacanjá Chan Sayab. The site's most prominent feature is a tall, exceptionally well preserved one-room temple perched atop a tall, steep mound. Strikingly, the temple has a giant tree growing directly out of its roof, with its roots grasped around the structure, like a hand around a ball. If the tree dies and falls or blows over, it threatens to bring the entire structure down with it. Lacandones identify the tree as a *ch'u te*, "the brother of the cedar," meaning it is likely a member of the Meliaceae family, that of tropical cedar and mahogany trees.

Emblem glyphs indicate that Lacanjá was closely allied with Bonampak. Knot-eye Jaguar, the father of the ruler who commissioned the mural of Bonampak, appears on a wall panel at the site (Sharer 1994:252), and inscriptions at rival site Yaxchilán indicate that a battle in AD 564 resulted in the capture of a lord from Lacanjá (Martin and Grube 2000:121). A similar fate seems to have fallen on another Lacanjá lord around AD 729, and, in fact, Yaxchilán came to dominate both Lacanjá and Bonampak during the eighth century (Martin and Grube 2000:123).

IF YOU GO . . . LACANJÁ The path to the archaeological site of Lacanjá is through the forest of the Lacandón Maya community of Lacanjá Chan Sayab, and your only chance of finding the site is by hiring a guide in that settlement. The trip leads you through primary forest and over a half-dozen small streams, a few of which have log bridges and some of which you must wade. The trip makes for a fine adventure in high forest with the best possible guides for the area.

PALENQUE

The ancient Maya built the city of Palenque on the edge of a chain of hills—the northern tail of the Chiapas highlands—overlooking the almost level valley of the Río Usumacinta. This location made Palenque a key link in trade between the Maya highlands and cities in the lowland forest and coastal plain. It likely also made the city an imposing site, perched on the sloping hills overlooking the farms and settlements on the plains below.

Many visitors consider the site to be the most graceful and beautiful of all Maya cities. Well-preserved buildings, carvings, and molded stucco make it one of the most popular archaeological sites in the Maya Tropical Forest. Built on a series of natural and human-made terraces, the city is remarkably compact but is surrounded by a tropical forest national park of 17.7 square kilometers (6.8 sq. mi.). The forest on the hills above the site is still dense and well protected. (The Arnold Schwarzenegger science fiction film *Predator* was filmed here in 1986 by Twentieth Century Fox.) Six year-round streams thread through the site, including one, the Río Otolum, that the city's ancient architects channeled with stone to create aqueducts complete with footbridges. The streams end in a delightful cascade of clear water and travertine just below the site.

As Schele and Freidel (1990:217) note, Palenque "has played a crucial role in the modern study of ancient Maya history and religion, as well as in the decipherment of their writing system." The site was explored by Spanish religious authorities as early as 1773 and in 1831 by an Irishman who adopted the unlikely name of Juan Galindo. Appointed governor of the Petén (which at that time included modern Chiapas), Galindo concluded after his examinations of Palenque that "Maya civilization had been superior to all others in the world" (M. Coe 1992:75).

Because the city's Maya occupants left behind a rich legacy of carved texts, focused especially on the dated succession of rulers (and justification for their authority), epigraphers and archaeologists have been able to reconstruct a detailed history of Palenque, while advancing the study of Maya hieroglyphs in general. We now know, for example, that the city's occupants referred to their home as Lakam Ha, "Big Water," and to their kingdom as Bak or Bakal, meaning "Bone" or "Skeleton."

Although excavations at the site have revealed pottery made as early as AD 100, Palenque expanded as a regional trade center between AD 300–600. The city's written history begins in AD 431 with a ruler named K'uk' Balam I, "Quetzal Jaguar." Recorded history ends with the ruler Wak Kimi Janaab Pakal in AD 799 (A. Coe 2001:262).

Most of the exposed structures of the site date from the Late Classic period (AD 500–900), when Palenque was ruled by Pakal the Great (who was buried beneath the Temple of the Inscriptions) and his son, K'inich Kan Balam II, who took over when his father died in AD 683.

Palenque lost a war to Bonampak in AD 603, to Calakmul in AD 611, and saw its ruler captured by the Maya of Toniná in AD 711, but the city went on to flourish during the late eighth century, reaching its zenith between AD 700 and 770. The site's last known recorded date comes from a vase made in AD 799. By AD 810, all ceremonial activity appears to have blinked out. Artifacts subsequent to that date are those of the Putun Maya, who lived in the abandoned ruins as they moved up the Río Usumacinta from the coastal plains. By AD 900, even they had abandoned Palenque to the encroaching forest (A. Coe 2001:264).

Today, Palenque is dominated by a half-dozen well-preserved structures, including the restored tower of the Palace, as well as the Temple of the Inscriptions with its graceful staircase to a large structure built on top. During the centuries that Palenque was occupied, the Maya painted the buildings red and decorated them with stucco painted green, yellow, and blue. The site is remarkable for the lack of free-standing sculptures that characterize so many Maya sites. Instead, the rulers and architects of Palenque focused on carved stone panels and stucco creations that were fixed to the inside or outside walls of the city's buildings. For example, just inside the door of the Temple of the Cross is a carved panel of a god smoking a cigar. The ornate cross inside the Temple of the Foliated Cross represents the Maya world tree, the ceiba.

The most dominant feature of the site is the four-story tower on the corner of the Palace, a building that once served as the primary residence and ceremonial center for the ruler of Palenque. Speculation about the use of the tower ranges from astronomical observatory to defensive lookout.

The Mexican archaeologist Alberto Ruz Lhuillier made the most remarkable discovery yet at Palenque. In 1947 he deduced that holes in a large stone slab in the structure atop the Temple of the Inscriptions were in fact lifting holds. The uprooting of this stone revealed a rubble-filled stairwell that descended into the depths of the building. After several years of work, Ruz and his colleagues discovered the tomb of the Palenque ruler, Pacal, who controlled the city from the age of 12 in AD 615 to the age of 80. Pacal's body had been placed in a huge stone sarcophagus capped with an intricately carved lid showing Pacal falling into the open jaws of the otherworld. (Chapter 3 of Schele and Mathews' *The Code of Kings* [1998] provides a detailed description of Pacal's tomb and its symbolism.)

IF YOU GO . . . PALENQUE Palenque is easily accessible by car, plane, bus, and train. Palenque's small airport has regular commercial service, and buses run regularly to the town of Palenque from many cities in southeastern Mexico, especially Villahermosa and San Cristóbal las Casas. The site is 8 kilometers (5 miles) west of the modern town called Palenque, where you will find a range of accommodations—from luxury hotels with swimming pools to backpackers' hammock-stringing spots. You can also stay near the ruins in one of several camping or cabaña spots. Palenque is visited by more than 370,000 people each year (Ricardo Hernández, personal communication, 2002).

YAXCHILÁN

One of the most impressive and imposing of the ancient cities in the Maya Tropical Forest, Yaxchilán is built on a series of tall hills in an omega-shaped meander of the Río Usumacinta, at the eastern border of Mexico's Selva Lacandona. Because it is surrounded on three sides by the river and protected to the south by other tall hills, Yaxchilán lay in a highly defensible position, a positive quality for the major city on the primary waterway of the Maya world.

Geography afforded Yaxchilán benefits in defensive position and commercial trade, but astronomy may also have played a part in the city's foundation. Art historian Carolyn Tate points out that the establishment of Yaxchilán around AD 300 came "during the leap in social and scientific development" that produced dynasties of Maya rulers who claimed godlike origins and reinforced their authority by erecting stone monuments citing their genealogical right to leadership, backed up with precise astronomical and calendric calculations (Tate 1992:4).

Tate notes that "they must have used the hills of Yaxchilán for years as observatories, which allowed them to measure the length of the year and see the passage of the planets" (1992:4). The structures of Yaxchilán are, in fact, oriented according to the summer and winter solstice. On the summer solstice, the sun rises between two hills in the Petén, the taller of which is the highest point visible from Yaxchilán. This event, marking the point in the year when the long summer days begin to shorten, allowed the leaders of Yaxchilán to schedule cyclical events. The two hills probably gave the city its name—Split Sky (Tate 1992:115). Backing up this possibility is the notation by Hernán Cortés of a site in the Usumacinta region called Izancanac, a term that can be glossed as "Place of the Split Sky."

From this strategic location in the horseshoe bend of the Usumacinta, the lords of Yaxchilán would have looked across the Usumacinta at the flat, agricultural land of the Petén. Yaxchilán's long and well-documented dynasty of rulers begins in the fourth century AD with the king Yat-Balam, "Penis of the Jaguar," whose descendants maintained unbroken control of the site for more than 500 years. They created alliances with the rulers of Bonampak and Piedras Negras, but also fought wars with Calakmul, Dos Pilas, Palenque, and Tikal (Webster 2002:281). Around AD 654, Palenque's leader, Pacal, captured the brother of Yaxchilán's ruler, Shield Jaguar. The last known ruler of Yaxchilán ascended to the throne around AD 800, but texts ceased to be produced in 808, indicating that trouble was afoot in the region. The site was likely abandoned by AD 850.

Yaxchilán is best known in Mayanist circles for the written data provided on the site's 125 monuments—among them 60 carved lintels, five hieroglyphic stairways, and 34 stelae (Tate 1992:38, 47). The lintels, stone slabs that lined the underside of doorways of the major buildings, depict the steady line of rulers—mainly father-to-son successions between AD 320 and 800. Among the scenes artistically carved on the lintels are Maya warfare, bloodletting, and ceremonial visions. One of the most striking (now located in the British Museum) commemorates the birth of a son to ruler Shield Jaguar II in AD 709. It shows the proud father holding a torch over his kneeling wife, Lady Xoc (Shark Lady), who is performing a ritual bleeding ceremony by pulling a rope braided with thorns through a hole in her tongue (Sharer 1994:245). Maya researcher Tatiana Proskouriakoff pointed out, in fact, that women played an important role at Yaxchilán, as evidenced by their frequent depiction on relief carvings.

The English explorer Alfred Maudslay took eight of Yaxchilán's carved lintels to Europe in the 1880s. Seven of these are now in the British Museum; the eighth was destroyed in the World War II bombing of Berlin. Another dozen lintels and four stelae are displayed in Mexico City's Museo Nacional de Antropología.

Other early explorers of Yaxchilán included Désiré Charnay, Teobert Maler, and Alfred Tozzer. Maler named the site Yaxchilán in a convolution of the Maya term for a nearby stream, Ya'al Chilan. Several nineteenth- and early twentieth-century researchers noted that the Lacandón Maya who were their contemporaries made religious pilgrimages to buildings at Yaxchilán, a practice that continued throughout the twentieth century. Leaving their weapons at the edge of the city and changing into clean tunics, they would pray and burn copal incense on top of the ancient stone altars. (In modern Lacandón cosmology, the True Lord, Hachäkyum, once lived in Palenque but later moved to Yaxchilán, where the Lacandones continue to pay obeisance to him.)

The Lacandones have always paid special attention to a headless statue in what archaeologists know as Structure 33. On the summer solstice, the rising sun illuminates this twice life-size depiction of Yaxchilán ruler Bird Jaguar IV, one of the city's last rulers, who sits Buddha-like in the center of the structure's main room. The statue's head rests in the next niche to the right. Modern Lacandón Maya say that this figure represents the god Hach Bilam, and that if the head is replaced on the torso the world will come to an end. Wisely, Mexico's archaeologists have left Hach Bilam's head separate from his body.

One other interesting note about the Lacandón view of the Yaxchilán region: Schele and Freidel (1990:480) point out that "Tom Jones (1985) provided convincing evidence that the Usumacinta was called Xocol Ha at the time of the conquest." "Xocol Ha" in Yucatec (and Lacandón) Maya means "Near the Water." By contrast, today's older Lacandones call the Usumacinta "Xoclah," from the name of the anadromous snook (*Centropomus undecimalis;* Spanish = *robalo;* Lacandón Maya = *xoclah*), which annually migrate from the Gulf of Mexico into the Usumacinta and its tributaries to spawn. The snook is the tastiest fish in the Río Usumacinta basin and one of the largest.

Another controversy surrounds the two piles of uniformly shaped stones mounded in the river in front of Yaxchilán. Schele and Freidel (1990:277) refer to "the huge stone pier that had been built over the river on its southern side." By contrast, structural engineer and amateur archaeologist James O'Kon, from Atlanta, Georgia, identified the ruins of bridge abutments on the river's shores and pointed to carved stone devices that may have guided the ropes for a three-span suspension bridge across the Usumacinta. O'Kon proposes that the stones that now lie in two mounds in the rush of the river were the pilings of a seventh-century, 600-foot-long suspension bridge that linked Yaxchilán with its affiliated site, now called La Pasadita, lying directly across the river in what is now Guatemala's Sierra del Lacandón National Park. A 1995 *National Geographic* note quotes O'Kon as stating that "when the river is at flood stage, from June to January, it's impossible to cross in a boat. It would be logical to build a bridge there" (*National Geographic* 1995).

Archaeological work at Yaxchilán began in earnest in 1972 and continues today under the guidance of Mexico's Instituto Nacional de Antropología e Historia (INAH). So far, workmen have discovered eight tombs and cleared 26 buildings, including two ball courts in the Main Plaza. Most of Yaxchilán's visible structures date between AD 450 and 808.

IF YOU GO . . . YAXCHILÁN Yaxchilán receives only 13,000 travelers per year, and most approach the city as the Maya did, by traveling on the Río Usumacinta. The best bet is to hire a boat and river pilot in the Chol Maya town of Frontera Corozal, Chiapas, a few miles upriver from Yaxchilán. Driving south on the Palenque–San Javier highway (also known as the Southern Frontier Highway), turn east at Km 25 to approach the riverbank town of Frontera Corozal. Chol Maya guides who live there will take you downriver to Yaxchilán in a long, painted wooden plank boat (most have canopies for protection from the sun) and wait for you while you tour the site.

The town of Frontera Corozal is worth a visit by itself. At dusk, after the day's work, young men on bicycles glide up and down the narrow, open streets of the town, calling to one another in glottalized Chol. The occasional stray dog lazily crosses the main road to avoid an approaching pickup truck, and at the base of the steep bank of the river, dozens of long wooden boats called *lanchas* are gathered like fish on a rope stringer, waiting for tomorrow's cargo and passengers. Men transfer cardboard boxes and plastic gasoline containers from the boats into waiting canvas-backed trucks, while boys jump from the sandbanks into the swift brown water of the river.

Frontera Corozal offers several cooperatively owned lodges of varying degrees of comfort and price, ranging from a spartan ecological campsite to the firmly established Centro Turístico Escudo Jaguar, with private baths in the rooms and television in the open-air *comedor,* where the staff speak Chol to each other as they take your order for *pollo asado* or tortilla soup.

You can also travel overland to Yaxchilán by hiring a Lacandón Maya guide in the communities of San Javier or Lacanjá Chan Sayab. Finally, if you have little time and lots of money, you can fly directly to the airstrip at Yaxchilán by hiring a single-engine plane in San Cristóbal las Casas, Palenque, or Comitán.

No matter how you get there, a visit to Yaxchilán is a treat for naturalists as well as archaeology buffs. It is one of the most mysterious sites in the Maya Tropical Forest, with structures hidden atop hills within dense forest. Archaeologists have cleared the site just enough to show off the largest buildings, but they have left the vast majority of the area in mature forest. The result is a delightful combination of nature and ancient architecture.

The omega formed by the Usumacinta at Yaxchilán is a haven for wild-life escaping deforestation in the Selva Lacandona, a situation that fills Yaxchilán with interesting animals. On a typical visit there in late January 2002, our team saw—during a two-hour visit—a troop of spider monkeys, a troop of howler monkeys (with babies), one coatimundi, a half-dozen toucans, one trogon, one scarlet macaw, four crocodiles (along the river), one poisonous fer-de-lance snake (called a *nauyaca* in Chiapas), one oven bird, one Royal Flycatcher, one kiskidee, one Black-and-white Warbler, one ant wren, and one small kingfisher.

POSTCLASSIC SITES IN THE SELVA LACANDONA, CHIAPAS

Today's Lacandón Maya moved into territory that would later become Chiapas, Mexico, from the Campeche/Petén area at the end of the eighteenth century. Previously, the lowland and montane tropical forest of the Selva Lacandona had been occupied by Maya who spoke languages in the Cholan family—among them Chol and Choltí. Discovered in the early 1500s during the first Spanish expeditions into the Selva Lacandona, these Postclassic Maya were given the name of one of their island cities—Lacam Tun, or Lacan Tun. Thus, the Maya inhabitants of the Selva Lacandona and southern and western Petén came to be known as Lacandones. The name was later applied to the Yucatec-speaking Maya who moved into the Selva Lacandona at the end of the 1700s. These early, Cholan-speaking Lacandones lived on islands in lakes and rivers of what is now the Selva Lacandona.

LACAM TUN (LAKE MIRAMAR) The site that provided the people of the Selva Lacandona with their name was Lacam Tun, located on the largest island in Laguna Miramar, a 79 square kilometer lake (30.5 square miles) in the southwestern region of the Montes Azules Biosphere Reserve. Lacam Tun is variously translated as "Fallen Stone(s)" or as "Banner Stones," the term used by the ancient Maya for stone stelae (Martin and Grube 2000:14).

Ceramic analysis indicates that the island was occupied from the Late Preclassic through Late Postclassic eras (Rivero 1992:80), but the site is best known for the history and architecture of its final occupants, the Choltí Lacandones.

Subsequent to the disintegration of Classic Maya civilization around AD 900, many of the surviving Maya communities moved into defensive positions on islands in lakes and rivers. One of the largest of these island communities was Lacam Tun, inhabited by Choltí-speaking Maya from at least the early 1500s through 1586. Pochutla and Nohpeten-Flores are other examples.

The Spanish conquistador Alonzo Dávila, a captain who reported to Francisco Montego of Yucatán, was the first European to see Lacam Tun. In 1529 and 1530, Montejo ordered Dávila to find the road that Hernán Cortés had cut through the forest five years earlier on his way to Nito to subdue a rebellious captain. Dávila happened upon Lake Miramar by chance and made his way to the island, but by the time the Spaniards got there, the Choltí Lacandones had fled in canoes and disappeared into the forest. Dávila reported 60 houses on the island (Villa Rojas 1966:29–30).

During subsequent decades, Choltí Lacandones made frequent attacks on Spanish and Christianized Maya settlements on the western edge of the Selva Lacandona. In reaction, the Spaniards launched a military expedition against them in 1559, led by Pedro Ramírez de Quiñones, who marched west out of Comitán. When the soldiers arrived at Lake Miramar, they built a brigantine to attack the island. As they had done 30 years previously, the Maya of Lacam Tun ran to their canoes and fled into the forest. Ramírez de Quiñones sacked the Choltí Lacandón settlement, then headed on to attack similar settlements at Topiltepeque (which he also found empty) and Pochutla, on Laguna Ocotal Grande, where a serious battle ensued between the Spaniards and Choltí Lacandones (see below).

Apparently, these Spanish attacks on the Choltí Lacandones were not enough to end raids on Colonial outposts, for in 1586, a third expedition, led by Juan Morales Villavicencio, similarly left Comitán to pacify Lacam Tun. Seeing that an attack was imminent, the Maya burned their houses and fled. The Spaniards killed the few inhabitants left behind, destroyed the community's crops, and cut down their orchards of cacao trees. Subsequent to this 1586 attack, the Choltí Lacandones abandoned Lacam Tun and created a new settlement at Sac Balam (see below).

Today, the island community of Lacam Tun is an unoccupied and isolated ruin dominated by stone walls, terraces, low pyramids, and a few decapitated, human sculptures. The site is interesting more for its history than for its existing structures, but a visit there is mysterious and exhilarating, partly because of the quiet surroundings of the huge Lake Miramar and partly because the entire island is still shrouded in natural vegetation. No larger than 5,500–7,200 square meters (0.55–0.72 hectares; 1.4–1.8

acres), the surface of the island is completely covered with human-made structures, dating from the Postclassic era. The Maya utilized natural rises on the island to construct pyramids of flat, loose stones, as well as low walls, terraces, and stairways (Rivero 1992). According to Colonial-era Spanish scribes, the Chol constructed wood and palm thatch structures on top of these stone foundations. Clearly, the majority of living quarters and all agricultural fields of the Postclassic inhabitants were on the shore of Lake Miramar. Today, the island is covered with vegetation, but you can make your way from plaza to plaza on narrow, overgrown trails.

The lake, Laguna Miramar, is worth a visit by itself. The water is extraordinarily clear—like an enormous swimming pool—and surrounded on all sides by forest-covered mountains. Where the mountains slope down to the water, their exposed white limestone cliffs contrast with the deep green of the tropical forest. Other than the gentle slosh of waves upon the shore, all is silent and absolutely still.

IF YOU GO . . . LACAM TUN Access to the ruins of the island fortress community of Lacam Tun is by boat only. Inquire for guides in the mixed Maya community of Zapata, which lies next to the town of San Quintín, due east of Lake Miramar. They will take you an hour and a half west by foot, where you can camp on the lakeshore. Your guides will use the fiberglass boats or wood canoes docked at the campsite to row you out to the island of Lacam Tun. Life jackets should be available in Zapata. Bring all the food and equipment you will need; there are no facilities on site.

POCHUTLA/LAGUNA OCOTAL GRANDE The Postclassic Choltí Maya site of Pochutla (sometimes called Tecpan-Pochutla) covers the entire surface of a 4-hectare (10-acre) island in Lake Ocotal Grande, the westernmost of three finger-shaped lakes in the northern panhandle of Montes Azules Biosphere Reserve. Pedro Ramírez de Quiñones, Oidor of the Audiencia de Guatemala, attacked Pochutla in 1559 as part of a Spanish colonial military attempt to eradicate unconquered Maya communities from the Chiapas lowlands. Arriving at the edge of Lake Ocotal Grande, the Spaniards constructed balsa rafts, while their 600 Chiapaneco Indian warriors (from today's Chiapa de Corzo) made cane floats. Thus prepared, they approached the island village and attacked. The Chiapaneco Indians unleashed showers of arrows as the 100 Spanish soldiers fired harquebuses point-blank into the Chol defense. Although the Choles attempted to counterattack by canoe, Spanish firearms forced them to abandon the lake completely. With their Indian allies, the Spaniards occupied Pochutla without further resistance. They found no one alive on the island: the women and children had hidden in the forest prior to the battle (Remesal 1966, vol. 4, bk. 10, chap. 12:1530; Cáceres López 1958, vol. 1:132).

The Spaniards' victory was short-lived, however, for the Choltí Lacandones reoccupied Pochutla. Five years later, though, a Dominican friar, Pedro de Lorenzo, who worked to Christianize Tzeltal and Tzotzil Maya families in the Chiapas highlands, received a visit from a former Pochutla leader, who apparently had fallen into disfavor with the community's leaders. He offered to accompany Friar Lorenzo to Pochutla to attempt to convert them. Lorenzo traveled to the island and remained there for three days, negotiating with the settlement's leader, Chan Ajaw. Not everyone was pleased with the friar's presence. On the second day, a group of men captured Lorenzo and prepared him for sacrifice. Others rescued the confused friar, who took advantage of the division in the community to entice Chan Ajaw and his followers to relocate in a distant settlement, where the church would provide them with food and material goods. During Lent of 1564, Chan Ajaw and the Pochutla inhabitants "of most importance" migrated to Ocosingo, where they were settled, baptized, and incorporated into the Colonial economic system (Nations 1979a).

Little is known of the Pochutla inhabitants who refused to relocate. Around 1573, 200 Lacandones from Pochutla and Lacam Tun raided the area west of Lake Petén Itzá, but as Scholes and Roys point out, "They were defeated and most of them were killed" (Scholes and Roys 1968:44).

Even today, it is obvious that the Choltís' island fortress of Pochutla was built for serious defense. Using naturally occurring boulders as foundations, the Choltís built walls of cut stone to create defensive walls around almost the entire circumference of their four-hectare island. High cliffs on the northern side of the island serve a similar defensive purpose. In the middle of the island, a half-dozen temple mounds mark the center of the community.

Modern Yucatec Lacandón Maya refer to the Choltí Lacandones of Pochutla in their oral history. In 1975, northern Lacandones from Mensabak (Chan K'in José Valenzuela) and Naja (Chan K'in Viejo) still called the lake *u petha' kah* (Outsiders' Lake) and said that long ago Spaniards killed all the people who lived there (Nations 1979a:73).

IF YOU WANT TO GO . . . POCHUTLA   Getting to the Postclassic site of Pochutla is no easy task. The site is six hours walk due west of the Tzeltal community of Palestina, in the northern Montes Azules Biosphere Reserve. A guide from that community can guide you to the Ocotales lakes, all of which have islands with ruins on them. Two years after the 1994 Zapatista revolt in Chiapas, the Mexican Army occupied the biological station built by Conservation International on Laguna Yanqui, next to Ocotal Grande. The army may or may not allow visitors to enter the area. If you make it to the lake, you must have a raft or canoe to row 45 minutes to the island fortress of Pochutla.

SAC BALAM

When the Choltí Lacandones of Lacam Tun abandoned their island fortress at Lake Miramar in 1586, they established a new settlement in a defensive position 50 kilometers (30 miles) to the southeast, at the base of a long mountain chain called the Sierra del Chaquistero. Spanish missionaries began to visit the Choltí Lacandones there as early as 1630, in attempts to pacify and Christianize them, but with no success. A 1693 attempt by two missionaries escorted by Chortí-speaking Maya warriors from Cobán, Guatemala also met with failure. Rather than listen to the friars' sermons, the Choltí tied the visitors to trees and left them there for five days. They then offered the missionaries the opportunity to worship Lacandón idols, but the friars thrust forth their crucifixes and repeated their account of the Catholic faith. The friars convinced the Choltí to send 12 emissaries with them to Cobán to see the benefits conversion had brought to their Chortí Maya cousins, but 10 of the 12 Choltí died during the trip. When the two survivors returned to Sac Balam without their comrades, the friars fled the town of Sac Balam and reported the failure of their attempt at peaceful conversion.

The result was a military expedition against Sac Balam two years later, in 1695, concurrent with the expedition against the Itza Maya of Nohpeten-Flores in the Petén. Troops closed in on the settlement simultaneously from Chiapas and Guatemala, but peaceful-minded Spanish priests beat the advancing army to the punch and occupied Sac Balam without conflict. The later arrival of more than 1,000 Spanish soldiers, allied Maya warriors, and more priests convinced the Choltí Lacandón that resistance was futile. They allowed the occupying force to clear the idols, dead fowl, and braziers from their temples and submitted to a perfunctory conversion to Christianity and to becoming loyal Spanish subjects.

The Spaniards constructed a wood fort and palisade around the settlement of Sac Balam and permanently occupied the site with a garrison of 30 soldiers, 15 allied Maya warriors, four priests, and several Christian Maya servants. The 500 Choltí Maya who lived in Sac Balam endured 15 years of taxes, disease, and forced labor. Some escaped into the forest to return to the old ways, others were finally relocated in 1712 to Retalhuleo, Guatemala, where their eventual deaths resulted in the extinction of the Choltí Lacandón population of the Maya Tropical Forest. The site of Sac Balam was abandoned and lay unknown and undiscovered in the forest for almost 300 years.

In May 1997, I accompanied a team of seven Mexican conservationists to follow clues in the reports of seventeenth and eighteenth century Spanish friars chronicled in the book *La Paz de Dios y del Rey,* by Jan de Vos (1980), to find the stone foundations of Sac Balam. Cutting a trail across the Sierra del Chaquistero, we identified stone foundations that are likely part of the settlement of Sac Balam. The site is exactly in the location specified by Spanish reports, is the only site identified in extensive searches of the surrounding forest, and displays architecture identical to that of Lacam Tun, the original town of the Choltí Lacandones.

Subsequent expeditions to the site that included historian Jan de Vos and Alejandro Tovalín, archaeologist with Mexico's Instituto Nacional de Antropología e Historia (INAH), cited similarities and some differences with the historical sources on Sac Balam and concluded that only further exploration and excavation of the site can undeniably demonstrate that the identified site is Sac Balam (Conservation International 1998).

The Sac Balam ruins consist of stone foundations covering 5 hectares (12 acres) beneath natural vegetation. With its back to the high cliff walls of the Sierra del Chaquistero, the site looks out over an enormous valley of lowland forest to the north. Like the site of Lacam Tun, on Lake Miramar, the site consists of loose stone construction, forming platforms with patios in between.

IF YOU GO . . . SAC BALAM Access to the Sac Balam ruins is difficult. You should attempt a trip there only with a well-prepared and well-equipped team and only with permission of Mexico's INAH and authorities of Montes Azules Biosphere Reserve. The site is accessible from the

Ixcán Ecolodge on the Río Lacantún, which lies on the southern border of Montes Azules. A hike of five difficult hours takes you over the crest of the Sierra del Chaquistero, through convoluted rock formations covered with a strange dwarf forest. Sac Balam is located directly below the sharp drop-off on the northern side of the sierra. Do not take this trip casually. Water is very scarce and the terrain is challenging. The only trail is that cut by the 1997 expedition.

CALAKMUL

CALAKMUL BIOSPHERE RESERVE Guatemala's Maya Biosphere Reserve and Mexico's Calakmul Biosphere Reserve join borders on the northern border of Guatemala's Department of Petén to form one of the largest blocks of protected forest in Latin America. The two reserves, and the two countries, are separated here by only a hand-cut path through the tall, semi-deciduous tropical forest that characterizes this region of the Yucatán Peninsula. Jaguars, jaguarundis, howler monkeys, and hawks move freely between the two reserves. The forest is dotted throughout by Maya ruins and numerous *bajos* (also called *akalchés*), and seasonally filled water holes called *aguadas,* which provide respite to the area's plentiful wildlife. The reserve is a mosaic of mature tropical forest, secondary growth, and savannas. Thirty percent of the bird species found here in the winter months are migrants from the United States and Canada (Ericson, Freudenberger, and Boege 1999:8).

To the east, the reserve borders the neighboring state of Quintana Roo, where other farming communities lie along its boundaries. To the south, Calakmul Biosphere Reserve rests atop the northern border of the Republic of Guatemala, locking onto the Maya Biosphere Reserve to create an international expanse of lowland tropical forest that hides a wealth of wildlife and ancient Maya cities.

Calakmul Biosphere Reserve consists of 7,252 square kilometers (2,800 sq. mi.) of legally protected area (of which 2,483 square kilometers (959 sq. mi.) are core areas and the rest buffer zones) located in the southeastern region of the state of Campeche. Covering almost 13 percent of the state's territory, it is the largest block of protected tropical forest in Mexico. Calakmul Biosphere Reserve was established by a Mexican presidential decree in 1989 and accepted into UNESCO's international system of biosphere reserves in 1993.

Some conflict has emerged between conservation proponents and local

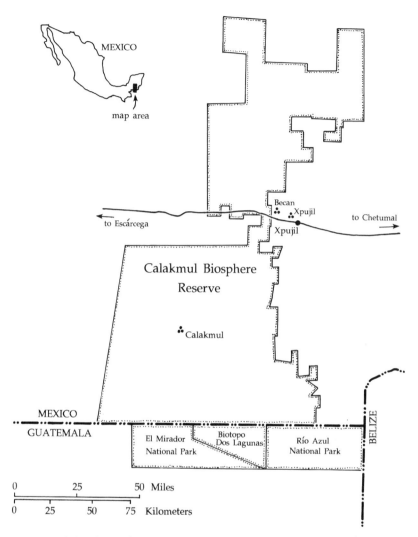

MAP 4. Calakmul Biosphere Reserve, Mexico

communities, because sections of the reserve's core zone overlap preexisting *ejido* boundaries and privately owned property. Agricultural fields push up against the reserve's western and northern borders. The reserve's core zones are divided into northern and southern sections, giving it the shape of a bottom-heavy hourglass divided by Highway 186, the primary land route between the Mexican cities of Escárcega and Chetumal, on the

Caribbean coast. The only legal activity allowed in these zones is scientific research.

The buffer zone of the southern section is made up of forest lands that belong to *ejidos* whose agricultural lands lie along the borders of the northern section of the reserve (Ericson, Freudenberger, and Boege 1999:8). Several of these communities were established in the late 1800s by Yucatec Maya fleeing the War of the Castes. During the 1940s, these communities received land grants that provided access to the chicle and hardwood forest in the southern reaches of Calakmul (Ericson, Freudenberger, and Boege 1999:13).

The Calakmul Biosphere Reserve sits atop the flat limestone shelf of the peninsula of Yucatán, which is covered with only a thin layer of soil. Surface water is extremely scarce. Land elevation within the reserve ranges from 100 to 300 meters (330–900 feet) above sea level. An annual average of 1 to 1.5 meters (39–59 inches) of rain falls during the months of June through November, with a pronounced dry season from December through May.

Scientists have identified a wealth of plant life and wildlife in the Calakmul Biosphere Reserve, including 1,600 species of vascular plants. Only 5 percent of the reserve supports humid tropical forest. Around half is covered with mixed high evergreen and semi-deciduous forest reaching 25 to 35 meters (83–116 feet) in height. Most of the remaining vegetation is low, semi-deciduous dry forest—the Yucatán Peninsula's famous scrub forest—which reaches 15 meters (50 feet) in height. Water-tolerant trees and plants appear in seasonally flooded depressions called *bajos,* the largest of which is El Laberinto, just west of the archaeological site of Calakmul (Gómez Pompa and Dirzo 1993; Folan, Marcus, and Miller 1995:279). Common trees include the *guayacán* (*Guaiacum sanctum*) and mahogany (*Swietenia macrophylla*). Logwood (*Haematoxolon campechianum*) is abundant in the *bajos.*

Scientists working in Calakmul Biosphere Reserve have identified 60 species of amphibians and reptiles (among them 17 species of snakes); 235 species of birds, of which 179 are residents and 56 migrants; and 94 mammal species, half of them bats but also including 16 species of carnivores and 15 of rodents. Five of the six cats of the Maya Tropical Forest and both spider and howler monkeys live in the reserve (Aranda Sánchez and Guzmán 1999). Calakmul Biosphere Reserve has large populations of white-lipped peccary (*Tayassu peccary*), tapir (*Tapirus bairdii*), ornate hawk eagle (*Spizaetus ornatus*), king vulture (*Sarcoramphus papa*), and jaguars (*Panthera onca*).

One striking feature of the reserve is the almost complete absence of permanent surface water. Precipitation in the region rapidly disappears into fissures in the limestone. Water accumulates only in ground depressions known in the Maya region as *aguadas*. Many of the 350 known *aguadas* in the reserve served as water sources for the several Maya cities that emerged in the territory now covered by the biosphere reserve, the largest of these sites being Calakmul itself.

Between AD 250 and 900, the land now occupied by the Calakmul Biosphere Reserve was one of the most densely inhabited regions of the Maya world. Within the boundaries of today's reserve lay Calakmul, the largest city of the Classic Maya era, and a series of satellite cities that joined with the larger site in a powerful political alliance.

In the early part of the twentieth century, this same region was the focus of extractive industries centered on chicle gum extraction and hardwood timber exploitation. Between 1901 and 1910, *chicleros* extracted and exported 10 million kilograms (22 million pounds) of chicle from Campeche State, representing half of Mexico's production. By the mid-1940s, the entire forested area of the state of Campeche was divided into chicle concession areas worked by 50 enterprises (Konrad 1999:99). Chicle production reached its peak during World War II, supplying soldiers' demand for chewing gum, and the industry diminished when the war ended. However, many chicle workers remained in the forest to create permanent farming settlements, and gradually a road and trail network extended over the area. Timber production overtook chicle extraction in economic importance after World War II, focused primarily on mahogany (*Swietenia macrophylla*) and tropical cedar (*Cedrela odorata*).

During the mid-1960s, much of the forested area formerly divided into chicle and timber concessions was deeded by the Mexican government to communities as *ejido* farms. The 1967 construction of the trans–Yucatán Peninsula highway from Escárcega to Chetumal prompted thousands of colonists to occupy forested land in the state, and by 1990 there were 72 *ejidos* and ranches in and around the Calakmul Biosphere Reserve, with a total of 24,000 inhabitants. Fewer than half of these individuals lived inside the boundaries of the biosphere reserve, however (Sánchez González 1999:113).

Most of the families in and around the reserve are not natives of

Campeche but immigrants from other regions of Mexico, chiefly the states of Veracruz and Tabasco. Most live in dirt-floored houses with palm or corrugated tarpaper roofs, and most are Spanish-speaking Ladinos, but they have been joined by Chol Maya families expelled from northern Chiapas by extensive beef cattle production and later by the 1980 explosion of the Chichonal Volcano in Chiapas. The 1994 Zapatista revolt in Chiapas pushed other Chol Maya families into the Calakmul region, to the point that they now outnumber native Yucatec Maya families.

Other residents include Maya from the Chiapas highlands—Tzeltal, Tzotzil—and Guatemalan highland Maya relocated by the Mexican government from refugee camps along the border of Guatemala with Chiapas, these latter the product of Guatemala's civil war during the late 1980s. The majority of these families are active milpa farmers and hunters, followed in number by those dedicated to cattle ranching. Together, this combination of hunting and deforestation, driven in large part by poverty and lack of economic alternatives, places heavy pressure on the reserve's natural resources.

CALAKMUL ARCHAEOLOGICAL SITE Located inside the biosphere reserve of the same name, the archaeological site of Calakmul protects the ruins of the largest city in the Late Classic Maya world. Calakmul was the capital city of Kaan, the Kingdom of the Snake, which Martin and Grube call "one of the most important and powerful of all Classic Maya kingdoms" (Martin and Grube 2000:101). The original Maya name for Calakmul itself was Oshtetun (Three Stones) (Simon Martin, personal communication, 1998).

Calakmul was the archenemy of Tikal, 100 kilometers (60 miles) to the south, and it eclipsed that city in the sixth and seventh centuries (Folan 1999:74; Martin and Grube 2000:101). Calakmul's rulers also fought ritual "star" wars with the leaders of Yaxchilán. A defensive wall around Calakmul indicates the seriousness of these conflicts.

At the same time, Calakmul's leaders were formidable politicians. They created alliances with other polities—installing, for example, the ruler of El Naranjo—to the point that their chief antagonist, Tikal, came to be almost encircled by cities affiliated with them. Calakmul's ruler, Yuknoom th Great, almost succeeding in consolidating control over the entire southe... Maya lowlands before he died in his eighties in AD 686. After conquering the Petén in 650 and defeating Tikal in 677, Calakmul was in turn twice defeated by Tikal (Martin and Grube 2000:109; Freidel and Guenter 2002).

The bulk of the site of Calakmul dates from the Late Classic, although archaeologist William J. Folan notes that certain early architectural features demonstrate that the site was an important Preclassic center as well (Folan 1999:74). This indicates that the early city of Calakmul missed or survived the calamity that struck the Preclassic city of El Mirador and, like its rival Tikal, went on to become a major power during the Classic era.

Calakmul is noted for the *sacbe* roads that connected it to friendly, neighboring sites. Built of white limestone rock and packed earth, the *sacbe* network created local, and long-distance, elevated platforms for foot traffic through a landscape that becomes a gummy mudpit during the rainy season. Because of these roads, runners and traders from Calakmul could have visited the city of El Mirador, 38 kilometers (23 miles) to the southwest, and continued on to El Tintal and Nakbe (Folan, Marcus, and Miller 1995). (El Mirador's Danta Pyramid is actually visible from the tallest structures of Calakmul, as is El Mirador's neighboring site, Nakbe.)

First discovered in 1931, Calakmul has been the primary research focus of William J. Folan, director of the Center for Historical and Social Investigation of the University of Campeche, Mexico, for 15 years. He and Jacinto May Hau identified 6,500 structures extending over 30 square kilometers (11 sq. mi.) in a seven-year mapping project (Folan et al. 1990). Folan and his colleagues estimate that the city was home to 50,000 or more people (Folan and Gallegos Osuna 1996:8).

Through subsequent, ongoing research under the auspices of Mexico's Instituto Nacional de Antropología e Historia (INAH), archaeologists led by Ramón Carrasco have located 117 stelae, the highest number for any Maya site (Sharer 1994:196). Also of major interest at the site is a system of *aguadas,* water reservoirs that appear to have been interconnected and to have provided water for the city's population of thousands. Calakmul has at least five major *aguadas,* one of which is the largest in the Maya world. A huge rectangular reservoir fed by a stream, the *aguada* measures 242 meters by 212 meters (794 feet by 695 feet) (Martin and Grube 2000:106).

IF YOU GO . . . CALAKMUL Calakmul is one of the least visited of the major Maya sites, despite the fact that access is easy, having improved greatly in 1993 when the government paved a narrow spur road to the center of the site from the major east-west highway that traverses the base of the Yucatán Peninsula. To arrive at the site, turn south off Mexican Highway 186 just east of the town of Conhuas, Campeche, stopping at the guardhouse to register with INAH authorities. Overnight lodging is available along Highway 186, or you may be able to camp at the site itself by requesting permission from INAH officials. There are no on-site food, water, or bathing facilities, but small campfires are allowed. Pack in everything you will need during your visit.

Letter from Calakmul

TO: William J. Folan and Lynda Folan
Center for Historical and Social Investigation
University of Campeche
Campeche, Mexico
FROM: Jim Nations
DATE: 21 January, 1998

Dear Willy and Lynda:

The trip from Campeche to Calakmul and back was excellent. The roads are good, and Santiago Billy was waiting in the town of Conhuas, as expected. I left the bag of oranges with your friend Don Ch'om, with your compliments.

Santiago and I drove on to the site that afternoon, and we asked permission of the chief INAH archaeologist, Ramón Carrasco, to camp on the grounds where your archaeological research cabins had been. No problem. At night, the bats whip in and out of the trees, dropping fleas, which rabidly attacked us as we sat around the campfire. We saw plenty of wildlife in and around the site, including *cojolitas,* ocellated turkeys, and the expected host of native and migratory bird species. (One of the Yucatec-speaking guards tried to convince us of the existence of the *sinsimito,* a Yeti-like creature said to inhabit the Calakmul forest, but we never spotted it.)

Only one of your archaeology cabins remains standing, and it now serves as the headquarters and sleeping quarters of the four INAH guards who are always on-site. They were fine fellows and allowed us to use some of their rain-caught water to bathe in.

We spent two nights talking with a friend we ran into in Calakmul—Simon Martin, an epigrapher from London. Santiago and Tom Sever and I had met him before in Yaxjá and Naranjo, Guatemala, six years ago. So, we learned about the latest developments in Maya glyph deciphering. The large site map you were kind enough to give me, Willy, was of great service. (The map appears to be rare, and everyone coveted it; I did manage to hang onto it, however.)

We explored the major monuments at Calakmul, plus the remains of the ancient water system. We found that from both Structure I and II, we could see the Danta and Tigre pyramids in Mirador, 45 kilometers [27 miles] away in northern Petén. As well, we could make out an additional site east of Mirador, which is likely Nakbe. (Nakbe is also visible from the top of Danta in Mirador.)

The INAH guards told us that the stelae count for Calakmul is now 117, and that three tombs were found during 1997. All three are on Structure II: if you climb the front set of stairs to the top, there is a V-shaped depression, then what appears to be a second, taller peak behind the first. All three tombs appear to have been found on this second, taller, mound of Structure II. Workmen were actively excavating one of the tombs last week, and Carrasco apparently reported (through the INAH guards) that he believes it to be that of the ruler who commissioned the construction of Structure II. So far, they have pulled 119 jade pieces from the tomb, as well as a number of poly-chromes that are currently being safeguarded in Campeche.

Santiago and I had plenty to eat; we hosted the INAH guards and Simon for several meals, and gave drinks and sandwiches to everyone we met along the way. On the last day, we visited Xpujil, and I dropped Santiago off at the bus station there for his trip back to Chetumal and Guatemala.

It was a fine trip, and I thank you for your help in putting it together. I en-joyed talking with you in Campeche, and I look forward to seeing you again there someday soon.

Let me know if I can help you in your work from here in Washington.

Abrazos,
Jim Nations

5   🌿   *Guatemala*

Introduction

For the Guatemalan equivalent of US$20 per day, a team of crusty chicle gum harvesters from the settlement of Carmelita, Petén, will guide you on a five-day horse and mule trip through a tunnel in the rainforest to the ancient Maya city of El Mirador. Notwithstanding the beauty and mystery of the 1,700-year-old city, the trip alone is worth the expense. Riding north out of Carmelita after an early morning breakfast of beans, tortillas, and the meat of a terrier-sized rodent called a paca, you pass through progressively denser rainforest that seems to go on forever. Through the occasional gap in the forest canopy, you watch the sun burn away the clouds overhead. Half the time, you and your fellow adventurers guide your horses through a dense swamp-forest called a *bajo*, where orchids stretch down from gnarled logwood trees, and exposed roots stretch across the trail like booby traps.

Twisting limbo-like in your perch atop a feisty mule, you rotate around hanging lianas and the buttresses of enormous ficus trees, trying to keep from falling out of the creaking leather saddle. The mules slog down the narrow trail for a full day before you reach your first campsite, a small pond and clearing in the forest called El Tintal. Those who know their Maya history recognize the 60-foot mounds on both sides of the campsite as the ruins of an abandoned sister city to El Mirador.

Beside the shallow pond that marks the site of El Tintal, you sleep in hammocks strung from the roof of open-sided structures covered with a palm thatch roof. Tired from a full day's walk, you gratefully fall asleep to the cacophony of insect sounds and frog calls that passes for quiet in the tropical forest. If you are wise, you have rigged a mosquito net to cover your hammock. But even then, you are careful not to sleep with your elbows pressed up against the thin mesh of the net. Thirsty Petén mosquitoes will land on your skin and dine on your blood through the net itself, and you will awaken with elbows swollen to the size of baseballs.

Archaeologists mapping the monumental buildings of El Tintal during the 1990s uncovered buried caches of smoothly polished jade and carved stone stelae glorifying the elaborately dressed rulers of this ancient city. Some modern travelers report that the spirits of the past have not abandoned the ruins the archaeologists uncovered. On trip after trip, visitors who sleep at El Tintal discover over breakfast campfires that each person in the group has spent a disturbed night of weird dreams and imagined visitations. Some muleteers attribute these experiences to the decade-old suicide of a chicle gum harvester who, spurned by his betrothed, hung himself from a tree that stretches over the shallow water hole. They say his spirit wanders the surrounding forest at night, seeking assistance. Other travelers report dreams of dark-skinned people who stand in the shadows at a distance, murmuring an unrecognizable language.

Early the next morning, on the second day of travel toward El Mirador, the mounted guide leads your group through increasingly taller forest, past large stands of nut-bearing cohune palm trees, in and under and around tree trunks and hanging lianas in a combination of hiking and contortions that exercises you from chin to toe. At the head of the caravan, your *chiclero* guide, Chepe Krasborn, goads his horse on with intermittent yelps and curses. Krasborn is a native of the Petén forest and has spent all of his 55 years here, bleeding chicle trees to export the valuable latex to chewing gum manufacturers in Europe and Japan. He knows the Petén forest as well as any man alive, with the possible exception of Luis Morales, who rides at the rear of the caravan, pulling on a rope that ties together three pack mules with the expedition's food, water, and camping gear. Also a lifelong resident of the Petén, Morales—at 60 years still a strong and vigorous man—has covered every square kilometer of Guatemala's tropical forest, working as a *chiclero*, allspice harvester, and, today, as your guide to the stone ruins of El Mirador.

Toward the end of the day, as dried leaves crunch underfoot along the trail, the group begins to notice tall mounds on the left and right. Krasborn points out a 60-centimeter-wide (2-foot) hole that drops straight into the ground on the side of the path—"A chultun," he says, "an ancient water cistern." Soon, the outlines of jumbled stone walls appear here and there just off the trail in the forest.

Within an hour, you emerge into a clearing to find a crude building made of rough-hewn boards and a corrugated zinc roof. This is the guardhouse of Guatemala's Instituto de Antropología e Historia (IDAEH), and the three guards who live here protect the site of El Mirador from grave robbers and looters. Your fellow travelers collapse into hammocks strung inside the house, and as their energy slowly returns, begin to ask questions of the bemused park guards. "How old is Mirador? Where did the Maya get their water? Why did the civilization collapse?"

After a long night of talk and, later, sound sleep, you arise early the next morning to the calls of a dozen species of tropical birds and the raucous, yelling growls of a troop of howler monkeys in the distance. Refueled with a breakfast of rice, refried beans, and black coffee with sugar, you follow the guards down the trail through a maze of earthen mounds and eroded stone walls into the city of El Mirador. A steep 10-minute climb brings you to the top of the tallest temple mound, and as you reach the cleared area above the forest canopy, a refreshing breeze cools the sweat that beads on your forehead.

Standing above the tropical forest that covers the Preclassic city of El Mirador, you find it difficult to envision what the city must have looked like in its glory, in AD 100. Today, the forest hides enormous mounds of earth—the eroded temples of what was once the largest city in the Maya world. Only atop the tallest of the mounds—the pyramids called Danta (Tapir), Tigre (Jaguar), or Monos (Spider Monkeys)—looking out over an ocean of tropical forest, do you see the other temples poking their heads through the canopy and get a sense of the absolute size of the city.

From your high perch on Danta Pyramid, you can watch the sun rise on the Maya Tropical Forest that radiates out from the mound in all directions, as far as the eye can see. Yet beneath the green waves of this forest canopy lie the bones and stones and distant dreams of a city that flourished for more than three centuries: traders hawking cotton cloth and fine-slipped pottery from the open-walled stalls of the marketplace, priests in wooden masks and macaw feathers chanting whispered prayers to a pantheon of gods, hunters straggling in from the edge of the forest with red brocket deer thrown over their shoulders. Once home to 40,000 Maya women, children, and men, El Mirador was abandoned 1,800 years ago to the eager regeneration of the rainforest.

Today, as the sun rises, El Mirador is mute. Only the distant roar of a howler monkey and the gliding circles of an orange-breasted falcon overhead remind you that El Mirador is still a place of life.

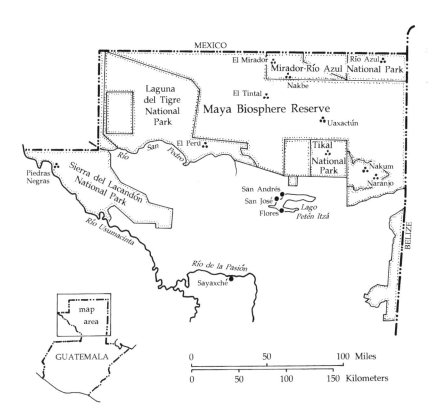

MAP 5. Petén, Guatemala

The Maya Tropical Forest in Guatemala

The Maya city of El Mirador lies in the heart of the Maya Tropical Forest, inside El Mirador National Park, which, in turn, is part of Guatemala's
Maya Biosphere Reserve. The Maya Biosphere Reserve, at 1.6 million hectares (16,000 sq. km.; 178 sq. mi.) is the keystone of the protected areas
of the Maya Tropical Forest and the largest protected area in Central
America. The reserve takes up the northern 44 percent of Guatemala's
Department of Petén, Guatemala's largest department, covering 36,000
square kilometers (13,900 sq. mi.)—as anthropologist Norman Schwartz
points out, a territory about the size of New Jersey and larger than the
Netherlands (Schwartz 1990:10).

For the thousand years between the time of the Maya collapse—
around AD 900—and the twenty-first century, almost all of the Petén was

covered by lowland tropical forest. Today, the forest covers the sawlike mountains—the Sierra del Lacandón—that parallel the Río Usumacinta in the western Petén, then dips into the boggy wetlands of Laguna del Tigre National Park in the extreme northwestern corner of the Petén, then sweeps southeastward across the mountainless plain of northern and northeastern Petén to reach across the international border into Belize.

Still, much of the forest we think of as virgin tropical forest in the Petén is, in fact, secondary vegetation—forest that sprouted in the abandoned agricultural fields of the ancient Maya and which was later intermittently dotted with the slash-and-burn plots of semi-nomadic farmers like the Lacandón Maya and Itza. These Postclassic era populations had so little effect on the forest that most of the Department of Petén has been covered with mature forest vegetation for more than a thousand years. Even a botanist would have trouble distinguishing which parts of this forest are original, primary vegetation, and which are thousand-year-old regrowth.

During the Postclassic era, the Itza Maya and related Yucatec-speaking groups occupied the Lake Petén Itzá region, and Chol- and Yucatec-speaking Lacandón Maya lived in the southern Petén until the seventeenth century and western Petén until the early twentieth century. The area was sparsely inhabited until the late 1960s.

During the nineteenth century, logging operations and a few cattle ranches brought income to some Spanish-speaking families who moved into the Petén, but only with the onset of the tapping and export of chicle latex did the Petén forest begin to yield solid income to more than a few hundred families. Chicle gum harvesting was the major source of income for Peteneros, as the region's inhabitants came to be called, from the 1870s through the late 1940s, when synthetic chewing gum base became the norm in North American chewing gum manufacturing. Nonetheless, the human population of the Petén in 1950 was only 15,880 children, women, and men (SEGEPLAN 1993:62).

Anthropologist Norman Schwartz points out that until 1970, 70 to 80 percent of the Petén remained densely forested. Since then, he notes, the Petén has been transformed from "an isolated, relatively peaceful hinterland" into "an increasingly well-populated, turbulent new frontier attracting landless campesinos from crowded Guatemalan highlands and Pacific coastal regions, well-capitalized cattle raisers, foreign and national logging companies, bureaucrats, revolutionaries, and foreign entrepreneurs eager to exploit forest resources, including oil" (Schwartz 1990:11).

Since the 1970s, waves of colonizing farm families from other departments of Guatemala—especially Baja Verapaz and Alta Verapaz and the drier departments of southeastern Guatemala—have poured into the Petén in search of farmland. These families have developed a culture of deforestation, corn farming, and cattle ranching that is transforming the thousand-year-old forest into a mosaic of fragmented patches, abandoned pasture, and agricultural clearings. Between 1960 and 1986, the department's human population skyrocketed from 26,000 to 300,000, "an increase," as Schwartz points out, "of over 1,000 percent in 25 years" (Schwartz 1990:257). By 1998 the population of the Petén was estimated at 500,000 people (Fort and Grandia 1999). By the beginning of the twenty-first century, officials were placing the department's population at 600,000. Unofficial, and probably more accurate, estimates reach 700,000-plus inhabitants in the Petén.

In 2003 and 2004, officials working under programs financed by the Inter-American Development Bank and World Bank mapped and legalized landholdings that Q'eqchi' families had colonized and cleared for farming. Ladino cattle ranchers moved in behind the legalization teams and, with government land survey maps in hand, began to buy up the newly deeded plots from the Maya families. The Q'eqchi' accepted the cash and moved farther north to clear new forest plots inside the Maya Biosphere Reserve (Liza Grandia, University of California–Berkeley, personal communication, January 2005).

It seems clear that the only climax forest that will last long into the twenty-first century in the Petén will be that protected in the region's national parks, biosphere reserves, and biotopes, and a few remnants on inaccessible cliffs and hilltops. Nonetheless, the forest that remains is large and impressive. The Petén's protected areas surround hundreds of ancient Maya cities, the most important of which are discussed later in this chapter. Before describing them, however, we should look at the people who currently live in this region of the Maya Tropical Forest.

Modern Peoples in the Guatemalan Petén

The majority of the inhabitants of the Department of Petén today are Spanish-speaking Ladinos from southern Guatemala, primarily from the dry southeastern region of the country. Second in number are the Q'eqchi' Maya, immigrants from the Department of Alta Verapaz. Approximately 25,000 Spanish-speaking Peteneros live in the area, many of them descendants of the original Spanish settlers in the Petén or of Mexican families who fled to the wilds of northern Guatemala during the nineteenth and early twentieth centuries.

Least numerous of all are the region's only original indigenous inhabitants, the Itza Maya. All other Maya groups in the area—the most numerous are the Q'eqchi'—are recent immigrants.

THE ITZA MAYA

Speakers of a dialect of Yucatec Maya, the Itza Maya have lived in the Department of Petén for at least 700 years. Before the Spanish conquest, in the sixteenth century, they shared the Petén with Chol-speaking Lacandón and Acala Maya, who lived south of the Itza in the region of the Río de la Pasión. These groups were exterminated by Spanish warfare and disease in the seventeenth century. Yucatec-speaking Lacandón lived along the Río Usumacinta and Río de la Pasión until the late 1940s, when they moved across the Usumacinta into Chiapas to join other Lacandón families already there. The Itza, then, are the only autochthonous group of the 600,000–700,000 current inhabitants of the Petén. Many of the 2,800 inhabitants of the town of San José, Petén, on the northwestern shore of Lake Petén Itzá, are descended from the Itza, but only 100 or so still speak the Itza language, and only half of those speak it fluently (Hofling 1996:109).

The ancestors of the Itza were likely the Chontal-speaking Putun Maya, who inhabited the Laguna de los Términos region of what is today the state of Tabasco, Mexico. During the Classic Maya era, the Putun served as intermediaries in trade between the Maya and the Nahuat-speaking states of the Valley of Mexico. From their communities in the river and wetland area at the western base of Yucatán, the Putunes sent canoes deep into the Maya forest, down tributaries of the Río Usumacinta to trade in such cities as Ceibal, Altar de Sacrificios, Yaxchilán, El Perú/Waka', and Piedras Negras. They also sent seagoing canoes around the coast of Yucatán to sites along the Caribbean coast. J. Eric S. Thompson called them "the Phoenicians of the New World" (Thompson 1970:7). Because Putun traders spoke both Nahuat and Yucatec, as well as their original Chontal Maya, they likely served as sources of information for both groups. (Modern Lacandón Maya of Chiapas still disdain other Maya languages as *putun t'an*, "garbled language.")

At the end of the Classic era, Putun Maya began to occupy territory in the Yucatán Peninsula. By AD 900, they had taken over the city of

Chichén Itzá. (*chi* = mouth; *chen* = well; thus, Mouth of the Well of the Itza, a reference to the Great Cenote at Chichén Itzá). A century later, however, a rival Itza group had developed in the competing city of Mayapán. This rival group eventually took over Chichén Itzá, and the Itza of Chichén abandoned their city to flee southward. According to oral tradition, they straggled through the forest to a large lake and settled on an island. The island became known as Peten Itza (*Peten* = island; thus, "the island of the Itza," a place known today as Flores, Petén, Guatemala). Grant D. Jones's book, *The Conquest of the Last Maya Kingdom* (1998), is the definitive book on the history of the Itza Maya.

With the Spanish invasion of the Maya world in the sixteenth century, the Itza population underwent the same collapse experienced by indigenous populations elsewhere in Middle America. Many Itza died of introduced diseases, such as pulmonary plague and yellow fever. Nonetheless, around 100,000 Itza still lived in the area around Lake Petén Itzá when Hernán Cortés happened upon them in 1525. Cortés was on his way from Mexico City to Nito, Honduras, to subdue a rebellious Spanish captain. He landed his ships near Coatzacoalcos, Mexico, and traveled overland through modern Tabasco and Petén with hundreds of Spanish soldiers and Chontal Indian bearers. (It was on this trip that Cortés beheaded and hung the last Aztec emperor, Cuahtemoc, and Tetlepanquetzal, Lord of Tlacopan, whom he had brought along as hostages from the already conquered city of Tenochtitlán, later to become Mexico City. He accused Cuahtemoc and Tetlepanquetzal of plotting against him [Pagden 1986:367; Morley and Brainerd 1956:115]).

Cortés arrived at Nohpeten, or Taj Itza, as the Itza variously called the island, and visited the king, Ajaw Kan Ek' It was during this visit that Cortés left his lame horse, Morcillo, with the Itza, promising to retrieve him on his return trip (see Chapter 2). But Cortés continued on his way south and returned to Mexico by sea. The Itza were left alone for another century.

In the early seventeenth century, Spanish Franciscan friars began to visit the Itza, hoping to convert them to Catholicism. But, as Philip Ainsworth Means points out in his 1917 history, this was "a more or less desultory evangelical affair, and no real vigor was injected into [the conquest of the Itza] until a commercial motive (the building of the Yucatán-Guatemala road) was introduced" (Means 1917:58).

The Itza were finally conquered by firearms-bearing Spaniards on March 13, 1697, making Nohpeten the last Maya city to fall during the Spanish conquest (G. Jones 1998:295 ff.). After this battle, the surviving Itza fled into the forest. Gradually, they returned to the northern shore of

Lake Petén Itzá, where they settled in the town that became today's San José. Today, the town continues to serve as the center of the surviving Itza people and culture.

During the 1930s dictatorship of Guatemalan president Jorge Ubico, the governor of the Petén prohibited the Itza from speaking their native language, an edict that schoolteachers enforced with corporal punishment (Hofling 1996:111). But the language survived within individual households, and in 1991 the Itza began a revitalization movement that today seeks to preserve the Itza language and forest-based tradition. Men such as Julian Tesucun Q'ixchan have begun teaching Itza Maya to elementary school children in San José.

In 1991 Reginaldo Chayax Huex, Feliciano Tzul Colli, and other Itzas obtained a 50-year lease from the Guatemalan government for 36 square kilometers (14 sq. mi.) of tropical forest north of San José, immediately south of the Biotopo El Zotz, one of the core zones of the Maya Biosphere Reserve. Called the Bio-Itza, the reserve is located in the buffer zone of the biosphere reserve, on property that belongs to the municipality of San José, some 24 kilometers (14 miles) north of the town center. Physical limits for the reserve were established in 1993. Within the Bio-Itza, the Itza community works to keep alive traditional agroforestry techniques and to reforest the area to preserve their traditional connection to the tropical forest (Atran 1993a; Chayax et al. 1998). Aided by Conservation International, The Nature Conservancy, the Centro Agronómico Tropical de Investigación y Enseñanza (CATIE), Cultural Survival, Eco-Logic, the Global Environmental Facility, and Scott Atran of the University of Michigan, the Bio-Itza committee has hired guards and constructed two rustic dormitories and a kitchen for ecotourists.

The reserve's success in conserving a small piece of the Itza's traditional tropical forest home is obvious from a 2003 satellite image of the Petén region. The Bio-Itza stands out as a square block of green vegetation pegged onto the southern border of the Maya Biosphere Reserve, like a comma accenting the reserve's survival.

〰️ The Lacandón Maya in Guatemala

Although the Itza Maya are the only surviving inhabitants of the early populations of the Petén, they once shared the territory with their Lacandón Maya cousins, now better known for their settlements across the Río Usumacinta in the Selva Lacandona of Chiapas (see Chapter 4). Historical sources indicate that the Lacandón Maya moved into Chiapas from the Petén during the late eighteenth and early nineteenth centuries, although some families remained in Guatemala until the late nineteenth century (Nations and Nigh 1980).

In 1862 the Archbishop of Guatemala charged the Capuchino friars of Antigua, Guatemala, with the state of the souls of the people of the Petén, including the little-known Lacandones. The government of Flores, Petén—at that time a town of 2,000—had maintained some contact with the Lacandones since 1837, when a government official visited them and designated Bor Menché, one of their leaders, the governor of all Lacandones. Unlike the government, the church had paid no attention to the Lacandones at all.

To remedy this situation, in 1862, three Capuchino friars traveled from Antigua to Flores—at that time a trip of three weeks—and on to Sac Luc, later called La Libertad. At the end of March, they traveled several months by canoe on the Río de la Pasión, Río Chixoy, Río Lacantún, and Río Usumacinta.

Fray Lorenzo de Mataró wrote an account of the trip when the group returned to Antigua in September 1863. The following year, he returned to the area and during four months baptized 674 people and confirmed 244 marriages. Lorenzo's efforts were apparently better received by the church hierarchy than by the Lacandones themselves. Twenty-five years after the friar's trip, when the German explorer Karl Sapper passed through the area, he reported that "just to mention the word Capuchino was enough to make the Lacandones turn and run" (de Vos 1988a:73–74).

During the nineteenth century and first half of the twentieth century, families of Lacandón Maya continued to live in the forested region that is today the Sierra del Lacandón National Park. With its lakes and forested hills, the region is a mirror image of the northern Selva Lacandona, of Chiapas, Mexico, where 600 Lacandones live today. The Selva Lacandona and Sierra del Lacandón are, after all, the east and west halves of the watershed of the Río Usumacinta, and it is no surprise that Lacandones felt comfortable moving back and forth across the river they know as Shoklah, for the large, tasty snook (*Centropomus undecimalis*) that swim in its waters.

Both the archaeological and historical records document the presence of Lacandones in the Guatemalan Petén from the earliest records to the twentieth century. Archaeologist Joel Palka conducted a survey of late-nineteenth-century Lacandón Maya settlement sites in the Pasión River Basin during the 1990s, identifying centuries-old settlements through clusters of large mango trees and Lacandón artifacts (Palka and López Olivares 1992; Palka 1996). Guatemalan archives from the decades 1840–1890 indicate that

Lacandones in the western Petén traded honey, wax, tree gums (probably copal incense and natural rubber), cacao, and tobacco with Ladinos from La Libertad, Petén, and Tabasco, Mexico (Schwartz 1990:115).

According to Guillermo López Carrazcosa, a resident of Carmelita, Petén, many of the Lacandones who remained in the Petén forest during the early twentieth century crossed the Río Usumacinta into Chiapas for good in 1944. López told me in 1989 that 60 Lacandón families had lived near Laguna Lacandón, inside today's Sierra del Lacandón National Park, until 1944, including a "100-plus"-year-old leader named Santo Domingo.

Also in 1989, I talked about Guatemalan Lacandones with a Petenero at a rural store in a settlement called Kilometro 107, on the road from La Libertad, Petén, to the town of El Naranjo, a road that parallels the eastern border of Sierra del Lacandón National Park. He told me that he and his wife lived near Laguna Lacandón, in Sierra del Lacandón, for three years in the late 1950s, working with an oil exploration company. When they left the region in 1959, he said, the area was still home to five Lacandón Maya—three women, two of them named María and Amalia, and two men, named Ramón and Domingo. Their settlement was called Makabilero/El Desempeño.

There is no doubt that Lacandón Maya families lived in the Sierra del Lacandón even before they lived in Chiapas, but other sources make clear that these particular five Lacandones had, in fact, moved into Guatemala from Chiapas. They show up in Baer and Merrifield's oral history of the Lacandón Maya (1971:91). In the early twentieth century, a group of northern Lacandones living in Chiapas moved across the Usumacinta into Guatemala and remained at El Desempeño until the late 1970s, when the two surviving women crossed the river to move among the southern Lacandones of Lacanjá Chan Sayab, Chiapas. They probably did this because one of the women was a southern Lacandón who had lived among northerners at Santo Domingo, Chiapas.

At the same time, anthropologist Norman Schwartz reports that "in 1960, there was one Lacandón family, residing in San Benito, left in Petén" (1990:318).

THE Q'EQCHI'

The most numerous indigenous people in the Petén today are the Q'eqchi' Maya, with 93,000 individuals, despite the fact that they are not original inhabitants of northern Guatemala. The Q'eqchi' homeland is the Guatemalan department of Alta Verapaz, in the narrow neck of Guatemala, where the Department of Petén joins the body of the country. Numbering at least 852,000 people in 2002, Guatemala's Q'eqchi' are the fourth-largest of the 21 linguistically distinct Maya groups in the country, but they cover the most extensive territory (R. Wilson 1995:21; INE 2002). This is the result of the Q'eqchi's pattern of out-migration from their original homeland, due to a complex of factors ranging from historical oppression to high fertility rates.

The vast majority of Q'eqchi' are rural farmers who grow corn and other crops using slash-and-burn agricultural techniques. One of the consequences of this pattern is that many Q'eqchi' villages in Alta Verapaz have encountered a serious shortage of land. As well, many Q'eqchi' supplement their income by serving in labor pools for Ladino and German-Guatemalan landowners who produce coffee and cardamom for export. Finally, the Q'eqchi' population grew rapidly during the twentieth century.

To escape this combination of degraded lands, colonial-like servitude, and population growth, many Q'eqchi' families have immigrated "to the vast areas of virgin forest in the north of the department and in the Petén and Belize" (R. Wilson 1995:38). The violence of Guatemala's civil war of the late twentieth century also pushed Q'eqchi' out of their original homeland and into forested areas of Belize and Guatemala. During the early 1980s, government forces destroyed approximately 100 Q'eqchi' villages in Alta Verapaz. Denounced as guerrillas, many Q'eqchi' were singled out for torture and murder; in some places, entire villages were burned and their inhabitants killed, leaving survivors to flee into the forest (R. Wilson 1995:219).

Pushed and pulled by these various factors, thousands of Q'eqchi' Maya families moved out of their original homelands in the Department of Alta Verapaz into the Department of Petén. During the 1980s, they began to settle in the tropical forest area that would become—in 1990—the Maya Biosphere Reserve. Even after the reserve was created, Q'eqchi' families continued to migrate into the forest, and hundreds of families illegally colonized the core areas of the biosphere reserve.

In the lowland forest of the Petén, traditional agricultural techniques that formerly served the Q'eqchi' in Alta Verapaz have evolved into destructive practices of deforestation. The Q'eqchi's production of chilies and corn for sale as cash crops degrades the land they clear and pushes families to continually expand into new forest areas, aiming the families toward a future that serves neither them nor the sustainable use of biological resources.

Anyone determined to point to a villain in this process would have to look back 100 years to the social and political movements that established Alta Verapaz as one of Guatemala's premier coffee production areas. During the last quarter of the nineteenth century, the central government of Guatemala declared almost half a million hectares (5,000 sq. km.; 1,930 sq. mi.) of Q'eqchi' homeland as "empty lands," thus allowing foreign, mostly German, entrepreneurs to create a coffee export empire based on Q'eqchi' land and labor (R. Wilson 1995:35). By the end of the 1870s, "there was no untitled land left in Alta Verapaz," and by 1885, two-thirds of the commerce in Alta Verapaz was in the hands of German coffee magnates (R. Wilson 1995:36).

Ethnographer Richard Wilson cites an 1867 letter to the president of Guatemala from the inhabitants of a Q'eqchi' community: "After having had our houses and farms, which are the fruit of our labor, taken away from us . . . the Commissioner of Panzos has forced us to plant coffee in the mountains where we grow corn. This appears to be nothing more than an attempt to exterminate us" (R. Wilson 1995:36).

It is unlikely that extermination was the goal of the coffee producers—they needed Q'eqchi' labor on their *fincas*—and the Q'eqchi' population continued to grow during the nineteenth century and into the twentieth. As Wilson indicates, citing anthropologist Richard Adams (1965), expanding coffee production created strong pressure on the Q'eqchi' to find land for food production. This pressure was ameliorated by their migration into the tropical forest of northern Petén and southern Belize.

This expansion into virgin territory continues today, fueled by the export production and population growth of the Q'eqchi', rather than by expulsion from their home territory. The population growth that pushes the Q'eqchi' and other families into tropical forests results from the high value placed on children in an agrarian economy, the lack of access to health care and contraceptives, and old-fashioned machismo that denigrates the right of women to make their own decisions about the number of children they bear. The average number of children per woman in the Petén is 7.1, one of the highest rates in Latin America (Grandia 1998).

PETENEROS

After Spanish soldiers conquered the Itza Maya on the island of Nohpeten/Flores in 1697, the surviving Itza fled into the forest and only gradually returned to claim their lands along the shore of Lake Petén Itzá.

The Spaniards, in the meantime, garrisoned 80 soldiers "and several Maya-speaking mestizo families from Yucatán and Guatemala" on the island to control the conquered region. These soldiers were later joined by other military families from Campeche and Yucatán and by 14 Spanish families, most likely from Antigua, Guatemala (Schwartz 1990:50–51).

By the beginning of the eighteenth century, the Petén was lightly populated with the descendants of these original settlers and others who joined them later. They created a mixture of Spaniards, creoles (Spaniards born in the New World), Itza Maya, Lacandón Maya, Indians and Blacks from Belize, and Indians and non-Indians from Yucatán. The Spaniards tended to marry only other Spaniards in order to maintain ethnic "purity" and a self-perceived social superiority, but by the end of the eighteenth century the various groups had intermarried sufficiently to create a population of Spanish-speaking Ladinos who would gradually come to be known as "Peteneros," people of the Petén.

Although most of the people of the Petén supported themselves through subsistence (milpa) agriculture, the primary land-based commercial activity was cattle raising, chiefly on the natural savannas of the central Petén. The farmers and cattle raisers were supplied, though, by "merchants who sold cloth, soap, wax, candles, sweets, and tobacco to the garrison; made profitable loans to the soldiers, acted as cattle dealers, and sold contraband sugarcane liquor (*aguardiente*) to the Indians from whom they purchased the cane" (Schwartz 1990:54). As late as 1778, however, the entire population of the Petén, including several hundred Lacandones hidden in the western forest, numbered only 3,000 individuals, three-quarters of whom were Indians (Schwartz 1990:53). The population of the region would not double to 6,000 for another 115 years.

The Petén's colonial era Indian majority was forced to perform free labor for their Spanish landlords and to plant and harvest grain and sugarcane in addition to their traditional Maya crops. Through the decades of the colonial period, though, Indian and Spanish cultural traits gradually blended together to create a truly Petenero culture. As Schwartz points out, "Indians learned how to handle livestock and to build Spanish-style structures, and the Spanish learned to live in Maya-style houses." Still, he continues, "Although Spaniards and Indians learned from each other, it is, of course, important to recall that most forms of production and their associated social relations were imposed upon the Indians by the Spanish" (1990:72).

As the colonial period plodded toward Guatemala's eventual independence from Spain in 1821, and well into the nineteenth century, the people of the Petén likewise plodded along economically by planting corn, sugarcane, and tobacco, raising cattle, and harvesting natural rubber and hardwood timber from the forest. It was not until the 1890s that a product appeared to change the economic landscape. This product was chicle gum, the latex of the inner bark of the *chicozapote* tree (*Manilkara zapota*). Chicle is harvested from wild trees dispersed in the forest. For almost 100 years, from 1890 until 1970, the Petén would be dominated by the extraction and export of chicle gum for use as the base in chewing gum.

Then, as now, chicle harvesters—*chicleros*—entered the forest in groups but worked as individuals. They climbed the *chicozapote* trees using ropes and metal spikes tied onto their boots, and cut herringbone hatch marks into the bark of the tree to drain three or four pounds of chicle latex from each tree into a paraffin-coated cotton bag hung on a peg at the tree's base. Back in camp, the *chiclero* boiled most of the moisture from the latex collected in a large, wok-like metal pot, then molded the hot substance into 10-kilogram (22 pound) blocks of chicle gum for export.

While chicle harvesting proved to be an important source of wages for Peteneros, most of the profits went to foreign—first U.S., later Japanese—corporations and the economic elite of the Petén, who contracted the harvesters and controlled exports and prices. Still, the chicle industry created an archetype for the Petén—the independent, rowdy, and forest-savvy *chiclero*—much the way the American West produced the archetype of the cowboy, who persists in the western mind today. In the mind of outsiders, and in that of many Guatemalans, a Petenero is still a tough, independent Spanish speaker who is wise in the ways of the Maya Tropical Forest.

Protected Areas

THE MAYA BIOSPHERE RESERVE

In 1987 the government of Germany offered to help Guatemalan president Vinicio Cerezo asphalt the only road connecting southern Guatemala with the Department of Petén, the country's northernmost department and, covering one-third of the nation, Guatemala's largest. Guatemala's first democratically elected president since 1954, Cerezo was also ecologically conscious. He was inclined to accept the Germans' offer but also concerned about the potential negative consequences the road improvement carried for the forest in the Petén. As a result, he turned to the recently established

Comisión Nacional del Medio Ambiente (CONAMA), headed by architect Jorge Cabrera, for a plan to protect the department's forest resources. Cerezo gave Cabrera 90 days to produce a technical study to conserve the ecosystems of the Petén, and Cabrera set to work, joined by a small team of Guatemalan and international conservationists, myself among them.

Plans to asphalt the road faltered during 1989, however, because the German Green Party began to question the wisdom of improving a road into a Central American tropical forest. Public opinion had also been focused on the Petén's tropical forest by a special issue of *National Geographic*, in which editor Wilbur Garrett proposed the creation of a multinational tourist network called the Ruta Maya (Garrett 1989). The publication galvanized the energy of conservationists and the tourism industry around a plan that would bring economic development to the Petén by conserving its tropical forests, traditional cultures, and archaeological history (Ponciano 1998:99).

Cabrera's 90 days to create a plan for protecting the natural ecosystems of the Petén gradually—and justifiably—expanded to a year, then to a second year of study, mapping, and planning. By mid-1989, the technical study team had hiked, walked, flown over, canoed, and ridden horses and mules over the entire northern reaches of the Petén. The technical study the group produced (Nations 1989) was delivered in late 1989 to Guatemala's Consejo Nacional de Areas Protegidas (CONAP), headed at that time by Andreas Lehnhoff. CONAP was created in 1989 as a subagency of CONAMA to manage Guatemala's emerging protected areas systems. (CONAP was absorbed into a newly created Ministerio de Ambiente y Recursos Naturales, Ministry of Environment and Natural Resources, at the beginning of the twenty-first century.) CONAP oversaw the transformation of the technical study into a proposed law for passage by the Guatemalan National Congress and signing by the president. A half-dozen Guatemalan conservationists, led by Cabrera, Lehnhoff, Santiago Billy, and Ismael Ponciano, lobbied the bill through the Guatemalan Congress, and in January 1990 the Congress passed Ley 5-90, creating the 1.6 million hectare (6,178 sq. mi.) Maya Biosphere Reserve, the largest protected area in Central America.

On the day the law passed, at a celebration party in Antigua, Guatemala, I reminded my fellow study team members that "the easy part" was over, and that the real work of creating the reserve on the ground, and protecting it, had just begun.

The Maya Biosphere Reserve has seven core areas, including four national parks and three wildlife reserves (called biotopes), that add up to

800,000 hectares (3,089 sq. mi.) of protected wildlands, as well as an 800,000-hectare (3,089 sq. mi.) multiple-use zone designed for the sustainable extraction of forest products, such as timber, *xate* palms, chicle gum, and allspice. By law, the national parks and wildlife reserves are intended to be free of human communities, reserved instead for biodiversity protection, tourism, and scientific research. In reality, 20,000 people live inside the reserve's nuclear zones, although much of the zones' biological diversity remains unaffected (Grunberg and Ramos 1998:8).

The Sierra del Lacandón National Park is characterized by a jagged mountain ridge (*sierra,* Spanish for "saw") that runs parallel to the Río Usumacinta for approximately 65 kilometers (40 miles), bordered on two sides by tropical savannas and lakes. The park is home to jaguars, harpy eagles, tapirs, a large population of howler monkeys, and until 1996 around 500 members of the Guatemalan Revolutionary Front, which conducted periodic firefights with the Guatemalan Army. The existence of these guerrilla fighters was one of the factors that prevented the Sierra del Lacandón National Park from being illegally deforested by colonizing farm families during the years of Guatemala's internal conflict. No campesino wanted to be encountered in the forested wilderness of Sierra del Lacandón by either the Guatemalan Army or the guerrillas, either of which would have been inclined to shoot first and ask questions later. Since the 1996 Peace Accords were signed, large sections of the Sierra del Lacandón National Park have been illegally colonized and deforested, especially in the extreme south and extreme northern portions of the park.

Sierra del Lacandón National Park has several outstanding features found nowhere else in the Maya Biosphere Reserve. The broken karst topography creates a series of cenotes in the southern reaches of the park— large sinkholes where the limestone floor has given way, leaving a gaping hole that exposes the water table below. Pozo Maya, also known as Juleki and the Abismo de Santiago, is one such place. We visited the site in June 1989 by stopping at a small settlement of 60 people called Los Esclavos, at kilometer 65 (39 miles) on the road from La Libertad to El Naranjo. Guided by a local immigrant farmer named Odilio, a team including botanist Juan José Castillo, Santiago Billy, and me traveled from Los Esclavos to Pozo Maya through what would later become Sierra del Lacandón National Park.

We drove as far as our four-wheel-drive Suzuki would take us on a muddy logging road, then hiked several more kilometers through tall forest to the edge of an enormous cenote. There, in the middle of the forest, we saw that the ground suddenly drops away into a limestone-sided hole that falls 150 meters (495 feet) directly downward. At the bottom of this cenote, deep green water mirrors the tropical forest above. Odilio told us that we were the first foreigners to visit the spot and that no one had ever climbed down to the water. Doing so would require serious rock climbing skills, but it would definitely be a manageable challenge for a professional climbing team.

The following day, Odilio put together a team of four guides and bearers from the settlement to take Juan José, Santiago, and me to Laguna Mendoza, three hours of hard hiking from Los Esclavos to the southwest. We carried a pair of two-man inflatable boats that we would later use to row out to the islands that our Instituto Geográfico Nacional topographic maps indicated as lying in the middle of Laguna Mendoza. Our goal was to evaluate the area for conservation potential and to explore the islands for Maya ruins.

Laguna Mendoza lies at the southernmost portion of Sierra del Lacandón National Park. Today, the area is surrounded by logging roads, colonists, and cattle ranches. In the late 1980s, it was still a wilderness filled with animals unaccustomed to human visitors. Waking up on an early morning on the shore of the lake, I wrote in my field book that "the voice of Laguna Mendoza is a howler monkey barking from the shore, the songs of a hundred birds, and the wind wrapping gently around the tropical forest that borders each island in the middle of the lake."

We used our small inflatable boats to row out to the islands, propelling the boats through the lake's clear water with crude paddles that Odilio had quickly hacked out of fallen trees with a machete. Eight of the nine islands we counted were completely overgrown with forest, with Spanish moss hanging over the water from tall trees along the islands' edge. We saw scarlet macaws, howler monkeys, and toucans and counted dozens of crocodiles floating like driftwood in the water.

We went ashore on the largest of the nine islands, having heard from our guides that it had served during the early 1980s as a hideout for the Guatemalan guerrilla forces that used Sierra del Lacandón as their base. Our guides told us that in 1982 Guatemalan Air Force jets had bombed the island, killing 300 guerrillas and family members and destroying the shelters the families had constructed beneath the island's forest canopy. We found the vegetation on the island regrowing in a tangled bloom of new growth, but the older trees were scorched from the flames of the attack. We found no bones or debris in the thick mat of vegetation.

Leaving Laguna Mendoza the next day, we hiked northwest into a seasonally inundated savanna that locals call Campo Verde. The area was total wilderness, with scores of spider and howler monkeys, guans, curassows, and deer. We came upon one group of 20 spider monkeys eating leaves and nuts in a ramon tree, but they were so unaccustomed to seeing humans and so unafraid of us that they continued eating nonchalantly as we took photos.

Even within the swampy areas of Campo Verde, we found traces of prehistoric Maya occupation. We saw a half-dozen unsacked house mounds in the middle of the low-lying *bajo* areas, yet another indication of a correlation between seasonally inundated swamp areas and Maya civilization.

After several nights in Campo Verde, we returned to the El Naranjo road and hiked northward to Laguna Guayacán, a lake that lies in the extreme northeastern corner of today's Sierra del Lacandón National Park. The lake appears on many maps as El Repasto, but *chicleros* and *xateros* who know the area call the entire area that surrounds the lake—the forest, lakes, and savanna—El Repasto and save the name Guayacán for the large lake that anchors this ecosystem. The lake itself is a kilometer across, surrounded on three sides by tall hills and on the northern shore by a huge swamp. This swamp, and the nearby seasonally inundated grassland called La Pita, are burned every year by hunters, who state that the fresh growth that results from the burn favors the tiny brocket deer they like to hunt there. El Repasto is also renowned among *xate* harvesters for the quantity and quality of *xate* that grows there, and by the natural beauty of the lake and abundance of wildlife.

Not far south of the lake, you can still make out the old airstrip cut in the 1950s by Esso when it was exploring for oil in the region. The company landed DC-3s on the gravel airstrip, which was partly recuperated in the 1980s for use as a clandestine guerrilla airstrip, where arms and food could be unloaded. Our guides told us that the pieces of aluminum wings scattered on the airstrip were the residue of an arms drop gone wrong. The guerrillas mistook their own supply plane for intruders and shot up the plane as it attempted to land.

The grassland swamps that surround Laguna Guayacán flood every September and lie under a foot of water until the end of November. During the subsequent dry season, hunters and *xate* collectors harvest crawfish from the grass and take them home to boil. The ground is also littered with mussels and the large apple snail (*Pomacea flagellata*), making it prime habitat for jabiru storks, the large white royal heron, and other waterfowl. From the surrounding hillsides, carpeted in tropical forest, visitors are constantly serenaded by the sound of howler monkeys. Sierra del Lacandón may, in fact, be one of Central America's best habitats for howler monkeys.

El Repasto is a three-edged ecotone; it includes a conjunction of grassland savanna with a lake-edge swamp characterized by *palo de tinte* (*Haematoxylum campechianum;* Spanish also = *palo de Campeche;* English = logwood; Lacandón Maya = *ek'*), a second marked by grassland savanna with oak forest, and oak forest with moist tropical forest. The large-leafed oak trees that grow intermittently in the grassland savanna called La Pita are *Quercus oleoides* (family Fagaceae), according to botanist Juan José Castillo Mont, now of the Universidad de San Carlos de Guatemala.

Years after the original expedition, Castillo Mont described the scene at La Pita and El Repasto as "a mirage." "That image of the landscape is difficult to forget," he wrote. "This vast, semi-inundated plain ending in a beautiful lake, Guayacán, and its dispersed clusters of *Acaelorraphe* gave the afternoon a sensation that could be confused with happiness and sadness at the same time. On the periphery and a little dispersed on the plain, the oaks and craboo trees (*Byrsonima crassifolia*) completed the beauty of the afternoon with those massive mountains known as the Sierra del Lacandón. Every time I think of the Sierra del Lacandón, I get nostalgic and worry that someday that scene will exist only in my imagination" (Juan José Castillo Mont, letter to the author, 2002).

In the extreme northwestern corner of the Maya Biosphere Reserve, bordered on two sides by Mexico, lies Laguna del Tigre National Park. At 3,400 square kilometers (1,312 sq. mi.)—larger than Yosemite National Park in California—the park creates the largest core zone in Central America and one of the largest protected areas in Central America. Laguna del Tigre occupies 20 percent of the Maya Biosphere Reserve. The park is a mixture of tropical forest and wetlands; it has probably 1,000 tropical lakes and a dozen rivers flowing through it. As the largest protected freshwater wetland in Central America, Laguna del Tigre warrants the term coined by Brian Houseal—the Pantanal of Mesoamerica—comparing it to the similar wetland region of Brazil.

Laguna del Tigre is Guatemala's largest Ramsar international wetland site and serves as a major flyway and wintering ground for migratory birds from the United States and Canada. (The 1971 Ramsar Convention on Wetlands of International Importance is named for the city in Iran where the convention was formulated.) By mid-2003, however, Ramsar officials were debating whether or not to remove Laguna del Tigre National Park from the Ramsar system, because of the large number of illegal migrants who had moved into the park to farm.

The Laguna del Tigre National Park is threatened by agricultural colonization in the south, by timber poaching from Mexico on the west and north, and by oil exploitation. In 1994, supported by funding from the World Bank's International Finance Corporation, a French-sponsored oil company called Basic Resources, Ltd.—later owned by Union Pacific, Anadarko and Perenco—built a 127-kilometer (76-mile) oil pipeline and accompanying road from inside the park to an oil refinery in La Libertad, Petén, just outside the buffer zone of the Maya Biosphere Reserve. The pipeline road introduced a new penetration route into the national park and biosphere reserve, bringing the threat of additional colonization and destruction (Bowles et al. 1999). Today, the colonists' settlements are like giant sponges, soaking up a widening circle of wildlife, fuelwood, and forest.

The one attempt by CONAP to relocate these illegal settlers on land outside the park ended in failure. In early March 1997, CONAP representatives reached an agreement with 40 of 700 families then occupying Laguna del Tigre to relocate their farms. However, the buses the families had boarded were halted while still inside the park by a campesino mob from other illegal settlements, who feared that they would be involuntarily relocated. The mob disarmed and held hostage a dozen Guatemalan policemen and demanded talks with CONAP. To obtain the release of the policemen, the governor of the Petén and the head of CONAP, Rodolfo Cardona, met with the campesinos, paid them several thousand dollars in cash "for food," and signed an agreement that they would not effect any relocations— voluntary or involuntary—from Laguna del Tigre (Hernández S. 1997a, 1997b). Several months later, government officials signed over the illegally seized lands to the invaders (Hernández S. 1997c). Many Guatemalan conservationists view this appeasement as the action that opened the national park to further illegal colonization, a process that continues today. By March 2001, there were 21 communities, with 3,800 people, living inside Laguna del Tigre National Park (Mancilla 2001).

Laguna del Tigre National Park also hosts, in its southeastern corner, Las Guacamayas Biological Station, dedicated to scientific research on the park's natural resources and wildlife (Billy 1999:35–38). The station began as a few tents pitched to house guards protecting the nests and young of the region's many scarlet macaws (*Ara macao*), but gradually developed into a formal research station.

Las Guacamayas Station also played a role in the tensions between conservation and illegal colonization. On March 31, 1997, urged on by the passive response of government officials to the hijacking of the buses moving the voluntarily relocating illegal colonists, a group of 60 armed men and 1 woman used the weapons seized from the policemen to invade and burn the thatch and pole structures of the Las Guacamayas Biological Research Station. The men took 13 Conservation International workers hostage and transported them downriver to the frontier town of El Naranjo. They sent a note to the office of Conservation International in Flores, Petén, demanding that the group cease defending the forest and allow new families to take over parkland for farms.

The late Carlos Soza Manzanero, then Conservation International's in-country director for Guatemala, played his cards brilliantly when he reported to the Petén authorities and the press—not the land-for-hostages demand—but a case of multiple kidnapping. When the hostage-takers (still holding the 13 Conservation International workers in a shed in El Naranjo) read the next day's newspapers, they saw themselves described as kidnappers rather than political leaders. Due to a spate of kidnappings of high-wealth individuals in Guatemala City during those months, convicted kidnappers in Guatemala were receiving mandatory sentences of 20 years to death.

In light of this news, the majority of the 60 hostage takers immediately abandoned town. The remaining leaders were left to sit down to explain their actions to Carlos Soza and a host of government authorities when they arrived in El Naranjo on April 2, two days after the mob had burned the station. The hostage-takers began their justification by stating that they were not kidnappers, that they had misunderstood Conservation International's goals in the national park, and that in addition to releasing the hostages, they would like to work with Conservation International to rebuild the biological station. Conservation International paid no ransom, met no demands, and went on to earn the respect of Guatemala's environment community by pressing formal charges against the five leaders of the attack—an action that few groups were willing to undertake during the late 1990s in Guatemala, due to the country's high level of violence and frequent vendettas.

During May 1997, Conservation International began reconstruction of the biological station (using brick and mortar) and initiated regular meetings with surrounding communities to create alliances where antagonism had existed. Today, Las Guacamayas Research Station is a full-blown tropical forest research site—with dormitories, showers, and an equipped laboratory—owned and operated by the Guatemalan conservation organization ProPetén. Subsequent to a 1999 Rapid Assessment Program expedition, Las Guacamayas took on international fame as an excellent site for scientific investigation (Bestelmeyer and Alonso 2000).

Las Guacamayas station also becomes an excellent sport-fishing site (catch and release only) in March, April, and May, when the Río San Pedro, on which the station is located, runs low and clear and the fish can see and attack fishing lures. By contrast, there is very little action in July and August, when the river is high, muddy, and filled with debris.

The large forested area of Laguna del Tigre National Park played a major role in the establishment of the Maya Biosphere Reserve. In the late 1980s, NASA remote sensing specialist Dr. Tom Sever produced a Landsat satellite image of the Río Usumacinta between Mexico and the Guatemalan Petén. The image clearly shows the political boundary of Guatemala, for the left side of the black and white image shows the almost totally deforested plains of the Mexican state of Tabasco, and the mostly deforested hills of the Selva Lacandona of Chiapas. Yet the straight, dark outline of the Petén is clearly visible, because of the vast expanse of forest still within the region, extending exactly up to the international frontier.

When Sever brought the image to Guatemala, Santiago Billy and I put it into the hands of Andrés Lehnhoff, then the executive secretary of CONAP. During an appointment with then-president Vinicio Cerezo in the Presidential Palace in Guatemala City a few days later, Lehnhoff rolled out the image on a table before the president. President Cerezo took a moment to figure out what the image illustrated, then exclaimed, "¡A la gran puchica!" a Guatemalan expression somewhat like "Son of a gun!" Realizing that Mexican deforestation had edged right up to the Guatemalan border and was already encroaching into the forest of the northwestern Petén, President Cerezo called to his assistant, "Get me the Mexican ambassador on the phone. We need to talk."

President Cerezo later shared the image with Mexican president Carlos Salinas in a binational meeting held in the Mexican town of Tapachula, Chiapas. Salinas acknowledged the implications of the image, but several officials traveling with him were so incredulous that so little tropical forest remained in Tabasco and Chiapas, Mexico, that they claimed the image must have been manipulated.

Several years later, during a meeting at his residence, former president Cerezo told Tom Sever and me that the image had been one of the primary elements that led him to push for the establishment of the 1.6-million hectare (16,000-km.; 6,178 sq. mi.) Maya Biosphere Reserve, of which Laguna del Tigre National Park, the forested area shown in Sever's satellite image, is a cornerstone.

Encroachment continues into Laguna del Tigre National Park. By summer 2001, the park had 13 communities inside it, with a total of 3,250 people. By May 2005, the number of illegal communities had grown to 20 (García 2005:4). Most are slash-and-burn farmers or cattle ranchers, activities that are not compatible with conservation of the area. Given that 68 percent of the population is under the age of 15, tensions over land use are likely to persist in the decades to come.

Between 1986 and 1990, fewer than 30 hectares (0.3 sq. km.; 0.12 sq. mi.) total of the park had been cleared, but invasions and deforestation increased between 1993–1995 to 805 hectares (8.05 sq. km.; 3.1 sq. mi.) per year. During 1995–1997, deforestation climbed to 1,626 hectares (16.26 sq. km.; 6.3 sq. mi.) per year (Sader, Coan, and Hayes 1998). Residents and neighboring Mexican communities also commonly poach wildlife, timber, and other forest products within the park's boundaries. By one estimate, 40 to 50 percent of Laguna del Tigre already may be lost for conservation use (García 2005:3).

The park has also become a major drop zone for the Colombian drug trade. During the 1990s, drug lords flew tons of Colombian cocaine from South America into clandestine airstrips in northern Mexico, where the drugs were off-loaded and secreted across the border in the United States. A renewed emphasis on drug interdiction slowed that trade, so drug traffickers flew the drugs from South America to northern Guatemala, specifically into the isolated reaches of Laguna del Tigre National Park. Pilots fly cocaine-filled planes from Colombia to the flat expanses of the park, land the planes, off-load the drugs for transport across the border into Mexico, then either abandon or torch the airplanes, leaving behind what one journalist called "an airplane graveyard" (Jordan 2004:A20).

The long, unguarded border of Laguna del Tigre also makes the park a major crossing point for migrants hiking into Mexico, headed to find work in the United States. In April 1999, a Guatemalan field biologist who worked for three weeks with Conservation International's Rapid Assessment Program research team in the extreme northwestern corner of Laguna del Tigre National Park reported that he saw an average of 60 people per day walking across the wetlands of Laguna del Tigre to cross the border into Mexico, including Nicaraguans, Salvadorans, Guatemalans, and even Chinese.

The story reminded me of a song we heard from a guide, Tomás Vargas, whom we employed in July 1989 on an expedition rowing up the Río Chocop in dugout *cayukos*. Sitting around a campfire on the riverbank after a hard day of rowing, Vargas spontaneously began to sing a slow, sad hymn in Spanish that used border crossings as a metaphor for entering Heaven.

> You won't need a visa
> when you enter into Heaven.
> The police along the way
> Will not steal the things you own.
> San Pedro will smile and welcome you
> As you walk through the sacred gates.
> You won't need a visa
> When you cross that sacred line.

In the extreme north of the Maya Biosphere Reserve, lying along the border of Mexico and Guatemala, is a complex of three large protected areas. The Mirador–Río Azul National Park protects major Maya archaeological sites and the drier tropical forest and the wildlife habitat that surrounds them. Separating the two blocks of land that form the Mirador–Río Azul National Park is the Biotopo Naachtún–Dos Lagunas, operated (like all Guatemalan biotopes) by the Centro de Estudios Conservacionistas (CECON) of the Universidad de San Carlos. The biotope covers 459 square kilometers (177 sq. mi.); Mirador and Río Azul combine to cover 1,010 square kilometers (390 sq. mi.). Together, the three-unit complex (sometimes collectively called La Danta) encompasses 1,470 square kilometers (570 sq. mi.) of undisturbed, moist, semi-deciduous tropical forest (Barrios 1995). On the ground, the entire block of forest is dotted with hundreds of Maya ruins, ranging from single house mounds to the major ruins of Mirador, Río Azul, La Muralla, El Kinal, Nakbe, Naachtún, and Zacatal.

Finally, in the south-central region of the Maya Biosphere Reserve lies the world-famous Tikal National Park, surrounding the Classic Maya site of Tikal, also a World Heritage Site and the focal point of most of the Petén's tourism. The site brings 200,000 national and international tourists to the Maya Biosphere Reserve each year. As a result, tourism is the single largest income producer for the Maya Biosphere Reserve, bringing in approximately US$35 million each year. (Tikal National Park is discussed again in the section on archaeology below.) Depending on the classification used, the forest of Tikal National Park is either subtropical moist (Holdridge et al. 1971) or tropical semi-deciduous (Pennington and Sarukhan 1968). Rainfall averages 1.3 to 1.5 meters (51–60 inches) per year. Like most of the Petén, the park experiences a marked dry season—February through May—although some rain will fall in almost every month. Ecologists Mark Schulze and David Whitacre conservatively estimate the number of tree species within Tikal National Park as 200 (Schulze and Whitacre 1999:174).

Attached to the southeastern edge of Tikal National Park is the 370 square kilometer (143 sq. mi.) Monumento Natural y Cultural Yaxjá-Nakum-Naranjo, which legally protects the forest resources and archaeological sites mentioned in the reserve's name (discussed below), as well as the two large, connected lakes known as Yaxjá and Sacnab.

In addition to the core areas that are national parks, the Maya Biosphere Reserve also has three wildlife reserves called biotopes. Two of these reserves lie alongside national parks. In the case of Biotopo Laguna del Tigre, the biotope is actually surrounded by Laguna del Tigre National Park. All three wildlife biotopes, and another in the reserve's buffer zone, are operated by Guatemala's Universidad de San Carlos, and all are areas dedicated to scientific research on tropical plants and animals. The already mentioned Naachtún–Dos Lagunas includes a rudimentary research station at the site called Dos Lagunas. The Biotopo Laguna del Tigre–Río Escondido is a 495 square kilometer (191 sq. mi.) block of wetland savannas and tropical forest with 300 lakes surrounded by the larger Laguna del Tigre National Park.

Like the other biotopes inside the Maya Biosphere Reserve, the Biotopo San Miguel La Palotada–El Zotz, with 495 square kilometers (191 sq. mi.), came into being in 1989 through Guatemalan congressional law (Decreto 4-89) to protect the lowland tropical forest that lies immediately west of Tikal National Park. These biotopes existed before the Maya Biosphere Reserve was declared and were surrounded by it as a result. The Biotopo El Zotz includes at least one large Maya ruin, called El Zotz, and several smaller sites. A graded road passes through the biotope, southwest to northeast, including a stop at the biotope's headquarters, maintained—as is the biotope itself—by the Centro de Estudios Conservacionistas (CECON) of the Universidad de San Carlos de Guatemala (Barrios 1995:83–84).

El Zotz has much of the wildlife associated with the slightly larger Tikal National Park, but human populations within the biotope and resulting illegal hunting hold down the number of easily visible animals. One exception is the cloud of bats, for which the site is named (*tzotz* is a Yucatec Maya name for bat). The bats fly in and out of caverns in a cliff near the CECON headquarters.

In the buffer zone of the Maya Biosphere Reserve, on the northern shore of Lake Petén Itzá, a small wildlife reserve of 7 square kilometers (2.7 sq. mi.), the Biotopo Cerro Cahuí, is dedicated to conservation of the ocellated turkey (*Agriocharis ocellata*) and its habitat.

Equal in size to the combined territory of the core areas of the Maya Biosphere Reserve is the reserve's multiple use zone, an 800,000-hectare (3,089 sq. mi.) expanse of tropical forest dedicated to the sustainable harvest of timber, *xate* palms, chicle gum, and allspice. Timber production focused on mahogany and tropical cedar is also allowed by law (Gretzinger 1998:111). The multiple use zone of the Maya Biosphere Reserve makes Guatemala second in the world in amount of certified sustainable forest production, just after Mexico. Guatemala currently has 100,026 hectares (386 sq. mi.) in community forest concessions.

Creating these community concessions was no easy task. When the Maya Biosphere Reserve was established in 1990, the region that became the multiple use zone was dominated by a half-dozen industrial logging concessions, privately owned, that focused on high-grading the most valuable timber—mainly mahogany and tropical cedar. A series of economic studies conducted for Conservation International by natural resource economist Jared Hardner and lobbying efforts by members of the communities of Carmelita and Oaxactún convinced CONAP to transform these industrial concessions into community concessions during the 1990s. More recently, archaeologist Richard Hansen's El Mirador project has proposed the incorporation of these community concessions into an expanded protected area—the Mirador Basin Special Protected Area—connected to the El Mirador–Río Azul (La Danta) National Park (FARES 2005). However, this move is resisted by community families who are currently employed and making money from the community timber concessions. USAID commissioned a study of the community concessions and their relation to protection of archaeological sites and came down on the side of the communities (Kunen and Roney 2004). It is still uncertain what will eventually happen in the area.

The important point about chicle, *xate* palms, and allspice in the multiple use zone is that all three are renewable natural products that can be harvested without killing the tree and without destroying the forest. *Xate* palm leaves can be cut every 90 days from the same palm. They are exported to Europe and the United States by the millions of stems for use in the floral industry. Florists prize the leaves because they stay green for 60 days after being cut and can be used as the green screen for cut flowers in flower arrangements. The *xate* industry employs thousands of harvesters and produces between US$4 and $7 million each year for Guatemala.

Allspice is produced by pollarding branches with berries from allspice trees, drying the berries, and exporting them for use in making pickles, pastries, pumpkin pies, and pickled herring. Income from allspice in the Petén fluctuates with the catch of herring in the northern Atlantic and Pacific, but produces approximately US$600,000 per year. Allspice and chicle gum harvesting is discussed at length in Chapter 3. The key point here is that chicle produces around US$2 million per year for Guatemala through exports to Japan and Italy, where it is used as the base for natural chewing gum.

How many other commercially valuable products grow in the forest of the Maya Biosphere Reserve is the subject of ongoing research. But these new potential products, like the currently harvested products, are all threatened by the advance of the agricultural frontier, by timber poaching, and by cattle ranching.

In the same pattern that threatens the tropical forests of Mexico and Belize, Guatemala's tropical forests are being cleared and burned by a three-stage process that begins with the construction of logging roads or oil roads, is followed by colonization of the newly penetrated area by farm families from other regions of the country, and frequently followed by cattle ranchers who follow the pioneer farmers through the forest, buying up small plots or natural forest to create large ranches to raise beef cattle.

The impetus for all these destructive activities can be summarized in two words: poverty and greed. Poverty drives dozens of people each day to leave other regions of Guatemala and migrate to the Department of Petén in search of land and new lives. Most of them come from the desert-like southeastern departments of Guatemala, followed by Q'eqchi' Maya from the Verapaz Departments and farm families from Guatemala's southern coast. They are pushed as well by heavily skewed patterns of landownership in other regions of Guatemala; a small percentage of the population controls the country's most fertile lands. Equally important is Guatemala's rapid rate of population growth, currently around 3.1 percent per year; it is even higher among rural families. Thus, Guatemala has an increasing number of rural families with no access to fertile lands and nowhere to go except to the tropical forest of the northern Petén.

As a result, the population of the Petén has grown from 25,000 to between 600,000 and 700,000 during the last 30 years. Most of these people have settled in regions south of the Maya Biosphere Reserve, but as
lands in the southern Petén are occupied and new logging and oil roads
are opened in the reserve, increasing pressure is being placed on the biosphere reserve itself.

The situation was exacerbated during the late 1990s by the return of
40,000 Guatemalan refugees from a decade of exile in Mexico. More than
100,000 Guatemalans fled the country during the late 1970s and early
1980s to escape Guatemala's vicious civil war. In 1996, 40,000 remained
in Mexico, some out of fear of the political situation in Guatemala, others
because they found that their previous lands had been occupied by prior
returnees or by population expansion that occurred during their absence.

As a result, a few refugee groups identified the forests of the Maya
Biosphere Reserve as their choice for homes in their native country. One
group of refugees identified a site along the Río Usumacinta as their chosen site for settlement. The area they picked, called El Quetzal, lies precisely at the point where the legal forest corridor connects the Montes
Azules Biosphere Reserve of Chiapas, Mexico, with the Maya Biosphere
Reserve of Guatemala. The prospects point to one of the ethical dilemmas
that conservation encounters in a world of politics and rising population.
Is it possible to accommodate refugees, colonizing farm families, cattle
ranchers, timber harvesters, chicle gatherers, tourists, and scientists, and
keep alive the biological diversity of the Maya Biosphere Reserve?

Major Archaeological Sites in the Guatemalan Petén

LA CORONA/SAK NIKTE'

What little is known about the recently discovered Late Classic site of
La Corona/Sak Nikte' is the result of three expeditions conducted during 1996, 1997, and 2005; a 1989 visit by Nicolai Grube; and texts found
on looted stone monuments from the site. Exploring for scarlet macaw
nesting sites in the northwestern Petén during 1996, Guatemalan conservationist Santiago Billy, U.S. researcher Kelly Reed, and their guides, Carlos Catalán and Luis Morales from Carmelita, Petén, came upon a Maya
site near a *chiclero* camp called Lo Veremos. Catalán had first encountered
the site during his years as a jaguar hunter. Exploring the area, the team

encountered numerous looters' trenches in the sides of temple mounds and one broken stela with hieroglyphs.

On an exploratory visit to the site later that year, 1996, Tom Sever, Dan Lee, Santiago Billy, and I, accompanied by the same guides, photographed the stela and explored the region with the aid of satellite images and a GPS. We found new mounds and climbed the largest structures. We returned to the site in May 1997 with Pancho Moro of Guatemala's Monumentos Pre-hispánicos of the Instituto de Antropología e Historia (IDAEH), and Ian Graham and David Stuart of Harvard's Peabody Museum of Archaeology and Ethnology.

Graham and Stuart identified four altars and one stela with glyphs at the site, which had several references to an individual known as Great or Red Turkey, a name found, as Graham describes it, "in only one other in-scription, on a Site Q panel in the Art Institute of Chicago." As Graham writes, "For the first time, a Site Q personage can be linked to a known site" (Graham 1997:46). One of the altars identified by Graham and Stuart carried a date of AD 656.

Site Q, named for the first letter of the Spanish word "¿Qué?" (What?), is an unidentified site, or sites, proposed as the provenience of a series of 30–35 finely carved limestone sculptures now found in museums in the United States. Discovery of the Great or Red Turkey glyph at La Corona led to speculation that the site was the elusive Site Q, or one of several sites known collectively as Site Q (Schuster 1997). Stuart, the Bartlett Curator of Maya Hieroglyphic Inscriptions at Harvard's Peabody Museum, identified a key locative glyph on Altars 1 and 2 from La Corona as Sak Nikte', "White Flower," indicating that this was the original name of the region in which La Corona lies, if not the name of the site itself (Freidel and Guenter 2002).

British epigrapher Simon Martin points out that inscriptions found at La Corona/Sak Nikte' in 1997 demonstrate close ties between the site and Calakmul (Mexico). One of these inscriptions "describes a ritual performed by the great Calakmul king Yich'aak K'ak' ('Fiery Claw') in the company of a vassal called Great Turkey, presumably the local ruler." Martin goes on to state that one of the finest Site Q museum pieces shows Great Turkey playing the Maya ballgame at Calakmul itself. "This connection strongly implies," says Martin, "that this panel, at least, came from La Corona or somewhere close by" (Martin 2000).

In April 2005, staff from the Proyecto Arqueológico El Perú/Waka', IDAEH, and Wildlife Conservation Society carried out additional research and mapping at La Corona and discovered a perfectly preserved, carved limestone panel that matches the style and story line of the well-known Site Q panels. According to the preliminary project report, the newly found panel serves as "the final proof that La Corona is actually Site Q" (Marken, Guenter, and Tsesmeli 2005:4). Nonetheless, some speculation remains that the kingdom of Sak Nikte' (Site Q) may have had multiple capitals, one of which was La Corona.

The panel discovered at La Corona during the April 2005 expedition refers to its dedication on October 27, AD 677, by K'inich Yook, king of La Corona, and shows him with a prince or king of Calakmul. The panel notes a visit by K'inich Yook during November AD 673 to the king of Calakmul, Yuknoom Ch'een, "the most powerful king of the Classic period" (Marken, Guenter, and Tsesmeli 2005:3). The authors of the expedition note that K'inich Yook, originally enthroned in AD 667, was reestablished as king in AD 675 after his return from Calakmul. They surmise that the center of La Corona was attacked by Tikal in AD 673, the same year that El Perú/Waka' was burned by Tikal, and that the trip K'inich Yook took to Calakmul may have been the result of a temporary exile from his home because of these wars (Marken, Guenter, and Tsesmili 2005:4).

Freidel and Guenter state that "politically and economically, Sak Nikte' [La Corona] was of immense strategic importance to the powerful Snake Kingdom, 'Kan' in Maya, with its capital during the Late Classic period being the enormous ruin of Calakmul, in southeastern Campeche, Mexico" (Freidel and Guenter 2002). They note that the site lay halfway between Calakmul and the lower reaches of the Río San Pedro Mártir "and its confluence with the greatest river of the Maya world, the Usumacinta."

"Through Sak Nikte' and other vassal cities on the San Pedro Mártir river system," write Freidel and Guenter, "the Snake Kings of Calakmul sought to command trade and tribute flowing on these major commercial arteries." They go on to point out that Sak Nikte' was likely ruled by subalterns of the kings of Calakmul, but that surviving texts indicate that they "used this center as a secondary capital and strategic base for operations against, and interactions with, the lands to the south and west" (Freidel and Guenter 2002).

Freidel and Guenter (2002) have identified a sculptured tablet known as the Dallas Altar as originating in Sak Nikte'. The tablet's text describes the arrival of three women from Calakmul in Sak Nikte' in AD 520, 677, and 721, the latter apparently in an action meant to reestablish Calakmul's presence in the Petén after two major defeats at the hands of the rival city Tikal. They point to the Dallas Tablet as indicating the importance of royal women during the Classic Maya civilization.

La Corona sits beside a crescent-shaped lake approximately 100 meters (330 feet) long. A main plaza is flanked by an acropolis and 12-meter-tall (40-foot) structures. Five smaller temples line up in a north-south row just to the southeast of the acropolis. Several mounds 4 meters (13 feet) tall appear along the western shore of the lake, and other platforms of cut stone lie between them. The western shore of the lake also has a rectangular cut in the bank that appears to be a canoe-docking area. A low stone mound sits just above the docking area.

Most intriguingly, NASA archaeologist Tom Sever found that LANDSAT satellite images of the La Corona area reveal two straight lines, possible *sacbe* roads, that meet in a T-shape just north of the site. During ground-truthing efforts in 1997, we found a low, linear ridge through the forest that may be the remnants of a road. The same area revealed what appears to be a stone-lined canal.

A half-dozen of the largest structures at La Corona were looted in 1980 by a team led by a Mexican named Concepción "Concho" Gonzales. According to one Guatemalan who worked on the looting team, Gonzales took back to Mexico "a lot of jade and stelae faces."

IF YOU GO . . . LA CORONA/SAK NIKTE'   Head for La Corona only with a guide, whom you can hire in the town of Carmelita. The guide will arrange a two-day horseback trip to the site for a modest fee. You will need camping gear, food, a water filter, mosquito nets, and good boots. There are no settlements along the way and nowhere to purchase food once you leave Carmelita. To get to the site, you will drive several hours west, northwest from Carmelita to the *chiclero* camp of El Junquillal, so named for a type of saw grass that grows in the large lake there.

The road ends at the lake, so you will have to arrange for guides and mules (for cargo) from Carmelita to meet you at El Junquillal. Traveling west out of El Junquillal six hours the first day, passing the Río Chocop and the Arroyo Jute and Arroyo Negro, you will arrive at the *chiclero* camp called Las Pericas for the first night's stay. The following day, a four-hour hike will take you into the site of La Corona, located next to the *chiclero* camp known as Lo Veremos.

EL MIRADOR

Largest of all Maya sites, the Late Preclassic site of El Mirador (circa 300 BC to AD 200) lies only 7 kilometers (4 miles) south of the border between northern Guatemala and Mexico, inside the Mirador–Río Azul National Park, one of the seven core areas of the Maya Biosphere Reserve. Satellite images of El Mirador show Maya *sacbe* roads radiating out from the city toward other Maya sites in Guatemala and neighboring Yucatán. The site is surrounded by huge, seasonally inundated *bajo* swamps, which likely played a major role in the agricultural support system for the ancient city.

But El Mirador was also key to early Maya trade networks. Archaeologist Robert J. Sharer speculates that "El Mirador served as a major redistribution node and probably controlled trans-Petén commerce in its heyday, especially the trans-peninsula trade between the Caribbean and Gulf coasts and exchange with the major highland power, Kaminaljuyu" (Sharer 1994:460). Thus, the site was the central hub in both east-west and north-south trade in the Maya world, serving as a central collection and redistribution point, much the way modern airport hubs such as Dallas–Fort Worth or Miami bring goods (passengers) to a central hub, then redistribute them to other places.

The existence of El Mirador was first reported in 1926, but the site was not excavated until the 1980s. Even today, though, most of the site is still covered with high forest filled with wildlife, a characteristic that makes visits to the site mysterious and adventurous. El Mirador was the largest Maya site of its time, and its Danta Pyramid, covering 18 hectares (45 acres), is the largest pre-Columbian structure in the New World. Danta reaches 70 meters (230 feet) and the Tigre Pyramid climbs to 55 meters (180 feet). During the city's heyday (150 BC–AD 150), these structures were coated with limestone plaster, decorated with giant stucco masks of Maya gods, and painted—probably red.

IF YOU GO . . . EL MIRADOR   Getting to El Mirador is an adventure, most of it done on old *chiclero* trails through the forest. To begin the trek, travel by car or bus to the town of Carmelita, north of Lake Petén Itzá, and inquire about guides and mules. There are no formal hotels in Carmelita, but for a small fee an ecocamp is available for hammock camping just outside of town. (Inquire in Carmelita.) A guided trip to El Mirador takes 13 hours each way, walking or on horseback, a trip best done over a minimum of five days (two days to get there, one day on site, two days return to Carmelita). Do not try to find the site without a guide; the dozens of old chicle and *xate* harvesting trails through the forest will quickly get you lost. Take a hammock, mosquito net, and tarp, or a tent and sleeping bag. No food is available on site, and water is usually scarce. Take enough food and water for the trail, and have a good water filter handy for use in the El Mirador *aguada* (one of the original Maya water reservoirs) when you get there. Gifts of food or flashlight batteries are welcomed by the IDAEH guards, who work 22 days on, 8 days off at the site headquarters, but there is no charge for visitors.

Wildlife is plentiful in the area, especially monkeys and all sorts of tropical and migratory birds. On a visit to the site in 1990, a pair of jaguars followed our wary group from Danta Pyramid back to the IDAEH guard camp, turning off the trail just as we reached our campsite.

NAKBE

What appears to be the earliest Maya city, Nakbe, was constructed on a site surrounded by seasonally flooded tropical forest, while much of the rest of the Maya world still lay smothered in wilderness. Excavations at Nakbe have revealed the best evidence yet of how monumental construction developed among the Maya, and Nakbe is the Maya Tropical Forest's best evidence for the beginning stages of monumental civic-ceremonial construction; its largest structures date from the Middle Preclassic (1000–300 BC) to the Late Preclassic (300–200 BC) (Sharer 1994:82).

Four of Nakbe's largest structures were erected during the Late Preclassic, 300 BC–AD 200. These and a hundred other stone buildings overlie the remains of a Maya village that dates to 1000 BC. The Maya buried the village with rock and rubble to create platforms, then constructed stone structures on top of the platforms. Nakbe's tallest (and earliest) pyramids reach 45 meters (148 feet).

Located 16 kilometers (10 miles) southeast of El Mirador, Nakbe predates that city, although a Maya causeway (*sacbe*), constructed later, connects the two sites. (Nakbe, in Yucatec Maya, means "Next to the Road.") During its heyday, Nakbe probably controlled east-west trade across the base of the Yucatán Peninsula, as Mirador and Tikal did later. Although the city remained the supreme power in the Maya world for centuries, it was eventually supplanted by El Mirador, whose importance was, in turn, overtaken by Tikal.

Archaeologist Richard D. Hansen, of the University of California, Los Angeles, has led excavations at Nakbe since the late 1980s. He notes that Nakbe's great plaza and pyramid complexes were constructed with sloping surfaces to allow rain to run off into reservoirs needed to supply large urban populations during the long dry season. He hypothesizes that "one

practical reason for building centers was to generate drinking water reserves" (Freidel, Schele, and Parker 1993:432).

IF YOU GO . . . NAKBE   There are no vehicle roads to Nakbe;
you can reach the site only by mule or on foot. Guides from the *chiclero* community of Carmelita will lead you on the minimum five-day trip
(two days in, two days out, with a full day at the site). The trail runs over,
through, and past other Maya ruins, as well as through large stands of
chicle and allspice trees. Be warned that water is scarce. Carry the water
you will need on the trip and be prepared to filter water from vegetation-
covered *aguadas* on the way to and from the site. Even after filtering, the
tannin-stained water tastes like a new herbal tea, but properly filtered it
will do you no harm.

NAKUM

Nakum is a large, unexcavated Late Classic site located east of Tikal and
north of Yaxjá. The 15 known stelae from the site reveal dates of AD 771,
810, and 849, making it contemporary with Tikal. Although rarely visited,
Nakum has been known since the early years of the twentieth century.
Frenchman Maurice de Perigny visited the site in 1905–1906 and again in
1909–1910 to clear and photograph it. Alfred Tozzer, a Peabody Museum
archaeologist and ethnologist of the Lacandón Maya, photographed and
mapped the site in 1910 and published the results in 1913 (Tozzer 1913).

Nakum consists of two large building complexes—a northern group and
a southern group—connected by a *sacbe* road called the Perigny Causeway. In the southern group, the Main Palace Acropolis rivals the Central
Acropolis of Tikal in size and number of structures. The long Palace D,
in the southern group, has 44 rooms. The solstice observatory group just
north of Palace D was designed to commemorate astronomical knowledge
and includes now-eroded monuments to solstices and equinoxes in front
of Temple A. The site's large water reservoir fills during the rainy season
and would have supplied thousands of inhabitants during the site's peak
years.

Archaeologist Nicholas Hellmuth calls the southern group of Nakum
"the most magnificently planned royal palace erected by the Petén Maya"
(Hellmuth 1978:95). Sharer speculates that the site may have served "as
an important trade link between Tikal and the Caribbean coast" (Sharer
1994:194).

IF YOU GO ... NAKUM To visit Nakum, travel first to Yaxjá and inquire at El Sombrero Ecolodge or the guardhouse of the Consejo Nacional de Areas Protegidas, which lies just north of El Sombrero, for a guide or directions to the site. During the dry season, you will be able to drive approximately 12 miles north from Yaxjá and park in front of the IDAEH guardhouse at Nakum. Government guards working at the site will guide you around the site.

Traveling to Nakum during the rainy season requires hiking or horses once you reach the Río Holmul, which you cross just before you enter Nakum. In 1992 we crossed the river on horseback, and the horses were swimming at least part of the time. You can camp at the site if you decide to stay overnight. Take your own food, camping equipment, and a water filter or sufficient bottled water to drink.

NARANJO

The Classic Maya site of Naranjo sits about 12 kilometers (7 miles) northeast of Lake Yaxjá, between the site of Yaxjá and the modern border of Guatemala-Belize. (A modern town with a similar name, El Naranjo, lies on the Río San Pedro in northwestern Petén.) Situated on the edge of a large wetland midway between the Holmul and Mopan rivers, Naranjo has several courtyard groups, 40 carved stelae, and a hieroglyphic stairway. The Austrian explorer Teobert Maler first reported the site in 1905.

The city of Caracol (inside modern Belize) attacked Naranjo in AD 626 and 627 and defeated the city decisively in AD 631 (Schele and Freidel 1990:177). After yet another attack on Naranjo in AD 636, Caracol's leaders forced the defeated townspeople of Naranjo to construct a hieroglyphic stairway to glorify their win. As Schele and Freidel (1990:179) note, "In their stairway, the surviving elite of Naranjo had a constant reminder of the hegemony of Caracol. That disgraceful monument was the last written record placed in public space for the next 40 years."

In AD 682, Naranjo reestablished a royal lineage when Lady Six Sky (aka Lady Wac-Chanil-Ahau), the daughter of the king of the southern Petén site Dos Pilas, married a noble of Naranjo. Eleven years later, her son, K'ak' Tiuliw Chan Chaak (aka Smoking-Squirrel), became king of Naranjo. Shortly afterward, with their royal dynasty reestablished, the nobles of Naranjo began to challenge nearby cities. They attacked Ucanal, a city probably allied with Caracol, thereby indirectly striking back at Caracol, and in AD 710 they attacked Yaxjá. By contrast, in AD 744 Tikal launched a "Star War" against Naranjo, capturing its leader, Yax Mayuy Chan Chaak. A stela at Tikal, dedicated four months after the battle, shows Naranjo's king bound and subdued, shortly before he was ritually slaughtered (Martin and Grube 2000:79).

The last dynastic date recorded at Naranjo is AD 849. The site of Naranjo shows no signs of excavation, but stelae lie about the plazas, and impressive walls—some still with their original stucco—outline a half-dozen Classic-era buildings. During its four centuries of existence, Naranjo was home to artists who produced some of the finest painted ceramics in the Maya world (Martin and Grube 2000:69).

IF YOU GO . . . NARANJO Visitors can drive to the site of Naranjo during the dry season and, with a four-wheel-drive vehicle, during all but the muddiest months of the rainy season, i.e., September through November. Take the dirt road about 20 kilometers (12 miles) northwest from the border town of Melchor de Menco along the Guatemala-Belize border directly to the site. Until the 1990s, few families lived along this road, but in recent years farmers and cattle raisers have settled along its length.

EL PERÚ/WAKA'

The large Classic Maya site of El Perú/Waka' is located on the northern bank of the Río San Pedro in northwestern Guatemala, inside Laguna del Tigre National Park, one of the core areas of the Maya Biosphere Reserve. Reported in 1961 by oil explorers, the site was partially looted in the late 1960s, and two of its stelae are now found in the Cleveland Museum of Art and the Kimbell Art Museum in Fort Worth, Texas. Ian Graham of Harvard's Peabody Museum surveyed El Perú/Waka' and produced a reliable map in 1969. The majority of the site's 40 identified carved monuments are still in place today, and new archaeological data are coming to light through a project begun in 2002 by David Freidel of Southern Methodist University and Héctor Escobedo of the Universidad de San Carlos de Guatemala. Freidel and Escobedo's work represents the first scientific excavation undertaken at the site and a major step in opening the site to sustainable tourism. In addition to holding a wealth of archaeological information, El Perú/Waka' is also worth visiting because of its location near the Río San Pedro and its abundant wildlife.

El Perú/Waka' was occupied as early as 500 BC, but activity reached a peak between AD 400 and 800, when the site ranked as a major city in the Maya world (*SMU News 2004*). El Perú/Waka' formed one corner of a triangle of major sites including Calakmul on the north and Tikal on the west (*SMU News 2004*). Freidel and Stanley Guenter have identified Stela 16 "as a posthumous portrait of the Teotihuacano general Siyaj K'ak', the most famous individual of the Early Classic period lowlands" (Freidel 2004). Stela 15, reassembled and replicated in fiberglass by the Freidel/Escobedo project, recounts the arrival of Siyaj K'ak' on January 6, AD 378, and his ceremonial activities with the king of Waka', K'inich Balam. Eight days later, Siyaj K'ak' conquered Tikal and replaced its king with Curl Snout, also known as Yax Nuun Ayiin I, the son of a leader from a city in what is now Mexico, and his locally born Maya queen. The alliance between Teotihuacán and Waka' continued until at least the end of the sixth century (Freidel 2004).

In turn, El Perú/Waka' was eventually defeated by Tikal in AD 743 (Skidmore 2003). According to Ian Graham, El Perú/Waka' also had strong commercial links to Palenque and cities in the Lake Petexbatún region. The site's 672 monumental structures cluster into seven groups, and many are constructed on natural hills to give them added height.

Archaeologist David Freidel reports that the ancient inhabitants called the site Waka', meaning "Stood-Up," in reference to the World Tree, which was named the Waka' Chan, "Stood-Up Sky." According to Freidel, "The lords of the city on their stelae have especially prominent, broad girdle elements of a god named Tzuk, 'partition' or 'dominion,' which decorates the trunk of the World Tree and which marks rulers as personifications of that tree" (David Freidel, personal communication, June 2001).

Surrounded by wetland savannas of Laguna del Tigre National Park, El Perú/Waka' is located on some of the most fertile, best drained soils in the Petén and has the highest forest in the northwestern Petén. The Laguna El Perú lies just west of the site and offers sightings of muscovy ducks (*Cairina moschata*), egrets, herons, and crocodiles.

Spider and howler monkeys are plentiful on the hike to the archaeological site, and scarlet macaws nest in the cantemo trees (*Acacia angustissima*; Yucatec Maya = *k'an te mo'* "yellow tree of the macaws") that dot the surrounding forest. The best months to see macaws nesting are April, May, and June, when parent birds are flying back and forth to bring food to the *pichoncitos* (chicks). (The young birds are born in late December or January.) After the young birds fledge in June, they join their parent birds to fly north into the forest until November, when they return to El Perú/Waka' to prepare nests for another clutch of eggs.

IF YOU GO . . . EL PERÚ/WAKA' The only year-round access to El Perú/Waka' is via the Río San Pedro, but you can boat there from either the west or east. To get there from the west, travel by car or bus to the town of El Naranjo, located on the Río San Pedro in northwestern Petén. Hire a boat and travel four hours upriver to the wooden boat dock and sign marked "El Perú."

From the east, you must drive over rough roads from the Flores/San Benito, Petén, area to the small Q'eqchi' community of Paso Caballos and hire a boat to take you to the El Perú/Waka' boat dock, a trip of only half an hour. Visitors to the Las Guacamayas Biological Station can arrange a boat 15 minutes downriver to the site. During the dry season, it may be possible to drive from the Flores/San Benito urban area near Lake Petén Itzá, past Laguna Larga all the way to Paso Caballos, on to the Las Guacamayas Biological Station, and on to El Perú/Waka'. But don't try this after the rains have begun.

If you travel by boat, you will arrive at a wooden boat dock on the river. Hike 20 minutes north on the wide trail to arrive at the IDAEH (Instituto de Antropología e Historia) headquarters, also used by the Freidel/Escobedo archaeological team. Palm-thatched structures are available here for overnight camping. The IDAEH guards will guide you on the one and one-half hour hike along a wide forest trail to the city of El Perú/Waka'. Sightings of scarlet macaws and spider monkeys are not uncommon on this trail.

PIEDRAS NEGRAS

Piedras Negras is a large Classic Maya site situated on the eastern bank of the Río Usumacinta that once served as the primary artery in the riverine traffic of the Maya world. The Maya name for the site was Yokib, "the Paw Stone" (Stuart 2004). Teobert Maler explored the site in 1895 and excavations by the University of Pennsylvania began during the 1930s, but research and reconstruction was only sporadic at Piedras Negras until recently. During the Guatemalan civil war of the 1970s and 1980s, the site served as a crossing point for guerrillas moving back and forth between Guatemala and Chiapas. Guerrilla fighters and their families planted corn in and around the ruins to supply themselves in the forest. More recently, in February 2005 heavily armed drug traffickers invaded the site and set up camp amid the pyramids, threatening archaeologists conducting research there (*Washington Post* 2005).

From inscriptions on monuments, the city can be dated as having flourished between AD 514 and 810. Many of the large structures at Piedras Negras had wood and thatch roofs, rather than the stone vaults found in contemporaneous sites such as Tikal and Yaxjá. Piedras Negras is best known for its sculptures, although visitors will find few of these visible at the site itself. Find them instead in Guatemala's Archaeological Museum in Parque Aurora, Guatemala City, and on loan to the University Museum of the University of Pennsylvania.

The numerous stelae originally found at Piedras Negras, however, served a key role in studies of Maya civilization, namely, as the raw data for the realization that Maya texts dealt with real political history rather than imagined events, astronomy, or religious myths, as previously thought. During the 1960s, archaeologist Tatiana Proskouriakoff realized that the dates on Piedras Negras monuments emulated the human lifespan. She used an uninterrupted series of 22 sculptured monuments to demonstrate that they illustrated the inauguration of new rulers and their wives in a continuous process of dynastic succession.

Investigation at Piedras Negras has revealed eight sweat, or steam, baths with masonry benches and small portals that served both as entryways and as drains to carry away the bathwater. The Maya produced steam by splashing water on heated rocks in stone hearths, which were lined with potsherds to reflect the heat of the fires. (A similar steam bath can be seen at Palenque, Chiapas, Mexico.)

IF YOU GO . . . PIEDRAS NEGRAS   Travel by river is the only way to get to Piedras Negras, but it makes for an excellent adventure. Travelers rafting down the Río Usumacinta in organized groups—usually from Yaxchilán or Frontera Corozal, Chiapas—sometimes stop on the Guatemalan side of the river and camp for the night on the sandy beach that lies below the site. They then continue downriver into Mexico to take out at La Palma, near Tenosique. Rapids below Piedras Negras prevent travelers from traveling upriver to the site.

You can also visit Piedras Negras from Guatemala by hiring a boat in the small community of Betel, which lies directly on the Río Usumacinta and can be reached by a road that parallels the Río de la Pasión. An easier approach is by car to the town of Sayaxché, where you can rent an aluminum boat with outboard motor that can make it to the site and back by traveling down the Río de la Pasión, then down the Río Usumacinta to Piedras Negras and back.

There are no accommodations at the site and no guards, so take water, sleeping bags, tents, and whatever else you require for a comfortable night. The site is almost completely covered in forest, with only a few trails and structures cleared of vegetation. One of the highlights of arriving at the site is examining the large, turtle-shaped stone that juts out from the beach over the rushing water of the Río Usumacinta. The meter-wide Classic-era carving depicts a seated man presenting gifts to a woman. It is easy to imagine that the large stone marked the site of a Maya loading dock.

RÍO AZUL

The Maya site of Río Azul covers more than a square kilometer on the bank of the river of the same name in extreme northeastern Guatemala, where Guatemala, Belize, and Mexico come together in a tri-national corner. The site flourished between AD 390 and 530, with 3,500 to 5,000 inhabitants, although it appears to have become subservient to Tikal just before those glory years with the capture and execution of eight of Río Azul's elite leaders (Sharer 1994:194). The city was abandoned for nearly a century between AD 530 and 600, then reoccupied under the leadership of the same family that had ruled it before.

Although the site has been mapped and partially excavated, revealing a series of tombs with glyph-painted walls, Río Azul remains overgrown and quiet today, with only a half-dozen visitors each year. Of the almost 500 structures at the site, the tallest temple, at 47 meters (155 feet), provides a view of unbroken forest in three countries. Subsequent to its discovery in 1962, the site was methodically looted and many of its tombs robbed of jade and ceramics that later ended up on the black market. Still, excavations between 1983 and 1987 uncovered valuable information and artifacts on the Early Classic period at the site.

Guatemala City's National Museum of Archaeology and Ethnology, in Aurora Park, displays a reconstruction of Río Azul's Early Classic Tomb 19 and some of the site's best ceramics. The display includes a rare, screw-top ceramic pot that held chocolate drinks, according to both deciphered glyphs painted on the pot and subsequent analysis by Hershey Food Laboratories of the food residue found inside.

IF YOU GO . . . RÍO AZUL The same road that passes through Tikal and north into Uaxactún continues 95 kilometers (57 miles) northeast to Río Azul and to a neighboring site, El Kinal. The road is passable with high-clearance vehicles, but only during the dry season, and you must take all food and supplies you need; there are no stores or settlements north of Uaxactún. The site of Río Azul is located inside Mirador–Río Azul National Park, sometimes referred to as La Danta Complex, along with the Biotopo Naachtun/Dos Lagunas.

NOHPETEN, TAYASAL, AND FLORES

Tayasal is a Classic-period Maya site located on a peninsula of land that juts into Lake Petén Itzá near the modern Petén capital city of Flores. At the peak of its development in the Late Classic (AD 500–900), the city may have been home to 22,000–32,000 people (Sharer 1994:471). Archaeologists also have found Postclassic house sites along the lakeshore of the Tayasal Peninsula, but this occupation was associated with the Late Postclassic city Nohpeten, which lies buried beneath the island city Flores. The early twentieth century archaeologist Sylvanus Morley used the name Tayasal to refer to the Classic-era ruins on the peninsula, thus setting the stage for years of confusion between that site and the Itza Maya ruins that lie beneath Flores. The city the Spaniards stormed and conquered in 1697 was on the island of Flores itself, and is referred to here as Nohpeten to distinguish it from the defunct Classic-era city Tayasal.

Nohpeten (now overlaid by the departmental capital city Flores) was founded around AD 1221, when Itza Maya who survived the sacking of the northern Yucatán city of Chichén Itzá—apparently by Itza from the rising city of Mayapán—moved southward into the Petén rainforest and settled on a series of islands in the region's lakes. The Itza controlled the island city of Nohpeten for another 475 years, until Spaniards attacked and destroyed the city in 1697. The captain of the victorious Spaniards, Martín de Ursua, renamed the sacked island Nuestra Señora de los Remedios y San Pablo, Laguna del Itza, later to be known simply as Flores, after a nineteenth-century politician who was killed by an anti-Liberal mob in Quetzaltenango in 1826.

Despite this whirlpool of contrasting names, the Itza Maya themselves were always clear on where they were: they called the island city Noh Peten, "Large Island," or Tah Itza, "Location of the Itza" (G. Jones 1998:7). This latter term, Tah Itza, was probably the source of the Hispanicized "Tayasal." The Itza called the lake itself Chal Tun Ha. The term "Petén Itzá" means "island [*peten*] of the Itza." Thus, "Lake Petén Itzá" is "Lake of the Itza's Island," and the Departamento del Petén takes its name from the Itza's island city. (In Itza Maya, the accent goes on the first syllable: *Peten Itza*, but the words have been Hispanicized to "Petén Itzá.")

IF YOU GO . . . TAYASAL RUINS   Ask in Flores about renting a taxiboat for the five-minute trip across the lake to the Peninsula of Tayasal. The boatman will wait for you while you climb to the top of the highest mound—still covered in regrowth vegetation—to the wood platform built in a tree at the very top. You will have a photo-perfect view of the island city of Flores and Lake Petén Itzá's two arms. Other than that, there's not much to see of the site itself—mostly mound after earthen mound, with no stelae or standing walls.

Flores, on the other hand, is a picturesque and pleasant town that is the gateway to tourism in the Guatemalan Petén. Early morning light hitting the dusty streets of Flores reveals the pastel colors of the town's houses and fills the sidewalks with men in cowboy hats and women walking down stone streets on their way to church. Sunlight reflects off Lake Petén Itzá to showcase water taxis plying their way back and forth across the lake, carrying schoolchildren and bicycles, men and women on their way to market, and fishermen seeking an elusive *blanco* for breakfast.

No Maya ruins are visible on the island of Flores itself, though a few stelae are mounted in the municipal park in front of the church at the top of the island. There is no doubt, however, that excavation beneath the sidewalks or patios of any spot on the island would expose artifacts of the Postclassic Itza community of Nohpeten that occupied the island until it was conquered by Spaniards in 1697. At the top of the island, you can visit the restored seventeenth-century colonial fortress built on top of Itza ruins by the conquering Spaniards. Today it houses the Centro de Información sobre Culturas y Artesanía del Petén (CINCAP), a museum and information center with exhibits, a handicraft store, and meeting room.

In 2003 a Flores-based water taxi driver (a *lanchero* in Spanish) named Miguel Betancourt Contreras told me that before the dirt causeway (*relleno*) was built in the early 1970s to connect Flores to Santa Elena, young couples would canoe around the island when the moon was full. Sometimes two men would paddle softly, one of them singing the island's traditional romantic songs to girls who caught their eyes. The *lanchero* sang one of these traditional songs in a soft, lilting voice:

Me gusta la leche,
Me gusta el café,

Pero no tanto como
tus ojos oscuros.

I love milk,
I love coffee,
But not as much
as your dark eyes.

The *lanchero* lamented the fact that with the construction of the causeway, this tradition had fallen by the wayside. The small televisions that now blink in the dark houses of Flores probably had an impact on this custom, as well.

In 1927 the surface of Lake Petén Itzá served as the landing site of the first airplane to arrive in the Petén—an amphibious craft piloted by the famous Charles A. Lindbergh. Lindbergh arrived here on a goodwill tour of Latin American countries, sponsored by the U.S. government, subsequent to his successful nonstop flight solo across the Atlantic in May 1927.

During the late 1990s, rowing crews in single and double shells began to take advantage of the lake's early morning glass-smooth surface. On many mornings by seven o'clock, rowers are skittering across the lake like water spiders on a jungle pond.

Lake Petén Itzá is surrounded by chains of hills on all sides, creating the setting for beautiful vistas of lime-green water and forest-covered hills. The island of Flores on an early morning is warm, fresh, and silent, with soft light coloring the houses of San Benito across the lake. Forest covers the hills in the background, and the Peninsula of Tayasal shows off the rippled texture of its tropical vegetation. Despite its violent history, Flores is today a place of peace and beauty.

TIKAL

Tikal is the quintessential Maya city. Located only 45 minutes north of the airport at Flores–Santa Elena, Petén, the site draws 200,000 visitors each year from Central America, the United States, Europe, South America, and Asia. Since its establishment in 1959 as one of Guatemala's first national parks, Tikal's 574 square kilometers (222 sq. mi.) have been a haven for lowland tropical wildlife. Tourists who leave without sighting troops of spider monkeys, toucans, and parrots are paying more attention to the stone ruins than to the animals overhead.

Tikal is one of the largest of the Maya cities and is the most extensively studied. Although the ancient city covers almost 125 square kilometers (48 sq. mi.) of the national park, the city's core area rests atop a series of long, low hills surrounded on the east and west by seasonally inundated forest (*bajos*) and on the north and south by constructed earthworks with moats. The defensive earthwork on the northern border separates Tikal from its neighboring city of Uaxactún. Tikal's strategic combination of flooded forest and defensive fortifications would have provided a first line of defense for the families who lived within the city and its surrounding farmland.

Including the merchants, traders, and farmers who lived outside the city's core, the population of Tikal reached 60,000 to 100,000 people during its peak in the Classic period (AD 200–900) (Sharer 1994:471; Martin and Grube 2000:25; Webster 2002:264). However, the city began in a humble fashion—as a settlement of swidden farmers, around 600 BC. Burials and stone tools of these early inhabitants were uncovered beneath the North Acropolis (on the northern side between Temples I and II in the main plaza) (Schele and Freidel 1990:131–132). Over time, the village became a city, marked by spasms of construction as the city's power and population grew. The city's inhabitants knew their home as Yax Mutal. More recent travelers in the region referred to the ruins as *ti ak'al,* "At the Waterhole," in reference to the site's many water reservoirs (Roberts 2004:46).

Tikal was one of several cities—its rival, Calakmul, in Mexico, is another, as is Uaxactún—that came to power as the city of El Mirador declined during Early Classic times. The basis of Tikal's power was trade and location. The low hills that provide the setting for Tikal contain the valuable resource of chert, or flint, used to make stone projectile points. Chert was a crucial trade item to the ancient Maya, who had no metal tools. Another factor that pushed Tikal to a position of power was modification of the surrounding seasonally inundated *bajos* for agricultural production. This transformation provided a steady food supply for the city's growing population.

But perhaps the most important of the factors leading to Tikal's power is the city's location at a critical portage point on the canoe-based trading route that passed goods from east to west, and vice versa, during the Classic era (Sharer 1994:208). Due west of Tikal, the Río San Pedro flows westward to connect to the mightiest of the Maya river highways, the Río Usumacinta, which—through its many tributaries—provides connections with sites as far away as Bonampak, Yaxchilán, Ceibal, and Altar de

Sacrificios. To the east, the Río Hondo and Belize River carried traders from the central Petén to the Caribbean and settlements along its coast, as far south as Honduras.

Tikal's combination of access to raw materials, a steady food supply, and control of a crucial trade route allowed the city to rise to a position of power that few other Maya cities could challenge. Nonetheless, Tikal fell under the control of political leaders from Teotihuacán, in the distant Valley of Mexico, during the late fourth century (Martin and Grube 2000:29). Most of Tikal's monuments were defaced, destroyed, or dispersed at this time, and Mexican-clad warriors began to appear on new monuments and painted ceramics. The Mexican spearthrower, a weapon called the *atlatl*, appeared in paintings and sculptures. Led by the warrior Siyaj K'ak', the Teotihuacanos killed the Tikal leader, Chak Tok Ich'aak (aka Jaguar Paw) in AD 378 and installed their own leader, Yax Nuun Ayiin I, also known as Curl Snout, the son of a Mexican leader, Spearthrower Owl, and his locally born Maya queen. Yax Nuun Ayiin I also married a Maya woman, and the alliance set in place between Teotihuacán and Tikal lasted for centuries.

By Early Classic times, a single dynasty had taken control of Tikal, jealously guarding their position of power. A succession of at least 32 kings and 1 queen ruled over the city and its zone of influence, until Tikal fell into disorder in the ninth century AD as part of the general Maya collapse.

The keystone elements of the ruins of Tikal today are the five temples whose roof combs tower over the surrounding forest canopy. Temples I and II face each other across the Great Plaza, which serves as the central feature and most visited location of the site today. Lying alongside the Grand Plaza is the North Acropolis. Construction began on this complex in Preclassic years and continued through the Late Classic. The tallest of the structures, at 76 meters (250 feet) including its platform base, is Temple IV, constructed in AD 741. Not only does Temple IV stand highest above the canopy of all Tikal buildings, it is also "the single largest construction of the Late Classic period" and the tallest Maya structure ever built (Martin and Grube 2000:49).

Two wooden lintels from the upper sanctuary of Temple IV relate one of several stories recorded at Tikal about its greatest military hero, Yik'in Chan K'awiil, who led the city between AD 734 and 746. In July AD 743, Yik'in Chan K'awiil defeated Jaguar Throne, the king of El Perú/Waka', in a battle that probably took place at Laguna Perdida, 65 kilometers (39 miles) slightly southwest. Yik'in Chan K'awiil captured the effigy of the defeated leader's patron god, Hobnal Kimi, the "drunken death god" and took it to Temple IV in Tikal (Martin and Grube 2000:49; Freidel 2004).

Not content to rest on his laurels, Yik'in Chan K'awiil was on the warpath again only six months later, when he attacked the kingdom of Naranjo and seized the city of Wak Kab'nal, taking captive the Naranjo king, Yax Mayuy Chan Chaak, who appears in Tikal's Stela 5. According to Martin and Grube, these victories broke a hostile encirclement of Tikal "that had endured for at least a century. Since both victims were leading Calakmul affiliates, their rapid defeat seems easiest to explain in the light of their patron's waning powers" (Martin and Grube 2000:49–50).

Because both El Perú/Waka' and Naranjo subsequently went dormant in the written record for the next three to four decades, they likely fell under Tikal's direct control as a result of these defeats. Simultaneously, Tikal went on to experience a determined construction boom and let its defensive earthworks go unused (Martin and Grube 2000:50).

The last dated stela at Tikal was erected in AD 869, only 40 years before the last dated one anywhere in the Maya world (Roberts 2004:48). Subsequently, the city went silent. David Webster notes that "right now, the most convincing collapse explanation we have for the Tikal kingdom is overpopulation and agrarian failure, with all of their attendant political consequences" (Webster 2002:274).

The first non-Maya to encounter the ruins of Tikal were probably the Franciscan friar Andrés de Avendaño and two fellow priests, in 1696. Walking back to Yucatán after a fruitless attempt to convert the Itza Maya of Lake Petén Itzá to Catholicism, Avendaño and his crew were lost in the Petén forest for a month, surviving on *zapotes* (mameys), leaves, and palm nuts. Avendaño later wrote that his group came upon a "variety of old buildings, excepting some in which I recognized apartments, and though they were very high and my strength was little, I climbed up them" (M. Coe 1993:99; G. Jones 1998:218–219).

Credit for the modern discovery of the site usually goes to Modesto Méndez and Ambrosio Tut, who were, respectively, the commissioner and governor of the Petén, when they led an expedition to Tikal in 1848 (W. Coe 1967:12). But Méndez and Tut were guided to the site by Itza Maya, who had known about the city all along (Atran 1993b:688).

The explorer Alfred Maudslay visited Tikal in 1881–1882 and produced detailed drawings of buildings and other features. Teobert Maler photographed the temples in 1895 and again in 1904, and carved his name on the inside doorway of a building in the Central Acropolis, where it is still visible today. Sylvanus Morley visited Tikal periodically between 1914 and

1928, and in 1956 the University of Pennsylvania began 15 years of excavation at the site, work followed since then, and today, by Guatemala's Instituto de Antropología e Historia (IDAEH) (Hunter 1986:44). Staffed by an interdisciplinary team that ranged from archaeologists to ornithologists, the work conducted by the University of Pennsylvania and IDAEH set the stage for later—and continuing—decades of work in both understanding the history of the Maya region and making its history, monuments, and natural wonders accessible to generations of visitors.

Water for the approximately 600 people who visit Tikal each day is brought in by truck from Lake Petén Itzá. Supplying water to the 100,000 people who lived here during the Classic era, especially in the middle of the dry season, would have been a daunting task. The Classic Maya solved this problem by excavating more than a dozen reservoirs, called *aguadas* in Spanish, which collected water draining off causeways and limestone-covered plazas. These reservoirs are marked on large site maps of the city, but visits to them reveal boggy, rectangular marshes covered with reeds. One of the original reservoirs, divided into smaller ponds, is still in use today, however. This is the reservoir located immediately behind the sculpture museum, on the trail between the central parking lot and the ruins. (From the 1950s until 1985, this same *aguada* served as home to the crocodile named Goliad, which bit two children and killed two Tikal park workers before being terminated by a park ranger [Campbell 1998:290–291].)

In the early 1980s, authorities constructed cement drainage canals in the forest surrounding the ruins in an attempt to mimic the Maya water collection system. This modern engineering attempt proved less successful at directing rainfall runoff than Tikal's ancient techniques, and they collect little water. The cement ditches nonetheless make good wildlife viewing trails through the forest.

IF YOU GO . . . TIKAL   If you fly into Flores–Santa Elena, as most visitors do, you will have your pick of the several dozen drivers who offer rides to Tikal as you walk out of the airport with your luggage. You can pick the style in which you wish to travel, ranging from a private taxi to a six-person van, to a converted school bus filled with 40 sweating tourists. The price varies according to comfort and your negotiating skills. You can also rent a car in the airport or arrange a ride to the site through your travel agent or hotel.

The ride 45 minutes north on an asphalted highway is pleasant. From the airport (or from your hotel in Flores), you will travel eastward along the southern shore of Lake Petén Itzá (though you won't yet see the lake), then turn north at the extreme eastern point of the lake to head straight toward Tikal. Your driver may suggest a stop along the road to shop at the crossroads community of El Remate, made up of small, thatch-covered huts of wood carvers who sell spoons, masks, and sculptures of forest animals. Begun in the mid-1980s, this industry has allowed a half-dozen families from El Remate to turn from forest farming to artisanship, from burning trees to carving hundreds of handicraft pieces from a single fallen tree trunk.

Traveling on toward Tikal, you will pass kilometer after kilometer of deforested land, passing through several villages where horses and pigs wander across the highway at inopportune times. Watch the ridge lines for the silhouettes of unexcavated Maya settlements and house mounds. The area is replete with them.

Finally you will arrive at a long wall of forest that marks the southern boundary of Tikal National Park. Ten minutes farther on, traveling now through mature tropical forest, you will stop at a gateway that halts traffic so visitors can pay their entrance fee at the guard post. The guards will also offer site maps and books, a commercial enterprise that allows them to augment their modest salaries.

A few kilometers farther north, you will drive past several rustic restaurants on the right (good food at very basic prices), then past the sculpture museum on the left before you turn into the Tikal parking lot. Your driver or guide will direct you toward the site or to one of the three hotels, if you are spending the night. A campsite near the parking lot offers space to hang a hammock or pitch a tent, as well as a building with showers, bathrooms, and sinks.

UAXACTÚN

Located 26 kilometers (16 miles) driving distance north of the ruins and hotels of Tikal, Uaxactún consists of two major groups of temples and palaces built on five low hills surrounding a modern community harvesting *xate*, allspice, and chicle also called Uaxactún (pronounced Wa-shak-*toon*). The Maya cities of Uaxactún and Tikal were the two major lowland forest polities to expand their power during the decline of El Mirador, 40 miles to the north. Schele and Freidel (1990:140) point out that "Tikal and Uaxactún moved into the Classic period as full equals, both ready and able to assume the role of El Mirador when that kingdom disintegrated." Located only a half-day's walk from each another, Uaxactún and Tikal led interconnected histories for a thousand years, from the Middle Preclassic through the Classic.

Neighborhood rivals for several centuries, the two cities changed history on January 16, AD 378, when, according to monuments at both Uaxactún and Tikal, Uaxactún lost a war to warriors commanded by Tikal's Siyaj K'ak', the immigrant leader from Teotihuacán who brought a large section of the Maya forest into the "political, cultural, and economic sphere of Teotihuacan, then at the height of its powers" (Martin and Grube 2000:29). The arrival of Sikyaj K'ak' in the Petén signaled the political and military dominance by Teotihuacán of a large section of what is today the northern Guatemalan Petén, and his victory over Uaxactún signaled the beginning of Tikal's domination of that city (Stuart 1998; Martin and Grube 2000:28–29).

Siyaj K'ak' apparently resorted to drastic measures to prevent any reprisals from the defeated royal family of Uaxactún. Modern archaeological excavations revealed the bones of five members of a Maya family buried in Structure B-8 at Uaxactún, leading archaeologists to surmise that after Siyaj K'ak' conquered the city, his forces sacrificed those members of the royal family not killed or captured in battle. Two adult women (one of them pregnant), a child, and an infant were buried at the foot of the building, which was then dedicated as a monument to the victory. The grave of the husband and father of the family, the defeated leader of Uaxactún, has not been found; he was likely carried back to Tikal for ritual torture and sacrifice.

Archaeological work on Uaxactún's Group E revealed the first known building construction arranged to create an astronomical observatory for the solar solstices and equinoxes. Standing on the east stairway of Pyramid E-7, east of today's airstrip, visitors can look east across the plaza of Group E to see the sunrise peek around the corner of the right-hand Temple E-3 on December 21 (the shortest day of the year), around the corner of the left-hand Temple E-1 on June 21 (the longest day of the year), and directly above the middle Temple E-2 on September 23 and March 21 (when day and night are the same length) (Sharer 1994:182).

An Early Classic mural found in Structure B-13, recorded during excavations of 1926–1937 but later destroyed, showed a flat-topped building with three women inside, and just outside two men greeting one another. One man is colored black; the other carries a central Mexico weapon, a spearthrower called an *atlatl*. The scene is evidence of the intrusion of Teotihuacán power in the Maya region, with direct impact on Uaxactún.

Fortunately, the murals, with more than 20 individuals displayed, were captured in drawings by Antonio Tejeda before they were destroyed by vandals sometime after the 1940s.

One of the latest dated monuments in the Maya Tropical Forest, Stela 12, was erected at Uaxactún in AD 889 (Martin and Grube 2000:30).

IF YOU GO . . . UAXACTÚN   Visitors with cars can drive through Tikal National Park directly to the town and site of Uaxactún, 26 kilometers (16 miles) to the north. An alternative route takes travelers north from the town of San Andrés, located on Lake Petén Itzá, through the community of San Miguel, then northeast through Biotopo El Zotz to Uaxactún. This latter road is notoriously foul during the rainy season, but pleasant— although bumpy—during the dry season.

The community of Uaxactún is situated along both lengths of a 1940s airstrip formerly used by C-47 Dakotas, surplus World War II airplanes, to pick up blocks of chicle and fly them to market. The Maya site is located within easy walking distance of the town, on hills above both sides of the airstrip. Groups A and B are located northwest of town, and Group E is due east of town. An IDAEH guardpost is located at the entrance to the community. Local families have opened several restaurants and a small Maya posada where you can spend the night.

YAXJÁ

The Maya city of Yaxjá was a large lakeside settlement perched on the northern shore of 27-meter-deep (89-foot) Lake Yaxjá, from which the site takes its name, "Green Water." Epigrapher David Stuart's phonetic reading of the site's name glyph demonstrates that the city's original Maya name has survived to the present day (Sharer 1994:194, 619). Yaxjá was one of the most densely populated Maya sites in the Maya Tropical Forest (Kelly 1996:114) and is the only site known to have had streets as well as causeways. One of the city's causeways leads down to the lake, where a modern boat dock likely sits on the same site of docks used by the Maya. In the east acropolis, the 10-story-tall Temple 216 provides a panoramic view of Lake Yaxjá, the surrounding forest, and the island site of Topoxte' (see below).

At its peak during the Late Classic era, an estimated 42,000 people lived in and around Yaxjá. Archaeologists working at the site have identified more than 500 structures, 9 large acropolis groups, and 40 stelae, 20 of them carved. The stelae and excavations indicate that Yaxjá was occupied from the first through the ninth centuries but flourished from AD 357 to 793.

Located in frequently contested territory between the giant rivals Tikal, Caracol, and Naranjo, Yaxjá was the site of several Classic-era battles. Stelae from the western Petén note that the boy king K'ak Tiliw Chan Chaak (aka Smoking-Squirrel) of Naranjo attacked Yaxjá in AD 710 during a campaign to establish dominance in the central Petén (Schele and Freidel 1990:189). The attack was part of a successful attempt to restore Naranjo's prestige after humiliating losses to Caracol. A year later, in 711, K'ak Tiliw Chan Chaak's warriors battled those of Yaxjá on nearby Lake Sacnab, "Clear Lake," located due east of Lake Yaxjá.

Pollen cores from Lake Yaxjá provide a record of human occupation at the site from 1000 BC through the Classic era, and through the collapse into Postclassic and colonial times (D. Rice and P. Rice 1984:13). The studies indicate that forests surrounding the site were essentially cleared by Early Classic times, when the population of the Maya Tropical Forest likely reached 4–5 million people (Deevey et al. 1979:298). Studies by archaeologists T. Pat Culvert, Vilma Fialko, Tom Sever, and remote-sensing specialist Dan Irwin revealed that the population of Yaxjá depended heavily on water control and agricultural development in the lowland areas called *bajos* that surround Yaxjá and cover 40 percent of today's Guatemalan Petén. As population grew around Yaxjá and other sites, deforestation led to erosion, which filled in the *bajos* and diminished food production (Gidwitz 2002:35).

The human population of the Yaxjá basin grew from an average of 25 people per square kilometer at the close of the Middle Preclassic (1000–300 BC) to an average of 211 people per square kilometer in the Late Classic (AD 500–900) (D. Rice and P. Rice 1984:17; Gidwitz 2002:28).

On the western end of Lake Yaxjá, a half-dozen various sized islands contain the remains of a Late Postclassic Maya settlement known as Topoxte.' The ruins include fourteenth-century stone pyramids and temples built in late Chichén Itzá, Yucatán style, with square columns and low, block-like structures. More than 200 house mounds and structures have been identified on the three largest islands (Bullard 1970:252). The Topoxte' islands were likely occupied during the Preclassic and Classic eras, but the architecture visible today comes from Late Postclassic occupation (Johnson 1985). Classic era glyphs indicate that when K'ak Tiliw Chan Chaak (Smoking-Squirrel) sacked nearby Yaxjá in AD 710, he dug up a recently buried Yaxjá ruler, Yax B'olon Chaak, and scattered his bones on one of the Topoxte' islands (Martin and Grube 2000:76). Prompted probably by the small spaces inside the buildings, local tradition holds that the inhabitants of Topoxte' were dwarfs.

The Postclassic Maya at Topoxte' apparently practiced sacrificial decapitation, as did their neighbors at Nohpeten and Lake Macanché (between Lake Petén Itzá and Lake Yaxjá). Archaeologists have excavated Postclassic human skulls buried in rows or facing each other at all three sites, bringing to mind the reported seventeenth century Itza Maya practice of displaying enemy skulls on stakes and modern Itza Maya rituals of venerating human skulls on specific ceremonial days in the town of San José, Petén (P. Rice and D. Rice 1985:181). Modern Itza still carry red-painted human skulls from house to house on specific Itza Maya holy days.

IF YOU GO . . . YAXJÁ   A spur road takes travelers 11 kilometers (7 miles) north from the Flores-Belize highway to Lake Yaxjá and the nearby archaeological site of Yaxjá. El Sombrero Lodge and EcoCamp has cabins and a restaurant on the southeastern shore of the lake. Despite the enticing beach and refreshing-looking water of Lake Yaxjá, visitors are warned to be extremely wary if they decide to swim in the lake. Crocodiles do live along the shore, and they have attacked tourists.

You can stay either at El Sombrero, which has rooms with beds and a restaurant, or camp at the Yaxjá archaeological site for free on two-story, open-walled, wooden platforms beneath palm roofs. The campsite has an excellent view of the lake, but you must bring your own food.

To get to the island site of Topoxte', you will need to rent a canoe to travel to the western end of Lake Yaxjá. When I visited the site with Guatemalan researchers various times during the 1980s and 1990s, we consistently found boa constrictors inhabiting the site.

EL ZOTZ

The ancient city of El Zotz (The Bat) lies inside a 495-square kilometer (191 sq. mi.) wildlife biotope of the same name on the western border of Tikal National Park. Unexcavated and largely unexplored, the site is situated near a large cliff filled with bats. They cloud the sky at dawn and dusk each day as they leave and return from feeding on forest nectars and insects. Access is by road: traveling north from Flores and San Andrés, turn east at the crossroads town of El Cruce a Dos Aguadas toward Uaxactún. This road is frequently impassable during the rainy season, even in four-wheel-drive vehicles.

6   🌿 *Belize*

Introduction

On the third day of the expedition to climb Little Quartz Ridge, we began to eat snails. The leader of our eight-person expedition into southern Belize had contracted six Mopan Maya guides from the farming community of San José, Belize. They would be our guides and help carry our food and gear, including plant presses used by the expedition botanist and the various backpacks of equipment used to gather data in this isolated area. Our Mopan guides knew the surrounding forest well. They had grown up here on the southern edge of the Columbia River Forest Reserve, clearing forest plots to plant corn, beans, and chilies. By contrast, we had arrived in their village with cardboard boxes of food in cans, boxes, and plastic bags—tuna, sardines, corned beef, instant rice, and cheese. We ate well during the first two days of the hike toward Little Quartz Ridge. We had brought enough food for all 14 of us, carefully calculated, including the Mopan guides. What we hadn't counted on was how voraciously the Mopan would devour the store-bought food. They were especially fond of the cheese.

On the third night, we camped beside a stream in an abandoned *chicleros'* clearing called Union Camp. We pitched our tents in a grassy field and built a fire just up from the stream bank. Our Mopan guides built a separate fire a few yards distant behind a ramshackle palm-thatched hut that looked like it was about to fall down. As we began talking about what to fix for dinner, the head Mopan guide approached our fire and sheepishly pointed out that all the food we had brought was gone, eaten up.

"You didn't bring enough food," he suggested. With a smile, though, he pointed out that the stream we were camped beside was full of jutes. He

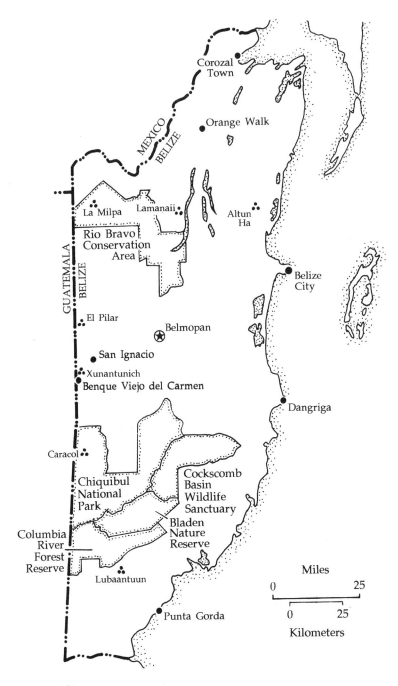

MAP 6. Belize

used the Belizean pronunciation, "hooties." Still pondering our miscalculation of food supplies, we walked over to the stream and shined flashlights into the water. Attached to the rocks on the streambed below were dozens of 3-inch-long conical snails. Scientists know them as *Pachychilus indiorum.* Throughout the Maya forest, they are called *jutes* in Spanish, "hooties" in Belize.

Jutes look like small, gray ice-cream cones. One end spirals to a sharp point, and the other opens like the mouth of a cave with a half-dome on top. In a contortion not unnatural for a snail, the living hootie keeps its body in the shell but sticks both its head and foot slightly out of the mouth to attach to underwater rocks and glean food passing by in the stream. Hooties are acceptable fare among the indigenous people of the Maya Tropical Forest, valued as protein when there is little else to be had.

Reluctantly, we plucked the hapless *jutes* from their watery home and dropped them into a blue *peltre* (pewter) cooking pot. Guided by our Mopan adviser, we filled the pot with stream water and put the pot on to boil. When the hooties had cooked for 10 minutes, we poured off the steaming water. Each of us gingerly selected a few piping hot hooties to begin the evening meal.

To eat a hootie, you take a rock and crush off the very tip of the hard, cone-shaped snail. Then, you place the larger, open end of the snail in your mouth and suck vigorously. The curled, black slug pops into your mouth with a rush of air. Then, you chew: gritty, dirt-flavored gristle. But it's protein, and it keeps your strength up after three days of climbing toward Little Quartz Ridge.

You can imagine the type of banter prompted by eight conservationists crunching and slurping boiled hooties.

"Hey, these are really just escargots, Maya escargots."

"You'd pay big money for these in a restaurant."

"Yeah, show me a restaurant that serves hooties and I'll buy you a bottle of wine to go with them."

"I think I'll skip the hooties and just drink the wine."

We were halfway through the bucket of boiled snails when Mick Fleming walked over to where the Mopan Maya were camped to ask the leader about some of the gear. As Mick turned the corner behind the dilapidated thatched hut, the Mopan froze. Three of them were holding 6-inch half-wheels of Gouda cheese, which they were eagerly gnawing on, while their friends awaited their turn.

"What's with all the cheese? Is this where all our cheese went?" Mick asked.

One of the Mopan, his mouth stuffed full of Gouda, mumbled, "What cheese?"

Slack-jawed and dejected but always a gentleman, poor Mick stumbled back to the campsite and took his place on a log around the fire.

"Pass me the hooties, please," he said.

Geography of Belize

Tucked into the eastern, Caribbean base of the Yucatán Peninsula, the nation of Belize hosts a delightfully diverse mosaic of Central American, Mexican, Caribbean, and Maya cultures. Yet all of this diversity—and a wealth of natural ecosystems and ancient Maya cities—is packed into the second-smallest country in Central America (Belize is about the size of Massachusetts), with the smallest population of any of the Central American nations.

Archaeologist Anabel Ford points out that at the peak of the Classic Maya civilization, around AD 900, the territory of Belize had five times the population that it does today (Ford 1995:1). Although the nation is twice the size of Jamaica, which has 2.6 million people, and larger than El Salvador, with 6.6 million people, Belize has never passed 300,000 inhabitants in modern times.

Belize is probably best known for its marine environment; it has the second-longest barrier reef in the world, after Australia's Great Barrier Reef. Belize's biodiversity-rich reef stretches 200 kilometers (120 miles) from the Mexican border in the north to the Sapodilla Cays in the Gulf of Honduras. The reef is as close as a few hundred meters offshore along the northern Ambergris Cay but more than 40 kilometers (24 miles) offshore at the southern Belizean town of Placencia. More than 450 sand and mangrove cays (pronounced "keys") dot the Caribbean Sea alongside the reef. Belize is one of the few places in the world—along with northeastern Australia, the Philippines, and Indonesia—where coral reefs and rainforest occur in such close proximity to one another and are so closely connected (Hain 1987:76). At the same time, the health of Belize's coral reef ecosystem is negatively impacted by deforestation of mainland tropical forests and the resulting sedimentation this destruction creates.

Belize's tradition of looking to the sea, rather than to the land, for livelihood has allowed the country to maintain much of its landmass in its original vegetation, including 55 percent (1,262,800 hectares; 4,876 sq. mi.) in natural forest. (The remainder of this original vegetation is savanna and native grassland.) Moreover, almost half of the country's forest is managed by the government or private owners for conservation or sustainable production (Brokaw et al. 1998:225).

Belize's wealth of lowland tropical forest, tropical savanna, wetlands, lagoons, mangroves, and upland pine forest keep alive 4,000 species of plants, 150 mammal species, 540 bird species, and 151 species of reptiles and amphibians, protecting the most intact complex of wildlife and natural ecosystems in the Maya Tropical Forest. The country's animal and plant life is especially diverse because the country is home to species from both the North and South American continents, as well as species from the Greater Antilles (Iremonger and Sayre 1994:35).

The nation's dense vegetation is dominated by lowland tropical forest interspersed with savannas of slender palmettos, scrub oaks, and fire-resistant pine trees. The vegetation becomes dryer as you move from the south to the north. The tall, moist forests in the southern districts receive an average of 4.5 meters (177 inches) of precipitation each year; the dryer north averages only 1.3 meters (51 inches).

In the heart of the country, almost in the center of an axis formed by lines running north-south and east-west, lies the Mountain Pine Ridge, an elevated plateau where pine forests grow atop the oldest exposed land surface in Central America. Farther south, the Maya Mountains cut like an elevated slash mark running southwest to northeast, rising to the highest elevations in the country. As David Rains Wallace points out, the Maya Mountains are a mass of granitic rock that has pushed through the limestone shelf of southwestern Belize to reach a height of 1,120 meters (3,675 feet) (D. Wallace 1997b:75).

On the Maya Mountains peak called Little Quartz Ridge, primitive plants called cycads keep alive a genetic tradition unchanged since the era of the dinosaurs. Described by one writer as looking "like pineapples on steroids," they are living fossils from the Mesozoic era, whose only surviving relatives grow on top of the tallest peaks of Guatemala's volcanic chain and on the mountains of western Cuba, giving rise to speculation that the plants survived ice ages and numerous climate change on the few mountaintops that stayed above water during repeated sea level rises (Owens 1996).

From the Maya Mountains' tallest point, Victoria Peak (1,127 meters; 3,699 feet), adventurous climbers can look westward to the flat shelf of the Guatemalan Petén and eastward toward the dozens of cays of the Caribbean Sea, interspersed along Belize's barrier reef.

A combination of low population density and rising income from international ecotourism has prompted a succession of Belizean governments to create new protected areas in the country. But challenges to the nation's wealth of biological resources still exist. During the late 1990s, government officials signed logging agreements with several Malaysian logging companies that high-graded the mahogany and tropical cedar stands of the southern portion of the country, and agriculture for citrus farming and slash-and-burn milpa farming continue to eat into the forest at the rate of 5 percent of the nation's forest cover each year (Barry and Vernon 1995:133).

A 1996 U.S. Agency for International Development study using satellite imagery estimated an annual forest loss of almost 25,000 hectares (61,775; 97 sq. mi.) per year between the late 1980s and mid-1990s, 90 percent of it on private lands or on national lands outside the nation's protected areas (White et al. 1996). Most of this deforestation came from agricultural development, ranging from large citrus plantations to the combined impact of many small milpas.

Government officials and environmentalists faced off in court between 2002 and 2004 over a Canadian-funded proposal for a nine-megawatt hydroelectric dam on the Macal River. The Chalillo Dam's reservoir will flood vital wildlife habitat in the Chiquibul National Park, the nation's largest protected area, and the neighboring Chiquibul National Forest, threatening the breeding ground of scarlet macaws and one of the last sound strongholds for the Central America tapir. Despite heroic efforts to prevent the dam's destructive development, Belizean and international conservationists have so far not won this pitched battle against a get-rich-quick scheme that will cost Belize dearly in both ecological and economic realms for years to come.

Belize's forest resources played the central role in the country's establishment. Spaniards were the first Europeans to claim title to the territory of Belize, which was still solidly inhabited by Maya communities when the Spaniards spied the New World. Despite the Spanish claim, British pirates were the first to actually occupy the area. They used Belizean inlets and bays to resupply their pirate vessels after patrolling for Spanish ships returning to Europe with gold and silver. During the late seventeenth century, British loggers began to live along the coast of Belize, taking advantage of the healthy stands of logwood (*Haematoxylon campechianum;* Spanish = *palo de tinte;* Yucatec Maya = *ek'*, "black"). They cut the logwood into lengths that fit into the holds of British ships, which transported the wood to England for use as a purple dye for clothing. As the British exported logwood to Europe, they imported African slaves as laborers, creating the first foundation for the Black Belizean population of today. As easy supplies of logwood dwindled, the British loggers turned increasingly to exports of mahogany (*Swietenia macrophylla;* Spanish = *caoba;* Yucatec Maya = *puna*).

Faced with the inevitable, Spanish authorities learned to tolerate the British interlopers on land they saw as their own. The Treaty of Versailles, in 1783, and the Convention of London, in 1786, confirmed the rights of British settlers in Belize, allowing them to legally cut mahogany as well as logwood, but Spain retained sovereignty over the region. The Spaniards also forbade the British to establish agricultural plantations or create local governments (Hall and Brignoli 2003:37).

But in 1798, a British ship gave chase to Spanish ships near Saint George's Caye, establishing British authority over what they came to call British Honduras and giving rise to a still celebrated Belizean national holiday. In 1862 the British government established the colony of British Honduras, led by a lieutenant governor who reported to the governor of Jamaica, another British colony. This subordination to Jamaica was eliminated in 1884, 13 years after British Honduras had become a crown colony (Hall and Brignoli 2003:45).

In 1973 British Honduras changed its name to Belize in anticipation of the 1981 Day of Independence from the United Kingdom, although the country remains part of the British Commonwealth. The Queen of England still graces the Belizean national currency, the Belizean dollar, which is pegged permanently at two Belizean dollars to one United States dollar.

In such a fashion, a combination of geography and history placed Belize in a long-term land controversy with neighboring Guatemala. Based on treaties from the Spanish colonial era, Guatemala has periodically voiced claims of sovereignty over 12,000 square kilometers (4,633 sq. mi.) of Belizean territory, representing about half of the nation's land area. Guatemalan officials recognized Belizean independence in 1991, after Belize agreed to voluntarily curtail its maritime claim to the sea lying south of the Sarstoon River, which serves as Belize's southern boundary with Guatemala. Nonetheless, Guatemala periodically revives its 140-year-old claim to southern Belize.

In reaction to the intermittent threat of a Guatemalan invasion, the United Kingdom kept several thousand soldiers and more than a dozen Harrier jets in Belize until 1994, when this military presence was scaled back to 80 UK military personnel and a half-dozen helicopters. The British troops utilize Belize as a jungle training camp in exchange for providing military aid and training to the Belizean Defense Force, which consists of around 1,000 Belizean troops (Lapper 2000).

Tensions between Belize and Guatemala have been exacerbated by an ill-defined physical border along Belize's western limit (Gonzales 2001:A3). Although the border has been defined on paper for more than 100 years, the boundary still is not physically marked on the ground. (The border between Mexico and northern Guatemala, for example, has long been de-lineated on the ground by a 10-meter-wide (33-foot) deforested swath cut through the forest.) In 1992 an expedition companion and I hiked from the Río Chiquibul inside the Guatemalan Petén across the undefined border and on to the Belizean archaeological site of Caracol, using an abandoned logging road. Once we left the newly emerging settlements in Guatemala, we saw no people other than our two Guatemalan guides until we got to Caracol.

The two Guatemalan farmers guided us as far as where they thought the border went, then left us on our own to proceed farther into Belize. Judg-ing by maps and walking distance, we declared a specific spot on the road as the demarcation line between the two countries and tied a piece of flag-ging tape on an overhanging branch in a symbolic marking of the border.

Having entered Belize "illegally," I returned to Guatemala several days later at the border-crossing town of Melchor de Menchos by simply walk-ing across the bridge that separates the two countries. I presented myself at the Guatemalan entry point as having never left the country. The Gua-temalan border guards waved me through with a shrug.

Because there still is no clearly marked physical border between Be-lize and the Guatemalan Petén, Guatemalan farmers frequently wander into Belizean territory—according to the Belizeans—and Belizean farmers encroach on the Petén (according to the Guatemalans). The dispute over where one country ends and the next begins led to the unfortunate death of several farmers during the 1990s, when villagers from one border com-munity raided their interloping neighbors in other, nearby communities in a jungle turf war.

In the early years of the twenty-first century, workmen finally began to physically delimit, clear, and mark the border between Belize and the

Guatemalan Petén, with help from the Organization for American States' Geographical Institute for Geography and History (Joseph Palacio, personal communication, March 2001).

Modern Peoples

The population of Belize is a colorful mix of Garífuna, Creoles, Yucatec Maya, Mopan Maya, Q'eqchi' Maya, Hindus, Chinese, British expatriates, German-speaking Mennonites, and U.S. expatriates, among others. The dominant language is a lilted, Caribbean-style English, although Spanish is overtaking English in the districts of northern Belize. Political power tends to concentrate in the hands of the Creoles, but such striking diversity within such a small population—the country has never surpassed 300,000 people—makes Belize a positive exercise in ethnic tolerance and intermarriage.

Since the country's independence from the United Kingdom in 1981, approximately 50,000 political and economic refugees from El Salvador and Guatemala have moved to Belize, gradually changing the country's Caribbean island style to one more like the rest of Central America. These Central American refugees now outnumber the 25,000 Maya and Garífuna Belizeans (Palacio 2001), pointing the country toward a future in which Spanish will overtake English as the dominant language. In the first years of the twenty-first century, just under half of the country's population spoke Spanish as their first language.

The 2000 official census of Belize cited a population of 249,000 people, but there are an additional 60,000 Belizeans living in the United States— almost 20 percent of all Belizeans—mostly in New York City. Seventy-five percent of these emigrants are Creoles (Barry and Vernon 1995:126).

THE GARÍFUNA

Sometimes known as Garinagu or Black Caribs, the Garífuna are descendants of indigenous Carib Indians who lived on the Windward Islands (primarily St. Vincent) of the Lesser Antilles, West Indies, before Spaniards arrived in the New World. The Caribs, who called themselves Kalipuna or Kwaib (hence the modern terms Garífuna and Carib) originated on the South American mainland but had taken over the islands from the original Arawak Indian inhabitants. These newer settlers mixed with Africans in

1635, when two Spanish ships carrying captured tribespeople from Nigeria shipwrecked off the island of St. Vincent and the survivors swam to shore (Eltringham, Fisher, and Stewart 1999:260). The Africans blended with the Caribbean Indians to produce the ethnic group now called Garífuna.

Although the Garífuna fiercely resisted domination by European colonists, Old World diseases and warfare had seriously reduced their number by the end of the eighteenth century. Nonetheless, English authorities were reluctant to allow a free Black society to exist in the midst of their island territories. In the wake of a failed rebellion against British rule, the Garífuna were exiled to the island of Baliceaux, where more than half of them died. In 1797 the British rounded up the 5,000 Garífuna women, men, and children who survived and transported them to Roatán, in the Bay Islands of Honduras (Rust 2001:104). Later that same year, the Spanish authorities of Honduras took 1,700 surviving Garífuna to the mainland, near the modern city of Trujillo, where they benefited the Spanish colony through their farming skills (Eltringham, Fisher, and Stewart 1999:260).

From mainland Honduras, the Garífuna expanded along the Caribbean coast, establishing communities in the Bluefields region of northeastern Nicaragua, near Livingston, Guatemala, and along the southern coast of Belize. Within Belize, they established settlements at Stann Creek (Dandriga), Punta Gorda, Hopkins, and Seine Beight (Dobson 1973:256).

The Garífuna migration into Belize was initially resisted by other ethnic groups already established there, and the British Superintendent tried to expel them in 1811, but an even larger contingent of Garífuna moved from Honduras to Belize in 1832. Their arrival, on November 19, 1832, is now celebrated nationally as Garífuna Settlement Day. Today, most of Belize's 11,000 Garífuna live in six villages located along the country's Caribbean coast, where they maintain their original language (Herlihy 1997:217).

CREOLE

The Belizean Creoles are largely Anglo-African, in contrast to the Garífuna, who are Amerindian-African. Representing about 30 percent of Belize's population, the Creoles trace their heritage to the mixing of early English settlers with African slaves. The Africans were involuntarily transported to Belize from Jamaica to cut timber between 1720 and the early 1800s (Barry and Vernon 1995:69). Through the years, the African-Jamaican-English married other Belizeans from a variety of ethnic groups to blossom as one of the predominant groups of modern Belize. Belize City, the largest city in the country, is 70 percent Creole. Most Creole Belizeans speak both English and Creole, a patois amalgam of languages based on English but nonetheless difficult for non-natives to understand.

Not all Creoles are dark-skinned. Instead, most Belizeans who identify themselves as English-speaking, non-Maya, and non-Mestizo would likely call themselves Creole, a distinction that is increasingly seen as cultural rather than racial. Creoles live mostly in the District of Belize, which includes Belize City, and they tend to dominate the country's political offices and administration.

MESTIZOS

The most numerous group in Belize are the Mestizos, at more than 40 percent of the population. As Spanish-speakers—though most of them are bilingual in English as well—the Mestizos are displaying greater power in local and national politics, gradually making inroads into arenas long considered the domain of the Creole Belizeans. The Mestizos' base population moved into northern Belize after the mid-nineteenth-century Caste War of Yucatán, when the Yucatec Maya rebelled against their Mexican overlords and—urged on by a talking cross—"came within a hair's breadth of driving their white masters into the sea" (Reed 1964:vii).

Beginning in 1847, Mexican families filtered into northern Belize and the Guatemalan Petén to escape the rebelling Maya. By 1857, the northern Belizean town of Corozal counted 2,000 refugees from the war, among them Spanish-speaking Mestizos, non-rebelling Yucatec Maya, and disaffected rebels seeking peace and stability under English rule (Chenaut 1989:73–74). In subsequent years, this base population mixed with other ethnic groups of Belize, including the late-twentieth-century influx of refugees from the war in El Salvador. Still, the two northernmost Belizean political units, the Districts of Corozal and Orange Walk, as well as the western District of Cayo, continue to be dominated by Spanish-speaking Belizeans of Mexican origin (Chenaut 1989:75).

MOPAN MAYA

Around 3,000 Mopan Maya live today in the District of Toledo, in southern Belize, and in western Belize in the District of Cayo. Historically, the Mopan lived in south-central and southeastern Petén, Guatemala, as well as in southern Belize (Schwartz 1990:33). Like their linguistic cousins, the

Yucatec-speaking Lacandón and the Itza Maya, the Mopan were part of an extensive group of Postclassic and colonial era Maya that J. Eric S. Thompson called the Chan Maya (Thompson 1977). The Mopan of Guatemala and Belize numbered 10,000–20,000 during the colonial era of the sixteenth and seventeenth centuries, but they had been seriously decimated by disease and war with the Spaniards and finally reduced by Spanish authorities into settlements in southeastern Petén and southern Belize (Schwartz 1990:35). Later, most of Belize's Mopan communities fled the territory to escape the British, joining up with family members in the Petén (Barry and Vernon 1995:79; G. Jones 1998:19–22).

Then, in an 1866 reversal, more than 100 Mopan from the settlement of San Luis, Petén, migrated into Belize's Toledo District to escape forced labor and taxes. In southern Belize, they settled near Pueblo Viejo and San Antonio, a region that is still the epicenter of Mopan settlement in Belize (Wilk 1997:57). Today, most of Belize's Mopan Maya maintain traditional rural lives, producing corn, rice, beans, cacao, and honey. In the Mopan community of San José, Toledo District, where Santiago Billy and I conducted interviews in 1990, the families planted 2–4 hectares (5–10 acres) of milpa each year, half of it from newly cut tropical forest, half from milpa regrowth.

Q'EQCHI' MAYA

The 12,000-plus Q'eqchi' Maya of southern Belize had their origins in southeastern Guatemala, in the mountains of Alta Verapaz (population figures from the 2000 census; Liza Grandia, personal communication, 2004). Many Q'eqchi' were expelled from southeastern Guatemala during the 1860s and 1870s, when German, English, and Ladino coffee planters took over traditional lands of the Q'eqchi'. By 1890 German companies owned more than 300,000 hectares (741,300 acres; 158 sq. mi.) of Verapaz territory, and 61 percent of all Guatemalan exports moved through the hands of merchants in Hamburg, Germany (Wilk 1997:50).

In reaction to loss of their land and legal maneuvers that forced Q'eqchi' to work on German coffee plantations, the Q'eqchi' began to move into southwestern Belize and the Guatemalan Petén. One large group began working on the plantations of a German entrepreneur named Bernard Cramer, who speculated in land in Toledo District during the second half of the nineteenth century. One of his sons, Herman Cramer, employed Q'eqchi' laborers to produce coffee shaded by rubber trees, as well as nutmeg, mace, allspice, and achiote. His major success came with cacao shaded by plantains and bananas; he exported 19,455 kilograms (42,800 pounds) of cacao in 1906 (Wilk 1997:61). Although the original Cramer plantations have been bought and sold by numerous owners through the decades, a single section of 14,600 hectares (36,000 acres; 146 sq. km.; 56 sq. mi.) of mostly forested land, called the Dolores Estate, still exists in the southwestern corner of Belize, the largest block of private land in Toledo District (Wilk 1997:61).

Of 36 major villages in Toledo District, 29 are inhabited by Q'eqchi'. The porous Belize-Guatemala border allows the Belizean Q'eqchi' to maintain close ties to relatives and constant trading networks with the 750,000 Q'eqchi' who live in neighboring Guatemala. In some communities, Q'eqchi' and Mopan Maya divide the surrounding farmland in harmony.

During the 1990s, the Q'eqchi' allied themselves with the Mopan Maya in a land rights movement to claim a Maya homeland in Toledo District. Together, the two Maya groups founded the Toledo Maya Cultural Council in 1978, an organization that represents the 14,000 Q'eqchi' and Mopan of Toledo District in southern Belize. The Council petitioned the government of Belize to establish a 202,347-hectare Maya homeland (500,000 acres; 2,024 sq. km.; 781 sq. mi.) to establish secure tenure on traditionally claimed land (TMCC and TAA 1997:5). Part of the impetus for this movement was the granting by the government of Belize, since 1993, of 17 logging concessions covering 202,347 hectares (500,000 acres) on traditional Maya land in southern Belize. Many of these large concessions went to Southeast Asian logging operations (TMCC and TAA 1997:5,123).

The Maya land rights movement has been resisted by Belize's Garífuna and Black Creole, who question why the Maya have rights to government-donated land when their ethnic groups do not, even though they have been in Belize for a longer period of time.

MENNONITES

One of the seemingly more incongruous groups of the family of Belizean people is the Mennonite population of northwestern Belize. Belize's approximately 9,000 Mennonites descend from the sixteenth-century Anabaptists, a religious group that dates to the Protestant Reformation. The group was led by a Dutchman, Menno Simons (1492–1559), hence the name Mennonites. (The more familiar Amish of the eastern and central United States later evolved from the Mennonites.) The Mennonites' pacifist tendencies led to governmental restrictions in the Netherlands and they moved first to Switzerland, then to Prussia and to Russia in the late eighteenth century, from which some families emigrated to the Great Plains of the United States and Canada during the 1870s. The outbreak of World War I led to restrictions in teaching their German-Dutch dialect, which prompted a move to Ciudad Cuauhtémoc, in the Mexican state of Chihuahua. Government restrictions in Mexico led to a move to British Honduras in 1957–1958, where they were joined by fellow Mennonites from Manitoba, Canada. The Mennonites became Belizean citizens upon the country's independence from Great Britain in 1981.

Twenty-first-century Belizean Mennonites are divided into conservative and progressive groups. The progressive families freely use electricity and motorized vehicles, while their more conservative brothers and sisters eschew them, preferring animal-drawn carts and kerosene lanterns (Eltringham, Fisher, and Stewart 1999:207). The Mennonites' six major settlements in Belize are Blue Creek, Shipyard, Little Belize, Barton Creek, Spanish Lookout, and Progresso. Of these settlements, Blue Creek is the most open to the modern world and Little Belize, Barton Creek, and Shipyard are the most traditional.

Belize's Mennonites speak a patois dialect called Low German or *Plattdeutsch,* but learn formal German in order to read the German Bible and sing hymns. In school, the children learn English as well, and many Mennonites learn Spanish from their neighbors.

The men and boys wear straw cowboy hats and overalls, and the women and girls wear conservative cotton dresses, white hosiery, and tight-fitting cotton bonnets, making the families look more like Pennsylvania farmers than Central American homesteaders. Their communities are orderly and successful, and the Mennonites grow much of the food the rest of the Belizean people—and visitors to Belize—consume.

Mennonites produce more than half of Belize's corn and rice; those of Spanish Lookout are Belize's primary producers and wholesale distributors of milk and commercial poultry (Jantzen 1989:666). Yet the Mennonites' agricultural practices have raised serious questions about environmental impact. When Mennonite farmers buy new land, they clear it by attaching a giant ship anchor chain between two tractors and pulling down the tropical forest, acres at a time. They pile the vegetation into tall pyres and burn it in fires so large they show up on satellite images. The farmers utilize the resulting cleared land to raise crops such as sorghum maize, corn, and rice in full-scale agribusiness style, with silos, barns, and barbed wire fences.

As contributors to the conservation survey *Parks in Peril* state it, "Mennonite farmers have completely transformed the [northern Belize] landscape for intensive agriculture. Using bulldozers, pesticides, herbicides, fertilizer, and a fierce work ethic, they have left scarcely a tree standing" (A. Wallace and Naughton-Treves 1998:225).

OTHER BELIZEAN GROUPS

Finally, in an interesting historical footnote, a group of die-hard former Confederates immigrated into the southern Belize district of Toledo after the American Civil War, where they established sugar plantations, mills, and rum distilleries 10 kilometers (6 miles) in from the Caribbean coast (as well as at the archaeological site of Lamanai). Their community, called the Toledo Settlement, struggled to survive during the period 1867–1870, using imported East Indian laborers, but by 1910 most of the former Confederates had abandoned the area. By contrast, the East Indians stayed on to become major players in the development of Toledo District (Wilk 1997:56).

The most recent influx of immigrants into Belize arrived during the 1990s, when Taiwanese and Hong Kong Chinese purchased Belizean passports in a controversial program of "economic citizenship" (Barry and Vernon 1995:xvii).

Protected Areas

Belize began creating protected areas as early as the 1960s, but the national protected areas system came into being only in 1981. Supported by an emerging national environmental movement and funded by cooperating governments and international conservation organizations, Belize's protected area system had grown by 1995 to 142,077 hectares (351,072 acres; 1,420 sq. km.; 549 sq. mi.) in national parks, 4,316 hectares (10,665 acres; 43 sq. km.; 17 sq. mi.) of natural monuments, 44,399 hectares (109,711 acres; 444 sq. km.; 171 sq. mi.) of nature reserves, 42,614 hectares (105,298 acres; 426 sq. km.; 165 sq. mi.) of wildlife sanctuaries, 99,155 hectares (254,013 acres; 991 sq. km.; 397 sq. mi.) of private reserves, and large expanses of marine reserves in the Caribbean Sea offshore (Barry and Vernon 1995:137). Not counting the country's marine reserves, Belize's public and private protected lands exceed 3,324 square kilometers (831,759 acres; 1,299 sq. mi.)

An equally large system of national forests—20,720 square kilometers (8,000 sq. mi.)—exists alongside this expanse of protected areas, but the forest reserves are logged and occasionally "degazetted" (removed from protected status) for use as agricultural lands. Between 1977 and 1991, the government of Belize de-reserved 341 square kilometers (132 sq. mi.) of national forest for conversion to agriculture (Smith 1991, cited in Brokaw et al. 1998:226).

The impetus for de-reserving national forests comes from rural families' demands for additional agricultural land and the general decline in national income from logging. Exports of primary timber, mostly mahogany, were the major factor in Belize's economy until 1950, when income began to drop because of overharvesting (Brokaw et al. 1998:227).

Although Belize's protected areas provide excellent opportunities for viewing wildlife, you can get closeups of your favorite rainforest critters at the well-designed and professionally managed Belize Zoo, located between Belize City and Belmopan on the Western Highway. U.S.-trained Belizean citizen Sharon Matola has dedicated her career to creating a humane exhibit of jaguars, crocodiles, peccaries, monkeys, snakes, and dozens of bird species. As one of the leaders in ecosystem protection in Belize, Matola designed the Belize Zoo as an instrument of education for both residents and visitors to Belize, a function it serves very well.

Each year, more than 17,000 Belizean schoolchildren visit the Belize Zoo, where they are taught conservation education by Belizean professionals (the zoo hires only Belizean workers), providing many of the children with the only environmental education they receive. The zoo got its start when a documentary film project ended with no plan to deal with the native animals it had photographed. Matola created a home for them, which gradually evolved into one of the best conservation education opportunities in Central America. All animals acquired since the zoo's inception have come from government confiscation of illegal wildlife, as injured animals unable to return to the wild, or were newly born on site. The Belize Zoo does not buy animals or take animals from the wild.

BLADEN BRANCH NATURE RESERVE

Created in 1991, the Bladen Branch Nature Reserve incorporates 400 square kilometers (97,000 acres; 152 sq. mi.) of the watershed of the Bladen Branch of the Monkey River, on the southern edge of the Maya Mountains, Toledo District, Belize. The area protects some of the most pristine ecosystems in Central America, much of it humid subtropical forest, despite the fact that loggers felled mahogany trees in some sections of the reserve during the 1940s. A portion of today's Bladen Branch Nature Reserve was designated Belize's first national park in 1990, but the newer classification, as a nature reserve, provides the country's strictest designation for protected areas. Bladen is the largest such reserve in Belize.

The Bladen Branch Nature Reserve—usually known in Belize simply as "the Bladen"—protects around half of the southeastern slope of the Maya Mountains. The main divide of the Maya Mountains serves as the reserve's northwestern border. The reserve follows the downward slope of the main divide of the mountain peaks (1,100 meters; 3,609 feet) (Iremonger and Sayre 1994:12). A series of creeks traces through the valleys that lead down from the mountains, feeding into the Bladen Branch, which flows into the Monkey River. The reserve is almost completely surrounded by other reserves and protected areas—the Columbia River Forest Reserve, the two Maya Mountains Forest Reserves, Deep River Forest Reserve, and to the north Chiquibul National Park. Unlike most protected areas in Latin America, the Bladen Branch Nature Reserve has no human communities within its boundaries.

The Bladen Branch Nature Reserve protects "more than a hundred species of mammals, 350 species of birds, 750 species of trees, and 1,500 species of flowering plants" (Barry and Vernon 1995:141). Expeditions carried out in 1993 identified 12 different vegetation types within the reserve's boundaries, ranging from tall forest to savanna and grassland, and found at least three plant species, including two trees, that appear to be new to science (Iremonger and Sayre 1994:28). Birds that are increasingly rare in the rest of the Maya Tropical Forest, including the crested guan (*Penelope purpurascens*) and great curassow (*Crax rubra*)—due to both habitat destruction and hunting—are still common in the Bladen (Iremonger and Sayre 1994:35). Together with the adjoining Columbia River Forest Reserve, the Bladen Branch Nature Reserve represents "the richest herpetofaunal region in Belize, including at least one endemic frog" (Iremonger and Sayre 1994:35).

IF YOU WANT TO GO ... BLADEN BRANCH NATURE RESERVE Access to the Bladen is restricted to researchers with legal permits and ecotourists on organized tours led by guides with special permission to enter the reserve. Seek information from Belizean conservationist organizations or from the country's major tour companies.

COLUMBIA RIVER FOREST RESERVE

Located in Toledo District, the Columbia River Forest Reserve protects 440 square kilometers (170 sq. mi.) of subtropical wet forest and subtropical lower montane wet forest on rugged limestone hills and low mountains in southwestern Belize. The reserve receives between 2.5 and 4 meters (98–158 inches) of rainfall every year. Botanists estimate that the Columbia River Forest Reserve may host 1,500 species of plants, "which would represent a high percentage of all plant species in the country" (Parker et al. 1993:9). A 1990 expedition to the Columbia River Forest Reserve noted the presence of a recently discovered species, the limestone rainfrog (*Eleutherodactylus psephosypharus*), which appears only in Belize, Guatemala, and possibly Honduras (Bird 1997:2).

Researchers have documented more than 232 bird species in the area, which represent more than 90 percent of the evergreen tropical forest bird species in Belize. The late ornithologist Ted Parker noted that due to massive deforestation elsewhere, the Columbia River Forest Reserve probably protects the largest remaining population of the keel-billed motmot (*Electron carinatum*) in the world (Parker et al. 1993:10). Scientists involved in the 1992 Conservation International Rapid Assessment Program expedition to the reserve noted that "the Columbia River Forest Reserve may support globally significant numbers of neotropical migrant [birds], especially during certain migratory periods (e.g., March–April)" (Parker et al. 1993:12).

The reserve's ecosystems are threatened from the south by farming communities of Q'eqchi' and Mopan Maya, who hunt and burn forest in the reserve to create farmland. Lying on the southeastern flank of the Maya Mountains, the reserve is the source of a half-dozen major streams, which combine to form the important Aguacate River, Blue Creek, Mojo River, and Río Grande, all of which flow into the Gulf of Honduras near the town of Punta Gorda. The reserve incorporates Little Quartz Ridge, which rises to 1,000 meters (3,281 feet) in the northern sector of the reserve. Named after the quartz-rich polyphyritic rocks found there, Little Quartz Ridge is an intrusion of igneous rock pushed up through strata of limestone (Bird 1997:1; Williams 1996:73). The area is characterized by montane palm forest dominated by a rare tall palm, *Colpothrinax cookii*, that is endemic to Central America and occurs only on quartz soils at high elevations (Bird 1997:1; Parker et al. 1993:10). Other than Belize, the palm is found only in specific mountainous areas of Guatemala, Honduras, Costa Rica, and

Panama. Little Quartz Ridge also has exceptionally high—perhaps the highest—bird diversity in Belize (Bird 1997:5).

IF YOU GO . . . COLUMBIA RIVER FOREST RESERVE Most tourists enter the Columbia River Forest Reserve through contact with tour operators in Belize City or Punta Gorda. Researchers or adventurers who are confident of their ability in the bush have entered through the Mopan Maya town of San José, where local guides can safely deliver them to the reserve and back. This requires a hike of three-plus hours, through milpas and regrowth, before the visitor encounters high forest to begin the several days' climb to the higher peaks.

RÍO BRAVO CONSERVATION AREA

The Río Bravo Conservation and Management Area (RBCMA) is a privately owned conservation and sustainable development area that covers 1,052 square kilometers (259,949 acres; 406 sq. mi.) in northwestern Belize. The area is owned and managed by a Belizean nongovernmental organization, the Programme for Belize (PfB), founded in 1988. The government of Belize has formally authorized PfB to manage the reserve as a freehold property in trust for the Belizean people in perpetuity. The Río Bravo reserve represents 4 percent of Belizean territory. PfB seeks to preserve the natural heritage and biological diversity of the country, produce sufficient cash return on sustainable development of their lands to pay for its perpetual care, and assist surrounding communities in sustainable economic development to further Belize's economic interests (Programme for Belize 2001). PfB's current activities include marketing of certified sustainable "green" hardwoods, chicle gum production, archaeological surveys, ecotourism, and a carbon sequestration project. All income from the organization's economic activities on PfB land is, by law, reinvested in the reserve's management.

The RBCMA lands encompass a variety of natural ecosystems, including lowland tropical moist forest, savanna, and wetlands. It has one of the largest surviving stands of mahogany in Central America—though the trees are still too young for harvest—and an intact assemblage of wildlife species that includes 70 species of mammals, 350 bird species, and 250 species of trees (Beletsky 1999b:37).

The area was formerly part of a large forest holding of the British firm Belize Estate and Produce Company, which had exploited the forest for commercial hardwoods for a century before selling it in the early 1980s. A Belizean entrepreneur purchased the land and divided it into three tracts. He kept one block of land for an ecolodge and sold the other two—amounting to 1,878 square kilometers (464,000 acres; 725 sq. mi.)—to a Houston-based cattle company, which planned to clear the land for pasture, and to Coca-Cola Foods, which intended to clear the land for orange trees to produce juice concentrate for export. In turn, Coca-Cola donated 170 square kilometers (42,000 acres; 66 sq. mi.) of its holdings to the Massachusetts Audubon Society to protect migratory birds. The Massachusetts Audubon Society worked with Belizean conservationists to establish the Programme for Belize, and with other international organizations—especially The Nature Conservancy—purchased an additional 445 square kilometers (109,960 acres; 172 sq. mi.) of land from the Belizean entrepreneur. Coca-Cola later donated another 202 square kilometers (49,914 acres; 78 sq. mi.) and PfB purchased another 116 square kilometers (28,664 acres; 45 sq. mi.) from a logging company. Finally, in 1998, PfB acquired 77 square kilometers (19,027 acres; 30 sq. mi.) to consolidate the reserve into a single continuous block, creating total land coverage of 1,010 square kilometers (249,571 acres; 390 sq. mi.) (A. Wallace and Naughton-Treves 1998:219; Programme for Belize 1998).

The Río Bravo Area forms part of the Northern Belize Biological Corridor, an area conceptualized as linking the existing protected areas of northern Belize in a path of natural and impacted, but biodiversity-friendly, landscapes. The Río Bravo Conservation and Management Area has been proposed as a biosphere reserve to the United Nations Educational, Scientific, and Cultural Organization (UNESCO), but discussions to achieve this classification are currently stalled.

COCKSCOMB BASIN WILDLIFE SANCTUARY

The Cockscomb Basin Wildlife Sanctuary was the first protected area in the world designated specifically for jaguar conservation. Researchers identify the area as having Central America's largest population of jaguars (*Panthera onca*)—an estimated 80 individuals—as well as 290 species of birds, including the scarlet macaw (*Ara macao*), chestnut-bellied heron (*Agamia agami*), and great curassow (*Crax rubra*). At least 85 species of amphibians, lizards, snakes, and terrapins ("a tremendously rich herpetofauna") are thought to live in the area (Rath 1990:4, 20). Researchers on a 1990 expedition to Cockscomb (Rath 1990) came upon a large temporary pond that was serving as a breeding site for "several tens of thousands" of Mexican tree frogs (*Smilisca baudinii*), as well as thousands of red-eyed tree frogs (*Agalychnis callidryas*).

Cockscomb received the designation of national forest reserve in 1984, and in 1986 the government of Belize declared 1,214 hectares (3,000 acres; 12 sq. km.; 4.7 sq. mi.) the Cockscomb Basin Wildlife Sanctuary/Forest Reserve. In late 1990, the government expanded the area to 41,440 hectares (102,398 acres; 414 sq. km.; 160 sq. mi.) of the watersheds it protects, and by 2002 the area had reached 51,800 hectares (128,000 acres; 518 sq. km.; 200 sq. mi.). The Victoria Peak Natural Monument, Belize's second-highest mountain at 1,122 meters (3,680 feet), adjoins Cockscomb and is administered as part of it. The Cockscomb consists of two separate basins, each a separate watershed, separated by a low ridge of hills (Rath 1990:4). Still, the area is referred to as the Cockscomb basin, because it is bordered on three sides by high ridges of hills and on the fourth by foothills of the Maya Mountains. The basin's many streams give rise to two of southern Belize's major rivers, South Stann Creek and the Swasey, which feeds into the Monkey River on its way to the Caribbean Sea.

During more than two years of field research, wildlife biologist Alan Rabinowitz radio-collared five adult male jaguars for up to 14 months inside the reserve, revealing that each regularly used territories of 29 to 42 square kilometers (11–16 sq. mi.), with overlapping ranges (Rabinowitz 1986:18). Females jaguars used about one-third the territory males did.

Protection of the area for jaguars also provides crucial habitat for other cats of the Maya Tropical Forest, specifically the puma (*Puma concolor*), ocelot (*Felis pardalis*), margay cat (*Felis wiedii*), and jaguarundi (*Felis yaguaroundi*). As well, Central American tapirs (*Tapirus bairdii*) live within the reserve. The Cockscomb Basin Reserve was logged in the past and much of the vegetation is secondary, but wildlife is abundant, reaching 500 species of larger animals in total.

IF YOU GO ... COCKSCOMB BASIN As Barry and Vernon (1995:140) point out, "Unless you have a four-wheel-drive vehicle, the only way into the Cockscomb Basin Reserve is a five-mile [8-km.] hike, backpacking all your food, since there are no stores." If you are driving, take the Southern Highway 26 kilometers (16 miles) south of Dangriga to the village of Maya Center, then travel 10 kilometers (6 miles) westward on a rough road to the Cockscomb visitors center, museum, visitors dormitory and cabins, and campgrounds. The reserve has more than 32 kilometers

(20 miles) of maintained trails for hikers and bird watchers, and excellent pools and waterfalls for swimming and cooling off. The Belize Audubon Society, which manages Cockscomb, advises visitors to bring "sturdy shoes, long-sleeved shirts, long pants, insect repellent, sunscreen, and plenty of water."

CHIQUIBUL NATIONAL PARK

Formerly part of the Chiquibul Forest Reserve, the Chiquibul National Park rests against Belize's western border with the Guatemalan Petén. Chiquibul National Park abuts the Reserva de la Biósfera Montañas Mayas (formerly known as Reserva de la Biósfera Chiquibul) in neighboring Guatemala. The Chiquibul River is born in the Maya Mountains of southern Belize, but passes almost immediately into the Guatemalan Petén, where it runs for 75 percent of its length before crossing back into Belize as the Mopan River. In Belize, it merges with the Belize River and travels through the San Ignacio Valley, Belize's breadbasket, then on through the country's two largest cities—Belmopan and Belize City. In 1991 Belize created the Chiquibul National Park and Chiquibul Forest Reserve—1,015 square kilometers (250,807 acres; 392 sq. mi.) and 768 square kilometers (189,773 acres; 297 sq. mi.), respectively—to protect this vital watershed. In 1995 Guatemala followed suit by establishing the Reserva de la Biósfera Chiquibul (618 sq. km.; 152,708 acres; 239 sq. mi.) on its side of the border, creating a mirror-image frontier protected area. Although the original goal of this binational protected area was to create an international corridor for wildlife, the Guatemalan side of the forest has been invaded by several thousand Guatemalans, who illegally practice slash-and-burn farming and cattle ranching within the boundaries of the protected area. Satellite imagery indicates that these farmers' agricultural plots encroach into Belize's Chiquibul National Park, and researchers in the region report that Guatemalan hunters frequently poach wildlife from the Belizean side of the border.

Belize's Chiquibul National Park covers 1,865 square kilometers (460,842 acres; 720 sq. mi.) in western Cayo District of central Belize. The Chiquibul National Park surrounds the important archaeological site of Caracol. Lying due west of the Maya Mountains, the Chiquibul National Park and the surrounding Chiquibul Forest Reserve rest on a layer of limestone strata, which conceals the vast underground Chiquibul Cave System. The system is made up of four caves linked by water flows, including the seemingly magical Chiquibul River, which courses through Belize, then goes underground to resurface across the border in the Guatemalan Petén, as if it were avoiding nonexistent border guards. The 55 kilometers (33 miles) of the Chiquibul Cave System that have been surveyed include the largest known passages and cave room in the Western Hemisphere (Reddell and Veni 1996:131).

The biological diversity and cultural resources of this region are yet to be fully explored. According to Matola and Platt (1998:24–25), "In a 1993 expedition to Doyle's Delight, a mountain peak near the southern border of Chiquibul National Park that at 1,124 meters [3,709 feet] is the highest point in Belize, a botanist from the Missouri Botanical Gardens collected more than 130 [plant] species never before reported in Belize, three of which were previously unknown in Central America."

Wildlife is also abundant, including the keel-billed motmot (*Electron carinatum*), scarlet macaw (*Ara macao*), ocellated turkey (*Agriocharis ocellata*), king vulture (*Sarcoramphus papa*), Central American tapir (*Tapirus bairdii*), spider monkey (*Ateles geoffroyi*), howler monkey (*Alouatta pigra*), jaguar (*Panthera onca*), ocelot (*Felis pardalis*), margay (*Felis wiedii*), and jaguarundi (*Felis yaguaroundi*) (Matola and Platt 1998:25).

IF YOU GO . . . CHIQUIBUL NATIONAL PARK   Chiquibul National park is accessible by road (see "If you go . . . Caracol" in the following pages), but entrance into Belize's extensive Chiquibul Cave system is restricted to those who obtain prior permission from the Department of Archaeology, located in the capital city of Belmopan. Potential spelunkers should inquire in that office.

MOUNTAIN PINE RIDGE FOREST RESERVE

The Mountain Pine Ridge Forest Reserve lies in the heart of Belize, almost in the center of an axis formed by lines going north-south and east-west. The reserve hosts what naturalist Les Beletsky calls "a striking, quite beautiful habitat—tropical pine forest" (Beletsky 1999b:7). The Mountain Pine Ridge is dominated by the mountain pine (*Pinus oocarpa*), a valuable timber tree in Belize. Established in 1944, the Mountain Pine Ridge Forest Reserve continues to be logged, although tourism lodges are also springing up on private inholdings within the reserve's boundaries. More than 150 species of birds have been documented within the reserve. Access to the reserve is via roads that drop south from the Western highway, usually at Georgeville or the town of San Ignacio, Cayo. The reserve covers 510 square kilometers (127,000 acres; 197 sq. mi.).

Archaeological Sites

ALTUN HA

The Maya city of Altun Ha, in northeastern Belize, was occupied for more than 1,900 years, from about 1000 BC to the time of the Maya collapse around AD 900. Most of the visible structures date from the Classic era, when the site's population peaked at approximately 3,000 residents (Sharer 1994:272).

Because of Altun Ha's location only 9 kilometers (5.4 miles) from the Caribbean Sea and the quantity of jade and obsidian artifacts recovered in the site's excavation, it is clear that the city was solidly tied in to the Maya trade network, interchanging trade goods from sites along the seacoast for items from Maya cities in the central lowlands. Although more than 500 structures have been identified at Altun Ha, the largest buildings—13 in number—are concentrated around two large, Classic-era plazas, today called A and B. Remarkably, carved stone stelae are not among the site's features.

However, archaeologists excavating the tallest structure in Plaza A found a wealth of Maya artifacts in a tomb dated at AD 550, including jade, flint, and fragments of a Maya codex. In the adjacent Plaza B, excavation of the site's largest structure, called B-4, revealed the largest carved jade piece yet found in the Maya forest. Discovered in the 1960s by David Pendergast of the Royal Ontario Museum, the piece measures 15 centimeters top to bottom (5.9 inches) and weighs 4.42 kilograms (9.7 pounds). It is a fully rounded jade head of the Maya sun god, K'inich Ahau, dating from around AD 600–650. The piece is now on view at the Museum of Belize on Gabourel Street in downtown Belize City, and a drawing of the stone graces the upper corner of every Belizean banknote.

A modern stone staircase on the western face of B-4 allows a nice climb to the top of the building, which at 18 meters (60 feet) provides a bird's-eye view not only of Plaza B and Plaza A but also of the surrounding forest. Archaeologist David Pendergast notes that the large, circular altar on top of Temple B-4 had a peculiar, sacrificial use: the Maya crushed carved jade pendants there and burned them in fires along with copal incense (Foster 1997:28). Structure B-4 is also famous as the logo of Belize's national beer, Belikin.

At least four reservoirs provided water for the human population of Altun Ha. The reservoir closest to the tall temple, B-4, was still being used in June 2002 as a secondary water source for the archaeological camp. A larger reservoir, known as Rockstone Pond, lies a five-minute walk down a vegetation-covered trail leading south from Plaza B. Rockstone Pond is a 4,700 square meter (50,500 square foot) reservoir of strikingly lime-green water, with strata of large limestone rocks around its edge, making it obvious that the reservoir was human-enhanced as a water source for Altun Ha. The Maya created a stone and clay dam to maintain the water level and lined the bottom of the reservoir with yellow clay (Foster 1997:29). In Yucatec Maya, Altun Ha means "Heavy Stone Water."

Large-scale archaeological work began at Altun Ha in 1964 through funding from the Royal Ontario Museum, and half of the recovered artifacts were taken to Canada. Subsequent research and restoration was led by Belizean archaeologists Joe Palacio and Elizabeth Graham. Funding has come from the government of Belize and the U.S. Agency for International Development, with a new influx of support during the early 2000s from the Belize Ministry of Tourism and the Inter-American Development Bank.

IF YOU GO ... ALTUN HA Altun Ha is located 55 kilometers (31 miles) northwest of Belize City on the Old Northern Highway which, having been replaced by the new Northern Highway, has fallen into slight disrepair. Because the road is sometimes one lane only and occasionally devolves from asphalt into dirt, you should proceed with caution. A 3-kilometer-long (almost 2-mile) loop road off the Old Northern Highway in the small settlement of Lucky Strike takes you directly to the site, where you can park by the guardhouse and handicraft shop. Take a hat and a water bottle. Because its main plazas have been cleared of vegetation, visiting Altun Ha on a humid, sunny day can be a sauna-like experience. A car is your best bet for getting to the site, but public buses and village transport trucks also serve the Old Northern Highway.

CARACOL

The site known as Caracol (the original Maya name appears to have been Oxwitzha', "Three Hill Water") sits on Belize's Vaca Plateau, a 500-meter-high (1,650-foot) shelf just north of the Maya Mountains. A logger, Rosa Mai, discovered the site in 1937, and archaeological teams conducted excavations between 1951 and 1958, followed by intensive excavation and research from 1985 until today by a team led by Arlen and Diane Chase.

At its peak around AD 650, Caracol was a densely populated settlement that relied on an enormous system of agricultural terraces to feed as many as 115,000–150,000 people living in an estimated 36,000 structures (A. Chase and D. Chase 1998:61, 72). The site covered 177 square kilometers (43,719 acres; 68 sq. mi.), all of it manipulated by the Maya into a combination residential-agricultural landscape. Arlen and Diane Chase (1998:61) call Caracol "an immense metropolis" that was simultaneously "a true garden city."

Caracol was founded as early as 600 BC, but it peaked during the Classic period, when the city had an extensive causeway system that allowed the Caracol Maya to distribute their monumental architecture over the landscape, rather than concentrate it all in one city center. Only 10 percent of the site has been surveyed and mapped, although work is ongoing.

The rulers and inhabitants of Caracol were seriously concerned with controlling agricultural soils and the flow of water. (Today, the region can be relatively dry for a tropical forest zone, with an average of 1.5 to 2.5 meters of rainfall [59–98 inches] per year.) Between AD 550 and 800, they constructed an estimated five water reservoirs per square kilometer and built stone terrace walls—some of them a kilometer long—to divert water and prevent soil erosion. They transported fertile agricultural soils to replace unproductive soils in terraced areas and produced a wide range of food and fiber crops, including perhaps cotton as a trade crop (A. Chase and D. Chase 1998:72). As the Chases note, the Caracol Maya must have adopted their extensive agricultural terracing and water-control system "as a means of attaining agricultural self-sufficiency in an era of population growth" (1998:72).

Caracol's success in farming allowed the city's leaders to engage in regional politics and military endeavors. One of Caracol's rulers, Yajaw Te' K'inich II, also known as Lord Water, took the throne in AD 553 and may have helped conquer the rival city of Tikal in 562. Another hypothesis holds, however, that it was Calakmul that conquered Tikal at this time, and that Caracol merely prospered during the 130-year silence that Tikal subsequently endured (Martin and Grube 2000:90). Tikal's leader, Wak Chan K'awiil (aka Double-Bird), was captured and killed during this war, ending his dynasty and interrupting the trade routes that had made Tikal prosperous and powerful. Schele and Freidel (1990:173–174) point out that the victory over Tikal "broke the back of Tikal's pride, independence, and prosperity," allowing other cities to rise in influence as a result. During this period, Caracol evolved from a minor capital to one of the major cities in the Maya world.

When Lord Water died in AD 599, control of Caracol passed to his two sons in sequence. The younger of these men, Lord Kan II, born in AD 588, assumed the throne in AD 618 and quickly formed an alliance with Calakmul to begin the campaign of war that led to the defeat of the Maya city of Naranjo, in today's neighboring Guatemala, in AD 631. (Schele and Freidel 1990:176).

Caracol's temporary dominance of the Petén robbed sites such as Tikal and Naranjo of their ability to record their own history, leading to a hiatus in the written record that lasted for 40 years at Naranjo and for more than 100 years at Tikal (Schele and Freidel 1990:172). Just over 60 years after their rise to prominence, however, Caracol's leaders saw their fortunes reversed. Naranjo and Tikal again rose as major forces in the Maya forest, leading to a decline of power at Caracol and the purposeful destruction of its monuments, followed by a 70-year paucity of written records at the site. The last known king of Caracol, Ruler XIII, erected a crude stela in AD 859 (Martin and Grube 2000:99). The city subsequently went silent.

IF YOU GO . . . CARACOL   Access to the site of Caracol is not easy, but the intrepid traveler with a four-wheel-drive vehicle will find the trip alone is worth the trouble. From Belize's Western Highway (the main road that traverses the country east to west), drop south at the town of Georgeville toward the forestry station at Augustine. The road continues south through San Luis to Caracol Camp, a trip of around 80 kilometers (50 miles). The view from the road allows you to appreciate the transition from the pine forest of the Mountain Pine Ridge Forest Reserve to the tropical moist forest of the Chiquibul Forest Reserve and Chiquibul National Park, which surround the Caracol Archaeological Reserve. At the Guacamayo Bridge, crossing over the Macal River, the exposed rock in the riverbed shows you Belize's granite basement, where the 3,000-meter (9,843-foot) blanket of limestone that covers Belize and most of the Guatemalan Petén has eroded away to expose the underlying strata (Coates 1997:32–33).

EL PILAR

El Pilar, in west central Belize, is an intricate and mysterious Classic Maya site that lies along the Belize-Guatemala border and extends westward into the forest of the Guatemalan Petén. An abundant supply of fresh water emerges as streams and natural springs from the 340-meter (1,115-foot) escarpment on which the monuments of El Pilar are located, creating one of the primary reasons the site was occupied for several thousand years—from the Middle Preclassic (1000–300 BC) until the Early Post-classic (AD 900–1200). The site has more than 25 plazas in a forested area of 40 hectares (100 acres), many of which have been partially cleared to create a garden-like atmosphere.

Anabel Ford of the University of California, Santa Barbara, has led a successful campaign to draw attention to El Pilar through projects that blend archaeological research, community development, and forest conservation in a model program for archaeo-ecological development in the Maya region (Ford 1998). Exhibits at the site demonstrate traditional Maya agricultural techniques and illustrate how ancient Maya house compounds were constructed. As a result, El Pilar is one of the most interactive Maya sites and an excellent spot for understanding how the ancient Maya actually lived.

The Belizean sector of El Pilar is located inside the 808-hectare (1,996-acre) El Pilar Archaeological Reserve for Maya Flora and Fauna, a well-manicured conservation area controlled by the Belize Archaeology Department. The Guatemalan section of the site, called Pilar Poniente, is controlled by Guatemala's Consejo Nacional de Areas Protegidas (CONAP) and the Instituto de Antropología e Historia (IDAEH). From the Belizean summit on the northwestern extreme of the site, you can sit on a covered vine-and-wood bench and look out over the Guatemalan Petén, which begins just 500 meters (1,640 feet) due west of where you are sitting. (Tikal is 32 kilometers (19 miles) due west of El Pilar.) The lookout here is known as Teo's Leap, for a 152-meter (500-foot) fall that Theophilo Williams, caretaker of El Pilar since 1983, accidentally took from this point. (He survived and is the site's most knowledgeable guide today.)

IF YOU GO . . . EL PILAR   From the major town of San Ignacio (Cayo), drive 5 kilometers (3 miles) to Bullet Tree Falls, where you can stop at the Amigos de El Pilar Café and Gift Shop and view a scale model of the site. Then, drive 11 kilometers (7 miles) on to El Pilar itself. Dozens of house mounds and old water holes dot the landscape between Bullet Tree Falls and the site. Once you arrive at the government guardhouse, stop to register and to engage a guide.

LA MILPA

The structures associated with the Maya city of La Milpa cover 78 square kilometers (30 sq. mi.) of lowland tropical forest inside the Río Bravo Conservation Area owned by the nonprofit conservation organization

Programme for Belize. La Milpa's size ranks it with Caracol and nearby La-manai as one of the largest archaeological sites in Belize. Although the main core of the site is not huge, its main plaza is one of the largest public spaces in the Maya world. The plaza is bordered by four pyramids, the tallest of which rises to 24 meters (79 feet). The site has 24 courtyards and two ball courts, with a total of more than 50 structures. La Milpa gained international attention in 1996 after the excavation of a fifth-century ruler's tomb that revealed an impressive jade necklace (Hammond 1997). Researchers have also identified 19 stelae (Tourtellot, González, and Belli 1999).

The first occupation at La Milpa dates from 400 BC, and the site appears to have grown until AD 500, when it experienced a century-long hiatus. It flourished again between AD 750 and 850, peaking at an estimated population of 46,000 individuals (*Belize Report* 1998:1; Tourtellot, González, and Belli 1999; Webster 2002:291). After the Maya collapse, the site was occupied by Postclassic groups, who used stones from the monuments to build foundations for pole and thatch structures in the site's main plaza. The foundations indicate that these temporary structures were similar to—and the size of—the god houses utilized by twentieth-century Lacandón Maya families.

La Milpa has two ball courts and several exposed *chultuno'ob*, water storage cisterns dug into the floors of the packed-earth plazas, which are surrounded by pyramids and residence buildings.

IF YOU GO . . . LA MILPA   You can obtain permission to visit La Milpa by contacting the office of Programme for Belize, in Belize City. The site is a three-hour drive from Belize City, but only a 15-minute drive (one-hour walk) from the well-appointed research station, also called La Milpa, which is operated by Programme for Belize inside the Río Bravo Conservation and Management Area in Belize's Orange Walk District.

LAMANAI

The Maya city of Lamanai, located on the shore of the New River Lagoon in north central Belize, is notable for being the only Maya center to survive the Classic Maya collapse and continue to function into the Spanish conquest (Schele and Freidel 1990:505). Indeed, the site has been almost continuously occupied since the Preclassic era, going through stages that include serving as an early Maya settlement, Classic Maya city, Spanish colonial outpost, nineteenth-century sugarcane production center, and today as an ecotourism site—a span of history that totals some 3,500 consecutive years.

Appropriately, the name "Lamanai," recorded as the site's original name by Franciscan missionaries in the 1650s, comes from the Yucatec Maya words for sunken crocodile (*lama'an ayim*). In keeping with its name, the site has coughed up numerous depictions of crocodiles, including figurine headdresses, decorations on ceramic vases, and a headdress on a 4-meter (13-foot) limestone mask on one of the temples.

The site is situated on the western shore of what appears to be a huge lake, complete with crocodiles, but which turns out to be a wide stretch of the New River, which rises in the Yalbac Hills of western Belize and flows into the Caribbean just south of the Belizean town of Corozal.

Construction began at Lamanai as early as the Late Preclassic. The site's largest structure, called N10-43, reaches 33 meters (108 feet)—10 modern-building stories high—and is one of the largest Preclassic structures in the Maya forest, though it was periodically modified, including during the Late Classic era, around AD 600 (Foster 1997:17). One of the smaller structures, called N10-27, dating from AD 608–625, has an incised stela in front of it, showing a ruler wearing a quetzal feather headdress. Excavations at the site's ball court, which dates from AD 900, revealed a cache of liquid mercury, likely imported from a site in today's Honduras (Webster 2002:293).

From the tallest structure at Lamanai you can look eastward down the southern reaches of the New River Lagoon and west, south, and north over a flat plain of tropical forest to survey the territory once ruled by the site's Maya lords.

More recent structures at Lamanai include the ruins of two sixteenth-century Christian churches (one is called Indian Church and has Maya stelae reset in front of it). Spanish friars established a mission at Lamanai in 1570 but abandoned it during a Maya revolt in 1630 (Ford 1998:16). More recent still is an 1866 red brick sugar-processing mill with a cane-crushing machine marked "Leeds and Company Foundry, New Orleans," which today has a 50-foot strangler fig growing out the top of its giant gears, as if it were possessed by an extraterrestrial parasite. The machine was the center of a sugar processing industry attempted by Confederates who abandoned the southern United States at the end of the U.S. Civil War. Nearby is a deep brick cistern, shaped exactly like an ancient Maya cistern called a *chultun*.

David Webster cogently sums up the remarkable history of Lamanai in the book *The Fall of the Ancient Maya*: "Lamanai is in one sense the exception that proves the rule," he says. "It was never sacked by enemies, its sustaining river and lagoon never dried up, its agricultural fields still produced staple crops, and no epidemic disease could have ravaged nearby kingdoms while leaving it untouched" (Webster 2002:294).

IF YOU GO . . . LAMANAI   Lamanai is 60 driving kilometers (37 miles) from Orange Walk town in northern Belize, and you can drive there by traveling south from that community. You can also get to the site by renting a boat at the toll bridge on the road 11 kilometers (7 miles) south of Orange Walk town. The trip takes about an hour and a half, with a good stop for bird watching. The boat lets you out at the Maya site, and the driver will wait while you tour the site and buy souvenirs in the local curio stands. The river here is famous for its tarpon (*Megalops atlanticus*), a large marine fish that migrates up freshwater rivers to breed. You can rent a boat to fish for these, as well as for plentiful *blancos* (*Petenia splendida*), called bay snook in Belize, and for a half-dozen varieties of smaller cichlids, locally called *mojarras* (*Cichlasoma* spp.).

Lamanai was professionally excavated and restored during 2001. Should you decide to spend the night at the site, the new Lamanai Outpost Lodge is a short walk from the ancient center.

LUBAANTUN

Lubaantun (Fallen Stones) is a small, late Classic Maya site in southern Belize that flourished for under two centuries—from AD 700 to 870 (Sharer 1994:275). Ceramics that include depictions of cacao pods have led researchers to conclude that Lubaantun served as a center for cacao production and export. Residents would have been able to transport their harvest to the Caribbean Sea via the Río Grande, which runs through a valley near the site. Although Lubaantun has two ball courts, it lacks the vaulted architecture and sculpture found at so many other Maya sites. Instead, the site's structures are built of medium-sized, rectangular stones, without the use of mortar. The tallest of these structures, at 15 meters (50 feet), gives the visitor a view of the Caribbean some 30 kilometers (17 miles) to the southeast.

IF YOU GO . . . LUBAANTUN   Access to Lubaantun is via Belize's Southern Highway toward Punta Gorda town. A right turn toward the village of San Antonio, then right again to San Pedro Colombia will take you to the site. Along the way, before the first turn off the Southern Highway, the small site of Nimli Punit is three-quarters of a mile off the main road. The site is known for its tall, thin monuments, most of which lie today under shaded palm canopies.

XUNANTUNICH

Xunantunich is a Late Classic site remarkable mostly for the sculptured stucco on its tallest structure and for its location on the Belize River in west central Belize, only a few kilometers from the Belize-Guatemalan border towns of Benque Viejo and Melchor de Mencos. Excavations carried out in 1960 revealed that some of the structures had been damaged by an earthquake during Classic Maya times, leading to a since discarded hypothesis that earthquakes caused the Maya collapse. Xunantunich was one of several satellite cities that thrived while the larger, previously more dominant sites declined during the final decades of the Classic period (Martin and Grube 2000:83). Xunantunich began to grow just as nearby Naranjo (8 kilometers (5 miles) to the northwest in today's Guatemala) was losing its power.

The 40-meter-tall (130-foot) Structure A-6, called El Castillo, "The Castle," has a remarkably well-preserved (and partially restored) stucco frieze near its top level. Glyphs on the frieze include those for the sun, moon, and Venus. The sculpture once extended around the entire building; today, only the work on the eastern side is visible. The surviving monuments of Xunantunich extend to AD 830 (Martin and Grube 2000:83). One interpretation of the name Xunantunich, in Yucatec Maya, is "Foreigner Lady Stones," but the name is of recent origin.

IF YOU GO . . . XUNANTUNICH   The site is an easy stop on Belize's Western Highway. A delightfully rickety, hand-powered ferry takes cars and pedestrians across the Mopan River. Once across, you will find the site approximately 2 kilometers (1.3 miles) up a hill, through the forest. A visitors center at the site has worthwhile exhibits.

PART THREE · **The Future of the Maya Tropical Forest**

The Future of the Selva Maya

Based on the work of conservationists, archaeologists, and historians, we know that the Maya Tropical Forest is one of the most biologically diverse regions on the planet and that during the pre-Columbian era, it hosted the most advanced civilization in the Western Hemisphere, that of the Classic Maya. All available evidence indicates that after a thousand years of successful adaptation to a tropical forest environment, Maya civilization disintegrated between AD 700 and 900 from an interrelated complex of factors—population growth, environmental degradation brought on by deforestation and erosion, increasing warfare, drought, and internal civil strife. The turmoil wrought by these interwoven factors led to the death or out-migration of 90 to 99 percent of the Classic-era Maya people (Webster 2002:328, Diamond 2005b:176–177). In the population vacuum created by this collapse, the vegetation of the Maya Tropical Forest gradually regenerated.

A sufficient number of Maya survived the collapse to begin to repopulate pockets of the region, although they never reached their former high population density or their previous level of cultural sophistication. Except for a few isolated exceptions, the Maya people ceased to use Classic-era hieroglyphic writing and time measurement. At the same time, though, the families who held on in the Maya forest maintained some cultural and ecological traditions of the Classic Maya era while they developed new ecological adaptations to their changed environment.

We also know that the Maya population was almost wiped out a second time when Spaniards invaded the Maya world during the sixteenth century—some 600 years after the Maya collapse. The Spanish conquistadores inadvertently brought a host of Old World diseases with them, and the resulting epidemics killed up to 90 percent of the Maya who were living at the time. Only during the twentieth century—500 years after the conquest—did the number of Maya people finally increase to a level even half of what it had been during the Classic era. Yet even now traces of ancient Maya traditions continue to echo in the lives of these modern people.

Today, as in the time of the ancient Maya, the Maya Tropical Forest is again being cleared and burned. While the ancient Maya cleared the forest for food production and fuelwood, the modern iteration of deforestation is goaded along by logging, oil exploration, road construction, hydroelectric dam construction, colonization, slash-and-burn agriculture, export crops production, and cattle ranching. This modern wave of deforestation is driven by overconsumption of natural resources in the developed world—by the importation of the Maya forest's oil, timber, and beef—and in the Maya Tropical Forest itself by one of the most rapidly growing human populations anywhere in the world.

As a result, the cornucopia of biological and cultural diversity still found in the Maya Tropical Forest is countered by the immediate, real-world threats the region faces. A 2005 satellite image of the area shows huge blotches of deforestation spreading out from human settlements in concentric rings of destruction. In Mexico's Selva Lacandona, PEMEX (Petróleos Mexicanos) oil roads spread through the forest like spiderwebs, providing access for a growing number of farmers and cattle ranchers clearing land for corn and beef cattle. In Guatemala, population growth is bringing new penetrations of land-hungry colonists into the region's national parks and biosphere reserves (Fort and Grandia 1999). In Belize, Salvadoran refugee farmers, citrus plantation entrepreneurs, and Mopan and Q'eqchi' Maya clear forest for agriculture, while Mennonite farmers rip hectare after hectare of trees from the ground using giant anchor chains dragged between two bulldozers. The current rate of forest destruction in the Maya Tropical Forest surpasses 800 square kilometers (197,700 acres; 309 sq. mi.) per year (Nations, Bray, and Wilson 1998). In at least half the years, dry weather conditions, forest fragmentation, and burning for pastures and agriculture produce forest fires that inadvertently burn thousands of additional hectares of natural forest.

At times, efforts to ease environmental threats in one country are hindered by ecological damage in another. Wildlife, forest products, and—increasingly—human refugees flow across the frontiers of Mexico, Guatemala, and Belize as if borders did not exist. Mexicans from deforested areas of Tabasco, Chiapas, and Campeche poach timber and wildlife in core areas of Guatemala's Maya Biosphere. Guatemalan families clear forest in western Belize, and deforested slopes in southern Belize have created flash floods in communities of the southern Guatemalan Petén. Acid rain from Mexico's Coatzacoalcos oil refineries threatens ancient Maya ruins in the Guatemalan Petén and in Mexico's own Yucatán Peninsula (Nations, Primack, and Bray 1998).

Just as the three nations of the Maya Tropical Forest are increasingly tied into a larger, regional economy, so too are their national environments inextricably bound together. Increasingly, threats to the Maya Tropical Forest are recognized as regional problems that require regional solutions. These solutions include improved systems of protected areas, a renewed focus on local economic development, especially ecotourism, and improved health care, including reproductive health and family planning for the region's growing number of families.

The challenges the Maya Tropical Forest faces today are not unlike those that faced the people of the Classic Maya era. The region has the fastest-growing regional population anywhere outside of Africa (PRB 2004). Environmental degradation from deforestation and erosion are again on the rise. The region has certainly experienced its share of civil unrest (a Marxist insurgency in Guatemala from 1960 until 1996; the still unresolved Zapatista uprising of 1994 in Chiapas), although that is hopefully on the wane. The region has been spared only the drought and climatic change that factored into the Maya collapse, although recent El Niño events and the forest fires of the late 1990s and early 2000 provide a sampling of such events.

The more challenging problems in today's Maya Tropical Forest are economics and education. Poverty is impelling individuals who have few other options to clear the forest for cropland simply to keep their families alive. Because many of the region's indigenous, and sustainable, systems of agriculture have been abandoned, the expansion of extensive milpas across the forest is jeopardizing the natural ecosystems that support the region's environmental stability. Too frequently, pioneer colonists seed their harvested milpas in grass and sell the cleared land to cattle raisers for beef cattle pastures, then move farther into the forest to clear new land for crops (Nations and Komer 1983). The lack of schools and education, especially for young girls, and the lack of economic opportunities for rural women, lead to exceptionally high birthrates, which fuel both more poverty and population growth across the landscape.

Greed also factors into the region's current challenges. The expansion of the agricultural frontier is enabled by the construction of roads through forested areas and, sometimes, through national parks and biosphere reserves. In many cases, these roads benefit only oil companies or timber barons, who make their profits selling petroleum or tropical hardwoods on international markets. As their products flow out of the forest on newly constructed roads, farm families flow into the forest seeking land and new lives. They are people with nowhere else to go, and no economic alternative beyond exploiting the natural resources that their own lives depend on.

Creating and defending protected areas, defying the selfish appropriation of forest resources by the few, and creating viable education and economic alternatives for thousands of pioneer farm families have become the most important activities in the survival of the Maya Tropical Forest and the people who call it home. Today, conservationists are working on national, regional, and international levels to ensure the stability of the region's protected areas, combat destructive get-rich-quick schemes, improve law enforcement, intensify agricultural production in areas that have already been deforested, and create economic alternatives through ecological and archaeological tourism, small business enterprises, and the sustainable harvesting of renewable forest products.

Success in these endeavors can benefit local communities, the economies of the three countries that share the Maya Tropical Forest, and the survival of the plant and animal species that create its web of life. Confronting these challenges is not an easy task, but for the future of the forest's biological diversity and for the future of the families who depend on it for survival there is no task that is more important.

Protected Areas: Threats and Solutions

Conservation studies, workshops, and projects carried out in the Maya Tropical Forest during the past 20 years have demonstrated that creating and maintaining strong national systems of protected areas—national parks, wildlife reserves, and biosphere reserves—is an effective way to counter environmental threats to the Maya Tropical Forest's natural ecosystems. The region is making considerable progress in achieving this goal.

In Chiapas, the government of Mexico established the 3,312 square kilometer (1,279 sq. mi.) Montes Azules Biosphere Reserve in the Selva Lacandona in 1978. In 1992 President Carlos Salinas added 810 square kilometers (313 sq. mi.) to adjoining reserves, and the indigenous inhabitants of Chiapas have created a certified community conservation area, La Cojolita, that connects the Montes Azules Biosphere Reserve to Guatemala's Maya Biosphere Reserve through a narrow corridor of natural forest rich with wildlife.

In Guatemala, President Vinicio Cerezo and the Guatemalan Congress created the 16,000 square kilometer (6,178 sq. mi.) Maya Biosphere Reserve in 1990, a protected area the size of the country of El Salvador. On its northern border with Mexico, the Maya Biosphere Reserve connects with the Calakmul Biosphere Reserve of Quintana Roo, and to the east with the Río Bravo lands of the Programme for Belize (1,052 kilometers; 406 sq. mi.). Farther south along the border between Guatemala and Belize, two frontier parks protect the watershed of the Chiquibul River. Today, 80 percent of the common border between Belize and Guatemala's Petén lies under protected status, although the Guatemalan side is under serious threat from logging and illegal colonization (Peirce 1997; Matola and Platt 1998).

Taken together, this complex of protected areas in Belize, Guatemala, and Mexico creates what conservationists call the Maya Arch, providing legal, if not actual, protection for more than 25,000 square kilometers (9,650 sq. mi.) of tropical forest and related natural ecosystems. The building blocks of the Maya Arch are the national parks of each country and their five biosphere reserves: Montes Azules, Lacantún, Maya, Calakmul, and Chiquibul. This remarkable constellation of protected areas makes the Maya Tropical Forest one of the largest complexes of biosphere reserves in the Western Hemisphere, creating a natural corridor that supports a large number of endemic species, including 29 bird, 39 reptile, 11 amphibian, 19 fish, and 11 mammal species, as well as the largest population of jaguars north of the equator (CEPF 2003:9; Swank and Teer 1989).

Conservationists know that the nuclear zones and connecting corridors of the protected areas of the Maya Tropical Forest must be shielded from destruction if the region's wealth of biodiversity is to survive. The prospects for conserving the entire range of natural ecosystems of the Maya Tropical Forest are essentially zero, given the region's population growth rate and rate of deforestation, but sizable examples of the region's natural ecosystems will survive if the countries keep alive the region's current configuration of protected areas. However, outside these protected areas—and in several cases, within them—the rapid growth of human numbers, especially in rural farming areas, and accompanying infrastructure development portend continuing patterns of forest destruction wrought by road building, logging, slash-and-burn agriculture, and cattle ranching.

The most important step in preventing this destruction may well be what happens in the lives and communities of the families who live outside the reserves' boundaries. Regional trends during the past few decades and examples from countries such as Costa Rica indicate that almost all tropical forest outside of protected areas of the Maya forest will be cleared for farmland or pastureland. Some erosion of protected areas will also take place. One major threat to protected areas in the region appears in the Montes Azules Biosphere Reserve of Chiapas, Mexico, where illegal encroachment by farm families is steady and persistent. Colonists have established more than 30 illegal settlements in Montes Azules and its adjoining Selva Lacandona reserves since 1995 (CEPF 2003:166). National governments since President Salinas have been slow to forcibly evict squatters from protected areas for fear of setting off conflict with the Zapatistas, who continue to hold out in the area and demand land for campesino families (Nations 1994). As the former head of Mexico's Secretariat of the Environment, Natural Resources and Fisheries (SEMARNAP) said on a visit to the Selva Lacandona in 2000, "We are buying time until the political situation changes." The Montes Azules Biosphere Reserve is under heavy threat from additional invasions, especially along its southwestern and northern borders.

Colonist communities continue to expand in the southern and southwestern areas of Laguna del Tigre National Park, inside Guatemala's Maya Biosphere Reserve, as well, but the presence of ProPetén's Las Guacamayas Biological Station and work with surrounding communities by ProPetén and the El Perú/Waka' project have maintained forest cover in the southeastern region of the park. Forest along the eastern edge of Mexico's Calakmul Biosphere Reserve is being eaten away by illegal colonization from neighboring farm communities (Ericson, Freudenberger, and Boege 1999).

Development projects supported by government officials threaten other regions. Belize's Chiquibul National Park and Chiquibul National Forest are losing territory along the Macal River to a hydroelectric dam promoted by the government of Belize and a Canadian power company, Fortis. A periodically proposed Xpujil-Uaxactún-Tikal road through the Calakmul Biosphere Reserve and Maya Biosphere Reserve, ostensibly designed to improve tourist access to the area, would instead open the area to increased logging, colonization, and cattle ranching. The road would cut in half the largest remaining contiguous block of undisturbed ecosystems in the Maya Tropical Forest. A road proposed from Punta Gorda, on the Caribbean coast of Belize, to the Guatemalan Petén town of San Luis would cut through the traditional Maya region of Toledo District, Belize, opening the area to slash-and-burn farming, citrus plantations, and beef cattle ranching.

Threats to the Maya forest may also result from regional initiatives in economic development. The Plan Puebla-Panama, for example, is an ambitious US$20 billion, 25-year development program launched by the government of Mexico in 2000 to promote economic development and regional integration in a corridor that runs from the Mexican city of Puebla to the Republic of Panama. The plan calls for new infrastructure that includes 9,000 kilometers (5,565 miles) of new or improved highways and a Central American Electrical Integration System (SIEPAC) that would erect 1,818 kilometers (1,090 miles) of new electrical transmission lines to distribute energy from up to 25 new hydroelectric dams and power plants fueled by natural gas (IDB 2002). Eighteen of these proposed hydroelectric dams would be built in Chiapas, including major constructions on the Río Usumacinta, which archaeologists and conservationists state will result in the inundation of human communities, Classic Maya cities, and protected areas (Weiner 2002; Scatena 2004).

Smaller-scale activities also threaten the natural and cultural resources of the Maya Tropical Forest. Illegal logging and wildlife poaching have plagued the Maya forest for decades. Belizean loggers have been caught removing mahogany and tropical cedar from the Guatemalan Petén; Guatemalan loggers have been apprehended poaching Belizean timber and wildlife. Along the western edge of Guatemala's Maya Biosphere Reserve, professional hunters from adjacent Mexican *ejidos* pack mules across the unprotected border to hunt edible animals, which they salt down and transport back to Mexico to sell in urban markets. Ten Mexican crocodile hunters were arrested in 2003 inside Guatemala's Sierra del Lacandón National Park (Conservation International 2003:76).

Another danger comes from the increasingly frequent forest fires that have ravaged Mexico and northern Central America during the past 10 years. These fires have damaged large sections of remaining tropical forests in Mexico, Guatemala, Honduras, El Salvador, and Nicaragua. In the Maya Tropical Forest, only Belize seems to have been spared, with fewer than 500 square kilometers (193 sq. mi.) affected (CEPF 2003:15). These forest fires plague the area in the spring, when thousands of farmers and cattle raisers torch felled vegetation to get at the soil below. The farmers' goal is to plant crops to feed their families and sell the surplus in local markets; the cattle raisers seek new grasslands to raise beef cattle for Latin America's growing cities and for export to the United States. But among the by-products of their efforts are forest fires.

The fires are especially onerous during years of dry conditions wrought by El Niño. Rains that would normally fall in April or May to extinguish lingering blazes do not appear until a month later, and dry leaf litter on the forest floor adjoining agricultural plots spreads the fires into the forest canopy. In some years, whipped by hot, dry winds, the fires have spread across an estimated 6,500 square kilometers (1.6 million acres; 2,510 sq. mi.) of tropical forest in Guatemala, Mexico, and Belize (CEPF 2003:15).

The continuing growth in the number of farm families in Mexico, Guatemala, and Belize, combined with the construction of new roads for logging and oil operations, fragments the region's tropical forests into islands of forest surrounded by agricultural plots. Like a sponge cut into a dozen pieces, the fragmented forest dries much more quickly than whole forest plots, adding to the danger of fires.

To counter this threat, international agencies are assisting the governments of the three countries to extinguish the fires when they occur and to work toward fire prevention. The U.S. Agency for International Development has financed a series of programs to train firefighting teams over the past decade. National governments are also working to prevent scorched national parks and wildlife reserves from being illegally colonized by farmers and land speculators, as has happened in the past in both Chiapas and the Guatemalan Petén.

The saving grace of ecosystem conservation in the Maya Tropical Forest is each country's protected areas system and the growing cadre of professional conservationists. New conservation organizations emerge every year, joining those that have served as voices of sanity in the region for the past 25 years. Ecological consciousness is growing, if gradually, within the general public of all three countries of the Maya Tropical Forest, and protected areas are increasingly seen as economic forces because of expanding tourism.

Nonetheless, the three countries are in a race with time. What we will likely end up with by the mid-twenty-first century is a diminished network of smaller national parks and wildlife reserves that are totally surrounded by agricultural lands and pasture. Much of the connectivity of these protected areas will be lost, producing islands of biological diversity that will continue to erode. This is not to say that we should despair and give up. Many positive actions are being moved into place to keep alive the biological and cultural heritage of the Maya Tropical Forest. To begin with, some of the key protected areas of the region still maintain their ecological integrity and deserve special attention from conservationists.

Among the most promising sites for the long-term conservation of natural ecosystems in the Maya Tropical Forest are the following:

- The Bladen Branch Nature Reserve in the Maya Mountains of southern Belize. The reserve has no permanent human communities inside or along its edges, because it is surrounded by a national park and other forest reserves. Nonetheless, hunters do enter the area from neighboring Guatemala and from communities in Toledo District. During the dry season, animals are drawn to the constant water sources of the reserve's larger rivers, providing hunters with easy access to edible birds and mammals (Iremonger and Sayre 1994:35). Protection measures in the Bladen are just beginning and should be redoubled. The reserve still requires boundary delimitation and construction of guard stations.
- Ornithologists point to the Columbia River Forest Reserve, Toledo District, Belize, as a key priority for neotropical migratory birds. As the late Ted Parker wrote in 1993, "Large tracts of relatively undisturbed forest such as the Columbia River Forest Reserve will become increasingly important to numerous neotropical migrants as the evergreen forests in adjacent countries become reduced to small and widely scattered fragments" (Parker et al. 1993:13). And as researchers on the 1992 Conservation International Rapid Assessment Program expedition to Toledo District wrote, "Our studies strongly suggest that the most species-rich plant and animal communities in Belize occur in the wet forests at 600–900 meters on the windward slopes of the southern Maya Mountains in the Toledo District" (Parker et al. 1993:14). Air photos and field verification demonstrate that this is one of the few large, continuous tracts of relatively undisturbed tropical forest left in Middle America.
- The Tzendales region of the Montes Azules Biosphere Reserve and adjoining Lacantún Biosphere Reserve is the best preserved section of the complex of protected areas in the Selva Lacandona of Chiapas. Protected on the south by the Río Lacanjá and on the west by a large tract of relatively intact forest, the Tzendales region holds great promise for long-term survival if it can be protected from illegal colonization.

- The Mirador-Calakmul region of northern Petén, Guatemala, and southern Campeche, Mexico, is the largest block of contiguous forest in the Maya region. Lack of road access into the area and the lack of surface water have prevented the region from falling prey to spontaneous colonization by farm families seeking land. If the region remains roadless, the Mirador-Calakmul forest should survive forever.

What all of these surviving areas have in common is isolation from human settlements. They represent the center regions of larger blocks of protected areas in the three nations of the Maya Tropical Forest. Preventing road construction and the colonization and cattle ranching that follow it are the most important factors in keeping these areas alive.

At the same time, we should not write off all other areas of the Maya forest. Solid, promising conservation work can still be achieved in a number of crucial regions of the forest. Small islands such as Tikal National Park and Palenque will survive because of the economic contributions they make to local and national economies. As ecological and archaeological tourism increases in the Maya Tropical Forest, other protected areas will demonstrate their economic value and their importance and protection should increase. Gradually, political leaders are coming to realize that instead of denying their citizens access to economic resources, national parks and biosphere reserves are the economic resources that drive local and regional economies. The fact that the economic benefits of protected areas depend on protecting their natural and cultural resources for visitors makes these resources crucial elements in supporting human communities and national economies.

Archaeology: Threats and Solutions

Threats to the natural areas of the Maya Tropical Forest are mirrored by threats to the region's cultural history. A visit to almost any Maya site will reveal the ugly cut of looters' trenches across the midsection of unexcavated tombs and temples. Professional artifact hunters and local people seeking extra money prey on unguarded sites in the Maya forest, digging into the sides of promising mounds in search of ancient burials that will yield ceramics and artifacts to sell on the black market. Sites that are looted in such a fashion, and the artifacts that result, lose much of their scientific value, depriving the rest of the world of the information that would have resulted from careful, professional excavation. Maya archaeologist Robert Sharer points out that "a looted Maya site is like a jigsaw puzzle that has had most of its pieces destroyed and the shapes and colors on most of the remaining pieces erased. No one could reassemble such a damaged and altered puzzle" (Sharer 1996:8).

Modern laws in Mexico, Guatemala, Belize, the United States, and European countries make it illegal to export or import ancient Maya artifacts, but wholesale looting still occurs. Government authorities almost never examine luggage and packages leaving the Maya forest countries on airplanes or buses, and few illegally exported artifacts are captured during impromptu searches at customs points in the United States and Europe.

Also, a major loophole exists in the system. While it is illegal to take ancient artifacts out of Mexico, Guatemala, and Belize, it is not illegal to possess them within the countries themselves. As a result, looters of Maya sites find ready markets for polychrome pottery, jade objects, and flint artifacts within their own countries. In Guatemala City, I once visited a house that had two rooms filled from floor to ceiling with shelves of large polychrome ceramics looted from Maya sites. Although the Guatemalan owners of Maya antiquities are requested to register their artifacts with Guatemala's Instituto de Antropología e Historia, few of them do so for fear that the artifacts will be confiscated in the future.

Archaeologist George Stuart, recently retired from the National Geographic Society, estimates that 1,000 ceramic artifacts are illegally exported from the Maya Tropical Forest every month, a number seconded by UCLA archaeologist Richard D. Hansen (Hansen 1997:48). These artifacts move through the forest and down the region's muddy roads on established networks. Frequently, looters take advantage of trade in legal commodities such as timber, chicle, and *xate* palms. In the late 1980s, in Carmelita, Petén, I saw this process in action. A Santa Elena–based *xate* palm contractor was hiding looted Maya ceramics beneath bundles of *xate* being prepared for transport to San Benito, Petén, and on to Guatemala City. When I pulled out my camera to photograph the scene, the contractor's workmen quickly hid the ceramics behind the doors of a warehouse. (This same contractor was arrested two years later for selling illegally cut mahogany, but dozens of unscrupulous dealers like him still operate in the Maya forest.)

Some of the artifacts dug from tombs in the Petén make their way across the northern border of Guatemala into Mexico. Mexican foremen slip across the unguarded border into Guatemala to hire local men as diggers, who turn over the excavated goods to the foremen for transport back to Mexico. There, eager purchasers await the shipment. Mule drivers in the Petén told me that Guatemalan looters are paid "por indio," that is, according to the number of human figures on the ceramics they find. For an especially fine ceramic piece, a looter may receive US$40 and the go-between US$200 to US$500, but the same piece can fetch more than US$100,000 when sold in a U.S. gallery to a private collector or museum (Hansen 1997:48).

Modern looters use gasoline-powered chainsaws to cut the facade from large stone pieces such as stelae. (In past decades, they used long, manually powered two-man saws.) If the resulting facade is too large to be hauled on a mule, they dice it into smaller pieces for reconstruction at the point of purchase.

While the beauty of Maya artifacts fuels illegal looting of the sites, the popularity of visiting Maya sites helps control looting. Ecotourism is good for site protection. On an expedition to Mirador in the early 1990s, I heard a mule driver casually comment to his companion that it was getting increasingly more difficult to loot sites in the area "because of the all the tourists who are coming and going."

Cultural Diversity: Threats and Solutions

In the twenty-first century, the Maya Tropical Forest is home to a mixture of traditional Maya communities and communities whose inhabitants migrated to the region at a later date. The remaining autochthonous families include the Lacandón and Chol Maya in eastern Chiapas, the Itza Maya of northern Guatemala, and the Mopan Maya of Belize. Several highland Maya groups have moved into the Maya forest during the past century, including Tzeltal, Tzotzil, and Tojolabal Maya into the Selva Lacandona of Chiapas, Q'eqchi' into the Guatemalan Petén and Belize, and highland Guatemalan Maya war refugees into the Calakmul Biosphere Reserve.

Surrounding the Maya families of Belize are Spanish, German, Garífuna, and English-speaking families. In Mexico and Guatemala, the Maya inhabitants are surrounded by at least 800,000 Spanish-speaking Mestizos, descendants of mixed Spanish-indigenous families. For the most part, indigenous groups and those of other ethnic groups get along without major problems. Discrimination is based more on economic factors than on ethnic history. In some communities—Zapata in Chiapas, Mexico, and El Cruce de Dos Aguadas in Guatemala, for example—Maya speakers and Spanish speakers live side by side in harmony. In other areas—Buen Samaritana in Guatemala is a good example—underlying ethnic-economic tensions cause communities to fission apart.

For the most part, though, the modern Maya blend traditions of the past with technology from the twenty-first century to forge new adaptations in a rapidly changing environment. Spanish-speakers, in turn, adopt beneficial Maya practices. The result is a farming and housing technology that, taken alone, presents few clues to distinguish the ethnic background of the families who live along the agricultural frontier.

Yet people everywhere are on the move, reacting to the increasing number of people, degraded homelands, new roads, and lax law enforcement. Population growth, land degradation, and market forces are pushing highland Maya families into lowland forests throughout the Maya tropical forest, turning upside down the rule that indigenous people and conservation are natural allies. The three clearest cases of indigenous communities who can be called conservationists in the Maya Tropical Forest are the Lacandones in Chiapas, the Itza in the Guatemalan Petén, and the Mopan in southern Belize. In all three instances, the groups are small in number, are still living on what remains of their traditional homeland, and are attempting to defend their forested territory against loggers, cattle ranchers, and invading Maya cousins alike. In a promising corollary, the Chol Maya who settled in Frontera Corozal in Chiapas are minimizing agricultural clearing in the surrounding tropical forest in favor of income from tourism and trade on the Río Usumacinta.

By contrast, many Q'eqchi' Maya families are expanding northward from their original territory into the Maya Biosphere Reserve and across the international border into Belize in search of forested land on which to produce corn for subsistence, cash crops, and beef cattle. In both the Guatemalan and Belizean cases, some of these families are moving into protected areas created to conserve biological diversity. Anthropologist Liza Grandia points out how community land tenure traditions can affect deforestation among the Q'eqchi'. In Belize, she notes, the Q'eqchi' maintain individual farming plots within their communities, and village elders monitor land usage, preventing individual families from selling off their family plots. As a result, the Belizean Q'eqchi' tend to think long-term and conserve their forest resources. By contrast, Grandia points out, Q'eqchi' farmers living in the neighboring Guatemalan Petén have no such community controls. They can and do sell their cleared forestlands to other farmers and to cattle raisers, then move on to clear additional national forestlands as a way to claim title to them. As a result, Q'eqchi' Maya families living in the Petén have a reputation for being professional deforesters (Liza Grandia, personal communication, October 2004).

Many of these colonizing families feel that they have a historical right to occupy forest areas. Challenged on his family's presence in a legally protected national park of Guatemala's largest biosphere reserve, one Q'eqchi' leader in the newly formed community of Paso Caballos responded, "This is the Maya Biosphere Reserve. We're Maya. What's the problem?" (Carlos Soza, personal communication, 1997).

The Q'eqchi' leader's response is an extreme expression of a recent social movement emerging in the Maya region. Known as Pan-Mayanism—el Movimiento Maya, in Spanish—it is, according to linguist Charles Andrew Hofling (1996:108), "one of the largest and most powerful revitalization movements in the world today." The Movimiento Maya gained momentum with the 1992 awarding of the Nobel Peace Prize to Rigoberta Menchú, a highland Guatemala Maya woman, in recognition of her struggle for indigenous rights during Guatemala's civil war. The Zapatista rebellion of 1994, in Chiapas, attracted even more international attention to the movement.

In its original intent, Pan-Mayanism is welcomed as a reassertion by Maya peoples of rights and traditions denied them by military governments, Ladino politicians, and dominant Spanish-speaking landowners during the last 500 years. In its extremist expression, however, Pan-Mayanism takes on the mantle of deforestation and land speculation in the name of a proud social movement.

Highland Maya communities are expanding into the lowland tropical forest in Chiapas, the Guatemalan Petén, and southern Belize, carrying the banner of Pan-Mayanism and a questionable historical claim that because the Classic Maya once occupied all this territory, it should be open to any Maya peoples today. In reality, during the Classic Maya, Postclassic, conquest, and colonial periods, the Maya Tropical Forest was occupied by Cholan (Chol, Choltí, and Chortí) and Yucatec speakers, which included the ancestors of today's lowland rainforest Maya, the Lacandón, Itza, Chol, and Mopan.

Combined with incongruous farming practices, market forces, and rapid population growth, this extreme expression of Pan-Mayanism portends an environmental and social disaster. While it is tempting to justify highland Maya invasions of lowland forests as a case of oppressed communities rightfully taking what has been denied them, it is the environment—and, subsequently, indigenous communities themselves—that suffer the consequences.

In March 2000, for example, 600 Guatemalan Q'eqchi' Maya invaded the southern Petén protected area called Salinas–San Román, which includes the archaeological sites of Ceibal, Aguateca, and Dos Pilas, near Lake Petexbatún, in the southern Petén. Using 150 chainsaws and 20 trucks, they set about felling the reserve's hardwood trees. Sixty Guatemalan university students of ecotourism who had the misfortune to visit the reserve that day were captured by the group, threatened with being burned alive, and told they would be killed if they reported what they had seen to the authorities (Tofalla 2000:6).

In lowland Chiapas, the expansion of highland Maya families into the traditional territory of lowland Maya peoples is already creating land disputes between indigenous Maya groups who would normally be allies. The movement of Tzeltal families from the Ocosingo Valley into the land grant of the Comunidad Lacandona is pitting thousands of invading Tzeltal Maya farmers against 700 Lacandón Maya, 3,000 Chol Maya, and 7,000 fellow Tzeltal Maya who have legal title to 6,410 square kilometers (2,475 sq. mi.) of lowland forestland in and around the Montes Azules Biosphere Reserve (Nations 1994).

During the 1994 Zapatista rebellion, the environment of lawlessness created by the military stalemate between rebels and Mexican army troops led to a half-dozen invasions of legal indigenous Maya communities by their neighboring Maya cousins, sometimes pitting Tzeltales against their linguistic brother–Tzeltales. When Zapatista spokespersons initially stated in press releases that their struggle aimed to secure land for the indigenous families of the Selva Lacandona, the elected representatives of the Comunidad Lacandona—one each from the Lacandón, Chol, and Tzeltal settlements that comprise it—immediately issued a public letter denying involvement in the rebellion and seeking government support for protection of their lands from Zapatista invaders.

The situation in the Maya tropical forest illustrates the politically correct but shortsighted view that Kent Redford of the Wildlife Conservation Society has called "the myth of the ecologically noble savage," the idea that indigenous communities can automatically be equated with conservation. As the case of the Maya tropical forest illustrates, the priority of many indigenous peoples is not conservation but land and rights to resources.

That reality should lead to a more sophisticated view of indigenous communities in the Maya Tropical Forest. This view was best expressed by University of Idaho anthropologist Tony Stocks: biological diversity may be conserved in traditional indigenous communities with secure land tenure, low population density, and low involvement in the cash economy, Stocks says, but in most other cases, increasing cash needs and high population growth rates are changing indigenous peoples' relationship with the eco- systems they inhabit (Stocks 1996:23). Geographer Bernard Nietschmann refined this concept into the rule of indigenous environments, which states that "where there are indigenous peoples with a homeland, there are still biologically rich environments" (Redford 1996:251).

In many cases, Maya indigenous communities of the lowland Maya Tropical Forest have become threats to biodiversity rather than guardians of the forest. But it is important to point out that an underlying element explains this situation. All but a few of the Maya groups currently in the Maya Tropical Forest are from displaced communities that are expanding out of their original homelands due to economic factors and population growth. The acquisition of their original homelands by outsiders during the past 500 years—in some cases during the past 100 years—set the stage for this out-migration. Hence, the qualifying phrase in Nietschmann's rule of indigenous environments: "where there are indigenous peoples *with a homeland,* there are still biologically rich environments [my italics]. "

This new perspective does not mean that the positive dialogue be- tween conservationists and indigenous peoples has run its course. On the contrary, indigenous people are still among the best hopes for maintain- ing large landscapes in a more or less natural state (Stearman 1996:264; Chapin 2004). But to benefit from this hope, conservationists must ad- dress the priority issues of indigenous peoples: land, resource rights, edu- cation, and health care.

In the Maya tropical forest, we can take specific actions to help achieve these goals:

- We can assist indigenous communities in securing legal title to their homelands so they can develop sustainable land-use practices on terri- tory they own and control. We must recognize, however, that having a homeland does not automatically end the destruction of biodiversity, if human and livestock populations continue to expand at rapid rates.
- We can learn from and help adapt indigenous agricultural systems to the reality of the twenty-first century. The reality is that we will watch

the world's population expand over the next 50 years to eight to nine billion people (PRB 2004). This population growth will require us to expand world food production, and we must do this in environmentally sustainable ways. The required increases in food production will have to come from land already under cultivation if the earth's remaining biological diversity is to survive. Tropical forests and tropical forest peoples will not endure if we feed the world's expanding population by increasing the amount of land under cultivation. Traditional indigenous agriculture, with its centuries of trial and error and human-guided diversity, could be one of the keys to increasing yields on existing agricultural lands (Toledo, Ortiz-Espejel, and Cortés 2003).

In the Maya Tropical Forest, we need to help local communities diversify their economic strategies, moving beyond the romantic notion of the Maya as Hombres de Maíz, Men of Corn. For example, "Today corn farming remains not just a way to feed the family, but an affirmation of Mayan identity" (Simon 1997:85). The idea that every Maya family has a genetic obligation to clear forest and plant corn runs counter to that family's survival and to ours as biological beings; deforestation rates and population growth have relegated this vision to history. Even more, in tropical Mexico, the economic viability of the Men of Corn died with the arrival of the North American Free Trade Agreement, NAFTA, which—like it or not—established a yearly, duty-free import quota of 2.5 million metric tons of corn into Mexico each year and a total phase-out of tariffs on corn imports over that amount during the next 15 years (Hufbauer and Schott 1993: 47–57). The political reality is that Mexico will now be importing corn from Iowa and selling microchips, vegetables, and oil in exchange. (The migration of thousands of Mexican farmers to the United States to find work is also related to this development.) The Central American version of NAFTA, the Central America Free Trade Agreement (CAFTA), launched into action in mid-2005 by the U.S. Congress, likely portends similar results for Guatemala.

But we should support projects that preserve and disseminate indigenous conservation traditions. In order to do so, we should assist indigenous groups to study these environmental traditions themselves. There is a great deal to be gained by paying young people a salary to study under their tribal elders and shamans instead of migrating to the city or another country to work as unskilled laborers (Plotkin 1993).

We also need a new generation of professionally trained field workers who are willing to learn indigenous languages, live in the field, and work with their indigenous colleagues to record the centuries-old information that is slipping away with the disappearance of traditional peoples and the acculturation of those who survive. Fashions in social sciences come and go, but accurate field data last forever. Aldo Leopold's warning about natural ecosystems holds true for traditional knowledge as well: "The first rule of intelligent tinkering is to save all the pieces" (Leopold 1989).

We can also promote cultural and biological diversity by working to defuse land conflicts between indigenous communities. Locally based human rights and conservation groups do this by financing and providing logistics for dialogue between the groups in their native languages. Once we assist the groups in coming together to talk, the outsiders should stay out of the way or, better yet, serve coffee.

It is also imperative that we work with non-indigenous, traditional forest dwellers, who sometimes display the type of conservation ethic frequently associated with indigenous communities. One of the best examples is that of the Mestizo chicle and allspice harvesters of Yucatán and the Guatemalan Petén. These groups can be conservationists for the same reasons that indigenous people can be: they want continued access to land and sustainable natural resources for their own economic survival.

The Challenge of Population Growth

We need to work on the challenge of population growth in the Maya Tropical Forest and throughout the world, including in our own societies. The best way to do this in traditional communities is to improve the status of women and educate young girls. United Nations studies indicate that when women in the developing world are allowed to make their own decisions about how many children they produce, they automatically produce one-third fewer children (Cain 1984; World Bank 1985; Jacobson 1993).

A key activity in decreasing population growth and achieving conservation is to increase economic opportunities for women. When women in the developing world earn money for their family, they are given more prestige within their family and within the community. As a result, they have more power to make decisions within the family, including the decision on how many children to produce. Increasing economic opportunities for women also aids conservation, because when women in the developing world produce money for their family, the family is less likely to have to degrade forests and fisheries in order to survive. People living in poverty become desperate people, and desperate people tend not to worry about the future of their natural environment. Educated, empowered populations are more likely to protect the natural resources they themselves depend on.

The education of young girls is another key activity. This education can be bilingual and it can—and should—include education in cultural traditions, especially traditions that promote the sustainable use of land and natural resources. These conservation traditions, expressed in native languages where they still exist, are what Hazel Henderson called "the cultural DNA" that can help create sustainable economies in healthy ecosystems (Gell-Mann 1994:292).

There are two key factors to remember about this situation. The first is that all of these activities—education, economic empowerment of women, and diminishing poverty—are activities that need to be carried out anyway, for the direct benefit of children, men, and women. The fact that these same activities help achieve the conservation of nature and dampen population growth is an added, positive benefit.

Just over 50 years ago, the human population of the earth was 3 billion people, and the earth still had vast regions of natural wilderness. Since that time, the population of the earth has more than doubled—to 6.4 billion people in mid-2004—and many wilderness areas have been reduced to remnants, among them those of the Maya Tropical Forest (PRB 2004). During these same decades, we have come to understand that the areas we seek to conserve are the same areas where human population is growing most rapidly. The world's biological diversity hotspots are also human population hotspots (Cincotta and Engelman 2000).

Today, 98 percent of human population growth is occurring in the developing world, in countries with the largest remaining areas of natural ecosystems. This coincidence of population growth and environmental degradation results from the fact that the biodiversity-rich areas are some of the most remote regions of the world. These are places where the lack of roads and infrastructure have maintained ecosystems in a relatively natural state, but also where families moving into these areas remain isolated from access to basic health care and reproductive health services (Cincotta and Engelman 2000).

Over the last 30 years, worldwide efforts to improve access to reproductive health and family planning have been hugely successful, saving the lives of millions of women and children and resulting in an unprecedented voluntary reduction in global fertility rates. Unfortunately, the benefits of these efforts have accrued mostly in urban environments, where population densities are higher and health providers' access to large numbers of families is easier. In rural areas, contraceptive use rates are lower, and fertility rates and maternal and infant mortality rates are markedly higher. Throughout the world, more than 350 million mostly rural couples still lack access to basic reproductive health care and information (Cincotta and Engelman 2000).

Governments, international organizations, and local nonprofit organizations must address the issue of human population growth in and around the national parks and biosphere reserves of the Maya forest in order to keep the region healthy for the benefit of current and future generations. Population growth rates in the Maya tropical forest—especially among indigenous families—are among the highest in the world (CARE/CI 1995). In the Selva Lacandona of eastern Chiapas, the current population of 450,000 people is growing at the rate of 7 percent per year, due to both natural increase and in-migration from the Maya highlands, a rate of growth that will double the population within 10 years. Fifty-two percent of the population of the Selva Lacandona is under the age of 15 years (World Bank 1994).

Next door, in the Guatemalan Petén, the population of 600,000 to 700,000 is growing at the rate of 10 percent per year, also due to both natural increase and in-migration (INE 2001). But positive action produces positive results. When the Guatemalan conservation organization ProPetén initiated an integrated reproductive health program in the 1990s, the total fertility rate (average number of children born per woman) in the Petén was 7.8, one of the highest rates in Latin America (Grandia 1998; INE 2001). (The human replacement rate is 2.1 births per woman, which results in no population growth.) ProPetén began working with communities inside and along the boundaries of the Maya Biosphere Reserve, setting up health clinics that included voluntary family planning opportunities. Women of the communities flocked to the clinics seeking aid in spacing their children, and the fertility rate for the region began to decline.

ProPetén went on to train 80 local midwives in reproductive health and voluntary family planning and worked with national organizations to initiate a program called the Biósfera Mobil, "the mobile biosphere," which brought high quality, affordable health care to children and mothers in the region's isolated farming communities. The organization also began an environmental education program that was adopted by the Department of Petén's primary schools, and they initiated a radio program focused on improving agricultural production on land already cleared. Among the positive results of ProPetén's efforts was a dramatic drop in the average number of births per woman—from 6.8 in 1999 to 5.8 in 2002, "about as fast as human fertility can decline," according to anthropologist Liza Grandia, who helped monitor the results (Wilson Center 2004). ProPetén's success demonstrates that for their own health and for that of their children, women on the agricultural frontier of the Maya forest are eager to space the birth of their children, rather than reproduce as fast as nature allows.

Fortunately, the 1994 International Conference on Population and Development, the Cairo Conference, showed us how to achieve this goal: economically empower women, provide universal access to voluntary family planning, and educate young girls—all activities that dampen population growth. As a result of progress in these areas, growth rates are declining in almost every region of the world. But we will still see almost 3 billion people added to the earth's population by the year 2050, during the lifetime of many of the people reading this page (PRB 2004).

A key factor in this analysis is that providing education to both boys and girls in the developing world, working for the economic empowerment of women, and working to eliminate poverty do not "control" population. Instead, these actions create a voluntary situation in which people are allowed to do what they already want to do anyway. There is no demand for a one-child family; there is no attempt to control people's lives. Instead, people are simply allowed the opportunity to make their own decisions.

Numerous advantages result from combining conservation action with population action among rural families on the agricultural frontier. We know that poverty compels many of the citizens of these regions to misuse their biological resources. Lack of access to education, health, credit, and family planning condemns them to bare subsistence levels. The most dramatic impact of this situation is the expansion of cropland at the expense of natural ecosystems such as forests and wetlands, with a resulting eradication of the earth's biological diversity.

On the positive side, conservationists are already working with these families, taking trucks or boats or mules to get to communities and earning the families' trust by working with them to help improve their lives and natural resource use. Adding a population component to conservation projects in these communities allows us to expand the impact of our operations by building on activities and infrastructures that already exist.

Creating integrated population/environment programs also builds on what conservationists are good at, such as understanding the complexity of the population/environment interface, working with families in an environment of mutual trust, and setting up economic enterprises as alternatives to ecosystem destruction.

We have already discovered that we get more bang for the buck by working with women. University of California–Berkeley anthropologist Liza Grandia found in Guatemala that when men earn new income from alternative economic enterprises, such as nontimber forest products or ecotourism, they spend the money on bicycles, soccer games, and drinking. When women earn money from these new enterprises, they spend it on food, medicines, and education for their children. The fact that these activities also serve to dampen fertility is an added plus to something that already needs to be done (Grandia 1999).

It is also important to take into account the developed world's overconsumption as a cause of ecosystem destruction. The gorge-and-vomit societies of the developed world prompt environmental degradation in the tropical world by sending road machinery into forestlands in search of petroleum, commercial timber, and room to grow export crops, such as oil palm, soybeans, and beef cattle. The population of the United States increased by a factor of 3 during the twentieth century, for example, but our use of raw materials increased by a factor of 17 (Brown 2002). The U.S. population's appetite for tropical hardwoods and petroleum has played a significant role in the degradation of natural ecosystems in the Maya Tropical Forest.

Unless we directly address the corollary issues of human population growth and overconsumption, we are simply postponing the loss of biological diversity in the region's protected areas. We are also missing an opportunity to help improve the lives of families who live in one of the earth's most sensitive ecosystems.

The Promise of Ecological Tourism

In the long term, we must work to create viable economic alternatives for families currently relegated to burning up their countries' natural resources to keep their children alive. New sources of income through microenterprises based on ecotourism and sustainable forest products such as essential oils, handicrafts, and raw botanicals for the cosmetic industry can create vital income for rural families without causing the death of the few forest regions that remain. Promoting agricultural techniques that eliminate the need for fire would allow the growing number of rural families to feed themselves without torching their future.

The region's income from tourism promises even more benefits. The Maya forest is one of the few places on earth where visitors can look up from a thousand-year-old stone city to watch spider monkeys turning somersaults through a tropical forest canopy. This combination of tropical wildlands and ancient monuments brings hundreds of thousands of tourists to the Maya Tropical Forest each year, providing the basis for a multimillion dollar tourism industry that will be one of the chief elements in the Maya forest's survival. Tourism focused on the rare combination of ancient cities and tropical forests promises to be a driving force in protection in the Maya Tropical Forest. By demonstrating the economic value of these cultural and natural resources unimpaired, this archaeo/ecotourism is prompting both local communities and national governments to protect Maya sites and natural ecosystems from destruction.

Two good examples are the El Perú/Waka' project inside Guatemala's Laguna del Tigre National Park and the Mirador Basin Project that seeks to link forest protection and archaeological restoration in the northern Petén with similar efforts in the Calakmul Biosphere Reserve of Mexico (FARES 2005).

Between 1997 and 2000, more than 23.5 million tourists visited the nations of the Maya world, including Honduras and El Salvador, as well as Mexico, Guatemala, and Belize. Tourism is increasing in the region at 9 percent per year (Mundo Maya 2002). The combination of archaeological restoration and environmental conservation, when designed, planned, and carried out with the active participation of local communities, can be the saving grace of the future of the Maya forest.

Properly conceived and executed, ecotourism gives economic value to the ecosystem services and cultural resources that national parks and biosphere reserves provide, generates direct income for conservation efforts, creates direct and indirect income for local stakeholders, prompts local communities to support conservation, builds local and national constituencies for conservation, and promotes sustainable use of natural and cultural resources (Drumm et al. 2004:3; Christ et al. 2003:4).

The logic behind tourism as a positive force for conserving biological and cultural resources is simple: deforestation, wildlife poaching, and archaeological looting are driven by people's desire to feed their families and make money. Preventing the destructive force of these activities is a function of creating continuing sources of employment and income generation that depend on keeping the resources intact. "Tourism is an excellent means of fostering this circumstance: a campesino who captures a bird to sell to the pet trade will earn money once, but a person or organization that protects local nesting areas and provides food, lodging, and guide services to bird-watchers can earn income many times over" (Norris, Wilber, and Morales Marín 1998:330).

The tropical forests that remain in Mexico, Guatemala, and Belize bring invaluable financial and environmental benefits to these countries—and to the hemisphere at large—in terms of income from tourism, recreation, watershed protection, wildlife, new products, and climate buffering. As government representatives and financial decision makers increase their understanding of the economic and ecological benefits of natural ecosystems and cultural resources, we can expect them to increasingly push for the conservation of these resources.

Regional Incentives

Conservation professionals in the nations of the Maya Tropical Forest, however, are not waiting for the political and economic communities to act but are taking their own positive steps to keep the region's ecosystems and cultural resources alive. For example, national and international organizations and indigenous groups focused on the conservation of biological diversity in the Maya Tropical Forest joined together in June 1998 to create the Coalition for the Selva Maya (La Coalición de la Selva Maya). This organization temporarily took on the role of designated worrier for conservation of the region's biological and cultural resources, following a series of meetings convened in 1990 through 1998 by the Tropical Ecosystems Directorate of the U.S. Man and the Biosphere Program in coordination with the Central American Commission for Environment and Development (Comisión Centroamericana de Ambiente y Desarrollo, CCAD). Subsequent meetings of the Coalition for the Selva Maya in Flores, Petén, and Las Milpas, Belize, allowed the members of the Coalition to agree on the group's mission, vision, objectives, and roles.

Currently moribund for lack of funding, the Coalition for the Selva Maya has the potential to be a driving force in the conservation of the Maya Tropical Forest.

Lessons from the Ancient Maya

The Maya Tropical Forest today harbors both the seeds of its own destruction and those of its ultimate salvation. On the pessimistic side, the future of the Maya Tropical Forest threatens to be similar to its past: human demands on the natural environment surpass the region's carrying capacity, producing ecological and economic disintegration. Classic Maya civilization collapsed shortly after reaching its peak of population, power, and food production. The decline was rapid and final. The growth in the number of people finally outpaced the ability to produce food, especially as forested hillsides were cleared to produce more food, exposing thin soils to erosion. Then the longest drought in Maya history hit the region, effectively ending food production sufficient to sustain millions of people (Diamond 2005a, 2005b:176). Agricultural collapse wrought economic chaos, which in turn brought on political strife, more warfare, and attacks on the political elite. City-states began to war with one another, as is evident in the hasty breastworks built in sites such as Dos Pilas and Aguateca in the southern Petén.

Between 90 and 99 percent of the population of the Maya Tropical Forest died, victims of thirst, starvation, and warfare. A lucky few relocated to cities on lakes and rivers. Climatic, economic, and political factors wreaked havoc even in the places of final refuge, and the Maya who survived in the southern lowlands faded into the forest.

The impact of climate change—specifically, extended droughts—on the collapse of Maya civilization has a potential parallel in modern times. All but a handful of scientists acknowledge the existence of a global warming trend in the early twenty-first century. We already are experiencing the predicted increase in average global temperature. No one doubts that this gradual warming will produce drastic changes in human activities, at least in specific areas. In the Maya forest, we may already be seeing the forward edge of these changes, namely, in the form of more frequent forest fires. Extended dry periods, combined with the continuing tradition of slash-and-burn farming, produce massive fires in Chiapas, Yucatán, and the Petén each year. If global climate change produces droughts in the Maya region similar to those at the end of the Classic era, we may lose ever larger areas of the Maya Tropical Forest to fires. Archaeologist David Webster makes the point succinctly: "In many ways modern Maya people are re-enacting the demographic processes of the Classic collapse, as reflected in the massive recent deforestation of much of the Maya Lowlands that is visible even from outer space" (Webster 2002:348).

What can we learn from Maya history to prevent similar disasters in the future? Harvard biologist E. O. Wilson predicts that at best we are facing an environmental bottleneck that "will cause the unfolding of a new kind of history driven by environmental change. Or perhaps an unfolding on a global scale of more of the old kind of history, which saw the collapse of regional civilizations, going back to the earliest in history" (E. Wilson 1998:287).

"People died in large numbers," Wilson says, "often horribly. Sometimes they were able to emigrate and displace other people, making them die horribly instead" (E. Wilson 1998:287).

Wilson points out that archaeologists and historians explain the collapse of civilizations by pointing to "drought, soil exhaustion, overpopulation, and warfare—singly or in some permutation." But ecologists add another perspective, he says.

> The populations reached the local carrying capacity, where further growth could no longer be sustained with the technology available. At that point life was often good, especially for the ruling classes, but fragile. A change such as a drought or depletion of the aquifer or a ravaging war then lowered the carrying capacity. (E. Wilson 1998:287)

We face the challenge of maneuvering through the bottleneck of the next 50 years of population growth and overconsumption while maintaining as much as possible of the rest of life that accompanies us on earth (E. Wilson 2004:7–8). The challenge sometimes seems overwhelming. We know that tropical forests, oceans, rivers, and wetlands continue to be threatened by misuse and destruction, but we also know that there is hope for finding a sustainable future.

One sign of hope is the creation of huge, new protected areas like the Maya Biosphere Reserve in northern Guatemala, the Río Bravo lands of the Programme for Belize, and the Calakmul Biosphere Reserve in Mexico. We have learned that protected areas *do* keep alive natural ecosystems and biodiversity, that parks work. To quote one recent study, "Tropical parks have been surprisingly effective at protecting the ecosystems and species within their borders, despite chronic underfunding and land-use pressure" (Bruner et al. 2001:126).

The growing force of ecotourism promises to be another positive force in economic development and environmental protection. As individuals, we can support resource protection in the Maya Tropical Forest by visiting it. Properly managed, tourism brings financial and social benefits to local people, provides needed tax dollars to national governments, and demonstrates the value of protected areas to local and regional decision makers. The United States National Park System Advisory Board recently pointed out that a "fundamental premise" of national parks is that "public enjoyment and the protection of the natural integrity of the parks are far from being mutually exclusive; rather, they are mutually dependent" (Earle et al. 2004:4; Wade 2005). This means that visiting the Maya Tropical Forest can be an investment in protecting it. Still, all the normal caveats hold:

- Take only pictures, leave only money (minimize your footprints, literally and symbolically).
- Support local, mom-and-pop operations where you can.
- Be a positive ambassador from your own country. Listen and learn.

Knowing what to protect and why to protect it emerges from the biological sciences, biogeography, and archaeology, but keeping alive cultural history and the foundation of life on earth is a social science. It is a function of understanding human beings, their politics, and their economic needs. We have learned that working with people is crucial. We have learned that if we help local communities and national enterprises to create economic alternatives to cultural and ecological destruction, these communities and enterprises will protect the environment they call home. That is the crux of sustainable development and the central tenet of conservation in the twenty-first century.

As Tom Lovejoy pointed out several years ago, the choice is *not* between people and nature. The choice is between a future in which both people and nature prosper, or a future in which both people and nature go down the tube together (Lovejoy 1986:426).

Over my office desk, I keep a quote from Václav Havel, who was until 2003 the president of the Czech Republic, and I leave it with you as a parting challenge.

I can hardly imagine living without hope. As for the future of the world, there is a colorful spectrum of possibilities, from the worst to the best. What will happen, I do not know. Hope forces me to believe that those better alternatives will prevail, and above all, it forces me to do something to make them happen. (Morrow 1992)

*G*lossary

biosphere reserve: A type of protected area that seeks to balance conservation of natural areas with sustainable human development and scientific research.

Maya Biosphere Reserve: A 1,600 square kilometer (6,178 sq. mi.) protected area in the Department of Petén, Guatemala.

Maya Tropical Forest: A lowland forest region of the modern territories of eastern Chiapas (Mexico), Guatemala's Department of Petén, the southern part of the Yucatán Peninsula, and all of the nation of Belize.

Selva Maya: The Spanish language term for the Maya Tropical Forest, a lowland forest region of the modern territories of eastern Chiapas (Mexico), Guatemala's Department of Petén, the southern part of the Yucatán Peninsula, and all of the nation of Belize.

References Cited

ADAMS, RICHARD
 1965 *Migraciones internas en Guatemala: expansión agraria de los indígenas kekchíes hacia el Petén.* Guatemala: Seminario de Integración Social Guatemalteca.

ANGIER, NATALIE
 2003 At Last, Ready for Its Close-Up. *New York Times,* June 17, 2003: D1, D4.

ARANDA SÁNCHEZ, MARCELO, AND SALVADOR GUZMÁN
 1999 Fauna. In *Naturaleza y cultura en Calakmul, Campeche,* edited by W. Folan Higgins, M. C. Sánchez González, and J. M. García Ortega, pp. 65–69. Campeche: Centro de Investigaciones Históricas y Sociales, Universidad Autónoma de Campeche, Mexico.

ARIZPE, LOURDES, FERNANDA PAZ, AND MARGARITA VELÁZQUEZ
 1996 *Culture and Global Change: Social Perceptions of Deforestation in the Lacandona Rain Forest in Mexico.* Ann Arbor: University of Michigan Press.

ATRAN, SCOTT
 1993a The Bio-Itza. *Anthropology Newsletter,* October, p. 37.
 1993b Itza Maya Tropical Agro-Forestry. *Current Anthropology* 34(5):633–700.

ATRAN, SCOTT, AND EDILBERTO UKAN EK'
 1999 Classification of Useful Plants by the Northern Petén Maya (Itzaj). In *Reconstructing Ancient Maya Diet,* edited by Christine D. White, chap. 2, pp. 19–59. Salt Lake City: University of Utah Press.

BAER, PHILLIP, AND WILLIAM R. MERRIFIELD
 1971 *Two Studies on the Lacandones of Mexico.* Norman: Summer Institute of Linguistics of the University of Oklahoma.

BARRIOS, ROSALITO
 1995 *Cincuenta áreas de interés especial para la conservación en Guatemala.* Guatemala: Centro de Estudios Conservacionistas.

BARRY, TOM, WITH DYLAN VERNON
 1995 *Inside Belize.* Albuquerque, NM: Interhemispheric Resource Center.

BATES, MARSTON

1963   *Where Winter Never Comes: A Study of Man and Nature in the Tropics.* New York: Charles Scribner's Sons.

BELETSKY, LES

1999a   *Tropical Mexico: The Ecotravellers' Wildlife Guide.* San Diego: Academic Press.

1999b   *Belize and Northern Guatemala: The Ecotravellers' Wildlife Guide.* San Diego: Academic Press.

BELIZE REPORT

1998   La Milpa: Uncovering Rich Layers of Maya History. *Belize Report* 4(1):1–2.

BELIZE TIMES

1991   Not Scared of Hard Work. *Belize Times,* Sunday, June 2, 1991.

BERENBAUM, MAY R.

1993   *Ninety-nine More Maggots, Mites, and Munchers.* Urbana: University of Illinois Press.

BESTELMEYER, BRANDON T., AND LEEANNE E. ALONSO, EDS.

2000   *A Biological Assessment of Laguna del Tigre National Park, Petén, Guatemala.* Rapid Assessment Program Bulletin 16. Washington, DC: Conservation International.

BILLY, SANTIAGO

1999   Las Guacamayas Biological Station. In *Thirteen Ways of Looking at a Tropical Forest: Guatemala's Maya Biosphere Reserve,* edited by James D. Nations, chap. 6, pp. 35–38. Washington, DC: Conservation International.

BIRD, NICK M., ED.

1997   *The 1997 Little Quartz Ridge Expedition.* Executive summary. Belize: Forest Planning and Management Project, Belize Forest Department and Belize Zoo and Tropical Education Center.

BJORK, ROBIN

2001   Presentation at the La Milpa, Belize, Tri-National Selva Maya meeting of the Tropical Ecosystem Directorate of the U.S. Man and the Biosphere Program and the Coalición de la Selva Maya. La Milpa, Belize, February 21, 22, 23, 2001.

BLAKESLEE, SANDRA

2005   Colicky Baby? Read This Before Calling an Exorcist. *New York Times,* March 8, 2005: D6.

BOREMANSE, DIDIER

1998   *Hach Winik: The Lacandón Maya of Chiapas, Southern Mexico.* Institute for Mesoamerican Studies, monograph 11. Albany, NY: University at Albany.

BOTKIN, DANIEL B.

1993   *Our Natural History: The Lessons of Lewis and Clark.* New York: Perigee Books.

BOWLES, IAN A., AMY ROSENFELD, CYRIL KORMOS, CONRAD
REINING, JAMES D. NATIONS, AND THOMAS ANKERSEN
1999 The Environmental Impacts of International Finance Corporation
Lending and Proposals for Reform: A Case Study of Conservation and
Oil Development in the Guatemalan Petén. *Environmental Law* 29(1):
103–132.

BREEDLOVE, DENNIS
1973 Phytogeography of Chiapas. In *Vegetation and Vegetational History
of Northern Latin America,* edited by A. Graham. Amsterdam: Elsevier
Scientific.
1981 *Introduction to the Flora of Chiapas.* Part 1 of *Flora of Chiapas,*
edited by Dennis Breedlove. San Francisco: California Academy of
Sciences.

BRITO FOUCHER, RODULFO
1931 México desconocido: las monterías de Chiapas. *Revista Universidad de
México* 1(4):324–328.

BROKAW, NICHOLAS V. L., ANDREW A. WHITMAN, ROGER WILSON,
JOHN M. HAGAN, NEIL BIRD, ELIZABETH P. MALLORY, LAURA K.
SNOOK, PAUL J. MARTINS, DARRELL NOVELO, DOMINIC WHITE, AND
ELIZABETH LOSOS
1998 Toward Sustainable Forestry in Belize. In *Timber, Tourists, and Temples,*
edited by Richard B. Primack, David Bray, Hugo A. Galletti, and Ismael
Ponciano, chap. 15. Washington, DC: Island Press.

BROWN, LESTER
2002 Building an Eco-economy. Plenary lecture, June 8, 2002, Healthy Ecosystems, Healthy People Conference, Washington, DC.

BRUNER, AARON, RAYMOND GULLISON, RICHARD RICE, AND
GUSTAVO DA FONSECA
2001 Effectiveness of Parks in Protecting Tropical Biodiversity. *Science*
291:125–128.

BULLARD, WILLIAM R., JR.
1970 Topoxte: A Postclassic Maya Site in Petén, Guatemala. In *Monographs
and Papers in Maya Archaeology,* edited by William R. Bullard Jr. Papers
of the Peabody Museum of Archaeology and Ethnology, Harvard University, vol. 61. Cambridge, MA: Peabody Museum, Harvard.

BUTZER, KARL W.
1992 The Americas Before and After 1492: An Introduction to Current Geographical Research. *Annals of the Association of American Geographers*
82(3):345–368.

BYE, ROBERT
1993 The Role of Humans in the Diversification of Plants in Mexico. In *Biological Diversity of Mexico: Origins and Distribution,* edited by
T. P. Ramamoorthy, Robert Bye, Antonio Lot, and John Fa. New York:
Oxford University Press.

CÁCERES LÓPEZ, CARLOS

1958   *Historia general del estado de Chiapas.* 2 vols. Mexico City: Imprente Mexicana.

CAIN, MEAD

1984   Women's Status and Fertility in Developing Countries: Son Preference and Economic Security. Staff Working Paper 682, World Bank, Washington, DC.

CAMPBELL, JONATHAN A.

1998   *Amphibians and Reptiles of Northern Guatemala, the Yucatan, and Belize.* Norman: University of Oklahoma Press.

CARE/CI (CARE/Conservation International)

1995   *Análisis de los impactos ambientales actuales y potenciales del proceso de reintegración de los retornados a Guatemala y recomendaciones para su mitigación.* Informe Final. Guatemala: CARE, Conservation International.

CASTRO, FERNANDO

1988   Monografía de los peces del Lago Petén Itzá, Petén, Guatemala. Escuela de Biología, Universidad de San Carlos de Guatemala, Facultad de Ciencias Químicas y Farmacia, Guatemala, Guatemala. Manuscript, 16 pp.

CEPF (Critical Ecosystem Partnership Fund)

2003   *The Northern Mesoamerica Ecosystem Profile.* Washington, DC: Conservation International.

CHAPIN, MAC

2004   A Challenge to Conservationists. *World-Watch* 17(6):17–31.

CHASE, ARLEN F.

1993   Comment on Scott Atran, Itza Maya Tropical Agro-Forestry. *Current Anthropology* 34(5):689–690.

CHASE, ARLEN F., AND DIANE Z. CHASE

1998   Scale and Intensity in Classic Period Maya Agriculture: Terracing and Settlement at the "Garden City" of Caracol, Belize. *Culture and Agriculture* 20(2/3):60–77.

CHAYAX HUEX, REGINALDO, FELICIANO TZUL COLLI, CARLOS GÓMEZ CAAL, AND STEVEN P. GRETZINGER

1998   The Bio-Itzá Reserve: History of an Indigenous Effort to Conserve the Maya Itzá Community of San José, El Petén, Guatemala. In *Timber, Tourists, and Temples: Conservation and Development in the Maya Forest of Belize, Guatemala, and Mexico,* edited by Richard B. Primack, David Bray, Hugo A. Galletti, and Ismael Ponciano, chap. 21, pp. 317–325. Washington, DC: Island Press.

CHENAUT, VICTORIA

1989   *Migrantes y aventureros en la frontera sur.* Mexico City: Centro de Investigaciones y Estudios Superiores en Antropología Social, Secretaría de Educación Pública.

CHRIST, COSTAS, OLIVER HILLEL, SELENI MATUS, AND JAMIE
SWEETING

2003 *Tourism and Biodiversity: Mapping Tourism's Global Footprint.*
Washington, DC: Conservation International.

CINCOTTA, RICHARD P., AND ROBERT ENGELMAN

2000 *Nature's Place: Human Population and the Future of Biological Diversity.* Washington, DC: Population Action International.

COATES, ANTHONY G.

1997 The Forging of Central America. In *Central America: A Natural and Cultural History,* edited by Anthony G. Coates, chap. 1, pp. 1–37. New Haven: Yale University Press.

COE, ANDREW

2001 *Archaeological Mexico: A Traveler's Guide to Ancient Cities and Sacred Sites.* Emeryville, CA: Avalon Travel Publishing.

COE, MICHAEL D.

1992 *Breaking the Maya Code.* New York: Thames and Hudson.

1993 *The Maya.* New York: Thames and Hudson.

COE, SOPHIE D., AND MICHAEL D.

1996 *The True History of Chocolate.* New York: Thames and Hudson.

COE, WILLIAM R.

1967 *Tikal: A Handbook of the Ancient Maya Ruins.* Philadelphia: University Museum, University of Pennsylvania.

CONSERVATION INTERNATIONAL

1998 Informe de la tercera expedición al Sac Bahlan—Río Tzendales, Selva Lacandona, Chiapas. Tuxtla Gutiérrez, Chiapas: Conservación Internacional, Mexico, AC.

2002 A Conservation Strategy for the Selva Maya Biodiversity Corridor. Washington, DC: Conservation International. Third draft, January 2002.

2003 The Northern Mesoamerica Ecosystem Profile. Washington, DC: Conservation International.

CULBERT, T. PATRICK

1974 *The Lost Civilization: The Story of the Classic Maya.* New York: Harper and Row.

DAVIS, L. IRBY

1972 *A Field Guide to the Birds of Mexico and Central America.* Austin: University of Texas Press.

DEEVEY, E. S., DON S. RICE, PRUDENCE M. RICE, H. H. VAUGHAN,
MARK BRENNER, AND M. S. FLANNERY

1979 Mayan Urbanism: Impact on a Tropical Karst Environment. *Science* 206(4416):298–306.

DENEVAN, WILLIAM M.

1992 The Pristine Myth: The Landscape of the Americas in 1492. *Annals of the Association of American Geographers* 82(3):369–385.

DE VOS, JAN

1980   *La paz de Dios y del rey: la conquista de la Selva Lacandona.* Mexico City: Fonapas, Chiapas.

1988a *Oro verde: la conquista de la Selva Lacandona por los madereros tabasqueños, 1822–1949.* Mexico City: Fondo de Cultura Económica.

1988b *Viajes al desierto de la soledad: cuando la Selva Lacandona aún era selva.* Mexico City: Secretaría de Educación Pública.

1993   *Las fronteras de la frontera sur.* Mexico City: Universidad Juárez Autónoma de Tabasco, Centro de Investigaciones y Estudios Superiores de Antropología Social.

DIAMOND, JARED

2004   Lessons from Environmental Collapses of Past Societies. Fourth annual John H. Chafee Memorial Lecture on Science and the Environment. Washington, DC: National Council for Science and the Environment.

2005a The Ends of the World as We Know Them. Op-ed. *New York Times,* Saturday, January 1, 2005: A21.

2005b *Collapse: How Societies Choose to Fail or Succeed.* New York: Penguin Group.

DIARIO OFICIAL DE LA FEDERACIÓN

1998   Areas protegidas, Chiapas. *Diario Oficial de la Federación.* Mexico City: Gobierno Federal de la República de México.

DOBSON, NARDA

1973   *A History of Belize.* London: Longman Group.

DOBYNS, HENRY F.

1963   An Outline of Andean Epidemic History to 1720. *Bulletin of the History of Medicine* 37:493–515.

DRUMM, ANDY, ALAN MOORE, ANDREW SOLES, CAROL PATTERSON, AND JOHN E. TERBORGH

2004   *Ecotourism Development: A Manual for Conservation Planners and Managers.* Vol. 2: *The Business of Ecotourism Development and Management.* Arlington, VA: Nature Conservancy.

DUGELBY, BARBARA L.

1991   Chamadorea Palm Extraction in Petén, Guatemala: Incentives for Overexploitation. Master's thesis, School of Forestry and Environmental Studies, Duke University.

1998   Governmental and Customary Arrangements Guiding Chicle Latex Extraction in Petén, Guatemala. In *Timber, Tourists, and Temples: Conservation and Development in the Maya Forest of Belize, Guatemala, and Mexico,* edited by Richard B. Primack, David Bray, Hugo A. Galletti, and Ismael Ponciano, chap. 11. Washington, DC: Island Press.

DURNING, ALAN

1993   Supporting Indigenous Peoples. In *State of the World, 1993,* chap. 5. Washington, DC: Worldwatch Institute.

EARLE, SYLVIA A., ROBERT CHANDLER, LARRY MADIN, SHIRLEY
M. MALCOM, GARY PAUL NABHAN, PETER RAVEN, AND EDWARD
O. WILSON
2004 *National Park Service Science in the 21st Century: A National Parks
Science Committee Report to the National Parks System Advisory Board.*
Washington, DC: National Park Service.

ELTRINGHAM, PETER, JOHN FISHER, AND IAIN STEWART
1999 *The Maya World: Southern Mexico, Belize, Guatemala, Honduras, El
Salvador.* Rough Guides travel series. London: Rough Guides.

ERICSON, JENNY, MARK S. FREUDENBERGER, AND ECKART BOEGE
1999 Population Dynamics, Migration, and the Future of the Calakmul
Biosphere Reserve. Occasional Paper 1, Program on Population and
Sustainable Development. Washington, DC: American Association for
the Advancement of Science.

FARES (Foundation for Anthropological Research and Environmental
Studies)
2005 Mirador Basin National Monument: The Cradle of Maya Civilization.
http://www.miradorbasin.com/Resources/mirador.htm.

FOLAN, WILLIAM J.
1999 Patrimonio histórico-cultural. In *Naturaleza y cultura en Calakmul,
Campeche,* edited by W. Folan Higgins, M. C. Sánchez González, and
J. M. García Ortega, pp. 71–81. Campeche: Centro de Investigaciones
Históricas y Sociales, Universidad Autónoma de Campeche.

FOLAN, WILLIAM J., AND SILVERIO GALLEGOS OSUNA
1996 El uso del suelo del sitio arqueológico de Calakmul, Campeche. *Yum
Kaax: Boletín de Información Ecológica de la Universidad Autónoma de
Campeche* 2(3):7–8.

FOLAN, WILLIAM J., JOYCE MARCUS, AND W. FRANK MILLER
1995 Verification of a Maya Settlement Model through Remote Sensing.
Cambridge Archaeological Journal 5(2):277–284.

FOLAN, WILLIAM J., JACINTO MAY HAU, ROGERIO COHUOH MUÑOZ,
AND RAYMUNDO GONZÁLEZ HEREDIA
1990 *Calakmul, Campeche, México: su mapa, una introducción.* Campeche:
Centro de Investigaciones Históricas y Sociales, Universidad Autónoma
de Campeche.

FORD, ANABEL
1995 *The Ancient Maya of Belize: Their Society and Sites.* Santa Barbara:
CORI/MesoAmerican Research Center, University of California.
2001 Presentation at the La Milpa, Belize Tri-national Selva Maya Meeting of
the Tropical Ecosystem Directorate of the U.S. Man and the Biosphere
Program and the Coalición de la Selva Maya. La Milpa, Belize, February
21, 22, 23, 2001.

FORD, ANABEL, ED.
1998 *The Future of El Pilar: The Integrated Research and Development
Plan for the El Pilar Archaeological Reserve for Flora and Fauna,*

Belize-Guatemala. Department of State Publication 10507, Bureau of Oceans and International Environmental and Scientific Affairs. Washington, DC: U.S. Man and the Biosphere Program, U.S. Department of State.

FORT, MEREDITH, AND LIZA GRANDIA
1999 Population and Environment in the Petén, Guatemala. In *Thirteen Ways of Looking at a Tropical Forest: Guatemala's Maya Biosphere Reserve,* edited by James D. Nations, chap. 13, pp. 85–91. Washington, DC: Conservation International.

FOSTER, BYRON, ED.
1997 *Warlords and Maize Men: A Guide to the Maya Sites of Belize.* Belize City: Cubola Productions.

FREIDEL, DAVID
2004 Letter to University of Texas Press.

FREIDEL, DAVID, AND STANLEY GUENTER
2002 The Dallas Tablet, A Site Q Monument Revealed. Manuscript, Department of Anthropology, Southern Methodist University, May 2002.

FREIDEL, DAVID, LINDA SCHELE, AND JOY PARKER
1993 *Maya Cosmos: Three Thousand Years on the Shaman's Path.* New York: Quill/William Morrow.

GALLENKAMP, CHARLES
1987 *Maya: The Riddle and Rediscovery of a Lost Civilization.* New York: Penguin.

GARCÍA, EDUARDO
2005 Parque Nacional Laguna del Tigre, área desprotegida. *Inforpress Centroamericana,* 27 de mayo, 2005:3-5. www.inforpressca.com; accessed July 2005.

GAREL, TONY, AND SHARON MATOLA
1996 *A Field Guide to the Snakes of Belize.* Belize: Belize Zoo and Tropical Education Center.

GARRETT, WILBUR E.
1989 La Ruta Maya. *National Geographic* 176(4):424–479.

GELL-MANN, MURRAY
1994 *The Quark and the Jaguar: Adventures in the Simple and the Complex.* New York: W. H. Freeman/Henry Holt.

GIDWITZ, TOM
2002 Pioneers of the Bajo. *Archaeology,* January/February 2002:28–35.

GIES, FRANCES, AND JOSEPH GIES
1994 *Cathedral, Forge, and Waterwheel: Technology and Invention in the Middle Ages.* New York: HarperCollins.

GILL, RICHARDSON B.
2000 *The Great Maya Droughts: Water, Life, and Death.* Albuquerque: University of New Mexico Press.

GÓMEZ POMPA, ARTURO, AND RODOLFO DIRZO
1993 *Areas naturales protegidas de México.* Mexico City: SEMARNAP.

GONZALES, DAVID

2001 Scorched Forest Fuels Tension on Guatemala-Belize Border. *New York Times,* January 15, 2001: A3.

GONZÁLEZ PACHECO, CUAUHTÉMOC

1983 *Capital extranjero en la selva de Chiapas, 1863–1982.* Instituto de Investigaciones Económicas. Mexico City: Universidad Nacional Autónoma de México.

GRAHAM, IAN

1997 Mission to La Corona. *Archaeology* 50(5):46.

GRANDIA, LIZA

1999 Valuing Women's Work in Guatemala's Petén. In *Thirteen Ways of Looking at a Tropical Forest: Guatemala's Maya Biosphere Reserve,* edited by James D. Nations, chap. 7. Washington, DC: Conservation International.

GREENBERG, RUSSELL

1990 *El sur de México: cruce de caminos para los pájaros migratorios.* Washington, DC: Smithsonian Migratory Bird Center, National Zoological Park.

GRETZINGER, STEVEN P.

1998 Community Forest Concessions: An Economic Alternative for the Maya Biosphere Reserve in the Petén, Guatemala. In *Timber, Tourists, and Temples: Conservation and Development in the Maya Forest of Belize, Guatemala, and Mexico,* edited by Richard B. Primack, David Bray, Hugo A. Galletti, and Ismael Ponciano, chap. 8, pp. 111–124. Washington, DC: Island Press.

GRUNBERG, GEORG, AND VICTOR HUGO RAMOS

1998 *Base de datos sobre población, tierras y medio ambiente en la Reserva de la Biosfera Maya.* Centro de Monitoreo y Evaluación, Consejo Nacional de Areas Protegidas. Petén, Guatemala: CARE-Guatemala.

HAIN, JAMES H. W.

1987 Belize. *Oceanus* 30(4):76–83. Woods Hole Oceanographic Institution.

HALL, CAROLYN, AND HECTOR PÉREZ BRIGNOLI; JOHN COTTER, CARTOGRAPHER

2003 *Historical Atlas of Central America.* Norman: University of Oklahoma Press.

HAMMOND, NORMAN

1997 Waiting Time in Belize: Patience and Persistence at La Milpa. *Context* 13(1–2). Boston University Center for Archaeological Studies.

HANSEN, RICHARD D.

1997 Plundering the Petén. *Archaeology* 50(5):48–49.

HEINZMAN, ROBERT, AND CONRAD REINING

1989 Non-Timber Forest Products in Belize and Their Role in a Biosphere Reserve Model. Contracting report prepared for the Institute for Economic Botany, New York Botanical Garden, Bronx, New York. 48 pp.

HELLMUTH, NICHOLAS M.

1978　*Tikal-Copan Travel Guide: A General Introduction to Maya Art, Architecture, and Archaeology.* St. Louis, MO: Foundation for Latin American Anthropological Research.

HERLIHY, PETER H.

1997　Central American Indian Peoples and Lands Today. In *Central America: A Natural and Cultural History.* New Haven: Yale University Press, edited by Anthony G. Coates, pp. 215–240.

HERNÁNDEZ OBREGÓN, VÍCTOR HUGO, AND EDOUARD ADÉ BLANCHARD, COORDINATORS

1997　*The Lacandona Rainforest: A Vanishing Paradise.* Mexico City: Pulsar, with Editorial Jilguero.

HERNÁNDEZ S., RAMÓN

1997a Campesinos retuvieron durante 26 horas a autoridades en Petén. *Prensa Libre* (Guatemala), March 7, 1997, p. 3.

1997b Secretario ejecutivo de CONAP avala suspensión de los desalojos en Petén. *Prensa Libre* (Guatemala), April 5, 1997, p. 2.

1997c CONAP subvenciona a los grupos invasores en la Reserva de la Biósfera Maya, en Petén. *Prensa Libre* (Guatemala), April 9, 1997, p. 6.

HOFLING, CHARLES ANDREW

1996　Indigenous Linguistic Revitalization and Outsider Interaction: The Itzaj Maya Case. *Human Organization* 55(1):108–116.

HOLDRIDGE, L. R., W. C. GENKE, W. H. HATHEWAY, T. LIANG, AND J. A. TOSI JR.

1971　*Forest Environments in Tropical Life Zones: A Pilot Study.* Oxford, England: Pergamon Press.

HOWREN, ALLEINE

1913　Causes and Origins of the Decree of April 6, 1830. *Southwestern Historical Quarterly* 16:395–398.

HUFBAUER, GARY CLYDE, AND JEFFREY J. SCHOTT

1993　*NAFTA: An Assessment.* Rev. ed. Washington, DC: Institute for International Economics.

HUNTER, C. BRUCE

1986　*A Guide to Ancient Maya Ruins.* Norman: University of Oklahoma Press.

IDB (Inter-American Development Bank)

2002　Estado de Avance: Plan Puebla-Panamá. Washington, DC: Banco Inter-Americano de Desarrollo. http://www.iadb.org/ppp.

INE (Instituto Nacional de Estadística)

2001　*Salud, migración, y recurses naturales en Petén: resultados del módulo ambiental en la encuesta de salud materno infantil, 1999.* Guatemala: Instituto Nacional de Estadística.

2002　*Censo nacional XI de población y VI de habitación.* Guatemala: Instituto Nacional de Estadística.

IÑIGO-ELÍAS, EDUARDO E.

1996　Landscape Ecology and Conservation Biology of the Scarlet Macaw (*Ara macao*) in the Gran Petén Region of Mexico and Guatemala. Ph.D. dissertation, University of Florida.

IREMONGER, SUSAN, AND ROGER SAYRE, EDS.

1994 *Rapid Ecological Assessment of the Bladen Nature Reserve, Toledo District, Belize.* A Study by the Nature Conservancy, Belize Audubon Society, and the Ministry of Natural Resources, Belize. Arlington, VA: Nature Conservancy.

JACOBSON, JODI L.

1993 Closing the Gender Gap in Development. In *State of the World, 1993,* pp. 61–79. Worldwatch Institute.

JANTZEN, CARL R.

1989 The Mennonites of Spanish Lookout. *The World and I* 4(6):664–673.

JOHNSON, JAY K.

1985 Postclassic Maya Site Structure at Toposte, El Petén, Guatemala. In *The Lowland Maya Postclassic,* edited by Arlen F. Chase and Prudence M. Rice, pp. 151–165. Austin: University of Texas Press.

JONES, GRANT D.

1998 *The Conquest of the Last Maya Kingdom.* Stanford: Stanford University Press.

2001 *The Caste War of Yucatan.* Palo Alto, CA: Stanford University Press.

JONES, TOM

1985 The Xoc, the Sharke, and the Sea Dogs: An Historical Encounter. In *Fifth Palenque Round Table, 1983,* edited by Virginia M. Fields, 211–222. Palenque Round Table series, edited by Merle Greene Robertson, vol. 7. San Francisco: Pre-Columbian Art Research Institute.

JORDAN, MARY

2004 Pit Stop on the Cocaine Highway: Guatemala Becomes Favored Link for U.S.-Bound Drugs. *Washington Post,* Wednesday, October 6, 2004: A20.

KAMSTRA, J.

1987 An Ecological Survey of the Cockscomb Basin, Belize. Master's thesis, York University, Ontario, Canada.

KASHANIPOUR, RYAN AMIR, AND R. JON MCGEE

2004 Northern Lacandon Maya Medicinal Plant Use in the Communities of Lacanjá Chan Sayab and Naha', Chiapas, Mexico. *Journal of Ecological Anthropology* 8:47–66.

KATZ, SOLOMON H., M. L. HEDIGER, AND L. A. VALLEROY

1974 Traditional Maize Processing Techniques in the New World. *Science* 184:765–773.

KELLY, JOYCE

1996 *An Archaeological Guide to Northern Central America: Belize, Guatemala, Honduras, and El Salvador.* Norman: University of Oklahoma Press.

KONRAD, HERMAN W.

1999 Historia de la región. In *Naturaleza y cultura en Calakmul, Campeche,* edited by W. Folan Higgins, M. C. Sánchez González, and J. M. García Ortega, pp. 91–106. Campeche: Centro de Investigaciones Históricos y Sociales, Universidad Autónoma de Campeche.

KRICHER, JOHN C.
1988   *A Neotropical Companion: An Introduction to the Animals, Plants, and Ecosystems of the New World Tropics.* Princeton: Princeton University Press.

KUNEN, JULIE, AND JOHN RONEY
2004   Evaluation and Recommendations for Protection of Archaeological Sites within Community Forestry Concessions in the Multiple Use Zone of the Maya Biosphere Reserve, Petén, Guatemala. Draft document, United States Agency for International Development, Washington, DC.

LANDA, DIEGO DE
(1566) *Yucatan Before and After the Conquest.* Translated with notes by William
1978   Gates. New York: Dover.

LAPPER, RICHARD
2000   Belize Seeks Army Aid after Flare-up. *Financial Times* (London, Eng.), World News, Friday, June 16, 2000.

LAZCANO-BARRERO, MARCO A., AND RICHARD C. VOGT.
1992   Peces de la Selva Lacandona, un recurso potencial. In *Reserva de la Biosfera Montes Azules, Selva Lacandona: investigación para su conservación,* edited by M. A. Vásquez-Sánchez and M. S. Ramos, pp. 135–144. San Cristóbal las Casas, Chiapas: Publicaciones Especiales Ecosfera 1.

LEE, JULIAN C.
2000   *A Field Guide to the Amphibians and Reptiles of the Maya World: The Lowlands of Mexico, Northern Guatemala, and Belize.* Ithaca: Cornell University Press.

LEOPOLD, ALDO
1989   *A Sand County Almanac: Sketches Here and There.* Oxford University Press.

LINARES, OLGA F.
1976   "Garden Hunting" in the American Tropics. *Human Ecology* 4(4): 331–349.

LOVEJOY, THOMAS
1986   Diverse Considerations. In *Biodiversity,* edited by E. O. Wilson, Chap. 47, pp. 421–426. Washington, DC: National Academy Press.

MACLEOD, MURDO J.
1973   *Spanish Central America: A Socioeconomic History, 1520–1720.* Berkeley: University of California Press.

MANCILLA, MARIO
2001   Presentation at the La Milpa, Belize Tri-National Selva Maya meeting of the Tropical Ecosystem Directorate of the U.S. Man and the Biosphere Program and the Coalición de la Selva Maya. La Milpa, Belize, February 21–23, 2001.

MARCH, IGNACIO
1994   Diagnóstico actualizado de la Reserva Integral de la Biósfera Montes Azules, Chiapas. Chiapas, México: Sub estudio de Areas Protegidas de México, Estudio del Subsector Forestal del Banco Mundial. Unpublished report.

MARION, MARIE-ODILE

1991 *Los hombres de la selva: un estudio de tecnología cultural en medio selvático.* Mexico City: Instituto Nacional de Antropología e Historia.

1997 Indigenous Peoples of the Forest. In *The Lacandona Rainforest: A Vanishing Paradise,* coordinated by Víctor Hugo Hernández Obregón and Edouard Adé Blanchard, pp. 71–91. Mexico City: Pulsar, with Editorial Jilguero.

MARKEN, DAMIEN B., STANLEY GUENTER, Y. EVANGELIA TSESMELI

2005 Informe preliminar del proyecto de reconocimiento de La Corona, 2005. Guatemala: Proyecto Arqueológico El Perú-Waka', Parque Nacional Laguna del Tigre.

MARTIN, SIMON

2000 The Hunt for Site Q: Lost Cities and Hieroglyphs in the Forests of the Maya. Manuscript, September 2000.

MARTIN, SIMON, AND NIKOLAI GRUBE

2000 *Chronicle of the Maya Kings and Queens: Deciphering the Dynasties of the Ancient Maya.* London: Thames and Hudson.

MARTÍNEZ RUÍZ, JESÚS

1986 *Diversidad monolingüe de México en 1970.* Mexico City: UNAM.

MATOLA, SHARON

2001 Summary of Scarlet Macaw Field Investigations. Jersey Wildlife Trust. Unpublished document. February 2001.

MATOLA, SHARON, AND ELIZABETH PLATT

1998 One Forest, Two Nations: The Chiquibul Forest of Belize and Guatemala. In *Timber, Tourists, and Temples,* edited by Richard B. Primack, David Bray, Hugo A. Galletti, and Ismael Ponciano, chap. 2. Washington, DC: Island Press.

MCGEE, R. JON

1990 *Life, Ritual, and Religion among the Lacandón Maya.* Belmont, CA: Wadsworth Modern Anthropology Library.

MEANS, PHILIP AINSWORTH

1917 *History of the Spanish Conquest of Yucatan and of the Itzas.* Papers of the Peabody Museum of American Archaeology and Ethnology, Harvard University. Cambridge, MA: Peabody Museum.

MEDELLÍN, RODRIGO A.

1994 Mammal Diversity and Conservation in the Selva Lacandona, Chiapas, Mexico. *Conservation Biology* 8(3):780–799.

MEDELLÍN, RODRIGO A., ALFRED L. GARDNER, AND J. MARCELO ARANDA

1998 The Taxonomic Status of the Yucatán Brown Brocket, *Mazama pandora* (Mammalia: Cervidae). *Proceedings of the Biological Society of Washington* 111(1):1–14.

MÉNDEZ, CLAUDIO

1999 How Old Is the Petén Tropical Forest? In *Thirteen Ways of Looking at a Tropical Forest: Guatemala's Maya Biosphere Reserve,* edited by

James D. Nations, chap. 5, pp. 31–34. Washington, DC: Conservation International.

MILLER, R. R.

1988   Mesoamerican Fishes of the Río Usumacinta Basin: Composition, Derivation, and Conservation. In *Wildlife in the Everglades and Latin American Wetlands,* edited by G. H. Dalrymple, W. F. Loftus, and F. S. Bernardino Jr., pp. 9–10. Miami: Florida International University.

MOHOLY-NAGY, HATTULA

1978   The Utilization of Pomacea Snails at Tikal, Guatemala. *American Antiquity* 43:65–73.

MONTAÑEZ, PABLO

1971   *Jataté-Usumacinta.* Mexico City: Costa-Amic.

MORELET, ARTURO

(1857)   *Viaje a América Central (Yucatán y Guatemala).* Guatemala: Academia
1990   de Geografía e Historia de Guatemala.

MORLEY, SYLVANUS GRISWOLD, AND GEORGE W. BRAINERD

1956   *The Ancient Maya.* 3rd ed. Stanford, CA: Stanford University Press.

MORROW, LANCE

1992   I Cherish a Certain Hope: Vaclav Havel. *Time,* August 3, 1992.

MUNDO MAYA

2002   *Mundo Maya Sustainable Tourism Program.* Guatemala: Mundo Maya Organization, Permanent Technical Secretariat, InterAmerican Development Bank.

NATIONAL GEOGRAPHIC

1995   Engineer's Analysis: A Bridge to Maya Past. *National Geographic,* October 1995.

NATIONS, JAMES D.

1979a   Population Ecology of the Lacandon Maya. Ph.D. dissertation, Department of Anthropology, Southern Methodist University, Dallas, Texas.

1979b   Snail Shells and Maize Preparation: A Lacandón Maya Analogy. *American Antiquity* 44(3):568–571.

1994   The Ecology of the Zapatista Revolt. *Cultural Survival Quarterly* 18(1): 31–33.

2001   Biosphere Reserves. In *International Encyclopedia of the Social and Behavioral Sciences,* edited by N. J. Smelser and Paul B. Baltes, pp. 1231–1235. Oxford: Pergamon.

NATIONS, JAMES D., ED.

1989   Estudio técnico de la Reserva de la Biósfera Maya. Guatemala: Consejo Nacional de Areas Protegidas de Guatemala.

1999   *Thirteen Ways of Looking at a Tropical Forest: Guatemala's Maya Biosphere Reserve.* Washington, DC: Conservation International.

NATIONS, JAMES D., AND DANIEL I. KOMER

1983   Central America's Tropical Rainforests: Positive Steps for Survival. *AMBIO: Journal of the Royal Swedish Academy of Sciences* (Stockholm) 12(5):232–238.

NATIONS, JAMES D., AND RONALD B. NIGH
1980 The Evolutionary Potential of Lacandón Maya Sustained-Yield Tropical Forest Agriculture. *Journal of Anthropological Research* 36:1–30.

NATIONS, JAMES D., RICHARD B. PRIMACK, AND DAVID BRAY
1998 Introduction: The Maya Forest. In *Timber, Tourists, and Temples: Conservation and Development in the Maya Forest of Belize, Guatemala, and Mexico,* edited by Richard B. Primack, David Bray, Hugo A. Galletti, and Ismael Ponciano, chap. 1. Washington, DC: Island Press.

NAVIN, THOMAS R., M.D.
1989 Letter to James D. Nations from Dr. Thomas R. Navin, Public Health Service, Centers for Disease Control, Department of Health and Human Services, U.S.A., July 27, 1989.

NOLASCO PÉREZ, PEDRO
1966 Historia de las misiones mercedarias en América. *Estudios* 22(74–75). Madrid: Padres Mercedarios.

NORRIS, RUTH, J. SCOTT WILBER, AND LUIS OSWALDO MORALES MARÍN
1998 Community-Based Ecotourism in the Maya Forest: Problems and Potentials. In *Timber, Tourists, and Temples: Conservation and Development in the Maya Forest of Belize, Guatemala, and Mexico,* edited by Richard B. Primack, David Bray, Hugo A. Galletti, and Ismael Ponciano, chap. 22. Washington, DC: Island Press.

O'BRIEN, KAREN L.
1998 *Sacrificing the Forest: Environmental and Social Struggles in Chiapas.* Boulder, CO: Westview Press.

O'HARA, JENNIFER L.
1998 Monitoring Nontimber Forest Product Harvest for Ecological Sustainability: A Case Study of Huano (*Sabal mauritiiformis*) in the Río Bravo Conservation and Management Area, Belize. In *Timber, Tourists, and Temples: Conservation and Development in the Maya Forest of Belize, Guatemala, and Mexico,* edited by Richard B. Primack, David Bray, Hugo A. Galletti, and Ismael Ponciano, chap. 13. Washington, DC: Island Press.

OWENS, MITCHELL
1996 A Garden of the Slightly Macabre. *New York Times,* August 22, 1996: B1.

PAGDEN, ANTHONY, ED.
1986 *Letters from Mexico: Hernán Cortés.* New Haven: Yale University Press.

PAIZ, MARIE CLAIRE
2001 Presentation at the La Milpa, Belize Tri-National Selva Maya meeting of the Tropical Ecosystem Directorate of the U.S. Man and the Biosphere Program and the Coalición de la Selva Maya. La Milpa, Belize, February 21–23, 2001.

PALACIO, JOSEPH
2001 Presentation at the La Milpa, Belize Tri-National Selva Maya meeting of the Tropical Ecosystem Directorate of the U.S. Man and the Biosphere

Program and the Coalición de la Selva Maya. La Milpa, Belize, February 21–23, 2001.

PALENQUE RESOURCES

2005 Genealogy of Rulers at Palenque. *Palenque Resources.* http://www. mesoweb.com/palenque/resources/rulers.

PALKA, JOEL W.

1996 Lacandon Maya Culture Change and Survival in the Lowland Frontier of the Expanding Guatemalan and Mexican Republics. In *Studies in Culture Contact: Interaction, Culture Change, and Archaeology,* edited by James G. Cusick. Southern Illinois University Press.

PALKA, JOEL W., AND NORA M. LÓPEZ OLIVARES

1992 Sitios lacandones-yucatecos en la región del Río de la Pasión, Departamento de Petén, Guatemala. *Revista U Tz'ib* 1(3):1–7.

PARDO-TEJEDA, ENRIQUE, AND CECILIA SÁNCHEZ MUÑOZ

1981 *Brosimum alicastrum: A Potentially Valuable Tropical Forest Resource.* Xalapa, Veracruz: Instituto Nacional de Investigaciones sobre Recursos Bióticos.

PARKER, THEODORE A., BRUCE K. HOLST, LOUISE H. EMMONS, AND JOHN R. MEYER

1993 *A Biological Assessment of the Columbia River Forest Reserve, Toledo District, Belize.* Rapid Assessment Program Working Paper 3, Conservation International, Washington, DC.

PEIRCE, BRADFORD R.

1997 Ecotourism: A Feasibility Study in the Chiquibul. Final consulting report. Washington, DC: Conservation International.

PENNINGTON, T. D., AND JOSÉ SARUKHAN

1968 *Arboles tropicales de México.* Mexico City: Instituto Nacional de Investigaciones Forestales.

PLOTKIN, MARK J.

1993 *Tales of a Shaman's Apprentice: An Ethnobotanist Searches for New Medicines in the Amazon Rain Forest.* New York: Penguin Books.

POLISAR, JOHN, AND ROBERT H. HORWICH

1994 Conservation of the Large, Economically Important River Turtle *Dermatemys mawii* in Belize. *Conservation Biology* 8(2):338–342.

PONCIANO, ISMAEL

1998 Forestry Policy and Protected Areas in the Petén, Guatemala. In *Timber, Tourists, and Temples: Conservation and Development in the Maya Forest of Belize, Guatemala, and Mexico,* edited by Richard B. Primack, David Bray, Hugo A. Galletti, and Ismael Ponciano, chap. 7, pp. 99–110. Washington, DC: Island Press.

PRB (Population Reference Bureau)

2004 World Population Data Sheet. Washington, DC: Population Reference Bureau.

PRENSA LIBRE

1997 Darán tierras a campesinos invasores de biósfera Maya. *Prensa Libre,* April 20, 1997. Guatemala.

PROGRAMME FOR BELIZE
1998 Annual Report, Fiscal Year 1998. Belize City: Programme for Belize.
2001 An Opportunity for Positive Action. Belize City: Programme for Belize. Brochure.

PULESTON, DENNIS E.
1968 *Brosimum alicastrum* as a Subsistence Alternative for the Classic Maya of the Central Southern Lowlands. Master's thesis, University of Pennsylvania.

RABINOWITZ, ALAN R.
1986 In the Realm of the Master Jaguar. *Animal Kingdom* 89(2):10–21.
2000 *Jaguar: One Man's Struggle to Establish the World's First Jaguar Preserve.* Washington, DC: Island Press.

RATH, TONY, ED.
1990 The Cockscomb Basin Expedition, Final Report, June 11–18. Dangriga, Belize: Pelican Beach Resort.

RECINOS, ADRIÁN, TRANS. AND ED.
1950 *Popol Vuh: The Sacred Book of the Ancient Quiché Maya.* English version by Delia Goetz and Sylvanus E. Morley. Norman: University of Oklahoma Press.

RECINOS, ADRIÁN, AND DELIA GOETZ, TRANS. AND EDS.
1953 *The Annals of the Cakchiquels.* Norman: University of Oklahoma Press.

REDDELL, JAMES R., AND GEORGE VENI
1996 Biology of the Chiquibul Cave System, Belize and Guatemala. *Journal of Cave and Karst Studies* 58(2):131–138.

REDFORD, KENT H., AND JANE A. MANSOUR, EDS.
1996 *Traditional Peoples and Biodiversity Conservation in Large Tropical Landscapes.* America Verde series. Arlington, VA: Nature Conservancy, Latin America and Caribbean Division.

REED, NELSON
1964 *The Caste War of Yucatan.* Stanford, CA: Stanford University Press.

REID, FIONA
1997 *A Field Guide to the Mammals of Central America and Southeast Mexico.* New York: Oxford University Press.

REMESAL, FRAY ANTONIO DE
(1619) *Historia general de las Indias Occidentales y particular de la gobernación*
1966   *de Chiapas y Guatemala.* 4 vols. 3rd ed. Guatemala: Departamento Editorial y de Producción de Material Didáctico "José de Piñeda Ibarra," Ministerio de Educación.

RICE, DON STEPHEN, AND PRUDENCE M. RICE
1984 Lessons from the Maya. *Latin American Research Review* 19(3):7–34.

RICE, PRUDENCE M., AND DON S. RICE
1985 Topoxte, Macanche, and the Central Petén Postclassic. In *The Lowland Maya Postclassic,* edited by Arlen F. Chase and Prudence M. Rice, pp. 166–183. Austin: University of Texas Press.

RIVERO TORRES, SONIA E.
1992 *Laguna Miramar, Chiapas, México: una aproximación histórica-*

arqueológica de los Lacandones desde el Clásico Temprano. Tuxtla
Gutiérrez, Chiapas: Consejo Estatal de Fomento a la Investigación y
Difusión de la Cultura, Instituto Nacional de Antropología e Historia,
Gobierno del Estado de Chiapas.

ROBERTS, DAVID
2004 Secrets of the Maya: Deciphering Tikal. *Smithsonian* 35(4):42–52.

ROSENGARTEN, FREDERIC, JR.
1973 *The Book of Spices.* New York: Jove Books.

ROYS, RALPH
1931 *The Ethno-Botany of the Maya.* Middle American Research Series,
no. 2. New Orleans: Department of Middle American Research, Tulane
University.

ROYS, RALPH, TRANS.
1968 *The Book of Chilam Balam of Chumayel.* Reproduced from Carnegie
Institution of Washington publication 438. Norman: University of
Oklahoma.

RUST, SUSIE POST
2001 The Garífuna: Weaving a Future from a Tangled Past. *National Geographic* 200(3):102–113.

SABLOFF, JEREMY A.
1994 *The New Archaeology and the Ancient Maya.* New York: Scientific
American Library.

SADER, STEVEN A., MICHAEL COAN, AND DANIEL HAYES
1998 *Time-Series Tropical Forest Change Detection for the Maya Biosphere
Reserve: Updated Estimates for 1995–1997.* Maine Image Analysis Laboratory, Department of Forest Management, University of Maine.

SADER, STEVEN A., TOM SEVER, AND MICHAEL RICHARDS
1994 Forest Change Estimates for the Northern Petén Region of Guatemala—
1986–1990. *Human Ecology* 22(3):317–332.

SÁNCHEZ, IVONNE
2001 Presentation at the La Milpa, Belize Tri-National Selva Maya meeting of
the Tropical Ecosystem Directorate of the U.S. Man and the Biosphere
Program and the Coalición de la Selva Maya. La Milpa, Belize, February
21–23, 2001.

SÁNCHEZ GONZÁLEZ, MARÍA CONSUELO
1999 Población Actual. In *Naturaleza y cultura en Calakmul, Campeche,*
edited by W. Folan Higgins, M. C. Sánchez González, and J. M. García
Ortega, pp. 111–116. Campeche: Centro de Investigaciones Históricos y
Sociales, Universidad Autónoma de Campeche.

SAUER, CARL ORTWIN
1967 *The Early Spanish Main.* Berkeley: University of California Press.

SCATENA, F. N.
2004 Sierra del Lacandón National Park: Hydropower Development on the
Río Usumacinta. http://www.sierralacandon.org/.

SCHELE, LINDA, AND DAVID FREIDEL
1990 *A Forest of Kings: The Untold Story of the Ancient Maya.* New York:
William Morrow.

SCHELE, LINDA, AND PETER MATHEWS
1998 *The Code of Kings: the Language of Seven Sacred Maya Temples and Tombs.* New York: Touchstone/Simon and Schuster.

SCHLESINGER, VICTORIA
2001 *Animals and Plants of the Ancient Maya: A Guide.* Austin: University of Texas Press.

SCHOLES, F. V., AND R. L. ROYS
1968 *The Maya Chontal Indians of Acalan-Tixchel: A Contribution to the History and Ethnography of the Yucatán Peninsula.* Reproduced from Carnegie Institution of Washington publication 560. Norman: University of Oklahoma Press.

SCHULZE, MARK D., AND DAVID F. WHITACRE
1999 A Classification and Ordination of the Tree Community of Tikal National Park, Petén, Guatemala. *Bulletin of the Florida Museum of Natural History* 41(3):169–297.

SCHUSTER, ANGELA M. H.
1997 The Search for Site Q. *Archaeology* 50(5):42–45.

SCHWARTZ, NORMAN B.
1990 *Forest Society: A Social History of Petén, Guatemala.* Philadelphia: University of Pennsylvania Press.

SCIENCE
1978 Killer Bees: O Death, Where Is Thy Sting? *Science* 200:1140–1141.

SCIENCE NEWS
1999 Juice Put the Bounce in Ancient Rubber. *Science News* 156:31.

SEGEPLAN (Secretaría General de Planificación)
1993 *Plan de desarrollo integrado de Petén.* Vol. 1: *Diagnóstico general de Petén.* Rev. 1st ed. Guatemala: Secretaría General del Consejo Nacional de Planificación Económica.

SEMARNAP (Secretaría de Medio Ambiente, Recursos Naturales y Pesca)
2000 *Programa de Manejo, Reserva de la Biósfera Montes Azules.* Mexico City: Instituto Nacional de Ecología, Secretaría de Medio Ambiente, Recursos Naturales y Pesca.

SEMARNAT (Secretaría de Medio Ambiente y Recursos Naturales)
2000 *Programa de Manejo, Areas de Protección de Flora y Fauna Nahá y Metzabok.* Tuxtla Gutiérrez, Chiapas: Comisión Nacional de Areas Naturales Protegidas, Secretaría de Medio Ambiente y Recursos Naturales.

SHARER, ROBERT J.
1994 *The Ancient Maya.* Stanford, CA: Stanford University Press.
1996 *Daily Life in Maya Civilization.* Westport, CT: Greenwood Press.

SIMON, JOEL
1997 *Endangered Mexico: An Environment on the Edge.* San Francisco: Sierra Club Books.

SKIDMORE, JOEL
2003 Maya Queen's Tomb Found at El Peru. *Mesoweb Reports.* http://www.mesoweb.com/reports/waka.

SMITH, C.
1989 *Economic Aspects of Forestry Management in Belize.* Consultancy report for the Forest Department, Ministry of Natural Resources. Belmopan: Government of Belize.

SMU NEWS (*Southern Methodist University News*)
2004 Archaeologists Announce Discoveries at the Ancient Maya Site of Waka' in Northern Guatemala. May 6, 2004. http://www.smu.edu/newsinfo/releases/03186.

STEARMAN, ALLYN MACLEAN
1996 On Common Ground: The Nature Conservancy and Traditional Peoples: The Río Chagres, Panama Workshop. In *Traditional Peoples and Biodiversity Conservation in Large Tropical Landscapes,* edited by K. H. Redford and J. A. Mansour, pp. 237–250. America Verde series. Arlington, VA: Nature Conservancy, Latin America and Caribbean Division.

STEURY, BRENT
2003 *Protected Area in Peril: Punta Manabique Wildlife Refuge, Izabal, Guatemala.* Summary report of site assessment conducted by International Technical Assistance Program, U.S. Department of the Interior, in partnership with the U.S. Agency for International Development–Guatemala. Washington, DC: U.S. Department of the Interior.

STEVENSON, MARK
2001 Tropical Rain Forest Sprouts Battleground: Environmentalists Are Pitted against Leftists and Zapatista Rebels in Montes Azules. *Los Angeles Times,* August 4, 2001.

STOCKS, ANTHONY
1996 The BOSAWAS Natural Reserve and the Mayangna of Nicaragua. In *Traditional Peoples and Biodiversity Conservation in Large Tropical Landscapes,* edited by K. H. Redford and J. A. Mansour. America Verde series, pp. 1–32. Arlington, VA: Nature Conservancy, Latin America and Caribbean Division.

STUART, DAVID
1998 The Arrival of Strangers: Teotihuacán and Tollan in Classic Maya History. *PARI Online Publications,* newsletter 25, July 1998. http://www.mesoweb.com/pari/publications.
2004 The Paw Stone: The Place Name of Piedras Negras, Guatemala. *PARI Journal* 4(3):1–6.

SWANK, W. G., AND J. F. TEER
1989 Status of the Jaguar—1987. *Oryx* 23:14–21.

TATE, CAROLYN E.
1992 *Yaxchilán: The Design of a Maya Ceremonial City.* Austin: University of Texas Press.

TELLO DÍAZ, CARLOS
2004 *La Selva: crónica de un viaje por la Lacandona.* Mexico City: Joaquín Mortiz.

THOMPSON, J. ERIC S.
1966 *The Rise and Fall of Maya Civilization.* Norman: University of Oklahoma Press.

1970 *Maya History and Religion.* Norman: University of Oklahoma Press.
1977 A Proposal for Constituting a Maya Subgroup, Cultural and Linguistic, in the Petén and Adjacent Regions. In *Anthropology and History in Yucatán,* edited by Grant D. Jones, pp. 3–42. Austin: University of Texas Press.

TMCC and TAA (Toledo Maya Cultural Council and Toledo Alcaldes Association)
1997 Maya Atlas: The Struggle to Preserve Maya Land in Southern Belize. Berkeley: North Atlantic Books.

TOFALLA, MARVIN
2000 Deforestan parque nacional: secuestran a estudiantes y los amenazan. *El Gráfico* (Guatemala), March 21, 2000:6.

TOLEDO, VICTOR M., BENJAMÍN ORTIZ-ESPEJEL, LENI CORTÉS, PATRICIA MOGUEL, AND MARÍA DE JESÚS ORDÓÑEZ
2003 The Multiple Use of Tropical Forests by Indigenous Peoples in Mexico: A Case of Adaptive Management. *Conservation Ecology* 7(3). http://www.consecol.org/vol 7/iss 3/art 9.

TOURTELLOT, GAIR, JASON GONZÁLEZ, AND FRANCISCO ESTRADA BELLI
1999 Land and People at La Milpa, Belize. Paper presented at the sixty-fourth annual meeting, Society for American Archaeology, Chicago, Illinois, March 27, 1999. http://www.bu.edu/lamilpa (Boston University).

TOZZER, ALFRED M.
1903 Report of the First Fellow in American Archaeology of the Archaeological Institute of America. *American Journal of Archaeology,* suppl., 2nd ser., 7:45-47.
1907 *A Comparative Study of the Mayas and the Lacandones.* New York: Macmillan.
(1912) Spanish Manuscript Letter on the Lacandones, in the Archives of the
1968A Indies at Seville. In *Proceedings of the 18th International Congress of Americanists.* London. Reprinted: Nendeln/Liechtenstein; Kraus Reprint.
1913 *A Preliminary Study of the Prehistoric Ruins of Nakum, Guatemala.* Memoirs of the Peabody Museum of American Archaeology and Ethnology, Harvard University, vol. 5, no. 3, pp. 137–201. Cambridge, MA: Peabody Museum.

TRENS, MANUEL B.
1957 *Historia de Chiapas.* 2 vols. 2nd ed. Mexico City: Los Talleres Gráficos de la Nación.

UNESCOPRESS
2004 Nineteen New Biosphere Reserves Added to UNESCO's Man and the Biosphere (MAB) Network. www.unesco.org.

VILLA ROJAS, ALFONSO
1966 Los Lacandones. *América Indígena* 27(1–2); 28(1). Mexico City: Instituto Indigenista Interamericano.

WADE, BILL
2005 See Yellowstone This Winter by Coach Instead of Snowmobile. Op-ed. *Salt Lake Tribune* (Salt Lake City, UT), January 2, 2005.

WALLACE, AUDREY, AND LISA NAUGHTON-TREVES
  1998   Belize: Río Bravo Conservation and Management Area. In *Parks in Peril*, edited by Katrina Brandon, Kent Redford, and Steven Sanderson, chap. 8, pp. 216–247. Washington, DC: Nature Conservancy.

WALLACE, DAVID RAINS
  1997a   *The Monkey's Bridge: Mysteries of Evolution in Central America.* San Francisco: Sierra Club Books.
  1997b   Central American Landscapes. In *Central America: A Natural and Cultural History,* edited by Anthony G. Coates, chap. 3, pp. 72–96. New Haven: Yale University Press.

WASHINGTON POST
  2005   Guatemala City. February 26, 2005, p. A16.

WASSERSTROM, ROBERT
  1983   *Class and Society in Central Chiapas.* Berkeley: University of California Press.

WEAVER, NEVIN, AND ELIZABETH C. WEAVER
  1981   Beekeeping with the Stingless Bee, *Melipona beecheii,* by the Yucatecan Maya. *Bee World* 62(1):7–19.

WEBB, DAVID
  1997   The Great American Faunal Interchange. In *Central America: A Natural and Cultural History,* edited by Anthony G. Coates, chap. 4, pp. 97–122. New Haven: Yale University Press.

WEBSTER, DAVID
  2002   *The Fall of the Ancient Maya: Solving the Mystery of the Maya Collapse.* New York: Thames and Hudson.

WEINER, TIM
  2002   Mexico Weighs Electricity against History. *New York Times,* September 22, 2002.

WHITACRE, DAVID
  2000   Selva Maya corridors workshop. E-mail to James D. Nations, April 13, 2000.

WHITE, WILLIAM A., JAY RANEY, THOMAS A. TREMBLAY, MELBA M. CRAWFORD, AND SOLAR S. SMITH.
  1996   Deforestation in Belize, 1989/92–1994/96. Final report on USAID contract 505-0043-C-00-6006. Austin: University of Texas.

WHITMORE, THOMAS M., AND B. L. TURNER II
  1992   Landscapes of Cultivation in Mesoamerica on the Eve of the Conquest. *Annals of the Association of American Geographers* 82(3):402–425.

WHITMORE, THOMAS M., B. L. TURNER II, D. L. JOHNSON, R. W. KATES, AND T. R. GOTTSCHANG
  1990   Long-term Population Change. In *The Earth as Transformed by Human Action,* edited by B. L. Turner II, pp. 25–39. Cambridge: Cambridge University Press.

WILK, RICHARD R.
  1997   *Household Ecology: Economic Change and Domestic Life among the Kekchi Maya in Belize.* DeKalb: Northern Illinois University Press.

WILLIAMS, NICK

1996 An Introduction to Cave Exploration in Belize. *Journal of Cave and Karst Studies* 58(2):69–75.

WILSON, E. O.

1998 *Consilience: The Unity of Knowledge.* New York: Alfred A. Knopf.

2004 From Deep History to the Century of the Environment: The National Park Service as Environmental Leader. *George Wright Forum* 21(1):5–9.

WILSON, RICHARD

1995 *Maya Resurgence in Guatemala: Q'eqchi' Experiences.* Norman: University of Oklahoma Press.

WILSON, W. T., R. A. NUNAMAKER, AND D. L. MAKI

1984 Beekeeping in Mexico. *American Bee Journal* 124(6):446–449, 459–461.

WILSON CENTER

2004 Population-Environmental Piggybacking: Integrating an Environmental Module into Guatemala's Demographic and Health Survey. Washington, DC: Woodrow Wilson International Center for Scholars. http://www.wilsoncenter.org/.

WINSTON, MARK L.

1979 The Potential Impact of the Africanized Honey Bee on Apiculture in Mexico and Central America. *American Bee Journal* 119(9):642–645.

WORLD BANK

1985 Slowing Population Growth. In *Population Change and Economic Development,* pp. 66–86. New York: World Bank/Oxford University Press.

1994 Personal interviews with Felipe Villagran of World Bank. Washington, DC.

XIMÉNEZ, FRAY FRANCISCO

(1901) *Historia de la provincia de San Vicente de Chiapa y Guatemala de la*
1973   *Orden de Predicadores.* Guatemala: Sociedad de Geografía e Historia de Guatemala.

ZOGBAUM, HEIDI

1992 *B. Traven: A Vision of Mexico.* Wilmington, DE: SR Books, Scholarly Resources.

Index

Acacia angustissisma, 68, 209
Agkistrodon bilineatus russeolus, 71
agouti. See *Dasyprocta punctata*
Agouti paca: as bushmeat, 172; described, 52–53; hunting of, 53
agriculture, Maya, 20; highland Maya, 29; impact of depopulation on, 33–34. *See also* crops: Maya
Agriocharis ocellata, 198
Ajaw Kan Ek', 40, 179
alligator gar. See *Atractosteus tropicus*
allspice. See *Pimenta dioica*
Alouatta palliata, 57
Alouatta pigra: described, 56–57; in Sierra del Lacandón, 191
Altar de Sacrificios, 27
Altun Ha, 23, 248–249
Alvarado, Pedro de, 31, 33
amate, 95–96
Amazona albifrons, 68
Amazona farinosa, 68–69
animals: domesticated, 34; of the Maya Tropical Forest, 51–93; mythological, 90–93; and rainfall, 51
Annals of the Cakchiquels, 29
annatto, 96
anteater. See *Cyclopes didactylus*
ants: army, 84; in *Cecropia* trees, 100; leafcutter, 88–89
Apis mellifera, 86–87

Ara macao cyanoptera: and Chalillo dam, 230; described, 67–68; at El Perú/Waka', 209; at Las Guacamayas Biological Station, 192; poaching in Selva Lacandona, 141–142
Aramus guarauna, 84
Ardea alba, 118
Ariopsis felis, 82
Aspidosperma magalocarpon, 93
Ateles geoffroyi, 56–57
Atitlán, Lake, 29
Atractosteus tropicus, 82
Atran, Scott, 180
Atropoides nummifer, 71–72
Atta spp., 88–89
Attalea cohune, 104
Aztecs, 31

bajos, 172, 223
balche. See *Lonchocarpus longistylus*
balsam. See *Myroxylon balsamum*
barbasco vine. See *Dioscorea* spp.
Basic Resources, Ltd., 192
bats, 198, 224
bayal vine. See *Desmoncus orthocanthos*
beekeeping, 86
bees: attacks on scarlet macaws, 67–68. See also *Apis mellifera; Melipona beecheii*
Beletsky, Les, 66, 247

Belize: archaeological sites, 23, 27, 248–256; and coral reef, 228; geography of, 228; history of, 230–231; land dispute with Guatemala, 231–232; and logging, 237, 240; map of, 226; peoples of, 233–239; population of, 228; protected areas, 239–247; Spanish claims to, 230–231; vegetation of, 229; mentioned, 7, 8
Belize Audubon Society, 246
Belize Zoo: and crocodiles, 76; described, 240
Billy, Santiago: at Calakmul, 170–171; captured by guerrillas, 10–15; and La Corona/Sak Nikte', 200–201; and Maya Biosphere Reserve, 187; and peccaries, 65–66; at Piedras Negras, 3; at Pozo Maya, 188; and satellite image, 194; and *sisimite*, 91; and wasp bite, 85; mentioned, 55
Bio-Itza: history of, 180; size and location of, 43–44
biological diversity: and biosphere reserves, 16; and Central America, 49; and the Maya Tropical Forest, 48–49; roots in geological history, 48–49; in Selva Lacandona, 144
biosphere reserves: defined, 15–17; and Mexican legislation, 146
Biotopo Cerro Cahuí, 198
Biotopo Laguna del Tigre-Río Escondido, 197
Biotopo Naachtún-Dos Lagunas, 196
Biotopo San Miguel La Palotada-El Zotz, 197
birds, 66–69. *See also specific species*
Bjork, Robin, 67, 69
Bladen Branch Nature Reserve, 240–241, 267
blanco. See *Petenia splendida*
Blom, Frans, 28
Bonampak: description of, 149–151; discovery of, 149; as protected area, 146; mentioned, 23
Boremanse, Didier, 139

botfly. See *Dermatobia hominis*
Bothriechis schlegelii, 72
Bothrops asper: described, 71; bites, 85
Brito Foucher, Rodulfo: and definition of Maya Tropical Forest, 48; and logging camps, 48, 123–124
Bromelia penguin, 120
Brosimum alicastrum: described, 97–98, as food for monkeys, 120
Buot, Geneviéve, 74
Bursera simaruba, 101
Butzer, Karl, 33

Cabrera, Jorge, 187
cacao. See *Theobroma cacao*
Cairina moschata, 209
Calakmul archaeological site: described, 168–171; and La Corona/Sak Nikte', 202; mentioned, 23
Calakmul Biosphere Reserve: and coatimundis, 58; described, 164–168; and jaguars, 55; map of, 165; vegetation of, 166; wildlife of, 166–167
Camino Real, 36, 39, 42
Campbell, Jonathan A.: on crocodiles, 76; on iguanas, 77; on venomous snakes, 70
Cañon del Colorado, 119–120
cantil. See *Agkistrodon bilineatus*
Caracol: described, 249–251; and Naranjo, 207; and Tikal, 250
Carmelita, Petén, 172
Carrasco, Ramón, 169
Carrillo, Eduardo, 55
Caste War of Yucatan: and Belize, 235; and Calakmul Biosphere Reserve, 166; history of, 44
Castilla elastica, 108
Castillo Mont, Juan José, 188, 191
Catalán, Carlos: and La Corona/Sak Nikte', 200–201; on snakebite remedy, 73; on wasp bite, 85
catfish, 82. *See also specific species*
Cathorops aguadulce, 82
Cathorops melanolopus, 82
Cecropia peltata, 100

Ceibal, 27
Central American Free Trade Agreement (CAFTA), 275
Centro de Estudios Conservacionistas (CECON), 196–197
Centropomus undecimalis: described, 81; migration, 81; and name of Río Usumacinta, 82, 156
Cerezo, Vinicio, 186–187, 194–195
Cerro Cahuí. *See* Biotopo Cerro Cahuí
Chalillo dam, 230
Chamaedorea elegans, 109
Chamaedorea oblongata, 109
Chan K'in Viejo, 132, 161
Chan K'in Wildlife Refuge. *See* Refugio de Vida Silvestre Chan-K'in
Chase, Arlen and Diane, 249–250
Chayax Huex, Reginaldo, 180
Chechem negro. See Metopium brownei
Chelydra serpentine, 77–78
Chiapas, 8, 23
Chichén Itzá, 26–28
chicle: and Calakmul Biosphere Reserve, 167; described, 101; harvesting, 101–103, 186; importance in Petén, 176, 186; sustainability, 198. See also *Manilkara zapota*
Chilam Balam of Chumayel, 33
Chiquibul Biosphere Reserve (Guatemala), 67
Chiquibul National Park, 246–247
chok berries, 103–104
Chol Maya: and Calakmul Biosphere Reserve, 168; clothing of, 140; conquest of, 36; as conservationists, 144; history of, 139–140; language, 158; and Yaxchilán, 157
Choltí Maya: conquest of, 35–39; and Lake Miramar, 158–160; language, 158; and Sac Balam, 162–163
Chontal Maya, 26
Chultun, 173, 254
Cichlasoma octofasciatum, 81
Cichlasoma urophtalmus, 81
climate change, 26, 283–284

Coalición de la Selva Maya, 282
coatimundis. See *Nasua narica*
Cockscomb Basin Wildlife Sanctuary, 244–246
codices, 95
Coe, Michael, 26, 43
cohune palms. See *Attalea cohune*
colic, infant, 59
collapse, Maya, 25–27
Colorado, Cornelio, 119–120
Colpothrinax cookii, 242
Columbia River Forest Reserve: as key conservation area, 267; described, 242–243; mentioned, 225
Columbus, Christopher, 30
Columbus, Ferdinand, 30
Comisión Nacional del Medio Ambiente (CONAMA): and establishment of Maya Biosphere Reserve, 187; mentioned, 4, 282
Comunidad Lacandona: history of, 130–134; logging in, 132–133
Consejo Nacional de Areas Protegidas (CONAP-Guatemala): and colonization of Laguna del Tigre National Park, 192; and establishment of Maya Biosphere Reserve, 187; and forestry concessions, 198; mentioned, 6
Conservation International: in Belize, 242, 267; and the Bio-Itza, 180; and forestry concessions, 198; at Laguna del Tigre, 195; at Laguna Ocotal Grande, 162; and Las Guacamayas Biological Station, 193; and Rapid Assessment Program, 195
Convention on International Trade in Endangered Species (CITES): and jaguars, 55; and turtles, 78
copal. See *Protium copal*
Copan, 23
coral snakes, 72–73
Cortés, Hernán: and the Aztec, 31; and his horse, Morzillo, 40–41; and the Itza Maya, 40–41; and the Maya, 18, 19; in the Petén, 179–180

Crax rubra: and Bladen Branch Nature Reserve, 241; and *chok* berries, 103–104; tail feathers as fans, 84
Creoles, 234–235
crocodiles. See *Crocodylus acutus; Crocodylus moreleti*
Crocodylus acutus, 74–75
Crocodylus moreleti: described, 74–76; diet, 75, 78; and humans, 75–76, 219; and turtles, 78
crops: Maya, 33–34; introduction of Spanish, 33, 46
Crotalus durissus, 72
Cuba, 30
Culbert, T. Patrick, 25, 223
cultural diversity, 270–276
cycads, 229
Cyclopes didactylus, 52

Dasyprocta punctata, 52–53
Dávila, Alonzo, 159
De Córdova, Francisco Hernández, 30
De Vos, Jan: on La Constancia, 123; on logging in the Selva Lacandona, 124, 128; on Putun migration, 29
deer: species described, 53–54. See also *Odocoileus virginianus; Mazama americana; Mazama pandora*
deforestation, 260
Dermatemys mawii, 78
Dermatobia hominis, 87–88
Desmoncus orthocanthos, 97
Diamond, Jared, 26
Dicotyles pecari, 65–66
Dioscorea spp.: described, 96; as fish poison, 80
Dipsas brevifacies, 69
diseases: impact of Old World, 31–33, 259–260
Dobyns, Henry, 32
droughts, 25

Eco-Logic, 180
Eira barbara, 52
El Desempeño, 5, 6–7

El Kinal, 212
El Mirador: access to, 172–173; described, 20–21, 174, 203–205; and jaguars, 55
El Naranjo (town), 193. See also Naranjo archaeological site
El Peru/Waka': described, 208–210; at La Corona/Sak Nikte', 201–202; and tourism, 281; mentioned, 24
El Pilar, 251–252
El Quetzal, 200
El Remate, 220
El Salvador, 21
El Tintal, 172–173
El Zotz archaeological site, 224. See also Biotopo San Miguel La Palotada-El Zotz
Enterolobium cyclocarpum, 77
epiphytes, 105
Escobedo, Héctor, 208
Eugerres mexicanus, 81

fer-de-lance. See *Bothrops asper*
Fialko, Vilma, 223
Ficus crassiuscula, 108–109
Ficus spp., 95–96
fires, 265–266
fish, 79–82. See also *specific species*
fishing: and *Chamaedorea* palms, 80; at Las Guacamayas Biological Station, 194; and plant poisons, 80; traditional Maya, 79–80; with nets, 80; with traps, 80
Fleming, Mick, 227–228
Flores, Petén: conquest of Nohpeten, 42–43, 213; history of, 213–215; and horse statue, 41; and its Spanish name, 42, 213; mentioned, 28
fly, black. See *Phlebotomus* spp.
Folan, William J., 169–171
Ford, Anabel, 8, 228, 252
forest concessions, 198
fox. See *Urocyon cinereoargenteus*
Freidel, David: and El Perú/Waka', 208–210; and La Corona/Sak Nikte', 202

Frontera Corozal: description of, 157; history of, 133

Galictis vittata, 52
Gallenkamp, Charles, 20, 23
García, Rudy, 4, 5, 10, 12
Garífuna, 233–234
Garrett, Wilbur, 187
Garrett, Will, 55
geology, 46
Gill, Richardson B., 25–26
global positioning devices (GPS), 6, 7, 10, 13
Graham, Ian, 201, 209
Grandia, Liza: on Q'eqchi' in Belize, 236; on challenge of population, 271–272, 280; on Q'eqchi' in Petén, 177
Grijalva, Juan, 30
grison. See *Galictis vittata*
Grootenboer, Kees, 150
Grube, Nicolai, 200
Guacamayas Biological Station. *See* Las Guacamayas Biological Station
Guacamayas sin Fronteras, 68
guanacaste tree. See *Enterolobium cyclocarpum*
guano palm, 105–106
Guatemala: archaeological sites, 200–224; civil war of, 38; peoples of, 177–186; population growth, 199; protected areas of Petén, 186–200; and refugees, 200; mentioned, 18
Guayacán. *See* Laguna Guayacán
Guenter, Stanley, 202, 209
Guerrero, Ramón, 115, 120–121
guerrillas. *See* Unión Revolucionaria Nacional Guatemalteca

Hachäkyum: and mahogany trees, 132; and Yaxchilán, 155
Haematoxylon campechianum: described, 106; and history of Belize, 230–231; uses, 106–107
Hansen, Richard: on looting of archaeological sites, 269; and Mirador Basin Special Protected Area, 198; and Nakbe, 205–206
Hardner, Jared, 198
Harpia harpyja, 66–67
Harpy eagle. See *Harpia harpyja*
Havel, Václav, 285
Hellmuth, Nicholas, 206
Hernández Nava, José: attacked by bees, 87; flight to Laguna Miramar, 128
Hernández, Ricardo: on colonization of Montes Azules Biosphere Reserve, 117–118; flight to Laguna Miramar, 128; on La Constancia expedition, 115
Hevea brasiliensis, 108
hiatus, Maya, 21, 25
Honduras, 32
Houseal, Brian, 191
Hoz, Juan José de la, 76
Hubbell, Peter, 73

Ictalurus furcatus, 82
Ictalurus merdionalis, 82
Iguana iguana rhinolopha, 76–77
iguanas. See *Iguana iguana rhinolopha*
Ilopango, Lake, 22
Ilopango Volcano, 21–22
Iñigo-Elías, Eduardo E.: and economic activities in Selva Lacandona, 141–142; and scarlet macaws, 68
insects, 84–90. *See also specific species*
Instituto de Antropología e Historia (IDAEH-Guatemala): and El Mirador, 55, 174; and El Perú/ Waka', 210; and La Corona/Sak Nikte', 201; and Nakum, 207; and Uaxactún, 222
Instituto Nacional de Antropología e Historia (INAH-México): and Bonampak, 150; and Calakmul, 169–170; and Sac Balam, 163; and Yaxchilán, 156
Irwin, Daniel, 223
Itza Maya: as aboriginal inhabitants of Petén, 44; and the Bio-Itza, 43;

history of, 27, 39–43, 178–180; language prohibited, 180; population of, 43; revitalization of, 180; and *sisimite*, 90; mentioned, 19
Ixcán EcoLodge and Biological Station, 119

jaguars. See *Panthera onca*
Janzen, Daniel, 88
Jones, Grant, 179
Joya del Cerén, 22
jutes. See *Pachichilus indiorum*

Kabah, 26
Kaesner, Hank, 87
Kaminaljuyú, 21, 24
Kaqchikel, 27, 29
Karp, Harvey, 59
katydids, 84
K'iche', 27, 29
kinkajou. See *Potos flavus*
Komer, Daniel, 261
Krasborn, Chepe, 173

Lacam Tun: described, 158–160; history of, 158–160; and Lacandón Maya, 35; location of, 145
Lacandón Maya: agriculture of, 138–139; and animals in general, 52; and beekeeping, 86; and botflies, 88; and coatimundis, 58–64; corngrinding song, 135–136; description of, 134–139; and fishing, 80; in Guatemala, 5, 6, 180–182; and harpy eagles, 66; history of, 131; language, 134; and leaf-cutter ants, 89; in Mexico, 14; migration into Mexico, 38; and monkeys, 57; origin of name, 34, 38, 158; and ritual bleeding, 95–96; and toucans, 69; and turtle shells, 77; and wildlife refuges, 147–148; and Yaxchilán, 138, 156
Lacanjá archaeological site, 151
Lacanjá Chan Sayab, 57
Lacantún, 28, 35. *See also* Lacam Tun
La Cojolita Communal Reserve: legislation of, 147; location of, 145
La Constancia logging camp: described, 122–127; expedition to, 117–128; history of, 115–117, 122–126
La Corona/Sak Nikte', 200–203
Laguna Guayacán, 190
Laguna de Términos, 30
Laguna del Lacandón, 5, 6–15
Laguna del Tigre National Park: and biotopes, 197; colonization of, 192, 195; described, 191–195; fish of, 79; and Ramsar Convention on Wetlands, 191–192; mentioned, 17
Laguna del Tigre-Río Escondido biotope. *See* Biotopo Laguna del Tigre-Río Escondido
Laguna Mendoza, 28, 189–190
Laguna Miramar. *See* Miramar
Laguna Ocotal Grande, 28, 160–162
Laguna Puerto Arturo, 28
Lake Miramar: and Choltí Maya, 35–36; described, 145, 160; mentioned, 28
Lamanai, 253–255
La Milpa, 252–253
Landa, Diego de: on allspice, 95; on copal, 105
Las Guacamayas Biological Station: described, 192, 194; and hostage crisis, 193–194
Lee, Dan: at El Mirador, 55; with guerrillas, 4, 9, 13
Lee, Julian, 79
Lehnhoff, Andreas: and Maya Biosphere Reserve, 187; and satellite image of Río Usumacinta, 194
leishmaniasis, 89–90
Leopardus pardalis, 52
Leopardus wiedii, 52
Lindbergh, Charles A., 215
Little Quartz Ridge, 225–229
logging: in Belize, 230, 237, 240; early exports to Europe, 124–125; in the Maya Biosphere Reserve, 198; in Selva Lacandona, 123–125

logwood. See *Haematoxylon campe-chianum*
Lonchocarpus longistylus, 86
looting: of archaeology sites, 268–270; of La Corona/Sak Nikte', 203
Lovejoy, Thomas, 285
Lubaantun, 255–256
Lutra longicaudis: described, 65; and turtles, 78

macaws. See *Ara macao cyanoptera*
MacLeod, Murdo, 32
Maia, 30
Maler, Teobert: and Naranjo, 207; and Piedras Negras, 210; on ramon seeds, 98; and Yaxchilán, 155
mammals: of the Maya Tropical Forest, 52–93. *See also by scientific name*
Man and the Biosphere Program (MAB): and Mexican biosphere reserves, 146; and UNESCO, 15, 282
manatee, 93
Manilkara chicle, 103
Manilkara zapota: described, 101; use by Maya, 103
March Mifsut, Ignacio: on La Constancia expedition, 115; sketch of La Constancia, 126; and tapir, 125
margay cat. See *Leopardus wiedii*
Martin, Simon, 170–171, 201
Martínez Calderón, Israel, 4, 5
Mata, Ricardo, 67
Matola, Sharon: and Belize Zoo, 240; and botflies, 88; on coral snakes, 73; on crocodiles, 76; on jaguars, 54
Maudslay, Alfred, 155, 218
Maya: languages of, 45; rise of civilization, 19–22; recent history, 44
Maya Biosphere Reserve: and Bio-Itza, 44; history of, 186–187; map of, 175; size of, 175; and sustainably harvested products, 198–199; and timber production, 198; vegetation of, 176; mentioned, 5, 6, 17
Maya Mountains: location of, 47; and scarlet macaws, 68

Mayapan, 28
Maya Tropical Forest: defined, 47–48; future of, 259–285; history of, 18–45; biodiversity of, 47–50; and tourism, 196; vegetation of, 47–50
Mazama americana, 53–54
Mazama pandora, 53–54
McGee, R. Jon, 139
Medellín, Rodrigo, 144
Melipona beecheii, 86
Mendoza. See Laguna Mendoza
Mennonites, 237–239
Mensäbäk. See Metzabok
mestizos, 235
Metopium brownei, 100
Metzabok Flora and Fauna Protected Area, 147–149. *See also* Mensabak
Mexico: archaeological sites, 149–171; peoples of, 129–142; protected areas, 142–149
Mexico City, 18, 23
Micrurus diastema, 72
Micrurus hippocrepis, 72
Micrurus nigrocinctus, 72
migratory birds, 8
Miller, Frank: at El Mirador, 55; with guerillas, 4, 5, 10
Mirador. See El Mirador (archaeological site); Mirador-Río Azul National Park
Mirador Basin Special Protected Area, 198, 281
Mirador-Río Azul National Park, 196
Miramar. See Lake Miramar
mojarras. See *Cichlasoma* spp., *Eugerres mexicanus*
monkeys. See *Alouatta pigra; Ateles geoffroyi; Alouatta palliata*
Montego, Francisco de, 31
Montes Azules Biosphere Reserve: description of, 144–146; key conservation area, 267; and illegal settlers, 117; as location of Sac Balam, 38
Montezuma, 31

Mopan Maya: described, 235–236; as
    guides, 225–228; and Q'eqchi', 237
Morales, Luis: at El Mirador, 173; and
    La Corona/Sak Nikte', 200–201; on
    snakebite remedy, 73
Morelet's crocodile. See *Crocodylus
    moreleti*
Morzillo, 40–41, 179
mosquitoes: and botflies, 87; in Guate-
    malan Petén, 173
Mountain Pine Ridge, 229, 247
multiple use zone, 198
Myroxylon balsamum, 96

Naachtún-Dos Lagunas. *See* Biotopo
    Naachtún-Dos Lagunas
Na Bolom, 28
Naha Flora and Fauna Protected Area,
    147–149
Nakatsuma, Alfred, 4, 9, 10, 13
Nakbe, 20, 21, 205–206
Nakum, 206–207
Naranjo (archaeological site), 207–208.
    See also El Naranjo (town)
Nasua narica: as bushmeat, 58; chant
    to cure disease of, 59–64; described,
    58–59
National Aeronautics and Space
    Administration (NASA), 4, 10;
    Marshall Space Flight Center, 23;
    Stennis Space Center, 6
Nature Conservancy, The, 180, 244
Nietschmann, Bernard, 274
Nimli Punit, 256
Nito, Honduras, 18
Nohpeten: described, 213; Spanish at-
    tack on, 179–180; mentioned, 19, 28
North American Free Trade Agree-
    ment (NAFTA), 275

O'Brien, Karen, 114
ocelot. See *Leopardus pardalis*
Ocotales. *See* Laguna Ocotal Grande
Odocoileus virginianus, 53–54. *See
    also* deer
Olid, Cristóbal de, 31
Orbignya cohune. See *Attalea cohune*

orchids. *See* epiphytes
Oreochromys niloticus, 79
otter. See *Lutra longicaudis*
Oxyrhopus petola, 73

paca. See *Agouti paca*
Pachichilus indiorum: and calcium for
    curing, 64; and calcium for maize
    preparation, 83; as food source, 83,
    225–228; described, 82–83
Palacio, Joseph, 223, 249
Palenque: described, 151–154; dis-
    covery of, 152; history of, 152–153;
    mentioned, 23
Palestina, 133
Palka, Joel, 181
Palo santo, 107
Pan-Mayanism, 272
Panthera onca: attacks on humans,
    54; in Belize, 244; in Calakmul Bio-
    sphere Reserve, 55; at El Mirador,
    55; described, 54–56
parrots. See *Amazona albifrons; Ama-
    zona farinosa*
Paso Caballos, 210, 272
peccaries. See *Tayassu tajacu; Dico-
    tyles pecari*
Pepsis spp., 85–86
Peregrine Fund, 66
Perez, Juan, 30
Petén: colonization of, 177–178; contact
    era indigenous groups, 176; map of,
    175; modern peoples of, 177–186;
    population of, 176; protected areas
    of, 186–200; vegetation of, 174–175
Peteneros, 184–186
Petenia splendida, 81
Petén Itzá, Lake, 27, 213–214
Petróleos Mexicanos (PEMEX): 141,
    260
petroleum: exploitation in Laguna del
    Tigre National Park, 192
Phlebotomus spp., 89–90
Piedras Negras: described, 210–212;
    mentioned, 3, 6, 11, 23
Pilar. *See* El Pilar
Pimenta dioica: described, 94; har-

vesting, 94–95; and the Maya, 95;
sustainability, 198–199
Piper spp., 107–108
pirates, 37
Plan Puebla-Panama, 265
plants, wild, 93–110
Pliocercus elapoides, 73
Plotkin, Mark, 275
Pochutla: archaeological site of, 160–
162; conquest of, 36; mentioned, 28
Pomacea flagellata: described, 83; as
food source for humans, 83–84; as
food source for waterfowl, 190–191
Ponciano, Ismael, 187
Popol Vuh, 29
population: challenge of, 276–280;
of Classic Maya, 8–9; growth in
Guatemala, 199–200; growth in
Selva Lacandona, 141
Porthidium nasutum, 72
Postclassic Maya archaeological sites:
of the Maya Tropical Forest, 28; in
the Selva Lacandona, 158–164
Potamarius nelsoni, 82
Potos flavus, 52
poverty, 261
Procuraduría Federal de Protección al
Ambiente (PROFEPA-Mexico): and
illegal colonists, 118
Programme for Belize, 17, 243–244, 253
ProPetén, 278–279
Proskouriakoff, Tatiana, 211
Protium copal, 104–105
puma. See *Puma concolor*
Puma concolor, 52, 55
Putun Maya: as ancestors of Itza Maya,
178–179; history of, 26–29, 30; at
Palenque, 153

Q'eqchi' Maya: and Belize, 236–237;
and cacao, 99; and deforestation,
271–272; described, 182–184; history of, 182–183; and Petén, 177;
population of, 182, 184
Quiñones, Pedro Ramírez de: expedition against the Choltí, 34–35; at
Lake Miramar, 159

Rabinowitz, Alan, 245
ramon. See *Brosimum alicastrum*
Ramphastos sulfuratus, 69
Ramsar Convention on Wetlands: and
biosphere reserves, 17; and Laguna
del Tigre National Park, 191–192
Rapid Assessment Program: in Belize,
242, 267; in Guatemala, 79, 194
rattlesnake. See *Crotalus durissus*
Redford, Kent, 273
Refugio de Vida Silvestre Chan-K'in,
146
reptiles, 69–79
Rhamdia guatemalensis, 82
Río Azul, 212–213
Río Bravo Conservation Area, 243–244
Río Chocop, 196
Río de la Pasión, 5
Río Dulce, 18
Río Grijalva, 29
Río Jataté, 28
Río Lacantún, 118, 146
Río Motagua, 28
Río Usumacinta: as trade route, 113;
watershed of, 27, 115; mentioned, 3,
6, 7, 15, 23, 28
Rivero, Sonia E., 28
Rostrhamus socialilis, 84
rubber. See *Castilla elastica; Hevea
brasiliensis*
Ruta Maya, 15, 187
Ruz Lhuillier, Alberto, 153

Sabal mauritiiformis, 105
Sabal morrisiana, 105
Sabloff, Jeremy, 27
Sac Balam: archaeological site of,
162–164; conquest of, 37–38; estab-
lishment of, 159; history of, 162–163;
rediscovery of, 163
Sac Nikte'. See La Corona/Sak Nikte'
Salinas, Carlos, 194
San José, Petén, 43, 178
San Miguel La Palotada-El Zotz. *See*
Biotopo San Miguel La Palotada-
El Zotz
Sapindus saponaria, 108

Sarcoramphus papa, 127
Sawyer, Peter, 126
Sayaxché, 4, 5, 11, 15
Sayil, 26
Schlesinger, Victoria, 89
Schwartz, Norman: on history of
  Peteneros, 185; on Lacandones
  in Petén, 182; on Maya Biosphere
  Reserve, 175
Selva Lacandona: archaeological
  sites of, 149–164; biodiversity of,
  144; colonization of, 131–132, 141;
  defined, 114; economic activities in,
  141–142; hydrology of, 115; peoples
  of, 129–142; population growth in,
  141; protected areas of, 142–149;
  mentioned, 5, 28
Sever, Tom, 4, 23; captured by guerrillas, 9–13, 15; in Guatemala, 170; and
  jaguars at El Mirador, 55; and La
  Corona/Sak Nikte' satellite image,
  203; and satellite image of Río Usumacinta, 194–195; and wasp bite,
  86; and Yaxjá, 223
Sharer, Robert, 22, 25, 269
Sheets, Payson, 22
Sierra del Lacandón National Park:
  and Campo Verde, 190; described,
  188–191; and El Repasto, 190–191;
  as habitat for howler monkeys, 191;
  vegetation of, 191
sikismiki, 90–92
sinsimito, 170
sisimite, 90–92
Site Q. *See* La Corona/Sak Nikte'
Siyah K'ak', 24
snails: described, 82–84; as food for
  snakes, 69. *See also* jutes, *Pachychi-*
  lus indiorum, Pomacea flagellata
snakes: described, 69–74; venomous,
  70–73. *See also individual species*
snook. See *Centropomus undecimalis*
Soza Manzanero, Carlos, 193
Spaniards: arrival in New World, 30;
  impact of their diseases, 33; and
  oppression of the Maya, 34–35

Spector, Sacha, 84
Staurotypus triporcatus, 78–79
Stenorrhina freminvillei, 69
Stocks, Tony, 274
strangler fig. See *Ficus crassiuscula*
Stuart, David, 201, 222
Stuart, George, 269

Tabasco, Mexico, 18, 26, 33
tapirs. See *Tapirus bairdii*
Tapirus bairdii, 58
Tate, Carolyn, 154
Tayasal, 213–214
Tayassu tajacu, 65
Tayra. See *Eira barbara*
Teotihuacán, 24
Tesucun Q'ixchan, Julian, 180
Theobroma cacao: described, 98–100;
  feral, 100; history of, 99
Thompson, Basil, 33
Thompson, J. Eric S., 24, 27, 43
Tikal archaeological site: described,
  215–220; and La Corona/Sak Nikte',
  202; and Naranjo, 208; and Uaxac-
  tún, 221; mentioned, 22–24, 27
Tikal National Park: described,
  196–197; vegetation of, 196–197;
  mentioned, 17
Tintal archaeological site. *See* El Tintal
Toledo Maya Cultural Council, 237
Toltec, 26–27, 29
Toniná, 23
Topiltepec: conquest of, 36; location
  of, 28
Topoxté, 28, 223–224
toucan. See *Ramphastos sulfuratus*
tourism: archaeological, 280–282; eco-
  logical, 280–282; guidelines for, 285;
  and Maya Biosphere Reserve, 196
Tozzer, Alfred: ethnography of Lacan-
  dón Maya, 139; and Nakbe, 206; and
  Yaxchilán, 155
Trachemys scripta, 78
trade, Classic Maya, 21
Traveling Wilburys, 5
Turkey. See *Agriocharis ocellata*

turtles: of the Maya Tropical Forest, 77–79; as musical instruments, 77. *See also specific species*
Tzeltal Maya: colonization of Selva Lacandona, 140; forest clearing by, 143; population of, 140
Tzendales, 267
Tz'utujil Maya, 29

Uaxactún, 24, 220–222
Unión Revolucionaria Nacional Guatemalteca (URNG): and the Petén, 13–14; at Piedras Negras, 210; in Sierra del Lacandón, 190, 210; mentioned, 3
United Nations Educational, Scientific and Cultural Organization (UNESCO): and Belize, 244; and biosphere reserve, 15–17; and Mexican legislation, 146; and Montes Azules Biosphere Reserve, 130
United States Agency for International Development (USAID): and Belize deforestation study, 230; and forest fires, 266; mentioned, 4, 6
Universidad de San Carlos, 197
University of Pennsylvania, 219
Urocyon cinereoargenteus, 52
Urotheca elapoides, 73
Ursua, Martín de, 42
Uxmal, 26

Valenzuela, José Chan K'in, 161
Valley of Mexico, 18, 26–28
Villagutiérrez, Juan de, 18
vipers, 70–73

Waka'. *See* El Peru/Waka'
Wallace, David Rains, 49, 229
warfare: of the Maya, 26; modern guerrilla, 45
wasp. See *Pepsis* spp.
Wasserstrom, Robert, 34
water: and Calakmul archaeological

site, 169; and Calakmul Biosphere Reserve, 167; and *chultun,* 173; reservoirs, 25; and Maya sites, 27; and Montes Azules Biosphere Reserve, 145; at Nakbe, 205–206; at Tikal, 219
weather, 50–51
weaving: highland Maya, 46; Itza Maya, 39
Webster, David, 26, 218, 254, 283
Whitacre, David, 66–67
Wildlife Conservation Society, 201, 273
Williams, John N., 115
Wilson, E. O., 284
Wood, Percy, 125
World Heritage Sites, 17

xate: harvesting, 109–110; sustainability, 198–199. See also *Chamaedorea elegans; Chamaedorea oblongata*
Xunantunich, 23, 256

Yaxchilán: described, 154–158; history of, 154–156; location of, 147; as wildlife refuge, 158; mentioned, 11, 23
Yaxjá archaeological site: described, 222–224. *See also* Lake Yaxjá; Yaxjá-Nakum-Naranjo Natural and Cultural Monument
Yaxjá, Lake, 28
Yaxjá-Nakum-Naranjo Natural and Cultural Monument, 197
yellow fever. *See* diseases
Yucatán: conquest of, 30; diseases in, 31; geology of, 46; mentioned, 7, 8, 18, 21, 25, 26, 27, 28

Zapatista National Liberation Army (EZLN): and Chol Maya, 168; and land invasions, 148, 273; and Maya of the Selva Lacandona, 45; and Montes Azules Biosphere Reserve, 117, 134
Zotz. *See* El Zotz; Biotopo San Miguel La Palotada-El Zotz